RETURN TO
SBVMWD
LIBRARY

D1443220

Urban Planning
for Arid Zones

Urban Planning
for Arid Zones

AMERICAN EXPERIENCES AND DIRECTIONS

GIDEON GOLANY, Editor
Department of Architecture
The Pennsylvania State University

A WILEY-INTERSCIENCE PUBLICATION
JOHN WILEY & SONS, New York • Chichester • Brisbane • Toronto

OCLC# 6204752 921195

Copyright © 1978 by John Wiley & Sons, Inc.

All rights reserved. Published simultaneously in Canada.

Reproduction or translation of any part of this work
beyond that permitted by Sections 107 or 108 of the
1976 United States Copyright Act without the permission
of the copyright owner is unlawful. Requests for
permission of further information should be addressed to
the Permissions Department, John Wiley & Sons, Inc.

Library of Congress Cataloging in Publication Data:

Main entry under title:

Urban Planning for Arid Zones: American Experiences and Directions

   "A Wiley-Interscience publication."
   Includes bibliographical references and index.
   1. City planning—United States—essays.
2. Arid regions—United States—
essays.   I. Golany, Gideon.

HT167.U728   309.2′62′09154   77-10472
ISBN 0-471-02948-3

Printed in the United States of America

10 9 8 7 6 5 4 3 2 1

To Frida and Michael Klein,
grandparents of Ofer and Amir,
for their warmth and love

Preface

Research on arid and semiarid regions has been focused traditionally and primarily on such aspects as climate, water, soil, mineral resources, vegetation (or the lack thereof), and—more recently—the physiological and psychological dimensions of human behavior there. For some reason, research on architecture and land use has been minimal, and that on urban and regional planning in desert areas virtually nonexistent. It is my firm belief that, in this field, scholars and professionals have failed to learn the lessons silently taught us both by the vast and impressive historical experience of the numerous early civilizations that existed and thrived in semiarid and arid zones of the Middle East, northern Africa, Iran, Afghanistan, Pakistan, and central Asia and by the more recent and more limited experience of the modern, more technological arid-zone communities in these areas and in large parts of Australia and the southwestern United States. This volume is specifically undertaken to correct—or, at least, to begin to correct—the latter error by examining closely one of the unique and important modern urban planning experiences—the American one.

For the purposes of this book, I, as editor, define as arid zones those areas of the globe with an annual average precipitation insufficient to support dry farming without water importation; with very low humidity and thus severe dryness; with a large daily temperature range; and with relatively high amounts of solar radiation, especially during the summer months. Such areas, along with the semiarid zones, constitute a large portion of the world's land, and in some countries, such as those in the Middle East, constitute most of a given nation's territory. In other countries, such as the United States, such arid and

semiarid land, although not predominant, nonetheless consitutes a significant portion of the national land area. And it is worthwhile noting that, in the case of the United States, this arid portion—the Southwest—is growing considerably more rapidly than any other single section. Accordingly, there has been, because of the recently gained consciousness of the rapid depletion of nonrenewable resources and awareness of energy shortages in relation to the expanding population and development, an accelerating interest in urban and regional planning in the arid zones of America as well as of other nations. This interest will necessarily increase dramatically in a future short on energy and food.

The American case, although it lacks the historical dimension of, for example, the Middle East, is especially interesting and significant since it is characterized by sophisticated and rapid technological development, a high standard of living, and the intense involvement and large contributions of private enterprise—characteristics (and advantages) not fully shared by other arid regions. This book is intended to expose planners, developers, and decision makers of the United States and of the world in general to these unique and valuable experiences in the design and development of urban centers and other communities in the American arid zone. It is, furthermore, intended to introduce the reader—both professional and general—to the comprehensiveness necessary in the field of urban and regional planning of arid zones and to expose him or her to the differing viewpoints, unresolved arguments, and unanswered questions that prevail about desert planning. Finally, this book is intended to fill a very noticeable gap in the planning

viii

profession's literature. The book has thus been prepared in a pioneering spirt, a spirit shared by the editor and all the contributors.

The nineteen contributors differ in background and profession: some are architects; some are sociologists; some are environmental psychologists; some are engineers; some are physiologists; some are professional planners. The book is designed to bring together theoreticians and practitioners, those who have researched as well as those who have practiced community living in an arid zone. Some of the contributors were invited to present their ideas at a seminar, composed of faculty and advanced students from various disciplines, that I conduct annually under the auspices of the Department of Architecture of The Pennsylvania State University. This seminar provided an ideal first forum for some of the important issues that this book raises. I hope that the passage of time and the addition of many new voices—with additional expertise—have made this book not only a better forum but also an inspiration for further work, both theoretical and practical.

My sincere thanks are extended to Theodore F. Sheckels, doctoral candidate in the Department of English, who worked closely with me throughout all the stages of the editorial work, for his dedication and careful handling of the manuscript. I would also like to express my appreciation to Hope Stephan and Elizabeth S. Hodges, graduate students in the Department of English, who worked with me in editing parts of this volume. My thanks are also extended to Nancy L. Houtz for her conscientious typing of the text and to Kevin Scott and Michael Zanin for drawing and redrawing some of the illustrations. Special thanks are due to Dean Walter H. Walters of the College of Arts and Architecture and Professor Raniero Corbelletti, head of the Department of Architecture. Without their support this project could not have been realized.

In the belief that a comprehensive and coherent collection of essays on urban and regional planning in the American arid and semiarid zone may assist planners throughout the world, and that it will significantly contribute to a better understanding of the unique nature of planning in these increasingly important regions, I preface this volume.

GIDEON GOLANY

University Park, Pennsylvania
October 1977

Contents

Tables

Figures

Contributors

DANIEL AIELLO is currently a candidate for an advanced degree in architecture at the Arizona State University. His area of specialization is desert habitation technology, and the activities of the architectural firm, i² Environmental Consultants, of which he is a principal, reflect this expertise.

ROBERT B. BECHTEL is president of the Environmental Research and Development Foundation and is a professor in the Department of Psychology at the University of Arizona. He was educated at Susquehanna University and the University of Kansas, where he received his Ph.D. in 1967. His research, consulting, and city government service activity has been varied; much of it has recently been in environmental psychology, studying locales as diverse as Albuquerque, Kansas City, Cleveland, and the Arctic. Many of his findings have been published in professional journals and as chapters in such books as *Environmental Design Research and Practice* (1973) and *Designing for Human Behavior* (1974). His book *Enclosing Behavior* is scheduled for publication in 1977.

MATHEW J. BETZ is presently assistant academic vice president of the Arizona State University and professor of engineering there. He previously served for 7 years as associate dean of the Graduate College. Before receiving his Ph.D from Northwestern University in 1961, Dr. Betz served for 2 years as an associate professor at the University of Khartoum in the Sudan. He studied transportation problems there for his doctoral dissertation, and he returned during 1965–1968 as manager of the Sudan Highway Reconnaisance Project. More recently, as a member of numerous Transportation Research Board committees, he has studied varied aspects of

the transportation picture, particularly the financial ones. Much of his recent independent research, consulting work, and published studies concerns the American Southwest, particularly the Phoenix metropolitan area.

COURTNEY B. CLELAND is associate professor of sociology at the University of Arizona, with interests in community and regional change, including the sociology of the American Southwest. He has done research on retirement communities in Arizona, family life in rural Saskatchewan, and population shifts in the Great Plains. From 1950 to 1964 he was a member of the faculty at North Dakota State University. He is a graduate of Carleton College in Minnesota, Hamilton College in New York, and the University of Minnesota, where he earned his Ph.D. in 1958. Dr. Cleland is author or coauthor of more than 40 publications, including a paper, "Do we Need a Sociology of Arid Regions?" in the monograph *Social Research in North American Moisture Deficient Regions* (1968) and a chapter, "Mobility of Older People," in *Older People and Their Social World* (1965). His most recent article is a coauthored paper, "Occupational Changes in North Central New Mexico," which appeared in the April 1976 *Social Science Journal*.

JEFFREY COOK, currently professor of architecture at the Arizona State University, was educated at Mount Allison University, the University of Manitoba, the Royal Academy of Fine Arts in Copenhagen, and Pratt Institute, where he received his Master of Architecture in 1961. He has taught since then at the Arizona State University except for two sabbaticals. During the first, in 1966–1967, he made a study and lecture tour of England; the second, in 1974–1975, was devoted to a lecture tour of American universities, where he spoke on solar energy and solar architecture. Among his numerous published books, booklets, articles, and designs are several dealing with or done for the arid Southwest. He is currently writing a book tentatively titled *Solar Architecture*.

RICHARD L. CROWTHER, AIA, is the principal of Crowther/Architects Group and the affiliated Crowther/Solar Group, both of Denver, Colorado. He has specialized in optimized energy conservation, life support, and passive and active solar and natural energy systems for residential and commercial use since 1972. Before the establishment of Crowther/Architects Group, Mr. Crowther was the principal in other architectural firms for more than 40 years. Since 1955 he has designed over 20 solar buildings which have been constructed, including the National Science Foundation/Colorado State University solar-heated and solar lithium absorption-cooled house at Fort Collins (1974). He has lectured before various audiences for a number of years on the subject of passive and active natural energy systems and has served as a consultant to the American Institute of Architects, the National Academy of Science, the state of Colorado, and other professional and political bodies on solar energy matters. The author of *Sun/Earth* (1976), Mr. Crowther lists among his publications "Solar Energy: The Architectural Imperative" in the November 1975 *ASHRAE Journal* and "Energy-saving Ideas for Heating and Cooling a House" in the March 1976 *National Geographic*.

STANLEY F. GILMAN joined The Pennsylvania State University as a professor of architectural engineering in 1973, bringing 20 years of engineering experience in the heating, ventilating, and air-conditioning industry, much of it with the Carrier Corporation. He conducted air-conditioning research at the University of Illinois from 1947 to 1953 and received his doctorate there. Former president of the 32,000-member American Society of Heating, Refrigerating, and Air-Conditioning Engineers (ASHRAE), a licensed professional engineer, a patentee and professional consultant in his field, and a director of federally sponsored research on solar heating, Dr. Gilman has authored or coauthored more than 50 publications on heating, ventilating, and air conditioning.

GIDEON GOLANY is a professor of urban and regional planning in the Department of Architecture at The Pennsylvania State University. The holder of four advanced degrees, including the Ph.D. granted in 1966 by The Hebrew University in Jerusalem, Dr.

Golany taught at the Technion–Israel Institute of Technology, Cornell University, and the Virginia Polytechnic Institute and State University before coming to The Pennsylvania State University in 1970. He has served as a consultant in new-town planning and urban and regional planning in Israel, Virginia, and Pennsylvania. A member of several professional societies and the recipient of numerous honors, Dr. Golany's most recent publications include *New-Town Planning: Principles and Practice* (1976), *Innovations for Future Cities* (1976), *Strategy for New Community Development in the United States* (1975), *The Contemporary New Communities Movement in the United States* (1974) (coedited with D. Walden), and *New Town Planning and Development—A Worldwide Bibliography* (1973).

LEONARD GORDON, currently professor in and associate chairman of the Department of Sociology at the Arizona State University, has fused a career as a teacher and a career as a researcher at that university since the conferral of his doctorate by Wayne State University in 1966. His research has been in the very problems plaguing America's cities: school desegregation, racial and ethnic interrelations, and urban rioting. His involvement with the American Sociological Association and several regional professional groups reflects this research, as do his numerous publications, among them—of particular interest here—his examination of Phoenix's cultural mix in *The Multi-Ethnic Society* (1973) and his forthcoming general text, *Sociology and American Social Issues* (Fall, 1977).

GUY S. GREENE was trained in landscape architecture at the Iowa State University. He has worked, however, not in the American Midwest, but in the arid Southwest and in Saudi Arabia. He has executed numerous land use plans for residential and industrial developments and has designed the landscaping for numerous others. This landscaping work has ranged from the King Faisal Specialist Hospital and the Ministry of Agriculture and Water complex in Riyadh, Saudi Arabia, to the Hyatt Regency Hotel in Phoenix and the Pima Community College in Tucson. In Tucson he is currently, as an independent landscape architect, serving as a consultant to the Pima County Park and Recreation Commission and the Tucson Planning Department and working on a master plan for the Santa Cruz Riverpark and a park and lake area at the Ina Road Waste Water Treatment Plant. His work has appeared in numerous periodicals, including *Architectural Forum, Architectural Record,* and the *New York Times*.

DANIEL HILLEL, currently visiting professor of environmental sciences at the University of Virginia, has lectured in various capacities at many universities, primarily on soil physics. He is particularly active at The Hebrew University of Jerusalem, where he served as head of the Department of Soil and Water Sciences from 1967 to 1974. He has also served as special advisor on soil and water use to the governments of Burma, Cyprus, Japan, and the United States (through the Department of Agriculture), and he has been a member of several national committees on the environment in Israel. Dr. Hillel is the author or coauthor of over 100 articles, bulletins, and reports dealing with aspects of land and water use, especially in arid regions. He is now preparing for publication (with B. Yaron) *Soil and Water Management in Arid Environments: The Case of Israel.* An earlier book, *Soil and Water: Physical Principles and Processes* (1971), has been translated from English into French and Portuguese and will soon be available in Japanese and Spanish as well.

WILLIAM H. ITTELSON, from 1968 to 1975 professor of psychology and head of the graduate environmental psychology program at the City University of New York and currently a professor in the Department of Psychology and coordinator of the environmental psychology program at the University of Arizona, holds two advanced degrees from Princeton University, an M.S. in electrical engineering (1948) and a Ph.D. in psychology (1950). Before 1968, Dr. Ittelson taught at Princeton, at Brooklyn College, and, as a Fulbright fellow, at Kyushu University in Japan. He served from 1953 to 1968 as a research consultant for the Veterans Administration, and he has received several grants from the National Institute of Mental Health to study the effects on patients of mental hospital ward design and to design research training programs in environmental psychology. His numerous articles reflect these concerns and a special interest in problems of perception. He has recently authored or coauthored *Environmental Psychology: Man and His Physical Setting* (1970), *Environment and Cognition* (1973), and *Introduction to Environmental Psychology* (1974).

ELIEZER KAMON is presently professor of applied physiology and ergonomics at The Pennsylvania State University. A 1964 recipient of the Ph.D. from The Hebrew University in Jerusalem, Dr. Kamon taught at The Hebrew University's Institute of Biological Sciences, the University of Pittsburgh, and the University of Illinois before coming to Penn State. He also acted as a consultant for United States Steel, Eastman Kodak, Dow Chemical, and other large corporations. Dr. Kamon's research has particularly emphasized comparative ergometry and thermal physiology, and his most recent publications reflect this. Among them are "Ergonomics of Heat and Cold" in *Texas Reports in Biology and Medicine* (1975); "The Relationship Between Perceptual Information and Physiological Responses to Exercise in the Heat" in the *Journal of Human Ergology* (1974); and "Instrumentation for Work Physiology" in the *Transactions of the New York Academy of the Sciences* (1974).

ALLEN V. KNEESE is currently professor of economics at the University of New Mexico. Since the conferral of his doctorate by Indiana University in 1954, Dr. Kneese has taught at the University of California at Berkeley and at Stanford University, and he has served Resources for the Future, Inc., both as director of its water resources program and as director of its quality of the environment program. Dr. Kneese has also acted as a consultant for numerous national and international organizations, including the World Health Organization, the National Academy of Sciences, the Tennessee Valley Authority, and the Environmental Protection Agency. The most recent of his numerous publications are *Economics and Environment: A Materials Balance Approach* (1975) (with R. Ayres and R. d'Age); *Pollution, Prices, and Public Policy* (1975) (with C. Schultze); and "Water Demands for Energy" (with L. Brown) in the 1975 volume of *Natural Resources Lawyer.*

HELMUT E. LANDSBERG is presently professor of meteorology at the University of Maryland and chairman of its graduate program. After receiving his doctorate in geophysics and meteorology at the University of Frankfurt, he taught at The Pennsylvania State University and the University of Chicago. He then served in high-level positions with the U.S. Weather Bureau and the Environmental Science Services Administration. An active participant in numerous professional societies, Dr. Landsberg in 1975 accepted a presidential appointment to the National Advisory Commission on Oceans and Atmosphere. The author of a noted textbook on physical climatology and over 300 scientific papers, Dr. Landsberg is also the editor of two series: *World Survey in Climatology* and *Advances in Geophysics.*

BRADFORD PERKINS was educated at Cornell University, where he studied architecture and Latin American studies, and Stanford University, where he received a Masters in Business Administration. Mr. Perkins is currently the managing partner of the four North and South American offices of Llewelyn–Davies International, a worldwide planning and architectural organization. He has been the director of or a participant in 10 of the 25 new towns planned by LDI, including ones in the United States, Egypt, Trinidad, Jamaica, Colombia, Canada, and Iran. Before joining LDI, Mr. Perkins worked in construction management, management consulting, and architecture. With this combined background, he is a specialist in the physical, financial, and management planning of large projects. Mr. Perkins is also currently on the faculty of City College of New York College of Architecture and has authored over 40 articles on planning and development management topics.

JEROME H. ROTHENBERG has been with the U.S. Department of Housing and Urban Development in various capacities since 1970. He is currently program manager for modular integrated utility systems in the Division of Energy, Building Technology, and Standards of the Office of Policy Development and Research. Before joining HUD, Mr. Rothenberg was with the General Electric Company in its aerospace program, was chief of engineering planning for the design and construction of space simulation test facilities with the Stokes Division of Pennwalt Corporation, and was a member of the engineering faculty at Newark University. Mr. Rothenberg has designed equipment and facilities for the power industry, as well as for the chemical and process industries. He holds four patents and is a registered engineer in New York and Pennsylvania.

LAWRENCE WHEELER is presently a professor in and chairman of the Department of Psychology and a professor of optical sciences at the University of Arizona. Before coming to the University of Arizona, Dr. Wheeler taught at California State College at Hayward and at Indiana University, where he received his doctorate in 1962. A member of numerous professional and honorary associations, Dr. Wheeler has published and lectured widely on the necessary relationship between the behavioral sciences and architectural planning.

JOHN I. YELLOTT, visiting professor of architecture at the Arizona State University, is a graduate of The Johns Hopkins University in mechanical engineering. He has taught at the University of Rochester, the Stevens Institute of Technology, and the Illinois Institute of Technology, where he served as a consultant to the Manhattan Project at the University of Chicago and the Director of the Institute of Gas Technology. Between 1945 and 1954 he engaged in industrial research on the coal-burning gas turbine. Since 1955 his research has been devoted to solar energy use and control, and from 1958 to 1973 he operated the Yellott Solar Energy Laboratory in Phoenix. He is a fellow of several American and European societies, including the American Association for the Advancement of Science and Great Britain's Royal Society of the Arts.

Urban Planning
for Arid Zones

The Unique Features
of Arid Zones 1

CHAPTER 1

Planning Urban Sites in Arid Zones: The Basic Considerations

GIDEON GOLANY

This chapter offers guidelines for urban and regional planners interested in planning a new city in an arid zone such as the American Southwest. It focuses on the unique treatment required of the qualified planner because of the planning problems resulting from the special climatic stress of an arid zone. For the purposes of this discussion we classify these problems as social, economic, and physical.

Although environmental extremes, especially aridity, are common to all desert areas, their climates vary with factors such as the following:

1. The latitude of the area, which partially determines the amount of solar radiation and the range of temperatures.
2. The distance from the sea.
3. The absolute or relative elevation of a given area, which affects its aridity and also the amplitude of temperature between day and night.
4. The topography and geomorphology of the area, which distinguish it from its surroundings and determine its microclimate.

These variables act separately or together to determine first the general climate of arid zones and then the variations among them. In general, all arid zones have little precipitation and temperatures that fluctuate widely between day and night, but they can be further classified as (1) cold polar zones, as in Siberia; (2) cold, dry continental zones, as in central Asia and central Australia, and cold, dry upland zones blocked by high mountains; and (3) hot, dry zones, as in North Africa, the Middle East, and the southwestern United States.

In this chapter we are particularly concerned with the hot, dry zones, although part of our discussion may pertain to cold and dry continental zones as well. Therefore we define arid zones as areas with an average annual precipitation that does not support dry farming, very low humidity, an average annual rate of evaporation greater than the average annual rate of precipitation, great variation in daytime and nighttime temperatures, and relatively intense solar radiation, especially during the summer.[1]

Arid zones so defined comprise one third of the world's land.[2] A few of these "deserts" receive no rain at all, but most receive varied amounts of precipitation, and the aridity results from an evaporation rate that exceeds the precipitation rate. In addition, the rain that does fall in arid zones is torrential, turbulent, brief, and sparse and often causes floods because the intense, brief rainfall does not have time to seep into the ground. The absence of soil (caused by eolian erosion) and of vegetation decreases the ground's absorption of runoff and thus increases the potential speed of the water. Extensive soil erosion and its intense transportation result.

SOCIAL CONSIDERATIONS

Because of the demanding conditions under which arid-zone development occurs, entrepreneurs should possess a visionary attitude, a pioneering spirit, and a devotion to the task.[3] Arid-land development, like that in other newly developed regions, may be conceived in four conditions: adaptive penetration, pioneering settlement, planned development, and visionary transformation.[4]

Arid settlement and development in virgin areas require, as we noted, vision and pioneering spirit or ideological motives in the young, dynamic settlers for quite a long time after its initiation. Thus the first population pyramid will consist of young bachelors (18 to 30 years of age) and young married couples (20 to 30 years of age), with and without young children.

Planners must consider in detail the effects of such a demographic structure of the new arid city on requirements for space, services, and jobs. The young bachelors will certainly need numerous recreational facilities, active community centers, and various entertainment centers. Whatever other motives they may have, bachelor settlers usually move to an arid-zone city to save money: wages there are likely to be higher than in other regions. Good economical services, such as discount shopping centers, are necessary to meet the needs of this group. Young married settlers will also have special requirements, such as the medical needs of pregnant women and special green areas for relaxing and socializing. Many of these married couples will have children of nursery, kindergarten, or elementary school age. The required educational facilities must feature adequate, compatible active and passive space for outdoor and indoor recreation and entertainment for the children and their educators. These children will also need special medical services. The early settlers, especially the bachelors and married couples without children, of the arid-zone city are as mobile as the populations of company towns or new-town developments. The married couples with children tend to be less mobile because of the negative impact that changes of environment and school may have on their children.

Children in the higher elementary grades and high school are usually not among the early settlers, and their absence may prevent some families from joining the community in its early years. Those who do join, however, may need to bus their teen-agers to an adjacent, usually distant, community. The elderly too, including parents of the initial settlers, will not join the community in its early phases of development;

yet they may decide to settle there if housing, services, and other amenities exist to meet their needs and standards. Therefore planners of an arid-zone city should consider the spatial requirements, social management, and medical and other services needed by the elderly that must be developed at a later stage of the city's existence.

Overall, the society formed by the early settlers will be composed of young, dynamic, informal people who tend to accept and even encourage friendly contact and social integration, thereby diminishing social distinctions. Friendships among these settlers are usually lasting and later arouse a strong sense of nostalgia among them. For many settlers such emotions become sufficient cause for rooting their families at the site. Social distinctions and barriers (e.g., pioneers, oldcomers, and newcomers) will emerge again when former urban dwellers migrate to the new settlement. Such social groups may even be formed because of veterans' nostalgia for pioneering, their sense of accomplishment, and, for some, their feelings of superiority.

Housing plans must accommodate the various groups in terms of type, size, quality, and schedule of development. Rented houses or apartments (as opposed to purchased ones) must be provided for the early settlers to facilitate their move and their exploration of the feasibility of settling in a new community. Housing plans must also consider the unique structure of the society of an arid-zone city, affecting unit size, type, design, grouping, requirements for private and public space, proximity to other land uses, maintenance, and depreciation. Such consideration will also call the planner's attention to the frequent housing changes by the early settlers that will occur at a later date in the city's development because of increased living standards, family expansion, the polarization of social groups, and the need for environmental improvement. Urban rehabilitation may then be needed for the houses of the early settlers to prevent their deterioration into slum quarters.

If a city's planner and developer decide that the town must be a self-sufficient community as soon as possible, then they must plan for a rapid population growth in the early development phases. Planners must also consider the social services, educational amenities, and medical services such rapid development will entail; their spatial requirements; and their development schedule. Without efficient, simultaneous development, the population may be unstable. Furthermore, speedy development and construction may become part of a national image of the community that can attract various social classes. Initially, such rapid, large-scale construction will attract two groups of people: unskilled, single laborers (mostly men), who will be relatively well paid, and a few skilled, married people, who will also be well paid. Both groups will desire large shopping centers (which offer a variety of choices), diverse social and cultural activities, and special health and medical services.

Because of the intense solar radiation in an arid zone, the dryness, the dust pollution in the absence of vegetation, and the isolation of cities, efficient, comprehensive health services are necessary to meet both normal and urgent needs. Also, the duration of outdoor labor should be adjusted to avoid work during peak radiation hours. The same holds true for student activities in kindergarten, elementary school, and even secondary school. For health reasons, a possible need may exist for early retirement or reduced working hours for the elderly. Also, since evaporation in an arid region is high, greater consumption of water is required to maintain a healthy physiological condition.

Research is needed on nutritional and clothing requirements in an arid zone. In the latter case, skin treatment requires special consideration because of the aridity and the radiation. Thus planners should consider forming the desired albedo to reduce the effects of radiation. The same is true for cities: colors that absorb radiation are more satisfactory than those that intensify reflection. For example, trees not only break monotony, improve a city's visual image, create shadows, and have other desired advantages, but they also affect albedo and reduce reflection. Such reductions not only protect human skin but also reduce the chances of dehydration and protect the eyes.

One powerful psychological impetus behind arid-zone settlers that is usually ignored is the desire to be close to a natural, quiet, virgin environment and to identify with it. In addition to demographic structure and climate, planners must consider this desire—and the associated desire for isolation and quiet—and its social implications.

ECONOMIC CONSIDERATIONS

Any new settlement in vast, uninhabited arid zones will be isolated. To survive, new urban settlements in these zones must be self-contained and self-sufficient in employment, services, and all other daily needs. This self-sufficiency must be attained earlier in the

development of such settlements than in other cities and will require more of an investment than is usual in the early stages. The populating of these new settlements must also occur earlier than normal to justify economically the operation of services at such a high level. The relationship between development phases, population size, and the goal of self-containment mandates comprehensive planning, well-coordinated development, and the early allocation of financial resources. Because of the financial risks involved in the early phases of developing these new settlements, private developers probably will not undertake the task. Thus public and other nonprofit investment is crucial in such early phases, raising the issue of the need for public involvement in the development of arid cities as compared to nonarid ones. In this regard we should note that most arid land is public land, permitting more choices in site selection than with privately owned land.

Because of its unique isolation and climatic stress, a city in an arid zone may not have a conventional economic structure. The proximity of nonarid settlements supports the development of interurban economic and social activities and services, but arid cities cannot develop such complementary activities and services. The unique climate of the arid zone does, however, offer some advantages for the more intense planning, building, and development of such economically or socially important facilities as recreational and civic centers, industries requiring dryness, energy production plants, and greenhouses. Furthermore, these facilities are necessary to avoid the psychological isolation of the arid city's population and a negative image in the eyes of outsiders who may be potential migrants. Excellent and abundant social services as well as economic diversity will be required to achieve this goal. Inclusion of facilities such as a university, a good airport or other transportation systems, and cultural facilities will enhance the city's image.[5]

Except for company towns, arid cities should not depend on one economic element alone because such reliance does not offer job security and can accentuate the social and psychological isolation of residents. Rather, an arid city should be planned to have as diverse an economy as possible, which would ideally include industry, agriculture, and services. This mix will support heterogeneity in the settlement's land use, its population's age and sexual structure, its society, and its cultural activities.

The vast distances between settlements in arid zones increase expenses for transporting goods, especially building materials, between producers (mainly in nonarid regions) and the consuming site (in the arid region). Such costs must motivate the new arid-zone city to accelerate production and the provision of daily services with self-sufficiency as its goal. Similarly, the availability of large tracts of undeveloped land should stimulate large-scale industrial development and the provision of necessary associated services. Moreover, arid-zone sites developing some self-sufficiency will usually acquire regional functions in addition to local ones, offering such services as motels and restaurants, shops, repair facilities, storage areas, and gasoline stations for vehicles crossing the region.[6]

This related, sequential economic picture—necessarily including job opportunities—supports the belief that the regional development of arid zones on any scale must include a dominant urban settlement that supplies social, economic, and service needs. Without such a center, self-sufficient regional development may be either very costly or sporadic and disjunctive. Thus arid zones must be planned and developed as massive units rather than as small entities to ensure their operation and cultural unity, a vital factor in such development.

In developing virgin regions in general and arid zones in particular, public investment is necessary to attract private enterprise after the development has been initiated. The risky enterprise of pioneering requires large quantities of "front" money for developing infrastructure. Privately financed industrial development will not proceed unless it is preceded by infrastructure construction. Unless the public guarantees such an advance payment without planning any immediate benefit, private investors will always find more economically secure ventures in nonarid zones. Furthermore, if arid zones are to be developed in a regional context rather than sporadically, they must be treated comprehensively—a goal that can be achieved only by public investment. Thus it is not a coincidence that even in free economic market countries such as the United States, where private enterprise dominates construction, the federal government in 1976 spent much more in the arid-zone states than in those located in the humid northeastern United States.[7] Since it has also been found that climatic differences correspond to variations in *per capita* income among countries (i.e., the more arid land a country has the more likely it is to have a lower *per capita* income), regional development will require subsidies, possibly from international sources.[8] In Israel, for example, all investment for the early development of the Negev and most of

the later investment in the region have been public. Without public financing, it is doubtful that the Negev would have been developed or that private investors would later have joined in the enterprise. This same reasoning generally applies to all arid regions.

PHYSICAL CONSIDERATIONS

Careful observation of urban arid centers planned in the distant past reveals the conscious adjustment those cities made to their environment and its climatic stress. Since such observation has not yet been thoroughly summarized and analyzed in the literature, it is essential to introduce here some basic guidance for physical planners. In every case they must judge the applicability of these guidelines, for arid zones differ among and within themselves.

Few theories, if any, exist concerning site selection in arid zones. However, careful study of the urban building techniques that evolved in such zones during ancient civilizations reveals immense experience that could prove invaluable to modern urban planners. Planners and developers who are alert to the fact that misinterpretation of a site's character may be costly economically and, later, socially will be particularly interested in these lessons.

In arid zones, more than in humid regions, the physical elements are socially and economically crucial. For example, a poorly selected site may not only consume vast energy for air conditioning but may also interfere with the planned social use of the site and thereby weaken urban growth. On the other hand, careful site selection, close consideration of land forms, and physical planning properly adjusted to climatic stress can lead to living conditions that moderate the climate of the city. This section is an analysis of the most important conditions present in an arid zone and the special treatment and adjustments that planners must undertake or make in response to each of them.

Site Selection in an Arid Climate. Arid zones are characterized by various conditions that can be affected by different combinations of physical determinants. Planners must decide which conditions are desirable and adopt criteria designed to maximize them in selecting the best site for a new settlement. A listing of such criteria for use in site selection is necessary. Since most of the items on such a list will have effects in conjunction with the others rather than alone, it is important that each criterion be set against the others when a site is being examined. Primarily, the physical criteria for an urban site in an arid zone will include the following:

1. Land sufficient to accommodate the planned population.
2. Water resources for daily consumption by homes, industry, and services. (Cities featuring agricultural development will require water for irrigation.)
3. Accessibility via standard transportation systems.
4. Local resources to employ at least part of the city's population. (In some cases, the climate may be one of the resources.)
5. Comfortable climatic conditions for healthy living and working.

In the process of site selection for a new settlement in an arid zone, planners should be most concerned with the last criterion. Therefore the following discussion will focus on conditions that are related to comfort. Obviously, no site will meet all requirements for comfort, and any site selected will represent compromises among the desired optima. Some comfort-related conditions and their limits may become clear in the early stages of development and may be overcome with some minor investment, but the strong, natural ones should be treated seriously from the outset of the planning process.

Air temperature. Some site characteristics can help to increase or decrease air temperature. In arid zones, artificial lakes often serve as reservoirs for the urban area's water supply, recreational areas, and the life blood of irrigation. Careful location of the city relative to the lake, along with proper orientation vis-à-vis the prevailing hot wind, will, however, affect its temperature. When the hot, dry air is blown over water, the humidity of the air increases and its temperature decreases; thus the temperature of the prevailing winds will be reduced if the wind crosses the lake before reaching the city. Although the reduction may involve only a few degrees, it may suffice for comfort. In regions where such water use is possible, a zone of bodies of water may be planned around the city to reduce the air temperature.

Where bodies of water are rare or cannot be built, air temperature may be most tolerable at a site located above the surrounding lowland, where wind is more frequent and the air relatively cooler. Such a site may also present an attractive landscape, although a greater investment will be necessary to make it accessible. A careful study of the exact to-

pography of the region, along with its wind patterns, must be made to select the specific site. This research will help to find a site where temperature can be most significantly reduced.

An example of a bad site would be one at the base of a foothill, characterized by temperatures higher than those at the top of the same slope. Such a site will be affected by the adiabatic heating of air that occurs as air flows down the slope (Figure 1). Another bad location would be in a valley, where air overheats and inversion occurs (Figure 2).

In flat regions, arid vegetation encircling a site can reduce wind speed and dust storms and also lower the air temperature when it crosses this green zone's relatively cool shadows. Also, the reduction of passive open space within a flatland city may help lower the air temperature.

Overall, the most important means of reducing wind temperature, regardless of the topography, is the design of urban configurations. Thus a planner should remember that the ratio of total shaded space to space open to solar radiation will affect wind temperature significantly. For example, a city dominated by large, black asphalt streets and open parking areas is most undesirable because they absorb sunshine. On the other hand, narrow, winding alleys, which exist in many ancient arid cities, are shaded and therefore relatively cool.

Relative humidity. Relative humidity is another crucial criterion to be considered when selecting a site. Generally, in arid climates evaporation decreases ambient temperature, and the degree of dryness contributes directly to the perception of discomfort. In arid areas not too far from the sea, slopes facing toward the wind blowing in from the sea will be more humid than those facing in the opposite direction; therefore a site of the former type is preferable. Also, at higher elevations in arid zones, the humidity is relatively greater. Thus sites at the top of a mountain, on the upper parts of a slope, or at the top of an isolated plateau (e.g., Mesa Verde, Colorado) are preferable to lowland sites, as Figure 3 illustrates.

Problems of excessive dryness may also be reduced by creating large bodies of water (where water is found) within the city or by encircling or crossing the city with such bodies. Waterways within the city's pattern not only reduce dryness and moderate temperatures but also break the arid zone's characteristic visual monotony by introducing a new landscape.[9]

Soil structure. The combination of low humidity,

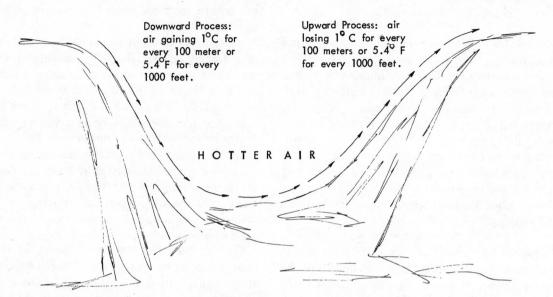

COLDER AIR

Downward Process: air gaining 1°C for every 100 meter or 5.4°F for every 1000 feet.

Upward Process: air losing 1°C for every 100 meters or 5.4°F for every 1000 feet.

HOTTER AIR

Figure 1. Adiabatic heating and cooling processes, demonstrating the desirability of an uphill site and the problems of a site at the base of a hill in an arid zone.

high temperature, and drastic differences between daytime and nighttime temperatures strongly affects the geomorphology and landscape of arid zones. This combination produces the sand common in these zones. The absence of vegetation contributes much to the instability of the sand, which is easily moved by the wind. The resulting dust storms may increase urban maintenance and accelerate the deterioration of buildings. Above all, such storms cause much human and animal discomfort as well as harm to vegetation.

A site at a higher elevation than the surrounding area may be less affected by dust storms. Airborne particles may abrade other bodies and, because of the vertical variation in their density, the effect of the particles will be greatest near the ground. Furthermore, urban planners familiar with the process of erosion may decide not only to select elevated sites but also to landscape the city with plants and water to minimize the effects of dust storms. Cultivation of the land surrounding the city should, however, be avoided unless the land is irrigated or planted to inhibit erosion. Since most urban surfaces are built up and compact, runoff is intense around the borders of cities, and the erosion there is relatively deep.

Exposure to radiation. Planners should consider carefully the orientation of sites relative to the sun. Sites on slopes facing south receive the most intense

solar radiation during the day, while those on slopes facing north receive the least. Sites on slopes facing east or west receive less radiation than those facing south but much more than locations on slopes facing north. However, slopes facing east usually receive solar radiation until noon, while slopes facing west receive radiation mainly during the afternoon, when the level of solar radiation is at its peak. These facts dictate the following preferred order of slope orientation in site selection: (1) northward, (2) eastward, (3) westward, (4) southward.

The planners and builders of ancient Mesopotamian cities seem to have shared these preferences in their selection of sites for residential areas. In Assur, the capital city of ancient Assyria (twentieth to sixth century BC), where the climate was hot and dry most of the year, high-class residential areas were built on slopes facing north because, in addition to being least radiated, these slopes enjoyed the cool northwest winds of the region.[10] Also, all the balconies in Abadan, Iran, a city dating from antiquity, face north to enjoy shade all day. On the other hand, farmers in the countries located on the northern shores of the Mediterranean used to plant grapes on slopes facing south to take advantage of the intense radiation.

Elevation. Relative humidity generally increases with absolute elevation above sea level. Since in-

A. LOW VENTILATION

A LOCATION IN THE BOTTOM OF A VALLEY
DOES NOT PROVIDE GOOD VENTILATION,
WHICH IS MOST NECESSARY IN AN ARID
AREA. FURTHERMORE, BECAUSE OF THE LOW
HUMIDITY AT THE BOTTOM OF THE VALLEY,
THE AIR WILL BE MORE ARID AND, THEREFORE,
HOTTER.

B. REFLECTION

REFLECTED SUN RADIATION WHEN COMBINED
WITH THE ABSENCE OF THE VENTILATION MAY
INCREASE THE TEMPERATURE IN THE VALLEY AND
IN THE CITY IF LOCATED THERE.

C. POLLUTION

SUCH A LOCATION BECOMES EVEN RISKIER
IF THE CITY WILL HAVE POLLUTING INDUSTRIES.
LACK OF INTENSITY OF VENTILATION COMBINED
WITH POLLUTION WILL RESULT IN MAJOR HEALTH
HAZARDS AT SUCH A SITE.

D. INVERSION

ANOTHER RISK IS INVERSION. WHEN THIS IS
COMBINED WITH VERY LOW OR NO VENTILATION
AND THE POLLUTION, AN AIR TRAP MAY RESULT.

E. FLOOD

ALTHOUGH RAIN IS VERY RARE IN ARID ZONES, IT
COMES IN LARGE QUANTITIES WITHIN A SHORT
TIME. THUS, A LARGE QUANTITY OF RUN-OFF
WILL DESCEND ON THE BOTTOM OF THE VALLEY
WHERE THE CITY IS LOCATED. SUCH STREAMS OF
WATER MAY BE COMBINED WITH LARGE QUANTITIES
OF MUD, ROCK, OR BOULDERS.

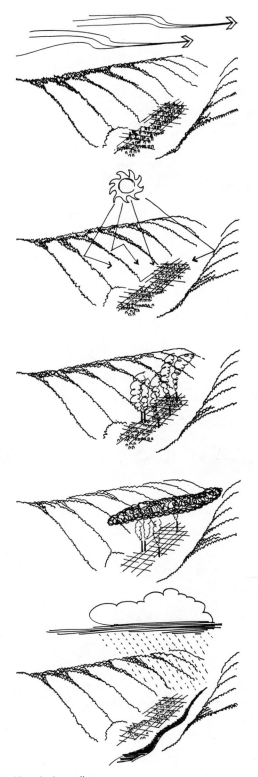

Figure 2. The problems associated with a site in a valley.

9

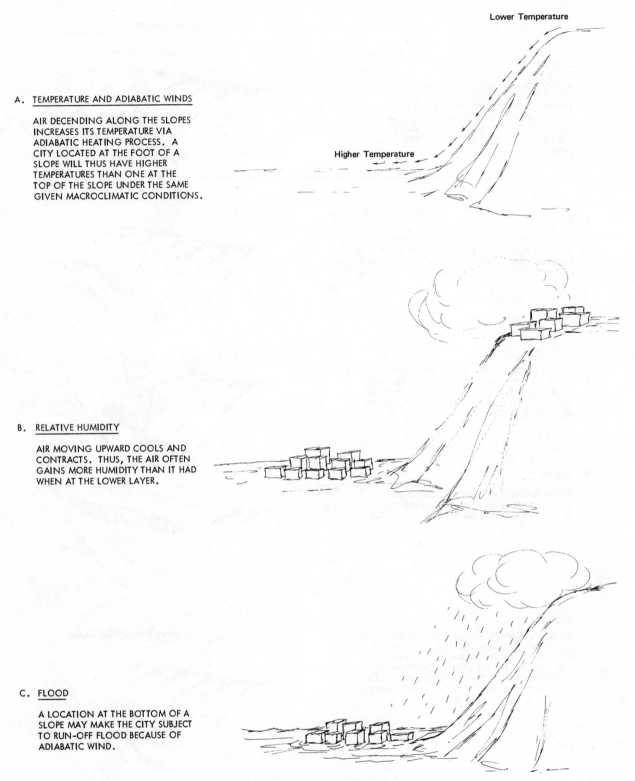

A. TEMPERATURE AND ADIABATIC WINDS

AIR DECENDING ALONG THE SLOPES INCREASES ITS TEMPERATURE VIA ADIABATIC HEATING PROCESS. A CITY LOCATED AT THE FOOT OF A SLOPE WILL THUS HAVE HIGHER TEMPERATURES THAN ONE AT THE TOP OF THE SLOPE UNDER THE SAME GIVEN MACROCLIMATIC CONDITIONS.

Lower Temperature

Higher Temperature

B. RELATIVE HUMIDITY

AIR MOVING UPWARD COOLS AND CONTRACTS. THUS, THE AIR OFTEN GAINS MORE HUMIDITY THAN IT HAD WHEN AT THE LOWER LAYER.

C. FLOOD

A LOCATION AT THE BOTTOM OF A SLOPE MAY MAKE THE CITY SUBJECT TO RUN-OFF FLOOD BECAUSE OF ADIABATIC WIND.

Figure 3. The advisability of locations on slopes and the problems facing urban locations at the bases of slopes.

10

creased relative humidity contributes to temperature reduction, an elevated new site may moderate temperature and thus provide comfort. A new site need not necessarily be atop a mountain or hill, however, because a site that is open in all directions may be hit by occasional strong winds and thus require special urban forms or protective vegetation. The slopes of a mountain may be high enough to effect the desired increase in humidity and decrease in temperature.

The elevation of a selected site relative to the surrounding lowland may also be crucial because of a city's need for ventilation. In addition, elevation offers a spectacular view of the environs, a landscape value that can be important in breaking the visual monotony of many arid environments.

Precipitation. The unique nature of precipitation in arid zones creates the following serious problems that require special treatment: intense erosion; land slides delivering large quantities of silt, mud, and rocks to major streams; and large amounts of runoff in a short time, creating major hazards and wide floodplains along the banks of streams.

In selecting a new site, planners should attend to the following points:

1. The natural drainage systems of the site must be able to function during the extreme periods of rainfall.
2. The site, especially its prospective built-up area, should not consist of any plains subject to periodic flooding (usually the banks of dry streams are attractive sites because of their flatness, but they are subject to flooding and should be avoided).
3. Urban construction in arid zones requires an investment for special systems of storm sewers to accommodate the rapid, heavy runoff. (Without such construction and investment, the streets of the city may flood during heavy rains, destroying houses and the streets themselves.)
4. Careful planning of the selected site and the natural water supply of its environs may be a great asset to the community, since good water control may improve both the landscape and the cityscape.

Accessibility. Access to the site during all the seasons of the year should be considered. One of the advantages of an arid-zone site is its good weather, which allows good air navigation year round. Yet the isolation typical of arid-zone cities supports the idea

that the best transportation system to develop first at the new site is aviation. In addition to providing easy access to the site, air transportation facilities usually cost less to build than a highway network leading to the new site. Moreover, cargo transport and passenger travel time are important factors in the development of a new site. Thus, when selecting a site for a new city, planners must also select a site for an airport nearby.

Surveying for highways and railroads and planning and constructing them require experimentation, large investments, and a lengthy span of time. Thus land transportation will probably consist initially of dirt roads that will remain dusty until construction is completed. In addition, many sections of highway that cross usually dry streams will require long bridges to maintain access to the new city during floods.

Water resources. Obviously, this criterion is fundamental for urban construction and a new city's operation because without water there can be no life on a new site.

The quality, quantity, and cost of tapping local water resources, such as rivers, streams, creeks, wells, runoff, or groundwater reserved in the form of fossil or fresh water, determine the site's possibilities. Many modern cities in arid zones have been built with drainage systems incapable of accommodating peak runoff. Ancient civilizations in arid zones, however, invented many devices to capture, divert, store, and use runoff and thus maximize urban growth. Runoff may, for example, enrich groundwater reserved for later use.

When local resources are judged insufficient, water may be imported from outside the locality if the political and economic problems can be solved. Although the quality of imported water and the requisite quantity, transportation, storage, and security are important considerations, willingness of consumers to pay for the water and to depend on outside sources is essential. Desalinated water from outside sources may be mixed with locally available saline water to maintain a quality usable for drinking and for industry, and thus increase the amount of locally available water. Beyond this mixing, there are devices for water desalinization: the price of the produced water will determine their use in an arid-zone city. Today this price is high for urban use and higher yet for agricultural use. The availability of low-cost solar energy in the future may decrease the cost of desalinization and broaden its use, which may allow the arid zone to become a new frontier for urban centers, as well as for agricultural production and villages.

Wastewater recycled from urban and industrial sewage may also be a possible source for reuse by industries, agriculture, or vegetation. Obviously, industries that consume large quantities of water, such as those processing food, should not be located in arid cities.

Recognizing human sensitivity to climatic stress as a serious problem, we have attempted here to help the planner to realize the significance of the criteria for new site selection in arid zones that are particularly pertinent to the issue of comfort. If followed, the guidelines suggested, will moderate the urban climate and increase human comfort there.

Site Planning in an Arid Zone. Dominating the landscapes of arid zones are special landforms that result from temperature amplitude, dryness, the nature of the rare precipitation, the lack of vegetation and the kinds of winds. For practical reasons, the characters of those forms must be studied and considered carefully when a settlement is planned and built on the selected site.

Because the prime physical requirement for an urban construction site is the availability of consecutive, relatively flat to moderately sloping tracts large enough to accommodate various urban land uses, we shall focus on arid-zone landforms that may meet this physical requirement. We shall also focus on those among these landforms that have potential initial water resources. Therefore, the arid-zone landforms discussed here are (1) piedmont, which consists of pediment and alluvial plain, (2) playa, (3) alluvial fan, (4) floodplain, (5) coastal plain, (6) the eolian landforms loess and sand dunes, and (7) mesa.

Piedmont. Piedmont, one of the most common distinct landforms, often constitutes a large portion of an arid zone. Piedmont is the entire area sloping down from a mountain to a low basin or playa. The upper part, just below the mountain slope, which sometimes includes the cliff surface, is called the pediment slope, while the lower part, which may extend back to the foot of the mountain, is termed the alluvial plain (or *bajada* or, sometimes, peripediment).[11]

Scholars do not agree on the definition of pediment.[12] In an arid region, however, it is typically a gently sloping surface formed on bedrock and lying between the mountain and the alluvial plain. The lower limit of the pediment is where its alluvial cover becomes continuous. The pediment is formed by the erosion of the mountain mass.[13] Commonly associated with pediments are coarse, crystalline rocks, notably granite.[14] The pediment, furthermore, often develops more than one drainage basin. Since its formation is dependent on hydraulic variables, patches of bedrock and alluvium cover the pediment, and much of its area is composed of eroded matter. The pediment can thus be viewed as an intermediate zone between zones of bedrock and alluvium.[15]

The size of the pediment varies enormously from a few square kilometers to hundreds of kilometers. The gradient of the pediment, dependent on such variables as faults, hydraulic factors, the nature of the deposited material, and its length, usually ranges between 0° and 11°.[16] Its relatively moderate topography and gradient, its position overlooking the surrounding area (which facilitates good ventilation and lower temperatures than prevail in the lowland), and the possibility of some natural water resources all make the pediment a good area for constructing new settlements. A pediment including more than one drainage system may, however, require special construction to permit access to the site.

The alluvial plain, which is the lower part of the piedmont between the pediment and the playa basin, is formed by material that eroded from the mountains and now covers the bedrock of the plain. This plain's gradient is very low, making transportation easy. Furthermore, because it is made of alluvium, the soil may be good for agriculture. An alluvial plain features large, unobstructed tracts of land that may make land assemblage easy, and its typically good drainage system may tolerate urban construction.

Playa. The playa is a landform that ranges in size from a few square meters to thousands of square kilometers and occurs in poorly drained, flat, dry lowlands or depressions with strata of fine sand, silts, clays, and salt.[17] The playa has a very insubstantial soil profile because of its relatively young age, and its water table is usually close to its surface. Because of the salt, the playa has no vegetation and is therefore subject to flooding after rain. Although the playa is usually dry, during wet seasons, some runoff may accumulate in shallow pools, but it becomes salty, especially when water begins to evaporate.[18] Playa lakes are usually located at the bottom of the piedmont and function as its lowest drainage basin.[19] The playa surfaces, described as "hard, soft, wet, dry, rough, smooth, flaky, puffy, salty, or nonsaline," differ from each other depending on the season, soil condition, and level of the water table.[20]

The flat landform and the closed drainage basin do not allow any drainage network to exist.[21] Although the playa is controlled principally by climate, the enclosed drainage basins are formed mainly by tectonic movements. Also, the basin may result from eolian processes such as the forming of hollows by deflation or the blocking of drainage by moving sand, or from volcanic activity, for example, the blocking of drainage by volcanic effusions.

Playas may accumulate elastic materials, mostly clay, silt, or granular particles, and inelastic saline sediments.[22] This accumulation of fine-grained sediments on the playa surface may result from the relative impermeability of the playa and from the eolian activities.[23] Such eolian erosion may also contribute to the formation of the playa. The intensity of eolian activity will depend on the soil structure and moisture level of the playa. Hard, crusty surfaces, with a high ratio of clay to other materials, are more resistant to deflation than are surfaces rich in salt. The wind will characteristically move some light grains, which will then settle in a dune formed within the playa or on its margins.[24] Sink holes and depressions may also develop in the playa when groundwater reaches the surface. Movement across the wide, deep sink holes may then be hazardous.[25]

The real importance of the playa lies in such minerals as salts (specifically chlorides), carbonates, sulfates, borates, and nitrates.[26] Its horizontal topography has, however, attracted speculation regarding transportation routes, military uses, and actual construction. Unfortunately the elastic soil and corrosive salt make it difficult to construct building foundations. For such construction to take place, drainage systems leading to the playa would have to be diverted, and dikes built to prevent flooding. Some construction, perhaps in the form of highways or railroads, may be possible in the playa. Moisture fluctuation, however, may still change the volume of soil, and hence it is desirable to elevate such roads and routes above the soil level.[27]

Alluvial fan. The alluvial fan is the only arid-zone landform caused by the deposit of materials by the fluvial system of a mountain. After radiating downslope, the mountain stream forms the fan, which begins at the stream's exit from the mountain and follows the divergent paths of the stream itself, as it deposits alluvial materials at the foot of the mountain. The lack of vegetation in arid zones causes fluctuation in the stream's drainage systems. Also, occasional heavy thunderstorms cause large quantities of materials to flow down from the mountain to its foot and thus produce expansion of the fan. Alluvial fans seem to be most highly developed where the possible areas of deposit are smaller than the mountain areas that feed them.[28] The morphology of the fan has three elements: abandoned areas of the existing fan surfaces, channels, and surfaces downslope of the channels.[29] Because of its origin in erosion and the form of the deposits there, an alluvial fan may hold some groundwater. Flooding, however, is still quite likely. To prevent the flooding of a selected site, planners must spend money to divert the alluvial fan's drainage at its apex, which is near the foot of the mountain. Even then, flood prevention may require control of the fan's locally developed channels. Since its drainage networks may change because of flood deposits of new mud, control must be exercised not only at the apex of the fan but also within the local drainage network.

An alluvial fan is important, for it provides large quantities of construction materials: silt and fine sand at the lower end, and boulders and mud in the other parts. Imaginatively used by a builder, these materials could provide unique features for a settlement. Because of their moderate topography, alluvial fans may also be good areas for settlements. These fans are large and gently sloping, feature good drainage, and are higher than the playa or the alluvial plain but lower than the mountains. The area may be 10 km in radius.[30] Sites of such a size can accommodate a city of 1 million people at an average density of 20 persons per acre. The gradient, rarely exceeding 10 percent, would be helpful in developing a city with suitable transportation networks, a landscape overlooking the plain, and good ventilation.

Floodplain. Floodplains are formed when rivers and streams deposit material on the plains adjacent to them. The floodplain of an arid stream may be extensive because of the relatively large quantities of water overflowing the stream within a short time. Floodplains may also be built in terraces by different flows. The extent of the floodplains in arid zones is also affected by the generally low topography, which allows the rivers to change course often. The deltas of such rivers are also part of the floodplain.

Although it may be terraced, a floodplain is poorly drained because of its flat topography and therefore may have a high water table for some time after a flood. In any event, the fluctuating drainage patterns are for the most part not apparent, making planning difficult. A floodplain, free of stones and large rocks, however, may have some good patches of soil for agriculture.

Highway construction across a floodplain requires long, elevated bridges with strong foundations to resist erosion by the large quantities of water. To cross without bridges, a highway must have a system to warn of anticipated floods and also to clear the highway of debris after a flood. Elevation of a highway on terraces is risky and not always effective because of the unique nature of rain in an arid zone.

Building materials indigenous in large quantities in the area include gravel, rock, and sometimes sand or clay. Because of the availability of these materials, and also its flatness, a floodplain often attracts settlers, who know that they can tap the water table of such plains. On the other hand, building there is hazardous unless the upper stream is totally controlled. Unfortunately, the construction of dams or reservoirs on a floodplain is especially difficult.

Coastal plains. Coastal plains are regions bounded by mountains on one side and the sea on the other side, and both of these bounds affect the strata, physical form, climate, and water system of such plains. They may be made up of various landforms such as beaches, tidal flats, floodplains, deltas, and ridges, all of which feature marine and alluvial sediments. Because of their location, these plains are composed of various soils, including silt, clay, and sand, in addition to rocks and gravel.

Coastal plains are sedimentary strata composed of sea shelf that has emerged and a margin of the continent. After emerging from the sea but before eroding, the coastal plain's surface is smooth and nearly featureless, sloping gently toward the sea.[31] The drainage is thus parallel. Older plains have more complex systems of drainage because of their more rugged topography. Most coastal plains, however, regardless of age, decline gently toward the ocean. Being close to the sea, they enjoy some humidity, dew, fog, and breezes. Because coastal plains merge mountains, rolling plains, beaches, shorelines, and the sea, the landscape is very attractive. The beach and shore may also be a good local resource attracting tourists to a new settlement.

The potential for capturing runoff from the mountains in reservoirs on the coastal plains and the possible water table there attract new settlers. Fresh water, if it is found on coastal plains, may be subject to the intrusion of salt water, especially when groundwater is extensively used and wells become depleted. Lakes, reservoirs, and ponds bedded by local impervious soils may be located in the lowland area of coastal plains to store fresh water. When a water table does not exist, septic tanks are suitable because the soil is not strongly consolidated.

The drainage systems of young coastal plains, which form parallel networks perpendicular to the shoreline, may necessitate the construction of grading and terracing for drainage when a highway is built near the upland part of the plain. A highway crossing close to the shoreline and parallel to it may have to cross the drainage system and the river deltas in the lowland part. In this case, flood warning systems or long, elevated bridges are necessary.

Coastal plains usually feature many materials suitable for use in construction, such as sand, gravel, and rocks. The soil there is suitable, however, for holding only small structures. Heavier ones may require such special features as piles or piers, depending on the soil structure.

The danger of tidal waves should be avoided by choosing for development on coastal plains sites that are high and reasonably far from the shoreline. Wide floodplains, deltas, or potential stream beds near the shore, as well as sites at the feet of mountains, where eroded materials usually collect, should also be avoided.

Eolian landforms. Eolian erosion transports particles of soil and deposits them far from their origin, thereby establishing new landforms. Unlike fluvial transportation, which may be a chemical as well as a mechanical process, eolian transportation is only mechanical. The density of transported particles is greatest nearest the ground, and they usually are carried no more than 4 ft above it.[32]

In general, hot, dry climates with their great temperature amplitudes foster eolian transport, which depends on wind velocity and force, particle size, the original structure of the rock or soil, air temperature, and the degree of aridity. Vegetation effectively inhibits such transportation where the soil will support plants.

Eolian transport occurs in two stages. First, deflation removes loose particles of soil. This stage is very common in arid zones because of the characteristic high temperature, soil aridity, and absence of vegetation. The removal of loose particles lowers one site, while the deposit of such particles builds up another. Thus new landforms are established in more than one area. The second stage is the abrading of other bodies by the carried particles, which polish some surfaces and add particles to those already in the air. Such wind abrasion, which is proportional to wind velocity, the density of the carried particles, and the height of particles above the ground, is responsible for creating various landforms.

Two common eolian landforms are loess and sand dunes. Loess has two main origins: glacial rivers and deserts. Both feature dry climates that foster deflation.[33] Consisting of silt (70 percent) and clay particles deposited far from their origin, loess may cover hundreds of square miles. Its thickness is inversely proportional to its distance from the source. Although loess soil exists in many places of the world, it is found most often in such arid or semiarid zones as the Sahara, southeastern Egypt, the Negev is Israel, Mongolia, and northeastern China.

Loess particles, ranging between 0.01 and 0.05 mm in diameter, are smaller than sand particles. Typical loess is soft, porous, and light in color, but the surface becomes harder than the interior as it retains rain.[34] Poorly drained horizontally and well drained vertically, loess easily erodes.[35] For the most part its topography rolls gently, but eroded areas of loess have a rugged topography and steep slopes. Loess soil, despite the potential erosion, is very good for agricultural use, when there is enough water.

Loess not only is a good landform for agricultural use but also is suitable for urban settlements, for it is reasonably good for construction. A subterranean structure here, for example, may be relatively humid and therefore cooler than one built on the surface. Septic tanks also work quite well because of good drainage in the subsoil.[36] Loess is also suitable for the construction of dams and water reservoirs; the soil can serve as a bottom layer because it is impervious. Moreover, loess can support the foundations of light and medium structures, but piles may be required for heavier construction. A layer of sand under the soil can, however, make development infeasible. Loess soil, we should note, occasionally contracts and expands after changes in air temperature, a feature that necessitates special treatment in designing for buildings, highways, or railroads. Highway construction, for example, requires special treatment along banks and cliffs: terraces and supports are necessary because of the great possibility of vertical erosion. Construction materials such as sand or gravel will, however, have to be imported.[37]

Sand dunes are composed of thin layers of particles resting on rock. Such layers cover between one quarter and one third of the world's deserts and sometimes form sand seas rather than isolated dunes.[38] Dunes are formed by the wind and vary according to its speed, direction, and turbulence.[39] (It is possible that the resulting friction, to which the erosion is due, is supported by electrical charges in the sand that cause the particles to rise.) The wind ordinarily does not carry the sand far from its source, and the ground at the dune site is usually covered with the jumping, bouncing grains, which distribute

themselves across the surface when the wind blows at a minimum of 11 mph.[40] Smooth surfaces facilitate the movement of sand particles, whereas rough surfaces lower the effective wind velocity. Stabilized sand dunes will develop a thin surface of loamy sand across their tops, but no sand dunes will develop drainage systems because they are characterized by rapid internal drainage and therefore lack seasonally high water tables near the surface.[41]

Sand dunes either are located along the coasts of seas, lakes, or rivers or occur inland. Dunes differ in their scale, magnitude, and effect on urban development. Coastal ones are limited, narrow, linear forms along the shoreline. They may stabilize with urban construction, thus eliminating their negative impact, as happened in The Netherlands and Israel. Widely distributed inland dunes are not necessarily linear. The sources of the sands that compose them may be old or present coastal shorelines, glacial plains, lake beds, river floodplains, or sandstone deposits. The different forms result from wind fluctuation, the velocity of the moving sand, and the relative humidity, which influence the sand's stability. These forms may include U-shaped (wind-drift), *barchan*, beach, transverse, and longitudinal. Urban development on such dunes must be accompanied by regional, rather than just local, treatment to reduce their negative impact.

When sand dunes are stable, they offer a good foundation for houses, other structures, or highways. However, since dunes easily transmit vibrations and can become hazardous for structures built on them if the wind erodes the dunes or their unstable particles abrade buildings and people, urban development on unstable dunes is not advisable. The wind, in fact, may also cause buildings or entire urban areas to become sand covered and thus seriously threaten human survival. If development is to occur, covering the sand's surface with vegetation to reduce the reflection of solar radiation, which adversely affects skin and eyesight, is recommended.

Septic tanks, which may reduce the need for special sewage systems in the new city, are suitable on dunes. However, the impact of such tanks on the water tables must be assessed in order to avoid ground pollution. Sand dunes may also be used as a sewage lagoon for the city. It is not advisable, however, to use them for solid waste disposal because the ground is thereby contaminated.

Trenching in sand dunes (e.g., for utilities systems) requires sheeting and therefore costs more than trenching in regular soil. In addition, pipelines installed in and covered by active dunes may later be subject to exposure and deterioration. On the other hand, the extraction and removal of sand in building is easy and may cost less than for regular soil. The planner must balance these costs and savings before selecting a dune site.

Mesa. Formed on eroded horizontal layers of limestone sediment, a flat-topped mesa stands as a conspicuous feature above its surroundings. The alternation of soft and hard horizontal layers forms sharp, straight cliffs that have some talus at their bases. These cliffs are formed when intense water erosion removes a soft layer and also weakens the base of the hard layer above it, causing its collapse. The size and the relative height of mesas vary from one place to another.[42] The horizontal top and acute cliffs make the mesa easy to defend and therefore attractive for settlements where this is a consideration.

Because of its elevation a mesa may be slightly humid and become a relatively green island within dry surroundings. Some water resources may also be found in the area, and the height provides good ventilation for the site. Moreover, settlements located at the top of a mesa enjoy an attractive view of a vast landscape. Mesas are, however, inaccessible and may require heavy investments for road construction. Again, therefore, the planner must balance costs and benefits before selecting a mesa site.

In our discussion of site selection, we were primarily concerned with climatic, environmental, and overall regional resources, as well as the general geomorphology and topography of the surrounding area as a whole. As we review the unique characteristics of the arid-zone landforms, we notice that their formation is due to common factors such as aridity, diurnal temperature fluctuation, wind dynamics, fluvial behavior, and soil composition, all of which must be well known to the planner if he is to make proper adjustments of the landforms to compensate for these factors. Each landform, as we noted, has its distinct advantages and disadvantages. Beyond these, the planner should examine each of the seven landforms discussed in this section with regard to the following:

1. The elevation, which affects relative humidity, wind ventilation, intensity of radiation, and the characteristics of the overall landscape.
2. The degree of adaptability of the landform to large-scale construction.
3. The quality of, quantity of, and proximity to water resources.

4. The character of the drainage system metamorphosis.
5. The accessibility of the site.

Generally, among these seven landforms, the piedmont, the coastal plain, and the mesa probably offer the planner the most encouraging prospects.

URBAN FORMS

To reduce or eliminate the unique climatic stress of an arid region requires reliance on special physical urban forms. In turn, however, these urban forms may create physical, social, or economic settings that create new problems and therefore also require adequate solutions. Thus the selection of a correct form cannot be a purely physical solution, but rather must be a comprehensive one. There are certain conditions in the arid regions (listed in Table 1) to which the new urban form must respond. To consider these conditions and their impacts, limitations, and stresses, or to use the conditions to advantage, we must outline the basic requirements of urban form in an arid zone.

While designing the physical urban form in an arid zone, a planner needs to consider ways to moderate the city's climate. Urban form and configuration cannot entirely change the regional climate, but can moderate the city's microclimate, especially in residential areas. The basic urban form must provide maximum shade and allow minimum reflection in streets, alleys, open spaces, or any other public spaces, as well as within houses during most of the day in all seasons. The new form should also minimize indirect solar radiation (especially reflection from the ground and walls) to avoid heating the air. Also, the form should moderate the effects of winds, which are hot during the day and cold at night. Used to provide natural ventilation, winds can increase humidity within the city's housing units and public spaces.

Throughout history, compact cities have been built for such reasons as to offer effective defense, to save land for agricultural purposes, or to foster social unity. Urban experience in the arid zones shows that such compact forms also are effectively adjusted to climatic stress. The necessity of human adaptation to arid zones brought about the development of these compact urban forms, which have microclimates more moderate than those of the environs. The narrow, winding alleys and streets, which block sunlight,

Table 1 Stressful Climatic Conditions, Their Impacts, and Their Solutions in Arid Zones

Condition	Impact	Advantages and/or Alternative Solutions
Intense solar radiation (especially in PM hours)	Reduction or elimination of outdoor social activities	Microclimate created within the city (domed areas; narrow, winding alleys; and specially designed houses)
	Potential encouragement of indoor familial and social activities	Recreation for winter and retirement communities
	Reduction in the productivity of labor	Maximally integrated pattern of land use
		Avoidance of large open spaces within the city where hot air can collect during the day
		Close proximity of urban services used intensely every day
		Compact structures and forms
		Use of subterrannean space for living and for working
	Physiological discomfort during outdoor movement	Ample, shaded public spaces
	Rapid decay of food	Construction of refrigerated storage
	Many cloudless days that provide large quantities of solar energy	Construction of devices to use solar energy
	Unusual timing of agricultural production	Economically successful agricultural communities with special adaptations to grow and market produce out of its usual season
High amplitude between day and night temperature	Problems in physiologically adapting to climatic extremes that limit the population to certain groups	Design and construction of special devices for energy storage and temperature exchange between day and night
	Discomfort and need for appropriate clothes and shelters	Design of shelters with tempered microclimates using natural or artificial systems
	Intense wind and turbulence	Wind catchment system for house ventilation
	Potential wind energy	Devices for generating energy from winds
Lack of vegetative cover	Increased radiation and reflection and intense negative impact of albedo	Selection and cultivation of xerophytes that require little or no water
		Use of xerophytes that do not require water as ground cover for open urban space
		Selection of light colors for every open space
	Creation of dust storms	Reduction of cultivated areas close to urban residences and reduction of open space within the urban conglomerate
	Increased boredom and feelings of isolation	Green zones of plants around and within the settlement to provide shade and to stabilize soil
Dryness (low humidity and deficit between extremely high evaporation and rare precipitation)	Negative impact on physiology of human beings, flora, and fauna	Little passive open urban space
		Special care for skin and eyes
	Thirst	Humidification of space within built-up structures (especially those for public gatherings)

17

Table 1 (*Continued*)

Condition	Impact	Advantages and/or Alternative Solutions
	Requirement of physiological adaptation and population limitation to certain groups	Recreation centers for asthmatic people
	Clear skies for most of the year	Development of excellent astronomical observations
		Good, relatively safe air navigation
	High evaporation of irrigated soil and quick salinization of intensely irrigated land so that agricultural production falters	Need for natural fertilization
	Consumption of water	Development of recycling systems for used water
		Avoidance of developing industries that consume large quantities of water
		Need for special nonaqueous chemical treatment of solid waste
	Eolian erosion and abrasion of structures and people	Landscaping with xerophytes

are relatively cool and also break stormy winds. Public gathering spaces such as bazaars or markets, which are covered, establish their own moderate microclimates. The bodies of water located in open spaces evaporate and therefore reduce the high temperatures.

Compact urban areas, if designed properly (Figure 4 shows some ways of doing this), can have microclimates that reduce dusty or cold nocturnal wind and solar radiation. A proper design conceives of neighborhoods as residential and service units, where daily functions are within walking distance. Such a design provides shaded space through which people from various places within the service unit can move and distributes services throughout the unit on a human scale adapted to the climatic stress. Compact neighborhood units are conceived of as single sections of the city, and the city as a whole is regarded as a chain (linear, polycentric, radial, or otherwise) of compact units. The public gathering spaces, in fact, can share protective or shading devices. Finally, all the separate urban units can relate to a central community center that by itself comprises a service center, a shopping center, and a residential area.

To be compact, any urban form must necessarily have high density; thus noise and other nuisances may be problems that should be reduced by paying special attention to spatial arrangements, especially the location of common space for playgrounds. To be compact, a physical unit will also feature the close proximity of land uses, such as places of work, residences, shopping areas, educational facilities, public offices, and community service centers. The sites chosen for these particular uses must reflect the goal of moderating climatic stress. Since compact forms, more than any others, foster intense social interaction and the integration of age groups, careful study and design are required to eliminate or at least reduce negative social effects.

A compact form can reduce the length of utility networks, the maintenance they require, and the expenditures of energy and thereby prove economical. However, such a form mandates special designs that may increase construction cost. On the other hand, a compact form decreases the traditional need for transportation systems and vehicles, further reducing construction and living costs.

Finally, to be compact, urban forms must comprise vertical rather than horizontal structures. The verticality of neighborhood units can be achieved, however, in two ways: the usual very tall structures and the relatively unusual subterranean ones. The latter can accommodate some housing units, a community center, shopping areas, offices, and any non-

A. GRID PERPENDICULAR AND PARALLEL
    TO EAST-WEST AXIS

B. GRID DIAGONAL TO EAST-WEST AXIS

ALTHOUGH THE GRID PATTERN MAXIMIZES RADIATION THROUGHOUT ITS STRAIGHT
STREETS, IT IS STILL POSSIBLE TO REDUCE THIS RECEIVED RADIATION THROUGHOUT
THE DAY BY ORIENTING THE GRID PATTERN DIAGONALLY TO THE EAST-WEST AXIS,
EVEN THOUGH SUCH A GRID STILL SUPPORTS THE DYNAMIC MOVEMENT OF THE AIR.

NORTH

C. NARROW, WINDING ALLEYS

D. NARROW, ZIG-ZAGGING ALLEYS

WINDING OR ZIG-ZAGGING NARROW ALLEYS RECEIVE MINIMUM SUNSHINE,
REDUCE THE EFFECT OF STORMY WINDS, ESTABLISH SHADOWED SPACE THROUGH-
OUT THE DAY WHICH PROVIDES A COOL AND COMFORTABLE MICRO-CLIMATE
AND ALSO STAYS RELATIVELY WARM DURING THE COLD NIGHTS IN THE ARID ZONE.

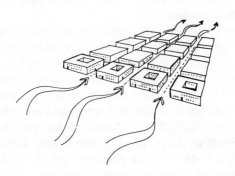

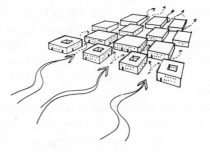

E. STRAIGHT, PARALLEL STREETS AND ALLEYS

F. STRAIGHT, BLOCKED STREETS AND ALLEYS

CITY STREET ORIENTATION AND HOUSING PATTERN ARE SIGNIFICANT AND MUST
BE CONSIDERED CAREFULLY BY THE PLANNER OF THE ARID-ZONE CITY.
STRAIGHT AND PARALLEL STREETS MAY OPEN THE CITY TO WIND VENTILATION;
IF BLOCKED, ONE MAY REDUCE A STORM'S EFFECTS. TWO FLOORS OF BUILT
UNITS WITH CLOSED PATIOS OPEN TO THE SKY WILL MAXIMIZE SHADOW,
MINIMIZE RADIATION, STILL RETAIN VENTILATION, AND REDUCE THE EFFECTS
OF STORMY WINDS.

Figure 4. Ways of properly designing an urban form in an arid region in response to solar radiation and wind.

polluting light industry. Subterranean structures can be constructed to provide a special microclimate that is more moderate than the one at ground level and should therefore be given special consideration. In addition, they save energy.

In general, then, planners of urban forms must consider the advantages of physical compactness and the proximity of land uses. They must also try to create a more moderate urban microclimate than that prevailing in the environs. Finally, they should consider the need for verticality (as opposed to horizontality) in designing urban configurations; this may require some subterranean construction.

CONCLUSION

Urban and regional planners should view the world's arid zones as potential locations for future urban expansion and for food production, and as energy resources. No matter what function these areas serve, the construction of settlements of different forms and functions which respond to the unique nature of a desert climate will be needed.

Arid zones were among the very first to establish villages and the first to develop cities of different forms and configurations, some of which have lasted thousands of years with no or minor interruptions until our time. These cities evolved their forms through the ages, carefully adjusting to the environment of the arid zone and its climatic stress. They have been excellent laboratories and, as such, are an asset to contemporary arid-zone planning. Unfortunately, these ancient lessons have been neglected. Our studies, however, can now begin to focus on the physical configurations of those ancient cities and should in the future consider in detail such aspects as site selection, subterranean houses, urban forms and configurations, land use, housing design, and, finally, water systems.

Regardless of the technological advancement we have achieved, planners of arid cities must develop unique physical configurations and forms to meet the climatic stress, for energy shortages and lack of funds are likely to make it impossible to solve all the city's problems with technology. In view of these very real economic conditions, the advantages of a compact city structure with relatively high density, covered or domed sections offering proper ventilation, the close proximity of all land uses, subterranean development, the use of special building materials and colors, innovative housing designs for

humidification and ventilation, and, finally, special cityscaping and landscaping to moderate the climate of the environs, all of which will create a man-made, controlled microclimate, must be considered. In other words, special devices in design have become vital. Unfortunately, we know very little, if anything, about these as yet.

Arid zones, we must remember, are highly sensitive environments. Any development thus requires comprehensive treatment of the area, preceded by diversified research and studies of the physical, social, economic, transportation, and other elements that must be incorporated into any final plan. Environmental issues must, however, receive special consideration. Among these, flood behavior and the dynamics of the physical environment (e.g., eolian processes, storms, and soil conditions) are integral parts of both the planning and the construction processes. In these processes, we need to remember that the impact of development on the arid zone's physical environment is remarkable because of its sensitivity. The impact can be positive if the plan influences the local climate favorably or stabilizes the physical dynamics, or it can be destructive if air, water, or land pollution results. Thus, study of the impact of development on the ecosystem of the arid zone must be a prerequisite to any planning and construction. Although the desert's resources (landscape, space, air, sunshine) appear to be inexhaustible, planners, recognizing that they are not, must identify the threshold of each of these resources and plan accordingly. More importantly, local residents and governments should be made responsible for guarding these resources.

Recent research on arid zones has caused some scientists to vacillate between optimism and pessimism, especially with regard to solar energy and the economics of water desalinization. This research, however, has focused mainly on such subjects as soil, water, climate, and agriculture. There have been very few studies on architecture and none on comprehensive city planning. Thus future research must focus on the unique features of the planning, construction, and operation of cities in deserts. The researchers must be concerned with the fact that the stress of the desert climate and the fragility of the environment require unique physical forms.

NOTES

1. Two criteria are to be considered in regard to precipitation and aridity: the annual average rainfall and its distribution. An annual

amount of 25 cm (or 10 in) of rain is considered to be the minimum required to support dry farming, but only if such an amount is distributed evenly throughout the rainy season. [See A. Holmes, *Principles of Physical Geology* (New York: Ronald Press, 1965), p. 769]. A zone so characterized may be viewed as bordering on being a hot, dry, arid zone, for below its norms an arid zone is established.

2. See Peveril Meigs, "World Distribution of Arid and Semi-arid Homoclimates," in *Review of Research on Arid Zone Hydrology* (Paris: UNESCO, 1953), pp. 203–210.

3. Some of the following social analysis is based on personal experience as an early settler and founder of an arid-zone kibbutz and as an interested observor of other arid-zone communities.

4. See Erik Cohen, "Man as the Initiator of Arid Zone Development: Social and Cultural Aspects," paper presented at the Symposium on Arid Zone Development: Potentialities and Problems, Boston, Mass., October 23–25, 1975, pp. 2–4.

5. Alexander Berler, "Social Policies for Israeli Development Towns," in *International Urban Growth Policies: New-Town Contributions,* Gideon Golany, ed. New York: John Wiley and Sons, in press.

6. For example, the Nabataeans, an ancient people who settled primarily in the arid land of the north Sinai, the Negev of southern Israel, and southern Jordan, established trading cities with very sophisticated, irrigated agricultural systems. More significantly, Ovdat, Mamshit, Rechovot, and the mountain fortress of Petra formed a chain of trading and agricultural cities along a major international highway running east–west and connecting North Africa, Arabia, and the Red Sea. Many of their sophisticated, innovative systems of irrigation, storing water, creating fertile soil, and using erosion and other arid-zone climatic factors for settlement survival must be studied to ascertain their applicability in our time.

7. Susan W. Stewart, "'Dollar Drain' Continues From Frostbelt to Sunbelt," *The Washington Post,* July 10, 1977, p. C4.

8. Allen V. Kneese and Jennifer Zamora, "The Future of the Arid Land," paper presented at the Symposium on Arid Zone Development: Potentialities and Problems, Boston, Mass., October 23–25, 1975, p. 15.

9. Early civilizations, for example, that accommodated large cities in arid zones developed along the great rivers: the Tigris, Euphrates, Nile, and Indus.

10. Paul Lampl, *Cities and Planning in the Ancient Near East* (New York: George Braziller, 1968), p. 17.

11. *Bajada* or *bahada* along with fans constitutes 21.4 percent of the southwestern United States, whereas in other deserts, such as the Sahara, it comprises only 1 percent. See Ronald U. Cooke and Andrew Warren, *Geomorphology in Deserts* (Berkeley and Los Angeles: University of California Press, 1973), p. 53; B. W. Sparks, *Geomorphology* (London: Longmans, Green and Company, 1960), p. 256.

12. Cooke, p. 188.

13. Arthur N. Strahler and Alan H. Strahler, *Introduction to Environmental Science* (New York: John Wiley and Sons, 1974), p. 381.

14. Cooke, p. 191.

15. Cooke, pp. 196–197.

16. Cooke, pp. 192–194.

17. Cooke, p. 215.

18. Sparks, p. 256.

19. The term *playa* or *dry lake* is used in North America; *sabkha,* in the Middle East.

20. Cooke, p. 218.

21. Cooke, p. 217.

22. Cooke, p. 217.

23. Cooke, p. 217.

24. Cooke, p. 223.

25. Cooke, p. 225.

26. Cooke, p. 216.

27. Douglas S. Way, *Terrain Analysis: A Guide to Site Selection Using Aerial Photographic Interpretation* (Stroudsburg, Pa.: Dowden, Hutchinson and Ross, 1973), p. 326.

28. Cooke, p. 175.

29. Cooke, p. 175.

30. Cooke, p. 175.

31. Strahler, p. 203.

32. Way, p. 261.

33. K. W. Glennie, *Desert Sedimentary Environment* (Amsterdam: Elsevier Publishing Company, 1970), p. 118.

34. Way, pp. 262–263.

35. Way, p. 279.

36. Way, p. 279.

37. Way, p. 283.

38. Cooke, p. 229.

39. Cooke, pp. 233–236.

40. Way, p. 261.

41. Way, p. 269.

42. Strahler, p. 202.

SUGGESTED READINGS

Amiran, D. H. K., and Wilson, A. H., eds. *Coastal Deserts: Their Natural and Human Environments.* Tucson: University of Arizona Press, 1973.

Aronin, J. E. *Climate and Architecture.* New York: Van Nostrand–Reinhold Books, Division of Litton Educational Publishers, 1953.

Danz, E. *Sun Protection—An International Architectural Survey.* New York: Frederick A. Praeger, 1967.

Givoni, B. *Man, Climate and Architecture.* Amsterdam: Elsevier Publishing Company, 1969.

McGinnies, W. G., and Goldman, B. J., eds. *Arid Land in Perspective.* Tucson: University of Arizona Press, 1969.

McGinnies, W. G., Goldman, B. J., and Paylore, P. *Food, Fiber and the Arid Land.* Tucson: University of Arizona Press, 1971.

Olgyay, V. *Design with Climate—Bioclimatic Approach to Architectural Regionalism.* Princeton, N.J.: Princeton University Press, 1964.

Rudofsky, B. *Architecture without Architects: A Short Introduction to Non-Pedigreed Architecture.* Garden City, N.Y.: Doubleday and Company, 1964.

Saini, B. S. *Building Environment—An Illustrated Analysis of Problems in Hot Dry Land.* Sydney: Angus and Robertson, 1973.

World Meteorological Organization. *Urban Climates,* proceedings of the Symposium on Urban Climates and Building Climatology, jointly organized by the World Health Organization and World Meteorological Organization, Brussels, October 1968, Vol. 1, Technical Note no. 108. Geneva: Secretariat of the World Meteorological Organization, 1970.

CHAPTER 2

Planning for the Climatic Realities of Arid Regions

HELMUT E. LANDSBERG

Over the last 30 years or so, UNESCO has paid a great deal of attention to the arid zones. There are two very good reasons why it has done so and why we too should begin to study these regions. First, many people have settled close to the arid zones, and, second, we are beginning to run out of land because mankind has been unduly prolific. In less than 50 years there will be nearly 6.5 billion people in the world, and it is going to be difficult to house and feed all of them. Therefore land of any kind is going to be at a premium, and there is an incentive to turn to arid and semiarid areas.

A 1975 UNESCO report describes fully these arid and semiarid areas. According to this report, these areas comprise one third of the earth's land and have 10 percent of its population. These people own one half of the world's cattle, one third of its sheep, and two thirds of its goats, and the prevailing climate places severe limitations on the water and food available for this livestock, since the rainfall is highly variable and other water resources are also intermittent and unreliable. Furthermore, this problem has been aggravated by both overgrazing and overpopulation, as unplanned agricultural settlements replaced nomadism over an interval of years of relatively abundant rainfall.[1]

This settlement pattern is one of the great problems of these areas, and to a large extent it has developed for political reasons. The countries that rule over many of these arid zones have steadfastly refused to accept the nomadism which provides a time-honored defense against recurrent arid conditions. As we will demonstrate later, arid zones are marked by times of feast and times of famine: there are years of abundant rainfall, and in those years everything is lush; and there are other years when rainfall is lacking and everything dries up. The solution that evolved in these regions was temporary occupancy—nomadism. The minute the wells dried up and the grazing gave out, the temporary residents would pack up and move somewhere else, where grazing and water were to be found. To certain political regimes, however, this adjusting process is anathema, because they cannot control nomadic populations that do not generally respect so-called national boundaries—assuming they can find such boundaries—and move to wherever they can find the proper environmental conditions for their families and their herds.

When these areas were under colonial rule, especially in Africa, the colonial governments did not interfere with nomadism, since the nomads generally passed from one colonial possession to another, rather than from one sovereign state to another. The Sahel south of the Sahara, for example, was at one time almost entirely under French rule. Now seven different countries are there. These countries all have well-marked borders, and they do not countenance a neighboring nation's tribe moving across them, even if the tribe has the resources to sustain itself. The new governments have simply said, "You people get settled, or else." "Or else" was usually a gun. Once settled in an area where, from time to time, nature does not cooperate, these once nomadic tribes faced problems.

In the recent good years, in the Sahel and in other parts of the world, people have multiplied. Furthermore, world agencies like the World Health Organization have contributed to the population increase by providing immunizations and other health services that were unavailable in these areas before. As a result, whereas once half of the children under five died from infectious diseases, many more of them now survive and have to be fed. Hence the natural balance that had established itself over many centuries, if not milennia, has been even further upset. As UNESCO states, "Mobility remains the basic element of effective adaptation to the exploration of sparse resources which are sporadic and short-lived. Yet by virtue of its nature, aims, and methods, the modern state, whatever its political options, is, owing to its very structure, against this mobility."[2] As a result, then, of both political and health-related factors, the human settlements in arid and semiarid regions face numerous problems. As UNESCO notes, human water and food supplies are by no means assured, and the housing thus far built has not coped effectively with the enormous amounts of solar radiation and has not been positioned to assure adequate ventilation. As a result of these errors in designing, the work capacity of the population has been severely limited by the enervating heat.[3]

We have to cope with these already existing problems, as well as plan for future ones that will inevitably develop as arid and semiarid regions grow in population.

THE CLIMATE OF ARID AND SEMIARID REGIONS

Defining Arid and Semiarid Regions. Table 1 reveals where the dry regions are to be found. In Africa there are 18 million km^2 of dry area; that represents 64 percent of the African continent. It is therefore not the place where we can expect much development. Asia has 16 million km^2 of dry land—39 percent of its total; Australia has 6 million km^2—81 percent of the continent; North America has 4 million km^2—17 percent of its area; South America has 3 million km^2—16 percent; and Europe has only a negligible amount.

These dry regions are characterized by the coincidence of a number of climatic extremes. The planner has to start with these basic realities. Usually planners are quite well informed: they look at the landscape, they have topographic charts, and so on, but they seldom reckon with the climate. They neglect it, thinking it will take care of itself. It does, usually with a vengeance.

Rainfall. The first climatic extreme is, of course, minimal rainfall. The world rainfall chart by the famous Munich climatologist Professor Geiger reveals where the arid and semiarid zones are. They can be found even in North America, where the western Great Plains are relatively dry.[4]

Variability of Rainfall. A second defining climatic characteristic is the extreme variability of rainfall. In the arid regions it is a rags-to-riches or feast-to-famine condition. For example, in the Sahel there can be as much rainfall in the best years—not on the average—as there is in Pennsylvania or elsewhere on the East Coast of the United States. But then there are other years when conditions are completely dry. Planners must cope with these wide swings, and that is not very easy. In the Book of Genesis, Joseph advises the Pharoah about 7 lean years to come and tells him to build warehouses and to store his grain. In the areas we are dealing with, this is easier said than done.

Sunshine. A third climatic extreme is the high mean duration of sunshine. It is high even in midwinter. Thus excessive sunshine is another problem that planners have to face, and again one not easily

Table 1   Geographical Distribution of Arid and Semiarid Land

Continent	Amount of Arid and Semiarid Land (million km^2)	Percentage of Total Land
Africa	18	64
Asia	16	39
Australia	6	81
North America	4	17
South America	3	16
Europe	1	1

Source: Peveril Meigs, "World Distribution of Arid and Semi-Arid Homoclimates," *Reviews of Research on Arid Zone Hydrology* (Paris: UNESCO, 1953), pp. 203–209.

dealt with when designing housing or any other structure. This sunshine is, however, not entirely unwelcome; in fact, some of it is needed for photosynthesis in plants and for other vital processes such as running machinery and lighting and cooling dwellings.

Solar Radiation. A fourth climatic extreme characterizing the regions under discussion is high levels of solar radiation intensity. This is, of course, an enormous energy resource. Here, again, the highest levels are found in northern Africa, parts of Asia (especially Asia Minor), parts of the American Southwest, most of Australia, certain parts of South America, South Africa, and Southwest Africa. The potential energy is quite stupendous. The only problem is that the radiation is intermittent, and it is difficult to cope with the interruptions caused by nightfall and occasional cloudy days. The planner must keep this climatic fact in mind because it will probably be impossible to increase the size or number of settlements in arid areas without using solar energy. It is, furthermore, an energy source that is available permanently, not for the next 100 years only, like, perhaps, Arab oil. Since cities are built to last for several hundred years, it is this kind of energy that will have to be developed in order to make the arid areas inhabitable.

Land Fertility. A fifth factor characterizing arid and semiarid regions is low land fertility. The planner has to provide for feeding a development's residents. In the dry areas the land is not fertile, and almost nothing in the world within our present technological knowledge can make it fertile. There are no soils to speak of in these regions, and we cannot grow anything without soil. People with large amounts of money, like the Saudi Arabians, may be able to grow food plants in greenhouses, but the cost of this is great compared to the outlay for ordinary agriculture.

High Temperatures. A sixth climatic extreme is excessively high temperatures. The arid regions are the areas of the world with the highest air temperatures— about 40° Centigrade (approximately 104° Fahrenheit) or even 50°C (122°F). These are temperatures beyond the body temperature of a human being. If we put a man out there, he would "sizzle." Planners designing in this area—in Persia, Arabia, North Africa, South and Southwest Africa, central Australia, regions east of the Andes, lower California, Arizona—will have to cope with these high temperatures.

Low Temperatures. A seventh climatic extreme coincident in arid and semiarid regions is quite low temperatures. Even in the Sahara Desert, from time to time, freezing temperatures of 0°C (32°F) occur. This, of course, applies to the arid zones of North America as far south as Mexico, to the desert regions of South Africa, to South America, and to inner Australia. In these areas temperatures go from one extreme to another. I recall my personal experience in the Sahara Desert during World War II. In the daytime the temperature was over 90°, and everything one wore was too hot, but at night the temperature was below freezing. There was, in other words, a range of 90 to 100°F in a single day. One had to have clothing of various weights, tent material, and blankets in order to cope with such a wide range of temperature. The planner will have to provide for these extremes just as the Army did. Here we are talking about maintaining cars, jeeps, trucks, and other machinery as well as human beings, and the rate of deterioration of machinery in an area with extreme diurnal as well as annual temperatures is unduly high.

Albedo. An eighth and last climatic factor is apparent in any satellite picture of the earth's surface. In such a picture the Mediterranean, because it does not reflect any light, looks black. On the other hand, the Sahara Desert, which reflects a considerable amount of light, is white. The difference between black and white is essentially a difference in "albedo," which is the precentage of incoming energy that can reflect in various wavelengths. Thus, if the albedo is 90 percent, the surface reflects 90 percent of the incoming energy. Seawater has an albedo of approximately 8 or 10 percent; water is therefore a very good absorber of energy. Desert or beach sand, in contrast, is a poor absorber of energy: it will reflect a considerable amount, its albedo measuring approximately 30 percent. Needless to say, arid regions tend to have high albedoes, that is, they absorb energy (including heat) poorly.

Political and Health Considerations. These eight climatic factors are coincident in arid or semiarid regions. The problems they collectively pose are complicated by political factors. Many developing nations are in these areas, and the people that live there are very poor. Therefore whatever housing is developed is usually developed by the government. Naturally, the minister of finance of a small, developing nation wants to spend as little as possible while attaining maximization of living space. Thus, climatically inappropriate and rather uncomfortable dwellings are built because they are inexpensive and use little land. The people are given very low priority. Whether or not they are productive does not seem to make any difference.

The climatic and political problems that have been mentioned are further complicated by the low level of public health in many of these areas. The tsetse fly and malaria mosquito pose important problems. In at least one country I visited, about 40 percent of the adult population is incapable of working simply because they are severely debilitated by both malnutrition and disease. When a nation has serious health problems, housing needs tend to be neglected because nutrition and health become the priority concerns.

THE DESERT LANDSCAPE AND IMPLICATIONS FOR PLANNERS

The Natural Landscape. Imagine a typical desert landscape with the Barchan dunes, miles and miles of them. These desert lands look very peaceful. When the winds get strong, however, they will begin to pick up dust particles; and when what the meteorologist calls "instability" exists, these dust particles will be carried up to very high levels—up to 2 to 3 km (approximately 10,000 ft)—without any effort. This is the meteorological condition popularly known as a sandstorm.

What does a sandstorm do to the people living on the ground? Very unpleasant things. There is nothing worse than to be caught in a *samoom* or *simoom* or *ghibli* (every tribe living there has its own name for a sandstorm). All one can do is hold on. The sand gets into a person's nose and eyes and mouth and throat, and it also gets into his home if it is not sealed off. The sandstorm is one of the realities of life, not just in the desert, but near it as well. It is one of the elements of the environment with which a planner has to cope when he designs.

The type and the amount of vegetation in a semi-arid country are other factors that the planner must consider. In the Sahel there is an average of about 7 to 10 in. of rain per year, but there are years when the area is completely dry and other years when it gets as much as 20 in.[5] Characteristically, there are a few shrubs and bushes; the rest of the land is dry, either completely dry or spotted with grasses that grow there during some seasons. Usually, in the rainy season the landscape becomes green in 2 days, and

then, 40 days after the rainy season is over, the green disappears and everything is dry again.

The rivers in arid and semiarid regions characteristically flow through vast stretches of dry land with some isolated tree growth near their banks. There are also isolated shrubs. If no rain gauges are available, an interesting sport is to count the number of shrubs per square kilometer. This indicates approximately how much rainfall there was recently, because each shrub has a root system that goes sideways and takes in every bit of water as it crowds out everything else. These rivers sometimes shrink with drought, so that maintaining a water supply is often a chaotic affair.

The planner must also be aware of the nature of oases. An oasis is centered on a water source, and there is often fairly lush vegetation. Geologically it is an unusually low area, and for this reason a confluence of water occurs if there is any water in the area. There are also wells that surface in the oasis area. Many of these wells are reasonably perennial and therefore will permit a permanent settlement. The oasis is dramatically different from its surroundings. In addition to water, it offers another thing that is extremely important—shade. There is nothing more precious than shade in arid and semiarid zones: it is the one commodity that nature rarely provides. Planners accustomed to working with landscaping will have to be aware that landscaping is practically impossible in a semiarid zone, except in an oasis.

In and near the oasis, one can sometimes acquire water by drilling wells. In fact, the colonial powers, as well as their successors, have drilled wells in a great many locations in the semiarid zones. They did something very risky. They did get water, and much of that water was fairly good, although some of it was (and is) a little brackish. The water, however, was "fossil" water, water that was stored there during the Pleistocene glaciations, when these areas were wet. It was old water that had seeped into the ground through the sand and remained hidden there on top of an impermeable layer somewhere underground. In drilling for this water, the colonial and subsequent governments were mining water, not using the surplus water that people use in the humid regions, water that otherwise would drain off into the ocean. Since this source of water, like any mine, can run dry, a planner relying on such wells has to ascertain what the water table is, how it is replenished, and how often it is replenished before he builds; otherwise, he may establish a settlement based on water in wells and then find in 10 or 15 years that the resource has been exhausted.

The Man-Made Landscape. The planner can learn many things by inspecting modern settlements in the arid zone. Typically, two things are noticeable. First, in certain directions the buildings have no windows; second, the walls are white. We will come back to these two items later.

An old Arabic city in Saudi Arabia reveals two other lessons: first, relatively little land is used for the settlement; second, the streets (as is true of every old settlement in arid countries, in the Near East as well as in Arabia, Algeria, and Tunisia) are narrow so that one building shades the other. A person can walk in some streets and think that he is walking in a canyon. As in a canyon, it is cool in these shaded streets because the sun does not reach there. Furthermore, a dark area will radiate against the sky and will therefore cool. Such an area not only does not gain any heat but also will in fact lose heat, so that it is possible to walk around at noon in these cities where the streets are laid out in the right direction and be relatively comfortable.

Man not only builds buildings, but also changes the landscape by farming and by raising animals. In the middle of the Sahel drought, an area that was quite green was evident from aloft. When the area was investigated, it was found to be fenced in. No livestock was allowed to graze, and no wild animals could enter to forage. That land stayed relatively green, the roots were preserved, what little rainfall occurred still took effect, and the vegetation was maintained. This occurrence reveals a great deal about sheep and goats. These animals are root eaters; when they do not get enough grass, they begin to dig down and eat the roots, thereby totally destroying the vegetation and often leading to what is called the encroachment of the desert. This, it should be emphasized, has not come about naturally: there is no evidence whatsoever that the desert migrates. If it seems to migrate, the reason is that man has laid the groundwork for desert migration through overgrazing and the introduction of large numbers of rodent-type grazers like sheep and goats into the area. The roots they devour would, if left intact, bind the soil and prevent it from blowing; when they are gone, the desert grows.

The experience of the United States in the Great Plains reveals that sheep and goats are not the only causes of desert encroachment. The Great Plains are in a semiarid region, but during the 1920s, with large amounts of rain, the area looked quite fertile and was therefore plowed up and converted into wheatland. Then a drought came in the 1930s, and wind erosion

began. It blew away a considerable amount of the soil of western Kansas, Nebraska, Oklahoma, and Arkansas. The residents were forced to become nomads and to migrate to other parts of the country. They had to pay the price for not living in accord with the general ecology of the country and for putting in either the wrong crop or the wrong animal. Since then we have learned some things; but in the last few years, with wheat at a premium, people again began to plow up these same areas. Now they are experiencing a relatively dry spell that could again lead to more soil blowing, the resultant loss of valuable soil, and the initiation of a vicious local ecological cycle.

THE PHOENIX, ARIZONA, LANDSCAPE AND ITS IMPLICATIONS FOR PLANNERS

Basic information regarding climate can be gathered for practically any dry area and can provide the planner with insights. Phoenix, Arizona, is one of this nation's largest cities in an arid or semiarid region. The data on it should thus provide especially pertinent insights.

Figure 1A gives us the amount of precipitation in millimeters (25 mm to 1 in.). We can see in the winter months from January to April a continuously downward trend. Then in May or June Phoenix really gets dry; after that, it has a wet season, thunderstorms mostly; then rain diminishes to rise again into December. This precipitation is essentially the amount of Phoenix's water income. A planner always has to worry a great deal about a locale's water income. An area has two sources of water: the sky and importation. If an area is allowed to import water, as the people in Arizona do from the Colorado River, the people in Mali do from the Niger, and the people in Egypt do from the Nile, a planner should take this into consideration. But, if we assume, just for the sake of argument, that someday the people in Ethiopia will become belligerent toward the Egyptians and cut off the Nile to spite them, that the Israelis and Jordanians will fight over the Jordan River and that the same kind of battle will take place on the Rio Grande between the United States and Mexico and on the rivers between the various states of the union, there will then arise very difficult problems with regard to importing water. The planner thus must rely as much as possible on an area's nonimported water income. He will have to watch this water

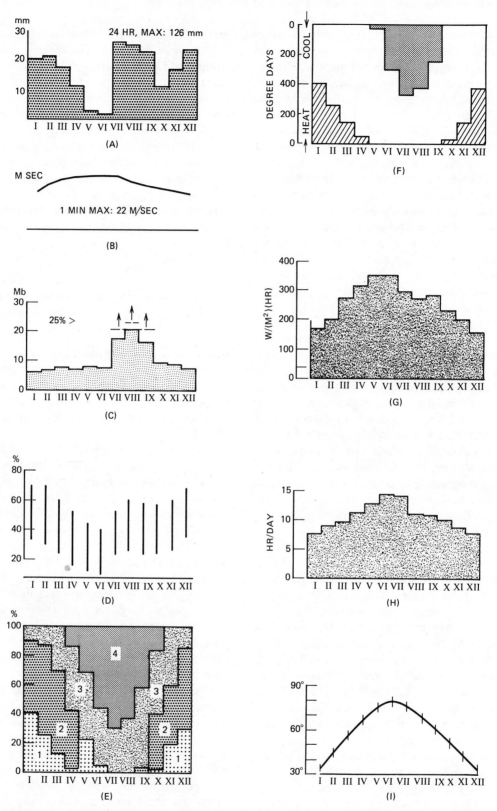

Figure 1. Climatic conditions by month in Phoenix, Arizona. Data from the U.S. Weather Bureau. (A) Precipitation. (B) Average windspeed. (C) Average vapor pressure. (D) Diurnal variation of relative humidity. (E) Temperature frequency. (F) Degree days above or below 65°F. (G) Solar energy on horizontal surface. (H) Daily sunshine. (I) Solar elevation at local noon.

income not just for 1 month or 1 year, but over a long period of time, if his plans are to make climatic sense.

Furthermore, the planner, in conjunction with governmental authorities, has to develop in every semiarid or arid area facilities for water storage. Moreover, these facilities must be protected against contamination and evaporation. The problem of evaporation is very serious because evaporation in a dry climate proceeds at an extraordinary rate and a good deal of water income can be just thrown away if the water is not covered. Thus, since ancient times, people have had cisterns in these areas as well as in others where water storage is problematic. Even in Bermuda, where there is plenty of water coming from the sky but no possibility, because of rapid evaporation and geological structure, of forming a groundwater table, people have tiles on their roofs, and every drop of water they collect is led into a cistern.

Figure 1B presents the average monthly wind speeds for Phoenix. They are generally very low, only 2 to 3 m/sec (approximately 3 or 4 mph), but they are a little higher in the summer than in the winter. This is a very important factor for the planner because in this particular city he will not be able to use the wind to dilute air pollutants: they just will not be carried away. Throughout Arizona, in my opinion, the people have already exhausted their air resource; they have long since exhausted it in southern California, where not enough ventilation is provided by the wind to put any more pollutants into the atmosphere. As a result in large portions of the American Southwest any process that puts air pollutants into the atmosphere has to be controlled at the source, a very expensive undertaking. The planner, however, cannot forget to also design for the occasional high wind speeds. The Phoenix area experiences heavy thunderstorms, and so, occasionally, there are winds that can be destructive—as high as 60 mph.

Another meteorological factor is represented in Figure 1C—the vapor pressure. As the chart reveals, the water content of the Phoenix atmosphere is very low, except in midsummer. When the vapor pressure gets above approximately 15 millibars, the environment is considered to be uncomfortable. The planner must be prepared to counteract this high Phoenix midsummer vapor pressure as well as the more usual low vapor pressure.

Figure 1D represents the monthly diurnal variations in relative humidity, the vertical lines connecting the high points and the low points. In the winter

Phoenix has fairly high relative humidities at night, but very low (30 percent) readings during the day; in the summer the humidity never goes much above 40 percent and often registers below 20 percent. This generally low humidity has an advantage and a disadvantage from the designer's point of view. The advantage is that he can use evaporative cooling systems in areas like this if there is sufficient water. In Arizona many air conditioners are based on evaporative cooling, and the city imports the water to operate them. The disadvantage, of course, is that any open water—in irrigation ditches, open lakes, reservoirs, and so on—tends to be rapidly lost. A good deal of the water behind the Grand Coulee Dam, for example, is lost because of rapid evaporation.

Figure 1E represents temperature frequency for the different months of the Phoenix year. Area 1 represents temperatures from 25 to 40°F, area 2 from 45 to 65°F, area 3 from 65 to 85°F, and area 4 above 85°F—four convenient steps. The first range represents a situation in which there is an absolute need for heating, and this situation exists in Phoenix significantly in November, December, January, and February. Heating may also be required in the second range, especially if the population is either sensitive to cold or is not working. In the fourth range and in the upper reaches of the third, cooling is required, and air conditioning is an extreme luxury because it uses four times as much energy as heating. That is a horrible ratio. In other words, it is much easier and cheaper to heat than to cool. Despite the cost, however, in these semiarid areas cooling is necessary for two reasons: one involves health, and the other, efficiency. If the environment is too hot, the productivity of workers goes down. To employ people usefully, it is necessary to extract as much labor from them as possible. As has been proved time and time again, if they do not feel comfortable, they either make errors, have accidents, or perform a comparatively small amount of work. In other words, if people are to work efficiently, they must be kept comfortable. The planner must keep this in mind.

Figure 1F presents a somewhat different plot of the temperature frequency, using 65°F as the separation point. Days on which heating will probably be required are indicated by the area marked with horizontal lines; days on which cooling will probably be required, by the "marbled" area.

As mentioned above, such heating and cooling require energy. Figure 1G represents the solar energy in Arizona on a horizontal surface in $W/(m^2)(hr)$. As the chart reveals, there is a very large amount of energy: even in January the sun provides nearly 200 $W/(m^2)(hr)$. Our present solar energy exploitation is about 1 percent of the potential but could probably easily be increased to approximately 5 percent. As the exploitation rate goes up, problems diminish because solar energy is free energy. We do not have to order it or worry about replenishment. It is there year after year: it is clearly reliable. One major problem encountered in relying on solar energy is caused by the seasonal variation in the amount of daily sunshine. This can be accurately charted, however, and solar energy devices can probably be adjusted to account for the variation. The planner must, therefore, be aware of the implications of the information relayed by a chart like Figure 1H.

Figure 1I presents another factor that a planner anticipating the necessity to cool must consider: the solar elevation at noon in the particular area. (A whole series of such curves for each hour of the day could have been drawn.) The solar elevation is extremely important for designers to note because the design of shading has to be based on this information.

Because so many of these factors deal with comfort, we need to explain what meteorologists mean by this term. Figure 2 is a comfort diagram. It plots relative humidity against temperature in degrees Celsius. The higher diagonal line represents the upper limit of survival. If there is a condition of 30 percent relative humidity and 45°C, people cannot take it: the body simply cannot throw off enough heat. Even in the hatched zone to the left of the diagonal, there is a strong possibility of heatstroke. Man learned the dangers inherent in the heatstroke zone by several painful experiences. During World War II the United States suffered a very large

number of casualties from heatstroke in the tropics of the Pacific; more recently, the Israelis and Arabs had many heatstroke victims when they were fighting their various wars in the Sinai Desert. The lower left-hand corner of the chart indicates the area of real comfort and also of maximum efficiency. In view of these facts, it should be clear that comfort is a fundamental concept, one that planners must be constantly cognizant of.

Although Figure 1 presents data for only one city, it is rather typical of arid regions. Thus the implications for planners and designers noted above are also typical. Similar information is easily available for other arid and semiarid regions. Every meteorological service in the world has, in one form or another, this kind of information. Often, however, it is not available in the form of a clear, easy-to-read graph. The National Climatic Center in Asheville, North Carolina, has all the data for this country in its computer library. Its computers will even graph the information on request. The thing to do before designing, therefore, is to acquire and carefully study the climatic data, as was done here for Phoenix.

CLIMATE AND ITS RELATIONSHIP TO DEVELOPMENT: A MODEL

Figure 3 is an elaborate diagram showing how the three important environmental factors of solar radiation, precipitation, and wind are related to developmental considerations. Radiation, first of all, produces photochemical reactions of two types: one in vegetation to create fiber; the other acting with a pollutant to create unpleasant environmental gases like the ozone in Los Angeles. Radiation also causes illumination and glare, two factors that cannot be neglected. To be dazzled by light is an unpleasant experience. Not only can it affect the eyes, but also it can cause migraine headaches in a number of people who cannot stand the slightest bit of glare. The temperature is also, of course, produced by the energy that radiates from the sun, and, together with the humidity (a derivative of the precipitation) and the ventilation (a derivative of the wind), affects a person's comfort in a given environment. This, in turn, influences the needs for heating and air conditioning.

In the center of Figure 3 a box enclosed by double lines represents the water supply; it is central because it is the critical and unique element needed to operate in an arid zone. The supply is derived from precipita-

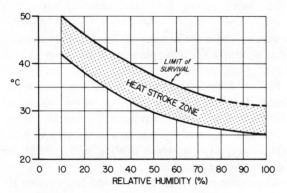

Figure 2. Comfort (temperature vs. relative humidity).

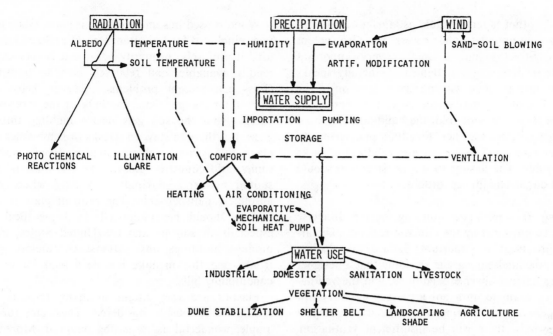

Figure 3. Climatic factors and their relationship to development.

tion, importation, and pumping. Pumping involves the use of either stored water from the rainy season or fossil water. Sometimes with pumping and almost always with importation, there are storage problems.

The bottom portion of Figure 3 details the uses of water in a developed arid or semiarid area. First of all, industry uses water: no kind of industry can be run without water, and the larger the industry, the more water is needed. If the plants in question are power plants, whether atomic or fossil fuel, they need water for cooling; if they manufacture steel or any other kind of metal such as aluminum, they need water. In addition, water is essential for domestic uses: washing, cooking, sanitation. Livestock needs water in considerable amounts. It is required for vegetation to stop desert migration, to provide shelter belts (a very useful defense against soil blowing), and to provide landscaping and shade. Finally, water is needed to irrigate the land used for agricultural purposes. In the United States, far more water is used in the West for irrigation than for all other purposes combined; in fact, agriculture in some areas would completely collapse and we would not be able to feed ourselves, let alone other peoples, if we did not have irrigation. Nor is the United States unique in depending so heavily on irrigation. In many countries in the Old World, irrigation has been the mainstay of agriculture for millenia. In China and Southeast Asia agriculture is also largely dependent on irrigation.

WHAT CLIMATIC FACTORS SHOULD GOVERN

Climatic factors should govern settlement design, building design, building materials, and energy sources used, as Table 2 indicates. All of these variables are important.

Settlement Design. Topography is an important variable because it governs what meteorologists call microclimate, climate on a very small scale. Topography also governs the air pollution potential, that is, the possibility of pollutant accumulation if there are pollutant sources. Such sources need not be in-

Table 2   What Climatic Factors Should Govern

Settlement Design	Building Design	Building Material	Energy Used
Topography	Architecture	Stone	Wood
Air pollution	Shading	Brick	Coal
potential	Landscaping	Building	Oil
Street layout	Shielding	blocks	Gas
Housing density	Ventilation	Concrete	Sun
Parks, open	Heating	Wood	Wind
spaces	Air con-	Glass	
	ditioning	Plastics	
	Insulation	Metals	
	Roofing		

dustrial; other agents, such as agricultural machinery, automobiles, and buses, are also potent sources. Street layout is another very important variable in designing a settlement. Generally speaking, we have to build with due consideration of the winds. Density of settlement is also a significant variable. If shade is desired, the buildings may have to be placed close together. Finally, a planner has to consider how much open space is needed for parks and the like. The answer to this question too should depend on the climatic conditions.

Building Design. The building design likewise should be governed by the climatic realities. The architecture itself is important, as are the shading devices, the landscaping, the shielding that a designer provides against adverse conditions, and the ventilation. For example, in a hot area that has very low wind speeds, if the housing is misplaced with respect to the winds, there will be insufficient ventilation. The heating and air-conditioning plants of a structure must be designed with the climate in mind. Another very important element in arid-zone building design is insulation, because it is the one thing that tempers extreme outside variations in climatic factors. The easiest way to reduce the variations between daytime and nighttime temperatures is to put something between the inside and outside worlds: insulation does just this. There are now new types of insulation, remarkably good, that will have the same effect as a 3 ft thick wall with one-ninth the thickness. Finally, the design of the roof is also very important. A roof can be used to collect water, as in Bermuda, if properly designed. The roof will absorb heat from the sun; and, if the roof is not properly designed, this heat will cause considerable trouble.

Building Material. The building material selected should also be governed by climatic considerations. A great many materials are available: stone, brick, building blocks, concrete, wood, glass, plastic, and metals. Each one of them will react differently to the environment: some protectively, some adversely. Using the wrong material in the wrong place, therefore, may cause trouble. A considerable amount of current construction in many arid areas is of necessity done in concrete because builders do not have stone and find the importation of building blocks too expensive. In view of this limitation it is essential to know the physical characteristics of concrete and the best ways to work with it.

Wood is used in some areas; so is glass. Glass is, in fact, employed far too often. Recent architecture has used it profusely, primarily because it is very cheap, readily available, and relatively easy to transport. Glass can present problems, however, because it traps solar energy. Once the bulk of the short-wave energy from the sun gets into a building through glass, it is there to stay. In Alaska or some other cold place, this is most welcome, but in planning for the sunny, arid countries, glass is the one material that should be used sparingly and only where it is absolutely indispensable. The ratio of glass to wall surface should be minimized. In some localities, especially in Europe and the United States, many modern buildings have almost completely glass fronts, and this mistake has been paid for in air-conditioning bills.

Plastics are very useful in many respects and should be seriously considered. They are, for example, wonderful as insulating material. Moreover, new varieties of plastics can introduce inertia into a design. Metal is very useful under certain circumstances, but not always. In Africa many aboriginal dwellings characteristically have thatched roofs, which, although not always completely waterproof, insulate and reflect solar radiation and therefore are good in that climate. The colonial powers, however, used sheet metal or corrugated metal in these same areas. This was a bad mistake because metal heats up tremendously and turns dwellings into ovens.

Energy Source Used. The choice of energy source should similarly be governed by the climate. In arid and semiarid regions the choices are somewhat limited. Wood and coal are too scarce; oil and gas are too easily exhaustible. But there remain the sun and the wind. Any design for the future in the arid and semiarid zones should make use of both of these energy sources. In some areas the wind is not very helpful, but, where there is a mountain or a hill, wind can be used.

SPECIFIC RECOMMENDATIONS

The Heat Island. When a city is built, the local environment is altered. One of the most important consequences is the inadvertent creation of a heat island. First of all, an urban area invariably absorbs more heat from the sun than does an undeveloped one because the building materials usually have an albedo lower than that of most natural land environments. Thus they necessarily absorb more energy. Second, an urban area rejects man-made heat because machinery, combustion processes, and man in a city are heat rejecting. Since the rejected heat has to be dissipated into the atmosphere, the air becomes warmer there than in rural environments.

In designing and building a city, there should be concern about this heat island. The more surfaces that are impermeable—built of concrete and asphalt, such as parking lots, streets, and the like—the greater this heat island will be. It was originally thought that heat islands existed only in high-latitude cities, but recent measurements have revealed that the phenomenon occurs in South Africa and Australia, even though these areas have less heat rejected by domestic fuel consumption for heating.

Shade. Helpful in alleviating the heat island is the creation of shade. It is important, therefore, to divert, if possible, water into vegetation for the creation of shade. The best vegetation providing the greatest amount of cooling consists of trees rather than grass, because, especially in semiarid regions, grass will dry out and consequently any cooling effect, both by reflection of energy and by evapotranspiration, will be only temporary. In the cities that have been built up in the arid Southwest of the United States—Tucson, Phoenix, and Las Vegas—the residents divert some of their water supply to trees. Perhaps not many places can afford this luxury, but, if possible, planning should include trees.

Figure 4 shows the effectiveness of another means of providing shade, the simple overhang. One can hardly overestimate the effectiveness of an overhang. At 25° latitude, only when the sun is at its lowest will

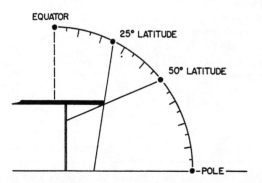

Figure 4. The effect of an overhang on sunlight at different latitudes. Redrafted after V. Olgyay, "The Temperate House," *Architectural Forum* **94**, no. 3 (March 1951), 184. Original based on this author's discussions with Olgyay.

light touch the upper half of the shaded wall or window. Only in high latitudes will the sun at its apogee penetrate, and these are the very latitudes where shading is usually unnecessary.

Windows. Numerous buildings throughout the Arabic world afford another clue as to how to reduce heat due to penetrating sunlight. These buildings feature no or few outside windows. The Spanish patio construction also features a minimum of windows on the exterior of the dwelling.

There may be psychological problems with eliminating all outdoor lighting, but a large number of persons in industry and in universities are working completely shut off from any outdoor light and performing very well. In several new buildings at the University of Maryland, all of the laboratories are in the center and are windowless. There have been no complaints from the persons working in these laboratories. People in many places work underground—in subway stations, for example—without complaining. They are quite comfortable.

If a designer does not want to go to the extreme of limiting or eliminating windows, he can make use of the outside shutter. This is an object that has been forgotten in many places. In the United States, outside shutters are usually mock shutters attached beside the window for decoration. In Europe, on the other hand, a very useful outside shutter called a *roulaux* can be rolled down to shut out the sun, cold, noise, and sometimes vandals too. The American Association for the Advancement of Science building in Washington, D.C., has an automatically regulated aluminum shutter system on the outside which turns with the sun so as to always exclude it. This requires several complex mechanisms and is undoubtedly beyond the average man's means. A shading device developed recently by Kaiser Industries keeps out 45 percent of the sunlight and is, in addition, relatively inexpensive. It has the additional advantage of also serving as an insect screen. American industry is coming up with more and more of these ideas, making shading affordable. If window screens are needed, the extra cost of combination shades and screens is small and purchases both insect protection and a certain amount of relief from sunlight.

Windows are also involved in ventilation, and they offer an additional opportunity for coping with the problem of cooling. The greatest absorber of heat in most buildings is the roof area; spaces directly under the roof act like a furnace. To combat this, insulation

Ceiling height

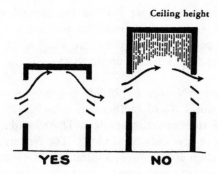

YES   **NO**

Figure 5. Window placement for ventilation. From D. H. K. Lee, *Physiological Objectives in Hot Weather Housing* (Washington: United States of America Housing and Home Finance Agency, 1953), p. 53.

can be placed under the roof or in the air chamber that is found there. Furthermore, it is possible to design the roof so that this space can be ventilated (if necessary with a fan), permitting the hot air to escape. A building design with the windows placed fairly high, which is not uncommon in some of the areas under consideration, provides this additional opportunity. Windows placed too low create a dead space under the ceiling and represent poor design. The key, as Figure 5 indicates, is to place the windows high. There are undoubtedly a number of other designs dependent on different window locations. They aim primarily at reducing indoor heat by improving ventilation. The planner has to be aware of the problems and should utilize a wind tunnel to determine optimal ventilation under circumstances simulating those of the region for which he is designing.

The Orientation of Towns. In a volume issued by the Swedish Building Research Institute and entitled *Teaching the Teachers,* Professor Ewald Liepold comments on ancient cities:

In the ancient world, the orientation of streets and buildings with respect to the winds was one of the most important problems of towns. Whoever has visited north Africa, for example, Tripoli, Libya, has certainly personally experienced the importance of wind orientation. Indeed, on days when the hot "Ghibli" blows from the desert, one does not feel it in the Arabic quarter which is closed in that direction. But in the modern quarter, one has trouble walking because the streets are oriented in the direction of the Ghibli. The Arabic section is opened toward the sea. It exploits during the hot season the sea breeze for cooling. Thus, natural conditions are used for climatization, an aim which can be attained by taking local climate into consideration.[6]

We can learn a great deal from these ancient Arabic cities: we can learn to build with the climate in mind. It is not, however, an easy lesson. Givoni had a difficult time at Haifa convincing the real estate interests and the city fathers not to block off the whole seafront with tall buildings that would have cut off the cooling sea breeze. He has designed for Haifa a seafront featuring buildings of various heights to permit the sea breeze to penetrate inland.[7] Unfortunately, the example of Haifa was not available for Chicago to follow. The lake breeze there is a natural air conditioner in summer. Since a number of very tall buildings were built along Lake Michigan, however, the breeze, which used to go at least a mile inland on a good summer day, no longer penetrates; it benefits only a thin layer two streets deep. This is not the way to build with climatic realities in mind.

The buildings of an arid-zone town can also be oriented vis-à-vis each other so as to promote cooling. Since the types of shadows that will be thrown by particular buildings are known, planners can, if it is desirable, design to use building shadows in lieu of shrubbery, deciduous trees, and the like.

Since the sun angles, the wind frequencies from

Table 3   Reflectivities and Emissivities of Some Typical Surfaces

Surface	Reflectivity (percent of solar radiation)	Reflectivity (percent of thermal radiation)	Emissivity (percent of thermal radiation)
Silver, polished	93	98	2
Aluminum, polished	85	92	8
Copper, polished	75	85	15
White lead paint	75	5	95
Chromium plate	72	80	20
White cardboard or paper	60–70	5	95
Light green paint	50	5	95
Aluminum paint	45	45	55
Wood, pine	40	5	95
Brick, various colors	23–48	5	95
Gray paint	25	5	95
Black matte	3	5	95

Source: D. H. K. Lee, *Physiological Objectives in Hot Weather Housing* (Washington: United States of America Housing and Home Finance Agency, 1953), p. 35. Lee's data are principally from *Handbook of Chemistry and Physics* (Cleveland: Rubber Chemical Publishing Company, 1949), pp. 2294–2296.

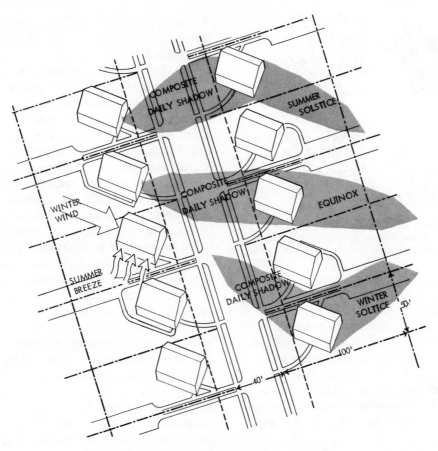

Figure 6. Housing orientation design for temperate zone.

various directions, and similar weather data are available, it is possible to design an optimal orientation for the particular environment. Such a design compromise—one which would be applicable to this nation's temperate region—combining maximal summer ventilation with optimal shadow is shown in Figure 6. The cold wind experienced in the eastern United States in the wintertime comes from the northwest. Therefore, on that side of a dwelling, maximum insulation and minimum fenestration are desirable. In the summertime, on the other hand, the object is to capture as much of the prevailing southwest winds as possible. A design would, of course, be quite different for an arid region, but the principle would be the same: discover the climatic realities and plan accordingly. Thus, near the desert, a plan should be designed to shut out the hot, dusty, dry desert winds and to let in the cool breezes, especially if the settlement is located anywhere near the seashore. If at all possible, terrain depressions where maximum contrasts invariably exist—the highest temperatures during the day and the lowest tempera-

tures at night—should be avoided. The ancients knew this; they always built on slopes because there exists the most even climatic conditions. Selection of the right slope vis-à-vis prevailing wind directions will provide more cooling ventilation. Buildings on the tops of hills, however, are exposed to undesirably high winds. If the area in question has hilltops, the planner should use them for the production of wind energy, remembering that a windmill is still a very useful device.

High Albedos. Table 3 and Figure 7 point the designer to the correct solutions to the albedo problem dealt with above. A dark surface will not reflect very much energy; rather, it will absorb it. A white surface, on the other hand, will, in both the infrared and the visible wavelengths, reflect most of the energy. This is very important for arid and semiarid areas. Desiring to increase the surface albedo, local people have painted everything white. Aluminum or aluminum paint, if affordable, can be used for the same purpose. Polished silver with a 93 percent

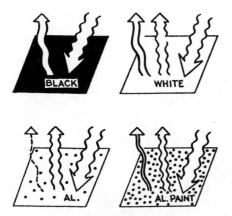

Figure 7. Albedos of four common substances. From D. H. K. Lee, *Physiological Objectives in Hot Weather Housing* (Washington: United States of America Housing and Home Finance Agency, 1953), p. 35.

albedo works very well but is, of course, extremely expensive. Ordinary white paint will reflect 75 percent of the radiation; aluminum, however, works in the infrared and thermal wavelengths as well as in the visible and is therefore preferable. Black paint, as Table 3 and Figure 7 show, reflects only about 5 percent of thermal radiation, so a planner must avoid any kind of dark material in semiarid areas. One must try to make the buildings as light as possible.

Water. The minimum water requirement for a working adult in a semiarid land is about 8 liters per day: that is what he needs in order to survive. In the old cities today, it is estimated that 60 liters of water per day per person is necessary for all purposes. In a modern westernized city, 250 liters of water per day per person is the estimated requirement. Moreover, that is just for domestic purposes; the figure does not include any industrial or agricultural use. Therefore, in the design stage, it is essential to find out what the water supply is, where it comes from, how reliable it is, and how much can be safely used and then match these data against the estimated needs. Any kind of vegetation decreases the gap between need and supply because, when the area does get rainfall, it is absorbed and reevaporated by the vegetation, instead of running off. The water may thus be recirculated.

CONCLUSION

Devotees of modern technology consider only the feasibility of producing any desired climate indoor anywhere on the globe. They do not reckon with the realities of resource use and energy considerations. Obviously, if one has to, one can heat a building at the South Pole, but this is a very profligate use of energy. Similarly, if one wants to settle and make productive a large number of people in an arid zone, air conditioning is not necessarily the best solution. My personal advice to planners in these areas is to watch nature. If you have ever been on the desert, one of the first things that intrigues you are the small lizards that live there by the thousands. You ask yourself, How do these creatures survive? It gets so hot, and they, cold-blooded animals, cannot possibly live without at least some adaptation mechanism. But the lizard does not have one. When it gets hot, the lizard runs around all night long, gets whatever food it needs, catches dew drops that deposit themselves during the nights (even on days when the temperature is above 90° the mercury may reach freezing during the night, so dew and even frost can form), and then goes at sunrise into its hole, which is about 20 cm below the surface. The diurnal high surface temperature does not penetrate that deeply, and the lizard stays very comfortable down there.

Why don't we do that? There is no good reason why we should not build underground, where the temperature is constant and the problem of ventilation is not prohibitive because it can certainly be handled by harnessing solar energy. Without a need for either air conditioning or heat, the cost of building will not be any greater than that for construction on the surface. One of my students who has studied areas in the United States (especially in Kentucky, Tennessee, and Arkansas) has concluded that building underground could result in tremendous energy savings by reducing the required winter heating and summer cooling. Thus, if I had to plan for the long-term use of arid and semiarid regions, I would "dig in."

A second piece of advice is not to take designs from other places and introduce them into arid and semiarid regions. The horrors of doing that are manifest in Las Vegas, where the designs are not at all adapted to the particular climate. We must instead work with the environment. We can manipulate the albedo (keeping the reflectivity at a maximum), we can manipulate the amount of shade to a certain extent, and we can manipulate ventilation. Once we realize what we can do, we have an arsenal to work with.

On the large scale, I do not see any real hope of a climatic change; so, where we can reforest or reestablish vegetation, we should do it, but that is a project that will take 20 or more years. We know that certain now-semiarid areas were forested before men cut down the trees because the lumber was valuable. It will now be an uphill struggle to rehabilitate these forests, partly because the soil has been washed away. Therefore the soil has to be rebuilt, layer after layer, first with very low-level vegetation, then with higher and higher types until finally enough good soil is available to support shrubbery and perhaps a few trees. We should not plant too densely: we are going to require a large amount of space for the necessarily large root systems. (A single tree may need almost an acre of land to get enough water.)

Finally, there is a need to limit population and prohibit certain kinds of industries. For example, a steel plant is out of place in a semiarid region because it uses an enormous amount of water. There are certain types of industries, however, that might easily be placed, with some restrictions, in an arid zone. We can profitably introduce electronic industries; in fact, they will probably do better there than in humid areas, where trouble with fungi and other things exists. An optical industry may be a possibility, although this will require the exclusion of dust. A variety of industries are acceptable because they are nonpolluting and use little or no water. Electronic assembly plants do not use much water; finishing industries are nonpolluting and require little water. These industries, however, need power, and that power will have to be provided. Both industrial development and population growth must be tied to the climatic situation and the concomitant available resources.

NOTES

1. UNESCO, "Obstacles to the Development of Arid and Semi-Arid Zones," *Nature and Resources,* **11,** no. 4 (October–December, 1975), 1–11.

2. *Ibid.,* p. 4.

3. *Ibid.,* pp. 1–11.

4. Rudolf Geiger, *Die Atmosphäre der Erde* (Darmstadt: Justus Perthes, n.d.), series of wall charts.

5. Helmut E. Landsberg, "Sahel Drought: Change of Climate or Part of Climate?" *Archive Der Metorologie, Geophysik Unb Bioklimatologie,* series B, vol. 23 (1975), 193–200.

6. Ewald Liepold, introductory remarks to National Swedish Institute for Building Research, *Teaching the Teachers on Building Climatology,* Counseil International du Bâtiment Proceedings, no. 25 (Stockholm, 1973), p. 16.

7. See Baruch Givoni, *Man, Climate and Architecture* (Amsterdam: Elsevier Publishing Company, 1969); *idem, Basic Study of Ventilation Problems in Hot Countries* (Haifa: Building Research Station, Technion—Israel Institute of Technology, 1962).

SUGGESTED READINGS

Gates, D. M. *Man and His Environment: Climate.* New York: Harper and Row, 1972.

Givoni, B. *Man, Climate and Architecture.* Amsterdam: Elsevier Publishing Company, 1969.

International Center for Arid and Semi-arid Land Studies. *Arid and Semi-arid Lands—A Preview.* Lubbock, Tex., 1967.

MacPhail, D. D. *The High Plains: Problems of Semiarid Environments,* Committee on Desert and Arid Zones Research of the Southwest and Rocky Mountain Division of the American Association for the Advancement of Science, Paper no. 15. Fort Collins, Colo., 1972.

Man's Responses to the Arid Ecosystem 2

CHAPTER 3

Physiological and Behavioral Responses to the Stresses of Desert Climate

ELIEZER KAMON

Engineers and physiologists whose main concern is man's adaptation to his environment have come to understand the interaction between man and his thermal environment. While the engineers have established the biophysical laws that govern heat exchange between man and his environment, the physiologists have gathered voluminous information on the body's functional characteristics under thermal stresses. The knowledge gained by the work done in these two disciplines provides us with the means to predict the strain put on man by the stresses of the environment and thus to design for his well-being and comfort. We need this capability because "deserts are no longer shunned. Man is increasingly exploiting desert regions for agriculture, travel, and warfare."[1] Since man's sensation of his environment—his feelings of comfort and of well-being—are strongly related to physiological responses to adverse environments, these factors underlie man's behavior when he is exposed to hot and cold ambient conditions, as he is in the desert.

Planners and architects interested in designing for human comfort in arid zones need to consider man's two main activities: work and leisure. Man's work can be impaired by unfavorable ambient conditions during working hours. Furthermore, discomfort during his leisure time can interfere with his performance on his job. The type of work, of course, has a substantial impact on the extent of man's interaction with his environment. Thus, when computing the total environmental effect, we must consider the two main types of work: (1) indoor, paced work, where, because man works at the demand of a machine, he may not be able to cope with the environment if the machine is not designed and paced correctly; and (2) outdoor work, where, because the heat load cannot be controlled, it is necessary to have appropriate rest periods under suitable conditions. In such circumstances, furthermore, the recreational facilities provided should take into account the needed relief from the inescapable exposure to the heat.

Although to a lesser extent, exposure to the cold should also be considered, since deserts, as Figure 1 indicates, are known to shift from very hot days to quite cold nights. However, arid zones are limited to dry ambient conditions, which are not as physiologically demanding as hot, humid environments.

Within this context of needs, we discuss (1) the biophysics of heat exchange, (2) the physiological responses to extreme heat and cold, and (3) some behavioral responses to exposure to unpleasant ambient temperatures. Before we turn to these topics, however, we must first discuss some general considerations.

GENERAL CONSIDERATIONS

Man, like other mammals, is constantly producing metabolic heat (M).[2] During work, M can increase tenfold. Since man is not 100 percent efficient, a large part of this energy is released as heat. This internally produced heat has to be transferred to the surface for dissipation. A small amount of heat is dissipated through the lungs. The main avenues of heat dissipation, however, are at the skin, and they are radiation, direct conduction, convection, and evaporation. Conduction requires surface contact, and this occurs mainly through the feet; however, since the feet are insulated, the heat conducted through them is negligible, leaving three main routes.

Figure 2 shows the range of ambient temperatures at which man's thermoregulation is physiological and the range at which it is behavioral. It can also be seen that the comfort zone is quite narrow and that a wider range of tolerable ambient temperatures exists because of the body's ability to respond to changing ambient conditions. However, man can tolerate an even wider range of ambient conditions because his behavioral thermoregulation involves the design of clothing and shelters, as well as innovations by his highly developed technology. Strained to the limit, man's physiological and behavioral thermoregulation allows him to maintain a body temperature of about 37°C during rest and up to 4°C higher during work. Since in very hot deserts the temperature can rise to 60°C during the day and can fall to below 0°C during the night, balanced heat exchange between man and his environment may not be reached when the metabolic rate (M) is too high for the body's systems to dissipate heat rapidly enough; when the surround-

ings are so hot as to add heat to the body by convection (C) and radiation (R); or when the surroundings are so cold as to suppress sweating, with the result that heat is rapidly lost from the body by R and C while M, despite its increase, is insufficient. Since convective (C) heat and radiative (R) heat can be transferred to the body if the air temperature is above the skin temperature, under certain circumstances quite common in the desert, the heat load on man will come from three sources, M, C, and R. In these cases the main avenue for heat dissipation is evaporation (Ev) at the skin surface.

The physical mechanisms of heat exchange, of course, are workable only if the physiological responses are operative. To maintain a temperature balance between the body and the environment under conditions of heat stress, internal heat must be transported to the skin surface (a task assumed by the circulatory system) and evaporative cooling must be accomplished by the sweat glands. The capacity of the heart to pump blood to the skin surface (particularly during work, when blood is also needed to facilitate muscle function) and the ability of the glands to produce and secrete the requisite sweat are limiting factors in such evaporative cooling. During extreme cold, on the other hand, the blood vessels constrict at the periphery to reduce heat dissipation. Increasing metabolic heat production by exercising or shivering can help to maintain the body temperature at its normal level.

The closer man gets to his maximal physiological

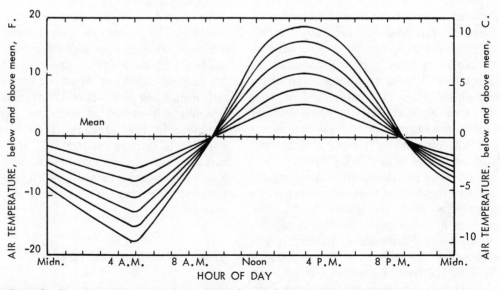

Figure 1. Diurnal temperature cycles in desert area. From E. F. Adolph and Associates, *Physiology of Man in the Desert* (1947; reprint, New York: Hafner Publishing Company, 1969), p. 120.

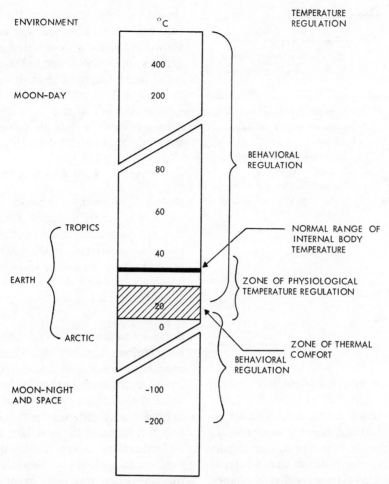

Figure 2. Control of body temperature by physiological and behavioral means. Adapted from J. D. Hardy, "Thermal Comfort and Health," *ASHRAE Journal,* **13,** no. 2 (February 1971), 49.

capacity because of physical exertion, the greater is the strain that will result from hot conditions. Thus, during physical work, when the intensity of the muscular activity is heavily taxing the heart, little of that organ's power is available to pump blood to aid in the transportation of excessive heat to the surface. With such a work load, even temperatures slightly above the zone of thermal comfort will be intolerable. With a light work load with body heat increasing because of a high external heat load, the strain on the individual is indicated by the heart rate. Under such circumstances, when the maximum heart rate (200 in young adults, 160 in older persons) is approached, relief from the stress and strain due to heat is sought. High heart rates are thus good indicators of strain caused by exposure to heat and physical work. When body heat accumulates because of insufficient heat dissipation, temperature rises, since core body temperature (T_c) is directly proportional to heat stored. Therefore T_c can also serve as a measure of strain resulting from excessive exposure to work and/or to heat.

The sensation of environmental temperature is related to skin temperature. An increase in skin temperature is proportional to a rise in air temperature. However, the rate of skin temperature rise is decreased by evaporative cooling. Perfused sweating with a reduced evaporation rate increases the temperature and also the dampness of the skin. Skin dampness correlates with feelings of discomfort. Thus changing ambient conditions can be described and quantified in psychological terms of sensation and discomfort even though these are based on physiological occurrences. Table 1 summarizes the major factors determining heat stress and physiological strain.

Table 1. Factors Determining Heat Stress and Physiological Strain

Factors Determining Heat Stress	Factors Determining Resulting Physiological Strain
Air temperature	Capacity for physical work
Skin temperature	Capacity for production of sweat
Ventilation of lungs	
Duration of exposure	Tolerance of rise in body core temperature
Conditions of recovery	
Air water vapor pressure	Capacity for circulation of blood to vital organs and skin
Skin water vapor pressure	
Metabolic heat production	
Clothing (amount and design)	
Air speed (and speed of movement of body)	
Mean radiant temperature (of solid surroundings)	
Effective surface area of skin (postural attitude)	

THE BIOPHYSICS OF HEAT EXCHANGE

Body temperature is kept within a narrow range because of the body's functional capacity to maintain a heat balance. This capacity is due to certain physiological responses, which are different under hot and cold stress situations. Therefore we will give separate consideration to each of these situations.

Heat Stress. Mounting heat can be of three types: metabolic (M), convective (C), and radiative (R). The main avenue of heat dissipation is evaporative cooling through the skin (Ev). Therefore the basic balance equation for constant body heat can be written as $M + R + C = Ev$. However, there are some relatively minor additions to this fundamental equation.

Man's sources of energy are hydrocarbons, some fats, and—to a small extent—protein. By burning these energy sources with oxygen, the body produces heat for energy: air is taken in, oxygen is extracted from the air, and this oxygen combusts with the foodstuffs. Thus a measurement of energy production can be derived from the amount of oxygen consumed: for each liter of oxygen consumed, about 5 kcal of energy is produced.

When a man is performing external work (W), such as walking uphill or lifting weights, the energy used in the vertical lifting of the body or the weight should be subtracted from the measured metabolic rate because it does not surface as heat. External work thus must be converted by the factor of 2.3 gcal/kg·m of work and subtracted from the metabolic heat. Changes in body temperature indicate changes in heat content or heat storage (S), which increases with a rise in body temperature and decreases with a fall in body temperature. Consequently, the complete heat balance equation is

$$(M - W) + R + C = (Ev + Er) + S$$

In this equation Er represents respiratory heat loss, which is relatively negligible.[3] Radiation and convection are the primary sources of the external heat load that man experiences in the desert. The radiation can be either from the sun or from the walls surrounding an object in a closed area. These sources need to be closely examined.

Solar Radiation. Although the air temperature in arid regions can be high enough to increase the convective heat gain to extremely uncomfortable levels, man's main burden in the desert is solar heat. Since the skies are clear for most of the year, solar radiant heat is quite substantial. Human skin absorbs only a fraction of the heat flux, and skin absorbance is, furthermore, lowest for the highest radiation flux. Figure 3 shows that the absorption rate inversely mirrors the solar heat flux, graphed as a function of wavelength. Skin absorption is somewhat higher for tanned (or black) skin, particularly in the visible wavelength range.

The method of computing man's heat absorption is similar to the meteorological methods of estimating radiant heat on vertical and horizontal surfaces. For man, the surface exposed to solar radiation depends on the posture assumed, which is most likely to be a standing or a walking posture in the outdoors. Solar radiant heat can be divided into direct and indirect radiation. The surface exposed to direct solar radiation is necessarily less than that exposed to indirect radiation in any assumed posture. Indirect radiation can be subdivided into diffusion and albedo: the first referring to scattered rays from the skies (including the scatter resulting from dust and water vapor), and the second referring to reflected rays from the terrain. The surface area exposed to direct solar radiation is about 20 percent of the total surface area of man, and the area exposed to the two types of indirect solar radiation is approximately 80 percent of the total. If a nude surface area of 2 m² is assumed,

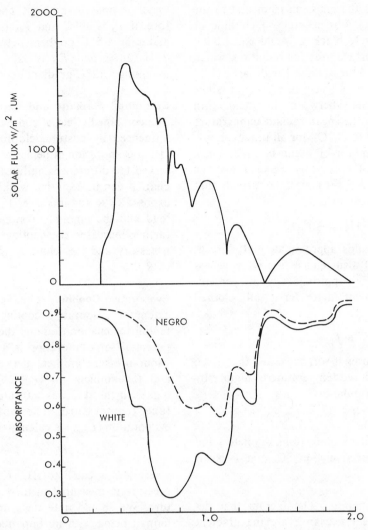

Figure 3. Spectral distribution of solar radiation and of absorption by white and by black skin. From D. McK. Kerslake, *The Stresses of Hot Environment* (Cambridge: Cambridge University Press, 1972), p. 62.

0.4 and 1.6 m² of a person's body are exposed to direct and indirect radiation, respectively.

The total radiant heat load is a function of the sun's altitude and zenith. Computations of expected radiant heat loads using a manikin are given by Roller and Goldman.[4] For example, between 12:30 and 1:00 PM the American southwestern sun is at a 60 to 70° angle, and the energy resulting from direct radiation amounts to 800 kcal/(m²)(hr) on horizontal surfaces and that from indirect radiation amounts to 130 kcal/(m²)(hr). Under these conditions the heat load on a walking man totals 120 to 160 kcal/hr. Some other calculations were made of the change in sweating resulting from an increased radiant heat load of 8°C. Sweating increased just as it would if

the convective heat load was increased by an amount equivalent to an 8°C rise in air temperature.

Indoor Radiant Heat. In a desert region enclosure, unless there is an internal source of heat such as a furnace, the only possible source of radiant heat is the overheated structure. The radiant heat exchange between man and the surroundings enclosing him is a function of the temperature gradient between the surrounding walls (T_r) and the skin surface (T_{sk}). According to the Stefan–Boltzmann law,

$$R = s_0 \cdot e \cdot AR[T_r + 273)^4 + (T_{sk} + 273)^4]$$

where R is the radiant heat flux in kcal/hr, s_0 is the Stefan-Boltzmann constant of $4.96 \cdot 10^{-8}$ kcal/

$(m^2)(hr)(°K)$, and e is the emission from and to the skin (or cloth surface). For example, if clothing or skin was almost entirely black, e would equal 0.95. AR is the effective surface area for radiation, which is about 75 percent of the standard nude area (1.83 and 1.65 m^2 for men and women, respectively). Since the expected difference between the mean skin temperature (T_{sk}) and the mean radiant temperature (T_r) is quite small (15 to 20°C), for all practical purposes, only the first power of T can be used. Thus, with the adjustment of s_0 for this use of T and the substitution for e and AR for males, the formula that can be used for R in kcal/hr is

$$R = 11(T_r - T_{sk})$$

Although clothing adds approximately 10 percent to the surface area, it also reduces the effectiveness of the radiant heat by approximately 30 percent. Therefore the adjustment factor for a fully clothed person will be

$$R = 7.8(T_r - T_{sk})$$

For industrial purposes it was suggested that T_r be derived from the measured temperature of a globe by using the following formula:

$$T_r = T_g + 1.8\,V^{0.5}(T_g - T_a)$$

where T_g and T_a are black globe (6 in. diameter) and air temperatures, respectively, in °C, and V is air movement in m/sec.

Convective Heat Exchange. The factors that determine convective heat exchange are the gradient between the air temperature (T_a) and the mean skin temperature (T_{sk}), and the wind speed (V). The best formula for C is

$$C = AC \cdot KC \cdot V^{0.6}(T_a - T_{sk})$$

where C is in kcal/hr and AC is man's available surface area for the convective heat transfer. The value of KC was found to be 7.2 measured in kcal units, and V was measured in m/sec. The expected air movements range from 1 to 4 m/sec (4 m/sec is approximately 9 mph or 14.5 km/hr). The product $AC \cdot KC \cdot V^{0.6}$ is thus between 12 and 28 for the expected wind velocities, assuming an average size male, but 0.89 less for an average size female.

Since thermoregulation results in the leveling off of mean skin temperature (T_{sk}), calculation of C is possible without precise measurement of T_{sk}. Under hot ambient conditions it can be assumed that T_{sk} is 35°C, under cold ambient conditions 31 to 32°C, and

under temperate ambient conditions 33°C. Therefore, if T_a is 40°C and T_{sk} is 35°C, C is computed assuming a 5°C gradient between T_a and T_{sk}. Or, if T_a is 20°C and T_{sk} is 32°C, C can be computed assuming a 12°C gradient between T_{sk} and T_a.

Combined Radiant and Convective Heat Loads. The combined effect of convective and radiant heat is influenced by posture, clothing, and wind velocity. Using evaporation of perspiration in g/hr, Givoni observed the differences outlined in Table 2. From this chart it can be seen that walking reduces the surface exposed to R and increases V, thus lowering the heat load and the amount of sweating. The increased V further increases the cooling. Thus less sweating is necessary and less clothing is required as a barrier to R.

Evaporative Cooling. The factors that determine the extent of evaporative cooling are the ambient potential for evaporation and the prevailing winds. The potential for evaporation is a function of the water vapor pressure gradient between the wet skin (P_{ws}) and the ambient air (P_{wa}). This potential will be highest if the skin was saturated at its prevailing surface temperature. The potential for maximal evaporation (E_{max}) is calculated by using the formula

$$E_{max} = AE \cdot KE \cdot V^{0.6} \cdot (P_{ws} - P_{wa})$$

where AE is equal to AC, KE is $2 \cdot KC$, and vapor pressure is measured in torrs at a specific temperature. We should note that, under hot conditions, a human being with no impaired functional responses will maintain a skin temperature of 35 to 36°C; this

Table 2.   Perspiration Rate in Arid Regions Under Different Conditions (g/hr)

Condition	Wind Velocity (m/sec)	
	1.0	2.5
Posture		
Sitting	341	306
Walking	259	226
Clothing		
Seminude	300	263
Clothed	191	122

Source: Data with adjustments from B. Givoni, *Man, Climate, and Architecture* (Amsterdam: Elsevier Publishing Company, 1969), pp. 64–65.

means that, in predicting C and E_{max}, additional constants are available such as the above skin temperature and its correspondent P_{ws} of 42 to 44.3 mm Hg.

Some heat, it should be noted, is lost through the lungs via both dry and evaporative heat exchange avenues. The loss is proportional to, first, the respiration rate, which is in turn proportional to the metabolic rate, and, second, the vapor pressure gradient between the lungs and the ambient air. Fanger's suggested formula for computing the respiratory heat loss shows, however, that it is negligible in hot environments.[5]

Heat Storage. In most cases heat storage is a transient phenomonon. During work the body temperature rises, only to level off at a temperature that is proportional to the work load. This means that there will be a rise in body heat content to a new level at which the body is at equilibrium unless overloaded with excessive external heat. The simplest approach to assess this transient heat storage is by measuring the changes in the core body temperature (T_c) and in the mean skin temperature (T_{sk}). Heat storage (S) can then be expressed as

$$S = 0.83 \cdot BW \, (0.67\Delta T_c + 0.33\Delta T_{sk})$$

where 0.83 is assumed as the specific heat of the body and BW is the body weight in kg. Here T_C and T_{sk} are measured in °C; S in kcal.

Dry Cold Stress. Since man's physiological mechanisms to cope with cold stress are not as effective as those that deal with heat stress, he resorts to behavioral mechanisms such as clothing and shelter in order to maintain his heat balance.

Since sweating is suppressed, the heat balance equation under cold conditions is reduced to the loss of metabolic heat (M) by radiation (R) and convection (C). This assumes that there is no change in heat storage and neglects conductance. However, the heat loss by respiration is substantial under cold conditions because of the temperature gradients and the vapor pressure gradients between the lungs, the ambience, and insensible perspiration. Belding suggests that we consider this heat loss as 25 percent of M.[6] Thus the heat balance equation will be $R + C = 0.75M$.

Outdoors, heat loss by R (basically to the sky) is quite substantial. The sky serves as a heat sink, and the loss can amount to 400 kcal/(m²)(hr). Convective heat will be a function of the T_{sk} to T_a gradient. The

external heat transfer will also be related to insulation. This can be expressed as

$$R + C = \frac{T_{sk} - T_a}{\text{insulation}} = 0.75M$$

Insulation is obtained from the air layers and the clothing around the skin. The given unit of insulation is the clo. The constant for the clo unit is 5.55 kcal/(hr)(°C) (established empirically); thus clothing insulation—I_{clo}— is defined as follows:

$$I_{clo} = 5.5 \, \frac{T_{sk} - T_a}{0.75M}$$

This equation indicates that as M increases, as it does during hard labor, the amount of insulation needed decreases. This is an important fact to consider in regard to physiological responses to cold.

Air movement reduces the value of clothing as insulation by eliminating the layer of still air above the cloth and by compressing the cloth, thus shrinking the air layer beneath it. As in the case of cold stress conditions, T_{sk} can be assumed to be constant at 33°C.

PHYSIOLOGICAL RESPONSES

The physiological responses of the body correspond to the strain caused by the stresses of the ambient conditions. These bodily responses help to maintain the heat balance (described in biophysical terms in the preceding section). The term "thermoregulatory responses" is often used to refer to this maintenance of heat balance.

Whereas cold ambient conditions call for heat conservation (primarily the responsibility of the circulatory system), hot ambient conditions demand heat dissipation, which involves both the circulatory and the sweating mechanisms. While the first acts to transport the internal metabolic heat to the skin surface, the second serves to dissipate the excessive heat through evaporative cooling. Successful dissipation of excessive heat results in body temperature equilibrium, whereas failure causes an elevated body temperature.

It is helpful to describe the physiological manifestation of the thermoregulatory responses in terms of engineering control systems. All control systems are characterized by a reference point in the controlling system and a feedback mechanism to it from the controlled systems. Man's controlling system is located in the brain, while the reference point is in the hypothalamus (the base of the midbrain). Feedback from the controlled system (the body) flows to the hypothalamus, where it is integrated and compared to "reference" information. Since the indicator of heat balance is body temperature, it is convenient to assume that the reference is a hypothetical "set point" temperature.

Figure 4 presents the body's "system" for controlling its temperature. A discrepancy between the integrated feedback and the "set point" causes the control mechanism in the hypothalamus to activate the effector mechanisms, that is, the various responses that compensate for the temperature difference. They are apparent to us as changes in circulation, metabolic level, and level of perspiration. There are two different channels through which these physiological responses can be activated—a channel for heat conservation (*HC*) and a channel for heat loss (*HL*).

Circulatory Responses. In general terms, the circulatory system may be divided into two large units: the central pump and blood depots, and the peripheral vascular system. These systems can be brought into play by changing the pumping rate of the blood, as well as by readjusting the blood distribution between the central depots and the periphery. The effectiveness of the control mechanism is demonstrated by the antagonistic adjustments to cold and heat.

The circulatory system responds to cold ambient conditions by constricting the blood vessels of the skin, thus increasing the central blood volume and reducing the heat flow from the core to the surface. The system responds to hot ambient conditions by dilating the surface skin vessels and, at the same time, constricting the vessels in the central system, so that blood is redistributed from the central depots to the skin. The adjustments to facilitate heat transfer to the periphery also include an increase in the rate of blood flow due to incremental increases in the pumping rate of the heart. The increased pumping rate results in an increase in stroke volume (*SV*) and an increase in pulse frequency (*HR*), which in turn cause a rise in cardiac output (*CO*). Since *SV* reaches its maximum level early in the functional adjustment of the heart, the increased *CO* is apparent mostly as an increase in *HR*.

Although the functional capacity of the circulatory system can increase substantially, strain resulting from the combined stresses of physical work and heat exposure is virtually unavoidable. Both stresses raise *CO*, but for different reasons. Muscular work dictates an increased blood flow to the muscles to meet the higher oxygen demand; heat stress dictates an increased flow to the skin to transfer the excessive heat. The strain induced by this competition for blood was noticed in the early observations by Adolph on man's performance in the desert. Marching under the sun, he found, increased the heart rate; this increase was linear with time as the heat load increased.[7]

Without any muscular activity, blood is pumped to the skin, where vasodilation occurs. The vaso-

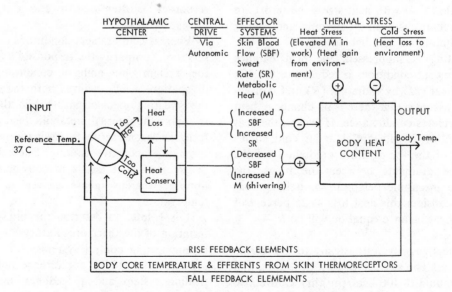

Figure 4. Physiological control system for body temperature.

constriction in the internal organs and the increased CO maintain the blood pressure close to its normal levels. The warm blood that reaches the skin raises the skin temperature, thus causing a higher skin-to-air temperature gradient (if the air temperature is not too high) in order to facilitate heat loss by both radiation and convection. If the air temperature is higher than the skin temperature, the rise in skin temperature lowers the air-to-skin temperature gradient, thus reducing heat flow into the body.

The immediate effect of muscular work is apparent in the vasodilation in the active muscles as well as in the skin. This requires more intense internal vasoconstriction and an increase in heart pumping rate. These heightened activities help to maintain the blood pressure and to allow a sufficient amount of blood to flow to the tissues where it is needed. Although prolonged work under heat stress conditions results in a gradual increase in CO, it seems that CO eventually stabilizes. The blood depots in the skin, however, increase; as a result, blood pressure and SV drop slightly. The reduced BP and SV are accompanied by increases in HR. These physiological changes are more severe during heavy work because the reduced SV is too large to be compensated for by the rise in HR; consequently CO drops during heavy work. When the strain of heavy work and heat is excessive, the drop in BP and the reduction in SV and CO can cause "failure" of the cardiovascular system (leading to fainting). Individuals with histories of heart failure, due to limited CO, require a greater redistribution of blood in order to maintain BP. More internal vasoconstriction compensates in such cases for the reduced CO.

Blood Volume and Body Fluids. Increases in blood volume, either during the hot season of the year or upon moving from a cold to a hot area, have been reported. However, most of these observations have been inconclusive. Logically, one would expect, upon exposure to heat, that blood volume (especially plasma volume) would respond to the increased demand for blood by the skin. Indeed, controlled laboratory studies show that acute exposure to heat raises blood volume, mainly because of the increased water content in the plasma.[8] This was explained by citing the diffusion from the interstitial compartment due to cutaneous vasodilation. It should be also noted that exposure to heat increases the amount of antidiuretic hormonal activity, thus reducing renal flow. This is helpful in conserving fluids and maintaining blood volumes at higher levels. Protein also seems to

be washed into the blood, and erythrocytes are added from different depots. However, this increase in volume (13 to 20 percent) was observed in hydrated, not physically active, men. Physical work, profuse sweating, and dehydration might cause a reversal and a reduced blood volume. In fact, men who have experienced continuous daily exposure to heat show, for about a week, plasma and blood volume increases; afterwards, there is a reversal and the trend is back to the preexposure volume. This phenomenon is also observed during periods of heat acclimation, when blood (mostly plasma) volume increases during acclimation but eventually returns to preacclimation levels.

Changes in BV to facilitate BF at the expense of the interstitial fluid and the return to normal preexposure levels may indicate that other peripheral adaptations were made to overcome the need for a larger BF. This adaptation could very well be in the state of the blood vessels, particularly in the renal system, where a change in the compliance and tone of the vessels could drastically alter the volume stored in them.

Cold stress reverses the fluid conservation phenomenon. Diuresis resulting from exposure to cold is a known phenomenon and is accompanied by unavoidable excretion of electrolytes. This reversal is also apparent in the drop in plasma volume and, to some extent, in blood volume, with an increase in hematocrit and the amount of circulating proteins. Such a phenomenon might be costly under desert conditions, where the fluid lost during the cold nights might already have sustained a deficit during the hot days. Furthermore, in the desert, where shifts from extreme heat to extreme cold occur, human response manifests itself in modified renal function (fluid shifts between compartments and spaces) because of the functioning of hormonal, nervous, and chemical systems at extreme levels.

The strain induced by the combined stresses of work and ambient conditions can be expressed in terms of the individual's maximum attainable HR (HR_{max}). The closer HR gets to a person's maximum, the less he can tolerate the conditions. While for some individuals a given task raises HR close to this limit, leaving only a small fraction of the HR to cope with the heat, for others the same work is less demanding and the resulting increase in HR is low enough that large reserves remain to cope with the heat. Since HR_{max} is dependent on age and sex, certain maximum values can be assumed. The measurement of HR under the given work and

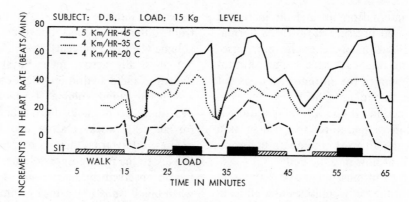

Figure 5. Heart rate during cycles of work and rest under three different ambient conditions. Redrawn from E. Kamon and H. S. Belding, "The Physiological Factors, Cost of Carrying Loads in Temperate and Hot Environments," *Human Factors,* **13,** no. 2 (1971), 159. Published by The Johns Hopkins University Press and reprinted with its permission.

ambient conditions, evaluated in relation to the expected HR_{max}, gives the measured HR as a fraction of HR_{max}.

A daily work load is generally considered acceptable when the average energy expenditure is between 300 and 360 kcal/hr for men and between 225 and 300 kcal/hr for women. Any task demanding more than the average should be interspersed with resting periods. Under acceptable work loads and nonstress temperatures, the average HR for work (or work and rest) is approximately 100 to 115 bpm. However, dry heat stress, where evaporation is free, will increase HR by roughly 10 bpm for each 10°C increase in T_a above 25°C. Thus an acceptable level of physical work at T_a 45° should result in an HR of between 120 and 135 bpm.

During prolonged work, HR will gradually increase with time, particularly during the work period, when a work–rest schedule is followed, as Figure 5 indicates. However, unlike the example shown in this figure, a rapid increase in HR beyond the level expected because of the work indicates an excessive heat load that will limit the individual's capacity to tolerate the ambient conditions.

Body Temperature. At the work load acceptable for a daily shift, HR increments are linearly correlated to the rise in core body temperature (T_c), as Figure 6 shows. This correlation is predictable since the increase in HR follows upon the need to increase the dissipation of accumulating heat, which, in turn, is revealed by the rise in T_c. Therefore the rise in HR over a period of time is a good measure of the increase in body temperature when a given work load under unfavorable ambient conditions is involved.

Mean skin temperature (T_{sk}) is linearly related to air temperature (T_a), but when T_a is above 35°C, T_{sk} tends to stabilize at that temperature unless the heat stored is rapidly increasing. Such T_{sk} stabilization is possible because of perspiration. Desert ambient conditions, however, may exceed the capacity of the sweating rate to keep pace. In such a case T_{sk} will rise as the accumulating heat is transferred from the core to the body's surface. This has some bearing on circulatory strain because, as T_{sk} rises, the $T_c - T_{sk}$ gradient is falling; therefore large volumes of blood must be pumped to the skin to relieve the heat. The conductance (K) of the metabolic heat can be expressed as

$$K = CI = \frac{M}{T_c - T_{sk}}$$

K is equal to the circulatory index (CI), which is 1 liter of blood per kilocalorie transferred per centigrade gradient (assuming the blood's specific heat to be 1°). It can be seen that K or CI will increase as the $T_c - T_{sk}$ gradient decreases.

Dehydration. A water deficit leads to a reduction in blood and plasma volumes. This is first apparent in the difficulty encountered by the circulatory system in transporting blood, resulting in increased viscosity rather than in reduced volume. This change is reflected in increased HR, as was noticed by Adolph and his associates (see Figure 7). Naturally, reduced circulatory capacity with increased HR and reduced SV leads to a rise in core body temperature. This apparent strain is in addition to the strains resulting from the stresses caused by impaired heat exchange.

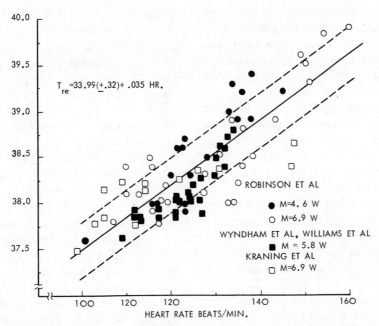

$T_{re} = 33.99(\underline{+}.32) + .035 \text{ HR.}$

ROBINSON ET AL

M=4. 6 W

M=6.9 W

WYNDHAM ET AL, WILLIAMS ET AL

M = 5.8 W

KRANING ET AL

M=6.9 W

HEART RATE BEATS/MIN.

Figure 6. Relationship between steady-state rectal temperature and steady-state heart rate for work requiring 5 kcal² min. Redrawn from E. Kamon and H. S. Belding. "Heart Rate and Rectal Temperature Relationships During Work in Hot Humid Environments," *Journal of Applied Physiology,* **31,** no. 3 (1971), 476.

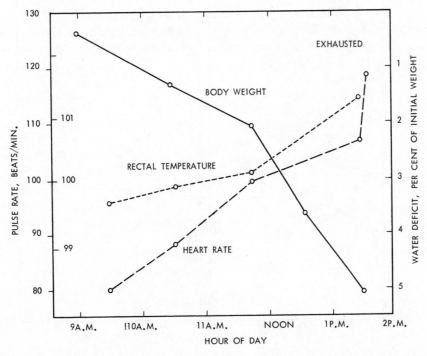

EXHAUSTED

BODY WEIGHT

RECTAL TEMPERATURE

HEART RATE

PULSE RATE, BEATS/MIN.

WATER DEFICIT, PER CENT OF INITIAL WEIGHT

HOUR OF DAY

Figure 7. Performance of man in desert without water and with the air temperature reaching 150°F. Redrawn from E. F. Adolph and Associates, *Physiology of Man in the Desert* (1947); reprint, New York: Hafner Publishing Company, 1969), p. 144.

Sweating. Human eccrine sweat glands are equipped to make adjustments for heat dissipation. They secrete their contents with relatively little electrolyte content, and, as they become more active, the sweat becomes more diluted. Sweating seems to depend on two factors: internal body temperature and skin temperature. These factors trigger the onset of sweating and affect its rate. Sweating in man has been shown to be a function of the change in core body temperature and, to a much lesser extent, in mean and local skin temperatures. Robinson was the first to demonstrate that the onset of sweating occurs, on the one hand, at relatively higher T_{sk} when T_c is low and, on the other, at relatively higher T_c when T_{sk} is low.[9] Later it was shown that the increase in sweating is about eight times larger for a unit of T_c increase than for a unit of T_{sk} increase. Additional local sweating occurs when local skin heating is added.[10]

Dehydration has little effect on sweating rate. Sweat glands do, however, exhibit signs of "fatigue." During the first 2 hours of exposure, a sweating rate of about 2 liters/hr can be achieved. The rate drops to less than 1 liter/hr a few hours later. If it is assumed that during prolonged heat exposures the average sweating rate of a man is between 1 and 1.2 liters/hr, constant sweating causes an average loss of about 10 to 15 grams of salt per day.

Acclimatization. Consecutive exposures to heat improve tolerance in that the physiological responses reveal reduced strain, as Figures 8 and 9 show. The first day of work under hot, dry ambient conditions results in a continuous rise in T_c, continuous increments in HR, and low sweating rates. With consecutive daily exposures to heat, however, these responses no longer show a continuous rise; HR, T_c, and T_{sk} tend instead to level off, with a substantial increase in sweating rate. These changes become possible probably because of the increased sensitivity of the sweating mechanism. As sweating commences at lower T_c and T_{sk}, the rise in these temperatures becomes less pronounced. This increased sensitivity also affects

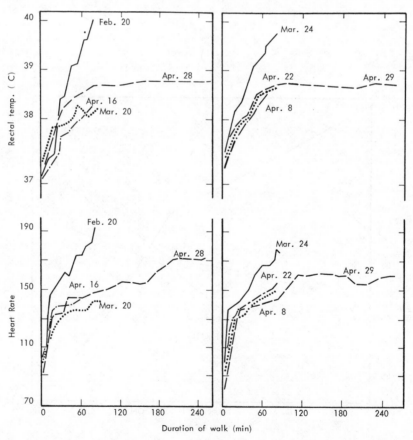

Figure 8. Heart rates and rectal temperatures of two subjects on selected dates of acclimatization. From S. Robinson, E. S. Turrell, H. S. Belding, and S. M. Hovrath, "Rapid Acclimation to Work in Hot Climates," *American Journal of Physiology*, **140** (1943), 172.

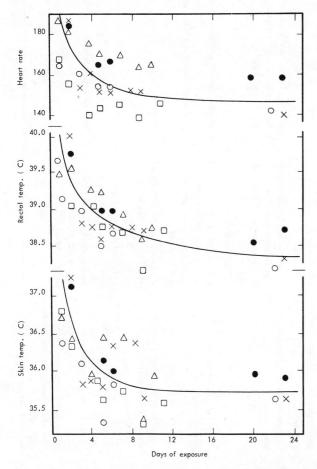

Figure 9. Heart rate and body temperature at end of treadmill walk on successive days of controlled exposure at 40°C. From S. Robinson, E. S. Turrell, H. S. Belding, and S. M. Hovrath, "Rapid Acclimation to Work in Hot Climates," *American Journal of Physiology,* **140** (1943), 170.

blood flow, since the flow rate rises with increases in T_c and T_{sk}. The increased sweating rate does, however, result in the dilution of electrolytes.

The Hazards of Heat Exposure. Even acclimated persons may encounter desert conditions in which an average sweating rate of 1 liter is insufficient and heat is therefore stored when the exposure is prolonged. Rise in body temperature of more than 6°C (T_c above 43°C) reduces chances of survival to less than 50 percent. The movement of bodily functions toward failure of the system to control body temperature is gradual. First, when blood is rushed to skin depots, the brain is deprived of an adequate supply. This causes the symptoms of heat exhaustion: giddiness, visual disturbance, increased *HR*, and reduced blood pressure. If, in addition, physical work is involved and a water deficit occurs (which could be accompanied by a salt deficit), symptoms of muscle cramps and muscle weakness are also apparent. Heat exhaustion can be treated by resting in a cool area and replenishing the body's salt and water. Severe cases, in fact, require intravenous administration of a saline solution.

Severe cases of heatstroke, indicating failure of the system to maintain heat balance, can occur in healthy, well-motivated persons. In these cases the circulatory functions operate normally while the body accumulates substantial amounts of heat. Eventually the core body temperature reaches hazardous levels, damaging the brain, and despite profuse sweating the body then fails to thermoregulate itself. Death is inevitable under such circumstances because of the brain damage, shock, hemorrhaging, and systems (kidney, liver) failure. Another phenomenon is the cessation of sweating when hyperthermia occurs. Heatstroke must be detected early enough so that immediate cooling can be provided. A study in Israel showed that heatstroke can occur at temperatures as low as 27.7°C dry bulb and 19.5° wet bulb and as high as 37.4°C dry bulb and 18.3°C wet bulb.[11]

The various heat-related disorders are summarized in Table 3. Severe cases characterized by impaired sweating should be treated mainly by cooling. This can be done by wetting the skin and blowing air on it to cause evaporative cooling, or by using ice packs if more intense cooling is required. Body massage may also be needed to increase blood circulation to the skin. The T_c should be frequently checked to avoid overcooling.

One of these disorders, heat syncope, is worth special mention. It is a transient phenomenon that afflicts unacclimated individuals after prolonged standing in the heat. The movement of blood to the legs results in hypotension and reduced brain perfusion. The ensuing fainting and the fall to a prone posture are sufficient to cause recovery because they lead to a resumption of normal circulation.

BEHAVIORAL RESPONSES

We know little about long-term behavioral characteristics due to exposure to hot ambient conditions. (The need to adapt upon transition from a temperate to a hot climate is covered under "Acclimatization.") In addition to the physiological changes to meet the heat stress, there is an obvious need to make some behavioral adaptation in the routine of daily

Table 3 Heat-Related Disorders

Clinical Designation	Etiological Category	Predisposing Factors	Physiological Malfunction	Clinical Manifestations	Treatment
Heat stroke	Thermoregulatory failure	(a) Abnormal tolerance for hyperthermia (b) Sustained exertion in young adults (c) Circulatory impairment in the elderly (d) Drugs (e.g. alcohol, atropine, amphetamines)	(a) Inadequate circulatory transfer of heat from core to skin (b) Failure of central drive for sweating	(a) Extreme hyperthermia (105°F or over) (b) Thermally induced disorders of cerebral function (c) Absence of sweating (not invariable)	(a) Immediate and effective cooling. (b) Treat complications (shock, renal shutdown, coagulopathy)
Heat exhaustion	Circulatory insufficiency	Dehydration from water depletion and/or salt depletion	(a) Competition between skin and core tissues for blood supply (b) Hypertonic contraction of ECF (water depletion) (c) Hypotonic contraction of ECF (salt depletion)	(a) Signs and symptoms of dehydration (b) Symptoms of cerebral circulatory function deficiency (c) Signs of hypovolemia and circulatory strain (d) Muscle weakness	Restore water and salt balance by oral or IV route
Heat syncope	Orthostatic hypotension	Standing immobile	Pooling of blood in dependent parts of body	Syncope	Rest in reclining position
Heat cramps	Salt depletion and water intoxication	(a) Profuse sweating (b) Drinking water without replacing salt	Lowered osmetic pressure of interstitial fluid of active skeletal muscles	Painful cramps in muscles used while working	Infusion of normal or hypertonic saline
Anhydrotic heat exhaustion	Chronic injury of eccrine sweat glands	(a) Prolonged exposure to heat (b) Skin trauma from sunburn or heat rash	Inadequate sweating for evaporative cooling	(a) Anhydrosis of affected areas of trunk and extremities (b) Hyperhydrosis of face and neck (c) Heat intolerance	(a) Avoid further heat exposure (b) Recovery usually complete on return to cool climate
Heat rash	Acute obstruction of eccrine sweat glands	Unrelieved exposure to humid heat with skin continuously wetted by sweat	Inflammatory reaction around obstructed glands	(a) Punctuate enythematous vesicles on affected skin areas (b) Prickling sensations upon heat exposure	(a) Intermittent relief from humid heat (b) Prevent secondary infection
Heat fatigue Transient	Acute behavioral disorder	Unaccustomed exposure to intense heat	Impaired performance of skilled tasks out of proportion to physiological strain	(a) Inability to concentrate on task, with performance decrement (b) Occasional acute anxiety state	Training
Chronic	Chronic behavioral disorder	Long residence in tropical climates by sojourners from temperate climates	(a) Psychosocial stresses major factor (b) Hormonal imbalance from heat stress postulated but not established	Deterioration in work performance and in standards of personal conduct	Recovery complete on returning home

activities. Taking a prolonged rest at midday and delaying some demanding activities until the evening are matters of course in hot climates.

The extent to which a man's quality of performance at work changes when he resides in a hot, dry climate is questionable. It appears that the dry desert climate does not change the efficiency of work at daily activities. Since research on this question calls for relatively short-term experiments, the easiest way to obtain meaningful results is to use humid rather than dry heat stress. Such results, of course, are not really applicable here. However, some observations made under humid conditions do have some relevance to the changes expected because of stress in general.

Studies on the effect of such hot ambient conditions have shown that they cause a tendency toward inattentiveness, which affects the accuracy of performance, particularly when perceptual and psychomotor activities are involved. Heat can bring about lassitude, which in turn is likely to increase the rate of accidents at work. Figure 10 shows the relationship between increased seasonal rise in ambient temperatures and frequency of work-related accidents in the Sahara Desert. The deteriorating performance can be attributed, to some extent, to insomnia due to the heat: sleeplessness or the lack of sound sleep can indeed affect performance. However, the extent of sleeplessness in hot climates is questionable.

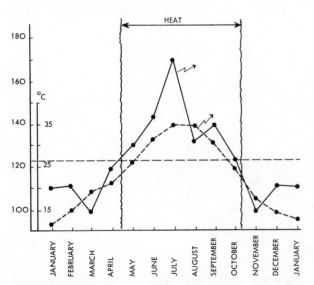

Figure 10. Industrial accidents by month. From G. E. Lambert, "Work, Sleep, Comfort," from *Environmental Physiology and Psychology in Arid Conditions: Review of Research* (Paris: UNESCO, 1963), p. 257. © UNESCO 1963. Reproduced by permission of UNESCO.

It should not be forgotten, however, that motivation is highly important in cases of behavioral adaptation. Either internal motivation or external motivation inspired by good supervision can increase performance under hot conditions, as Figure 11 shows.

Behavioral Adaptation. Responses to change in climatic conditions include the wearing of clothing and the construction of shelters. Although clothing is usually thought of in terms of warmth and protection against cold, its insulative value against heat should not be overlooked, in particular as protection from radiant heat. Cloth can repell radiant heat as well as reduce heat loss due to convection (C). During the heat of the day, clothing can reduce the external heat gain by 30 to 50 percent, depending on its thickness (reducing C) and design reflectance (reducing R). From the standpoint of design, hats, for example, are considered to have more protective value against the sun when they are wide enough to shade parts of the body.

Since the desert ambience is dry, clothing, while affording protection against heat, should not impair evaporation. This danger can easily be avoided by allowing for air flow under the clothing. Therefore thin, loosely fitting cloth, which can reflect R, protect against C (both to and from the body), and allow for sweat evaporation, is desirable. Oversweating, to the extent that the cloth is wetted, reduces the air layer between the cloth and the skin, thus lowering the convective insulation value of the cloth. For this reason cotton twill, with as little synthetic fabric as possible, is most desirable. Synthetic fibers should be avoided because they reduce the capacity of the fabric to act as a wick in transferring sweat through the cloth; this in turn reduces the evaporation from the surface of the cloth.

The insulative value of cloth is defined by its resistance, mostly to the loss of body heat. However, such resistance differs for different physical activities. If a given suit is comfortable at a T_a of 21°C (70°F) for a resting man, it will be comfortable for walking 5.5 km/hr (3.5 mph) at a T_a of 7°C (45°F). For a given T_a, the greater the inactivity, the less insulation from clothing is necessary. As mentioned previously, the insulation value is given in units of clo; and, as Figure 12 shows, for any given T_a, clo becomes less as M increases.

Sweating constitutes quite a serious problem in the cold, particularly when work ceases. Cooling by evaporation when M is not high results in a chill.

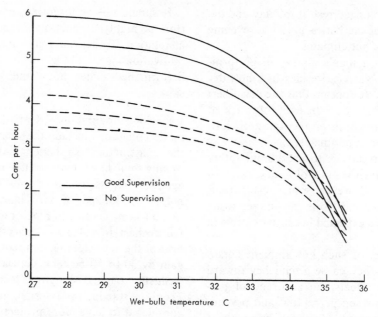

Figure 11. Production at different temperatures with good and no supervision. From C. H. Wyndham, "Research in the Human Science in the Gold Mining Industry," *American Industrial Hygiene Association Journal,* **35,** no. 3 (1974), 131.

Moreover, the sweat replaces the air, and thus the cloth's insulative power declines. Thick cloth improves insulation only if the air is compartmentalized, since such cloth does not allow for convection by air movement. Replacing the air compartments by liquid reduces the insulation substantially.

Wind reduces the thickness of the air film above the clothing, thus lowering its insulative value. The type of cloth used to make windbreakers is helpful in

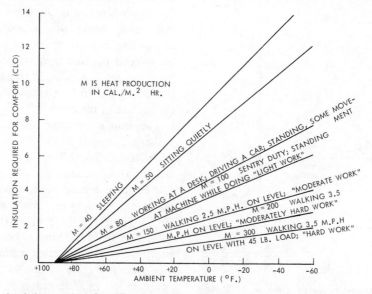

Figure 12. Insulation required for different activities at different temperatures. Redrafted from L. H. Newburgh, *Physiology of Heat Regulation and the Science of Clothing* (1949; reprint, New York: Hafner Publishing Company, 1968), p. 353.

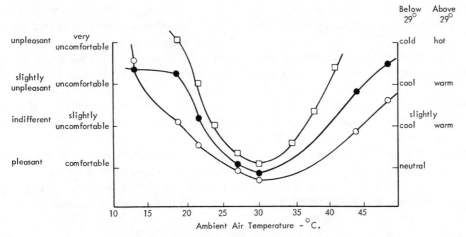

Figure 13. Subjective estimates of thermal comfort at different air temperatures. From A. P. Gagge, J. A. J. Stolwijk, and J. D. Hardy, "Comfort and Thermal Sensations and Associated Physiological Responses at Various Ambient Temperatures," *Environmental Research*, **1** (1967), 6.

protection against wind. Furthermore, the light windbreaker cloth can be useful in the desert as protection from cold at night and as a repellent of R during the day.

Psychophysical Responses. Behavioral modification in response to ambient conditions is guided by the sensation of the thermal environment. This involves the subjective sensation of warmth or coldness, the feeling of discomfort, and the impression of unpleasantness. It should not be overlooked that, although feeling cold and hot implies the existence of sensing mechanisms, the state of the mind (which is expressed in dissatisfaction with the environment) is definitely associated with the physiological changes that take place in response to the environment.

The scaling method shown in Figure 13 for charting thermal sensations was developed by several investigators. This figure clearly shows that thermal sensations of pleasantness or its opposite are functions of air temperature. The figure also indicates that the feeling of comfort is spread over a wide span of air temperatures, for, sensing temperature as neutral, we tend to accept it as pleasant. The neutral and pleasant air temperature is between a T_a of 28° and one of 30°C, which is a range where no thermoregulatory physiological responses are necessary. Interestingly enough, the comfortable temperature is higher in the summer than in the winter, and people residing in bitter climates felt comfortable at higher temperatures. Thus summer comfort was judged at

76°F and 77°F in the United Kingdom and the United States, respectively, 78°F in Singapore, and 81.5°F in Australia.

With regard to the physiological responses discussed earlier, it appears that, during rest, a drop in T_{sk}, accompanied by a drop in T_a, is associated with discomfort. A high T_a discomfort is associated with the apparent increase in sweating. During work, when the physiological responses are steady and core body temperature is up, the sensation of air temperature is still linked to T_{sk} rather than T_c or the metabolic rate. However, discomfort continues to be affected by the metabolic rate and any rise in T_c because these are correlated with the perspiration rate.

Radiant heat impinges on the skin and is therefore certain to add to the effective component of thermal sensation. Experienced outdoorsmen know the pleasantness of warming to the sun when the air is cool. The expected correlation would be between the radiant heat and the skin temperature; however, the situation is not that simple. Internal temperature has an effect on the intensity of the perception of the change in T_{sk}. Actually, the initial T_{sk}, which is dependent on T_a, affects the pleasant perception, as is shown in Figure 14. This figure charts the relations between pleasantness and irradiance, which increases the local temperature of the irradiated area (in this case, the forehead). Note that the optimal value depends on how low T_a is. Moreover, experiments irradiating a larger skin area have shown that there is spatial summation of sensation. Behavior will then be modified based on the heat absorbed, since the physiological responses are aimed at preserving man's homeostasis.

The effects of heat stress are also manifested in the ability (or inability) to perform mental and physical work. Most of the tests that showed deterioration in performance were carried out in humid, hot environments, and the tasks chosen for testing basically involved perception and reaction time. One would expect deterioration in perception, concentration, and reaction under conditions of humid heat. Some such deteriorations are summarized in Table 4. An early study carried out by McWorth showed deterioration in the performance of a telegraphic coding operation. It was noted that, although skilled coders performed better under heat stress than novices, their performance did deteriorate.[12] That motivation is important in overcoming the hardship of environmental stress has been reported on several occasions, one such report being that of Wyndham and his associates on physical work. The level of physical work—shoveling rock in mines—deteriorated with increased heat stress, but it deteriorated less with a good foreman who could motivate the workers.[13]

It should be noted, however, that the period of exposure is important. Individuals perform better under

Table 4. The Effect of heat on Psychomotor Performance

Task	Temperature (DB or DB/WB °C)	Exposure (hr)	Effect
Cognitive			
Arithmetic	21–60, 35/33	0.5–1.5, 6.5	None
	71–112	0.5 to physiological	Error up
	37/32	limit	Performance down
	38/24–43/50	2	Performance by incentive up
Visual judgment			
Matching pattern, coding	Up to 38/32	1	None
Vigilance			
Visual	30/25–63/47	0.3–2	None—detection rate up
	38/32–54/24		None—performance down
(Meters monitored)	63/47		None
Auditory	Vapor barrier suit > 38	1	None
Skill			
Code reception	41/35	3	Error up
Flight simulation	71–113, 43/25–60/29	1 to physiological	Error up
		limit	Performance down
Tracking			
1–2 dimensional	32/27–38/29	0.5–6	None
	71, 47/41, 52/35	0.5–2	Performance down but by incentive up
Central tracking	35/31–41/35	1–2	Performance down
Peripheral stimulation			
Rotary pursuit test	10, 38		Performance down
Reaction time			
Visual	33/48, 52/(31–36)	1–6	Reaction time shorter
To peripheral light	Up to 51/35	2	Increased misses
Serial reaction tests	(32–40)/(25–38)	1–2	Increased reaction time
Time estimation			
Counting, tapping	41/35, 38/32	1	Time judgment up
	Vapor barrier suit (T_c up 1–2°C)		Tapping rate up

Source: Adapted from W. F. Grether, "Human Performance at Elevated Environmental Temperature," *Aerospace Medicine*, **44** (1973), 747–755.

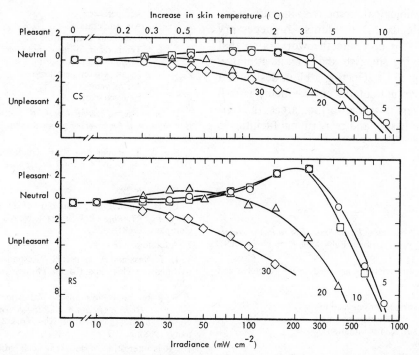

Figure 14. Estimates of pleasantness and unpleasantness compared to increase in skin temperature and irradiance. From L. E. Marks and R. R. Gonzalez, "Skin Temperature Modifies the Pleasantness of Thermal Stimuli." Reproduced from *Nature,* **247** (1947), 474.

short exposures to heat stress. Deterioration in performance becomes apparent only after prolonged exposure.

This deterioration can result in accidents. Accident frequency rises, as Figure 10 reveals, in the hot seasons. In reactions to visual and auditory stimuli, seasonal differences in performance have also been observed between the August values and the yearly average.

CONCLUSION

Since physiological strain due to heat exposure is a result of the sum of the metabolic and the external heat loads, these two factors should be considered in the designing of cities in arid areas. The heat load found in these areas can be alleviated by reducing the radiant heat flux and by improving the provisions for evaporative cooling. To do this, designs must call for large shady areas that allow breezes to pass through. Such natural methods of cooling are sometimes preferable to man-made cooling systems because air-conditioned rooms suppress sweating and leave the cooling to convection and radiation only. Outdoors,

natural cooling is an especially important factor when the need for cooling is immediately subsequent to heavy labor under hot ambient conditions.

The heat exchange between man and his surroundings is calculable, and the metabolic heat production during work is predictable. Consequently, it is possible to estimate the strain due to work and that due to existing external heat loads. Therefore, in the planning of cities for desert climates, the following factors should be considered: (1) the expected stresses due to the work load for a given facility; (2) the external heat load, particularly in relation to seasonal changes; (3) the provision of regional rest areas for each work site, based on the projected stress for the particular type of industry involved; and (4) the provision of regional arrangements for leisure and recreation.

Planning for the third and fourth items should take into consideration the observed strong correlation between man's feeling of comfort or pleasantness and his physiological responses. Thus discomfort is linked to sweating, but is modulated by skin temperature; and sensations of temperature and pleasantness are associated with skin temperature, but are modulated by the core body temperature. This discomfort accompanying physiological responses impairs work efficiency and leads to accidents. A necessary countermeasure is to motivate the workers so that they avoid becoming sluggish and remain attentive. This can be achieved by selecting a plant design that adds to the pleasantness of the environment, as well as to the attractiveness of the working areas, the resting areas, and the leisure and recreational facilities in the city.

NOTES

1. E. F. Adolph and Associates, *Physiology of Man in the Desert* (1947; reprint, New York: Hafner Publishing Company, 1969), p. 120.

2. Many specialized abbreviations are used in the formulae and text. These are summarized here:

AC	Effective surface for convection
AE	Effective surface for evaporation
AR	Effective surface for radiation
BF	Blood flow
BP	Blood pressure
BV	Blood volume
BW	Body weight
C	Convection
CI	Circulatory index
CO	Cardiac output
e	Emission from or to the skin or cloth surface
E_{max}	Ambient capacity for evaporation
Er	Respiratory heat loss
Ev	Evaporation
HC	Heat conservation
HL	Heat loss
HR	Pulse frequency
HR_{max}	Maximum pulse frequency
I_{clo}	Clothing insulation
K	Conductance
KC	Coefficient for convection
KE	Coefficient for evaporation
M	Metabolic heat
P_{wa}	Water vapor pressure for air
P_{ws}	Water vapor pressure for saturated wet skin
R	Radiative heat
S	Heat storage
S_0	$4.96 \cdot 10^{-8}$ kcal/(m²)(hr)(°K)
SV	Stroke volume
T	Temperature
T_a	Air temperature
T_c	Core body temperature
T_g	Temperature of measured globe
T_r	Mean radiant temperature
T_{sk}	Mean skin temperature
V	Air movement
W	External work

3. P. O. Fanger, *Thermal Comfort: Analysis and Applications in Environmental Engineering* (Copenhagen: Danish Technical Press, 1970), p. 107.

4. See W. L. Roller and R. F. Goldman, "Prediction of Solar Heat Load in Man," *Journal of Applied Physiology,* **24** (1968), 717–721.

5. Fanger, p. 28.

6. L. H. Newburgh, *Physiology of Heat Regulation and the Science of Clothing* (1949; reprint, New York: Hafner Publishing Company, 1968), p. 353.

7. Adolph, p. 208.

8. D. E. Bass and A. Henschel, "Responses of Body Fluids Compartment to Heat and Cold," *Physiological Review,* **36** (1956), 130.

9. S. Robinson, "Physiological Adjustments to Heat," in *Physiology of Heat Regulation and the Science of Clothing,* L. H. Newburgh, ed. (1949; reprint, New York: Hafner Publishing Company, 1968), p. 193.

10. It is interesting to note that acclimation is recognized by the apparent onset of sweating at lower T_{sk} and T_c than for the nonacclimated individual.

11. D. McK. Kerslake, *The Stresses of Hot Environments* (Cambridge: Cambridge University Press, 1972), p. 47.

12. N. H. McWorth, "Effects of Heat on Wireless Operation Hearing and Recording Morse Code Messages," *British Journal of Industrial Medicine,* **3** (1946), 143.

13. C. H. Wyndham, "Research in the Human Science in the Gold Mining Industry," *American Industrial Hygiene Association Journal,* **35,** no. 3 (1974), 113.

SUGGESTED READINGS

Kamon, E. "Ergonomics and Allied Sciences." In *Labor Department Yearbook.* Washington: U.S. Government Printing Office, in press.

Kamon, E. "Ergonomics of Heat and Cold." *Texas Reports on Biology and Medicine,* **33,** no. 1 (1975), 145–182.

Kamon, E., and Avellini, B. "Physiologic Limits to Work in the Heat and Evaporative Coefficient for Women." *Journal of Applied Physiology,* **41,** no. 1 (1976), 71–76.

CHAPTER 4

The Arid West and Human Responses to It

JOHN I. YELLOTT, DANIEL AIELLO

It would be pleasing to advocates of solar energy utilization to be able to state truthfully that the cities in America's arid West had been carefully planned to take advantage of their only inexhaustible energy resource, the sun's radiation. Unfortunately, this is not the case, because, like virtually all other cities in the United States, America's western population centers have developed with little or no attention being paid to the sun. It will be shown that a number of pre-Columbian settlements, on the other hand, were carefully oriented to take advantage of the winter sun's warmth and to minimize the impact of the sun's searing heat in summer. The cities that resulted from the westward march of the Anglos and the northward thrust of the Spanish soldiers and missionaries, however, have generally followed a north–south, east–west grid pattern that was easy for surveyors to lay out and for land developers to use in planning. The structures that they built may have been appropriate to the cities from which these builders came, but they generally ignored nature's demands in a region where sunshine is magnificiently abundant, rainfall is so scarce that most plants can grow only with the aid of irrigation, and both diurnal and seasonal temperature variations are far greater than those experienced in the East.

It is the writers' opinion that the real impact of the sun on the cities of America's arid West is still to be felt, and that it will be the impending energy crisis which will cause builders to work with nature rather than to use scarce energy sources and the highly developed technology of air conditioning and ignore

nature completely. The era of low-cost energy has already ended in the West, and the conspicuous expenditure of fluid fossil fuels that has characterized western life will have to come to an end as natural gas becomes extinct and oil doubles and then quadruples in price. The population of many of the western cities will continue to grow, particularly those in the southwestern states, but the structures which will house the newcomers will have to return to the principles of energy conservation that were practices by the wise people who preceded the Anglos and the Spaniards to this land.

THE ARID WEST

Climatologists are by no means in accord on what constitutes a desert, but most of them agree that an area in which the annual evaporation exceeds the precipitation deserves the designation "arid." For the purposes of this chapter, an annual rainfall of 20 in. or less will be considered adequate for this classification, and many readers may be surprised to learn that nearly half of the land area of North America falls within this category. "West of the Pecos" is an expression that gained wide popularity when the first westward migration was under way. It is appropriate to use it again here, because it is west of the 100th meridian of longitude, from Texas to Canada, that annual rainfall diminishes to the 20 in. level. The Pecos River in western Texas, wandering southeastward to its confluence with the Rio Grande, an-

61

chors the southern end of that meridian. Near its northern end, Fargo, North Dakota, lies virtually on the 20 in. annual precipitation isopleth.[1]

As one moves westward across the Great Plains, the annual rainfall falls to 16 and then to 12 in. as meridian 105 west is reached at Denver. There the Rocky Mountains rise, and from then on to the Pacific coastal ranges—between 120 and 125W, the pattern is one of snow-covered peaks and arid valleys. The minimum annual precipitation, between 2 and 8 in./year, occurs in the watershed (if that word is appropriate) of the Colorado River, between the 20th and 35th parallels of latitude and the 115th and 118th meridians of longitude. The Mohave Desert, encompassing parts of Arizona, Nevada, and California, has the distinction of including within its shifting boundaries the lowest (282 ft below sea level) and the driest (0 to 4 in. of precipitation per year) places in the United States.

Aridity generally exists in the "shadow" of high mountains, on their downwind slopes and, in the case of the American West, for several hundred miles eastward into the plains. Moisture-laden air blows inland from the Pacific Ocean, but the very high mountains of the Sierra Nevada and the Rockies remove much of this water vapor. Little remains to be shared with the low lands among the peaks or with the plains that extend without interruption to the east of meridian 105 until the much lower Appalachian

chain is reached between meridians 85 and 80. The influence of the warm, moist air from the Gulf of Mexico makes itself felt as one moves east of meridian 100, and annual precipitation increases steadily to reach its maximum, about 80 in./year, in the Blue Ridge Mountains. The fiftieth state, Hawaii, holds the record with 300 in./year on a mountain top in Hilo and 460 in./year at Mt. Waialeale in Kauai.

The population density in any part of the world varies with the availability of water, for all living creatures (with very few exceptions) must have water in order to live. Within the area of aridity just defined, between 100 and 118°W longitude, cities are few and far between, and they generally exist near one of the region's few rivers. Table 1 lists 19 cities, ranging in population (according to the 1970 census) from Casper, Wyoming, with 36,361 to Phoenix, Arizona, with 581,562, plus 8 cities in California.[2] Table 1 also shows the date of the founding of each city, the river or other adjacent water supply, and the reason for the founding of each. Figure 1 shows, in addition to these cities, the pre-Columbian Indian settlements, which were built a thousand years before Columbus or even Lief Ericson set foot on the North American continent. These settlements are of so much interest and value, since many of them show far more distinctive and sun-related patterns than do today's Anglo-dominated cities, that they will be discussed in more detail later.

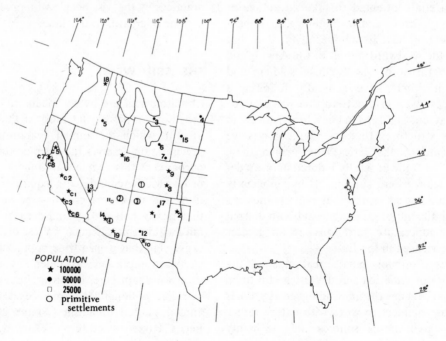

Figure 1.   Cities of the arid American West.

Table 1.   Origin of Cities in Arid American West

Map Number	City and State	Founding Date	Adjacent River or Other Water Supply	Reasons for Founding
1	Albuquerque, NM	1705	Rio Grande	Spanish fort and mission
2	Amarillo, TX	1887	Amarillo Creek	Cattle, railroad, oil
3	Billings, MN	1882	Yellowstone	Railroad division point, ranching center
4	Bismark, MN	1872	Missouri	Military outpost, ranching center
5	Boise, ID	1863	Boise	Military outpost, ranching center
6	Casper, WY	1888	North Platte	Railroad division point, ranching center
7	Cheyenne, WY	1867	None	Railroad division point, ranching center
8	Colorado Springs, CO	1871	Fountain Creek	Railroad center, health resort, air force communications center
9	Denver, CO	1861	South Platte	Railroad division point, mining center, transcontinental trail
10	El Paso, TX	1659	Rio Grande	Spanish fort and mission, railroad and trading center
11	Flagstaff, AZ	1876	None	Railroad division point, gateway to the Grand Canyon
12	Las Cruces, NM	1848	Rio Grande	Crossroad, ranching and trading center
13	Las Vegas, NV	1770	Colorado	Old Spanish Trail, gambling center
14	Phoenix, AZ	1870	Salt, Gila	Farming on irrigated land
15	Rapid City, Sd	1876	Rapid	Trading center for ranches
16	Salt Lake City, UT	1847	None (for potable water)	World center for Mormon Church, mining center
17	Santa Fe, NM	1609	Rio Grande	Earliest Spanish capital of Arizona territory, mission
18	Spokane, WA	1871	Spokane	Trading center, farming area
19	Tucson, AZ	1776	Santa Cruz (usually dry)	Spanish fort and mission
C-1	Bakersfield, CA	1851	Kern	Gold mining, agriculture, oil mining
C-2	Fresno, CA	1800	None	Spanish mission, mining center, farming area
C-3	Los Angeles, CA	1781	None	Spanish fort and mission
C-4	Oakland, CA	1850	San Francicso and Oakland Bays	Transportation and commercial center
C-5	Sacramento, CA	1839	Sacramento, American	Mining, commercial, and agricultural center
C-6	San Diego, CA	1779	None	Spanish fort and mission
C-7	San Francisco, Ca	1834	San Francisco and Oakland Bays	Northern end of Spanish-controlled territory, commerce and shipping center
C-8	San Jose, CA	1770	None	Spanish mission and fort

The average population in the arid West ranges from 2 to 20 people per square mile, but these figures are highly misleading, because there are vast areas of completely uninhabited—and uninhabitable—space, where the aridity is so great and the water supply is so small or even nonexistent that people simply cannot live there. With the exception of the Spanish-based settlements, Albuquerque, El Paso, Santa Fe, and Tucson and the California coastal cities, all of the communities in the arid West grew up after the War between the States. They arose during the great westward migration, and some, like Salt Lake City, were carefully selected and planned, whereas others simply grew up at a crossroads or a railroad division point that had, in those days, an adequate water supply.

Table 2. Population Growth of Cities in Arid American West[a]

Map Number	City and State	Year 1900	1920	1940	1960	1970	Rank (1970)
1	Albuquerque, NM	6,238	15,157	35,449	201,189	243,751	58
	Ratio to 1920	0.41	1.00	2.34	13.2	16.1	
2	Amarillo, TX	1,442	15,494	51,686	137,969	127,010	113
	Ratio to 1920	0.09	1.00	3.33	8.9	8.2	
3	Billings, MN	3,221	15,100	23,261	52,851	61,581	314
	Ratio to 1920	0.21	1.00	1.54	3.5	4.1	
4	Bismark, ND	3,319	7,122	15,496	17,670	34,703	NR
	Ratio to 1920	0.47	1.00	2.18	3.89	4.87	
5	Boise, ID	5,957	21,393	26,130	34,481	74,990	236
	Ratio to 1920	0.28	1.00	1.22	1.6	3.5	
6	Casper, WY	883	11,447	17,764	38,930	36,361	NR
	Ratio to 1920	0.08	1.00	1.57	3.40	3.18	
7	Cheyenne, WY	14,087	13,829	22,542	40,914	43,505	NR
	Ratio to 1920	1.02	1.00	1.63	2.96	3.15	
8	Colorado Springs, CO	21,083	30,105	36,789	70,194	135,060	105
	Ratio to 1920	0.70	1.00	1.22	2.3	4.5	
9	Denver, CO	133,859	256,491	322,412	493,887	514,678	25
	Ratio to 1920	0.58	1.00	1.26	1.9	2.0	
10	El Paso, TX	89,306	77,560	96,810	276,687	322,261	45
	Ratio to 1920	0.51	1.00	1.25	3.6	4.2	
11	Flagstaff, AZ	NA	3,186	5,080	18,214	26,117	NR
	Ratio to 1920	NA	1.00	1.59	5.72	8.20	
12	Las Cruces, NM	3,836	3,969	8,385	20,367	37,857	NR
	Ratio to 1920	0.97	1.00	2.11	5.13	9.54	
13	Las Vegas, NV	NA	2,304	8,422	64,405	125,787	115
	Ratio to 1920	NA	1.00	3.66	28.0	54.6	
14	Phoenix, AZ	5,544	29,053	65,414	439,170	581,562	20
	Ratio to 1920	0.19	1.00	2.25	15.1	20.0	
15	Rapid City, SD	1,342	5,777	13,844	42,399	43,836	NR
	Ratio to 1920	0.23	1.00	2.40	7.34	7.59	
16	Salt Lake City, UT	53,531	118,110	149,934	189,454	175,885	74
	Ratio to 1920	0.45	1.00	1.27	1.6	1.5	
17	Santa Fe, NM	5,603	7,236	20,325	33,394	41,167	NR
	Ratio to 1920	0.77	1.00	2.81	4.61	5.69	
18	Spokane, WA	36,848	104,437	122,001	181,600	170,516	80
	Ratio to 1920	0.35	1.00	1.17	1.7	1.6	
19	Tucson, AZ	7,531	20,292	35,752	212,892	262,933	53
	Ratio to 1920	0.37	1.00	1.76	10.5	13.1	
C-1	Bakersfield, CA	4,836	18,638	29,252	56,848	69,515	268
	Ratio to 1920	0.26	1.00	1.57	3.05	3.73	
C-2	Fresno, CA	12,470	45,086	60,685	133,929	165,972	83
	Ratio to 1920	0.28	1.00	1.35	2.97	3.68	
C-3	Los Angeles, CA	102,500	576,673	1,504,277	2,479,015	2,809,015	3
	Ratio to 1920	0.18	1.00	2.61	4.30	4.87	
C-4	Oakland, CA	66,960	216,261	302,163	367,548	361,561	39
	Ratio to 1920	0.31	1.00	1.40	1.70	1.67	
C-5	Sacramento, CA	29,281	65,908	105,958	191,667	257,105	55
	Ratio to 1920	0.44	1.00	1.61	2.91	3.90	
C-6	San Diego, CA	17,700	74,361	203,341	573,224	697,027	14
	Ratio to 1920	0.24	1.00	2.73	7.71	9.37	
C-7	San Francisco, Ca	342,800	506,676	634,536	740,316	715,674	13
	Ratio to 1920	0.68	1.00	1.25	1.46	1.41	
C-8	San Jose, CA	21,500	39,642	68,457	204,196	445,719	31
	Ratio to 1920	0.54	1.00	1.73	5.45	11.25	

[a] NA—Data not available in *The World Almanac* for 1976; NR—1970 population below 45,000, so not ranked.

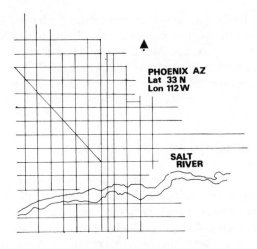

Figure 2.   North–south grid of Phoenix, Arizona, streets.

Figure 4.   The skewed grid of Las Vegas, Nevada—its older section dominated by early transportation routes.

It was not difficult to select the cities listed in Table 2, because few if any other settlements grew to deserve the name. The availability of water was one of the major reasons for the founding of many of these cities, with the oldest arising from the northward thrust from Mexico of the Spanish military and missionary explorers. Santa Fe, located quite close to the Rio Grande, and El Paso and Albuquerque, both directly on that great river, are the oldest cities on the list, followed by the coastal cities of California, which were founded when the Spaniards wanted to establish their claim to that land by actual military occupation.

The Anglo-founded cities generally began during the second half of the 1880s, when the lure of California gold attracted thousands of adventurous men and women across the Mississippi and the Great

Plains. Other thousands came around the horn by ship to California ports after they had been claimed from Spain and Mexico by the United States. Trails, and then wagon roads and railway lines, brought about the establishment of many of the inland cities, but it was the availability of water on a reasonably permanent basis that enabled the cities listed in Table 2 to grow and, with a few exceptions, to prosper. "Ghost cities," however, abound in the arid West, and they generally perished because their reason for existence, gold and silver mining, also expired. In their earlier years, many of these listed cities had enough water for domestic needs from flowing streams or from underground sources. Most of them, such as Denver and Phoenix, are now seeking additional water from distant rivers or lakes.

Virtually all of the cities listed in Table 2 were, as Figures 2 through 5 reveal, laid out on a north–south, east–west grid pattern, although in some cases the grid was turned 45° from the usual orientation. Few show the radial pattern that characterizes many of the great eastern cities, although Santa Fe, depicted in Figure 6, began as a collection of adobe buildings erected along trails that ran almost radially out from the central plaza. The California coastal cities laid out their original roads parallel to the ocean or bay

Figure 3.   Albuquerque, New Mexico—its older section dominated by the Rio Grande; its newer section following north–south grid.

Figure 5.   Boise, Idaho—its older portion oriented at 45° to the section lines due to Boise River.

Figure 6. Sante Fe, New Mexico—its radial pattern established by Spanish founders; dominated by landforms and the Rio Grande.

shores, but they changed to the north–south, east–west grid pattern as soon as they expanded into the valleys which lay beyond their original boundaries.

The Spanish explorers chose the Rio Grande Valley primarily because of its continuing and relatively abundant year-round supply of water. The Colorado River played no great part in their plans for exploring and then subjugating the western half of the North American continent. In fact, it was viewed primarily as an obstacle to their exploration, and its Grand Canyon was regarded not as one of "the Wonders of the World" but rather as an impassable barrier to their northward expansion. The first Anglo to explore the upper reaches of the Colorado, beyond what is now Lake Mead, was Lieutenant Charles Christmas Ives in 1858. In his report to Washington,

he stated, "The land is utterly worthless; having once entered it, the only proper course of action is to leave it as soon as possible. I doubt whether any other white men will ever pass this way again." Ives was quite wrong, of course, but he could not foresee the changes that a century would bring to pass.

THE CLIMATE OF THE ARID WEST

High levels of insolation, meager cloud cover, and aridity characterize much of the western half of the United States. Mean daily solar radiation in January is, as Figure 7 reveals, 300 Langleys/day (1107 Btu/ft^2. day) where the 90th meridian emerges from Mexico and diminishes to 175 Ly (646 Btu/ft^2. day) at the Canadian border. The isopleth denoting 100 Ly (369 Btu/ft^2. day) moves a short distance inland away from nonarid Seattle and Portland because of the high incidence of cloudiness in the Pacific Northwest. In July the 600 Ly (2214 Btu/ft^2. day) isopleth runs from the Gulf of Mexico to the Canadian border almost parallel to the 100th meridian. The insolation increases toward the west, reaching 650 Ly (2400 Btu/ft^2. day) in western Texas and New Mexico and then attaining 700 and 750 Ly (2583 and 2770 Btu/ft^2. day) in California's high Sierras. Insolation in summer is usually about 50 percent above the annual average, as shown by the June data for the 27 cities listed in Table 3. Insolation in winter is from 50 to 60 percent lower than the average, depending on local conditions such as altitude and cloud cover.

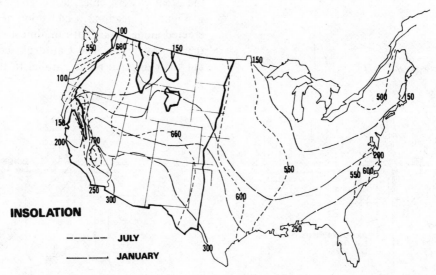

INSOLATION

- - - - - - JULY

———— JANUARY

Figure 7. July and January mean horizontal insolation (Ly/day) for the continental United States.

Table 3 Climatic Data for Cities in Arid American West[a]

Map Number	City and State	1	2	3	4	5	6	7	8
1	Albuquerque, NM	35	5310	512	303	76.0	35	79.0	4348
		107	12		726	4.0		35.0	
2	Amarillo, TX	35	3607	475	275	76.0	37	81.0	3985
		102	19		670	4.0		38.0	
3	Billings, MN	46	3567	375	160	61.0	20	70.0	7049
		109	12		625	6.0		35.0	
4	Bismark, ND	47	1647	369	157	59.0	10	72.0	8857
		101	16		590	6.1		45.0	
5	Boise, ID	44	2842	395	138	66.0	20	75.0	5809
		116	12		636	5.6		27.0	
6	Casper, WY	43	539	425	220	61.0	25	70.0	7410
		107	12		650	5.5		36.0	
7	Cheyenne, WY	41	6126	410	220	66.0	20	79.0	7278
		105	16		650	5.2		37.0	
8	Colorado Springs, CO	39	6173	370	250	70.0	25	70.0	6423
		105	12		600	4.9		30.0	
9	Denver, CO	40	5288	367	201	67.0	30	73.0	6283
		105	16		525	4.7		30.0	
10	El Paso, Tx	32	3918	536	333	80.0	40	82.0	2700
		107	7		729	3.2		33.0	
11	Flagstaff, AZ	35	6993	510	300	80.0	40	66.0	7152
		112	16		720	4.3		27.0	
12	Las Cruces, NM	33	3500	530	320	82.0	35	80.0	3000
		107	12		728	3.6		33.0	
13	Las Vegas, NV	36	2162	509	277	82.0	40	90.0	2709
		115	8		748	3.2		22.0	
14	Phoenix, AZ	34	1117	520	301	85.0	50	91.0	1765
		112	7		739	3.5		27.0	
15	Rapid City, SD	44	1165	392	183	63.0	20	74.0	7345
		103	16		585	5.6		43.0	
16	Salt Lake City, UT	40	4220	394	163	69.0	20	76.0	6052
		112	20		621	5.3		29.0	
17	Santa Fe, NM	36	7045	500	300	68.0	20	70.0	6006
		106	16		700	5.3		35.0	
18	Spokane, WA	48	2357	361	119	58.0	25	70.0	6655
		118	22		596	6.2		29.0	
19	Tucson, AZ	32	2584	518	315	85.0	50	85.0	1800
		111	12		699	3.4		28.0	
C-1	Bakersfield, CA	35	495	500	300	78.0	40	84.0	2122
		119	8		750	3.6		30.0	
C-2	Fresno, CA	37	326	450	184	78.0	46	82.0	2611
		126	11		682	3.8		36.0	
C-3	Los Angeles, CA	34	122	450	243	73.0	54	73.0	2061
		118	13		645	4.0		50.0	
C-4	Oakland, CA	38	8	410	150	66.0	49	67.0	2870
		122	18		650	4.6		69.0	
C-5	Sacramento, CA	39	17	450	174	77.0	46	75.0	2419
		122	16		682	3.2		46.0	
C-6	San Diego, CA	33	10	380	244	68.0	52	69.0	1458
		117	11		497	4.7		68.0	
C-7	San Francisco, Ca	38	8	410	150	66.0	49	63.0	2700
		122	16		650	4.6		75.0	
C-8	San Jose, CA	37	70	420	160	71.0	45	70.0	2700
		122	16		660	4.4		60.0	

[a] 1—Latitude and longitude; 2—elevation (ft) and annual precipitation (in.); 3—annual average insolation (Ly/day); 4—daily average insolation (Ly/day), January and June; 5—possible sunshine (percent) and cloud cover (on scale of 0 to 10); 6—daily average temperature for January (°F); 7—daily average temperature for July (°F) and relative humidity (percent) at noon; 8—number of heating degree days.

In fact, if it were not for the influence of cloud cover and water vapor in the atmosphere, insolation on horizontal surfaces would necessarily follow lines of latitude, with altitude acting as an upward modifier in the Rocky Mountain states. The percent of possible sunshine is characteristically high in the arid West precisely because cloud cover during daylight hours, expressed on a scale of 0 for an absolutely clear sky to 10 for a completely overcast sky, is low compared to the rest of the United States. The West's highest cloud cover, from 5 to 6 on the Weather Bureau's scale as evaluated visually by its observers, is found along the northern tier of the western states.

Average summer temperatures are high, ranging from 60°F in the northern plains and high-altitude regions to 85° in Phoenix and 80° in the cities of western Texas. Winter average temperatures are much more variable, ranging from a low of 10° in Bismark to 50° in Phoenix and Tucson. Wet-bulb and dew-point temperatures, not given in Table 3 but readily determined, are generally lower than in the eastern half of the United States.[3] Since relative humidities are generally more readily understood, they are listed in Table 3 for noon on average July days. In winter the humidity ratio (weight of water vapor per unit weight of dry air, pound per pound or kilogram per kilogram) is always so low that the moisture content of the atmosphere is not an important factor in determining human comfort. In summer, however, humidity is very important, because few people are comfortable in an atmosphere at an otherwise suitable temperature if the humidity ratio is so high that little moisture can be lost by evaporation.

RESPONSES TO THE SUN

Arid California. The largest by far of the 11 states that lie west of meridian 100 is California, which, with its 156,361 mi², is exceeded in size only by Alaska (566,432 mi²) and Texas (262,134 mi²). In population, California now stands first among all the states, having passed New York for this distinction in the decade between the 1960 and 1970 censuses. As of 1974 its population was estimated to be nearly 21 million, larger than that of all but 30 of the world's nations. In latitude, California extends from 32.5°N along the Mexican border to 42° where Oregon begins; in longitude, the span is from 114°W at Parker Dam on the Colorado to 124°W at Cape

Mendocino, on the Pacific coast just south of Eureka. All of California's major cities come within the arid classification, since even the "City by the Bay," San Francisco, has an annual rainfall of only 15.6 in. and Los Angeles, the third largest city in the United States, has only 12.8 in. The five largest cities in the state are either on the Pacific coast or within 40 mi of it, yet the precipitation which they receive is comparable to that which falls on the Mountain States from Denver to Tucson.

California's great central basin is both arid and fertile, and its amazingly large agricultural production is supported entirely by irrigation through a network of canals that carry water from the definitely nonarid northern portion of the state. Los Angeles obtains a large portion of its municipal water supply from the Colorado River through an aqueduct which runs from just above Parker Dam to Lake Matthews, some 40 mi east of the city. Two other lengthy aqueducts, now nearing completion, will bring more water to Los Angeles from the rivers that now flow toward the sea from the high Sierras. San Francisco receives most of its drinking water from the Hetch Hetchy Reservoir in Yosemite National Park, about 140 mi east of the city.

California's seacoast cities were founded by the Spaniards to militarily defend their vast territories from possible inroads by the English from the Pacific Ocean and by the Russians, who were moving southward from Alaska. Almost the only traces of the Spanish heritage are the missions, which still stand two centuries after their construction by the Jesuits and their often unwilling Indian converts. The best known of these is San Juan Capistrano, completed in 1776; others in this remarkable chain are Santa Cruz (near San Jose) and San Jose de Guadalupe (across the bay from San Francisco), both completed in 1791, and Mission San Francisco, completed in 1823 near Sonoma just north of San Franscisco Bay, the most northerly of the Spanish settlements.

It would again be gratifying to be able to say that the architecture of the missions reveals an understanding of the impact of the sun on buildings in the arid West, but this is not the case. The missions were all virtually identical to those that the Jesuits had built in their native Spain. Fortunately, the high ceilings, covered patios, and courtyards which had served them well in southern Europe were equally effective in Mexico and in California. Virtually all of the Spanish-built villages were walled to provide protection from the Indians, who, in most cases, were less than enthusiastic about the invaders who laid claim to the land and enforced their claims with small but well-armed bands of soldiers.

California is called "the Golden State" not because of the gold mines which gave rise to the boom that began in 1849, but rather because of its rainfall pattern. Most of the state receives its precipitation in the winter and spring, and as a result the rolling hills turn green. Then the rains cease, and the hot summer sun turns the grass brown. The moisture that blows in from the Pacific Ocean frequently ends as snow on the tops of the high Sierras which run along the eastern border of the state, and virtually all of this snow drains down through a multitude of streams and rivers into dozens of small lakes. The most arid portion of California lies in the great valley between the coastal range and the Sierras and in the true desert, which extends southward and eastward from the southern end of the Sierra Nevada. Here is to be found Death Valley, more than 280 ft below sea level, a spot that receives about 2.0 in. of rain annually. The highest temperature recorded in the United States was 134°F, experienced at Death Valley on July 10, 1913.

A factor that will become very important as the sun's impact begins to be felt in California is the orientation of its coastline, which runs northwesterly from San Diego until it reaches the San Francisco Bay area, where it turns toward the north. Most of the population of California is to be found in the coastal cities and towns, and virtually all of them grew from settlements in which the major streets paralleled the coast. Thus tens of thousands of homes face toward the southwest or the northeast, rather than toward the south or the north. This is fortunate, because much of the coastal area is cloudy in the morning and clear in the afternoon. Thus rooftops and walls that face the southwest are well disposed to receive the sun's rays when they break through the overcast.

The vast expansion which swept over southern California after World War I followed the north–south, east–west grid that characterizes most western cities. The expansion carried the coastal cities into the relatively flat areas beyond the coastal mountain ranges, and, as soon as the terrain permitted, the old, familiar north–south, east–west grid pattern was reestablished. California appears to be more conscious of the true energy situation than any other state, probably because its residents have seen their own fossil fuel resources pass the peak of productivity and begin to recede. For example, Southern California Gas Company, when it was founded, obtained 98 percent of its natural gas from California sources with only 2 percent imported from other states. Now the situation is exactly the reverse, and 98 percent comes from other states and from Canada, which has informed its American customers that gas exportation will be subject to 30 percent annual reductions until it is shut off completely.

Local California cities, such as Davis, home of a major branch of the University of California system, have adopted building codes that will permit no structure to be erected which is not energy conserving in its very design. The statewide building code implements ASHRAE building standard 90-75 in one form or another.[4] Attention will necessarily be paid to the sun in the Golden State because the residents will be compelled to do so by the combined forces of economics, public opinion, dwindling energy supplies from all sources, and, finally, law.

The Past. Although modern man has had the technology to enable him to ignore natural forces (except the lack of water) and to build almost any kind of structure in an area that is arid, sunny, and given to wide fluctuations in atmospheric temperature, the first semipermanent residents of much of the Southwest did not possess this technology, and so their dwellings had to come to terms with the natural forces that surrounded them. A surprisingly large number of Indian tribes inhabited the southwestern plains and deserts, and about a thousand years ago, they created a number of extraordinarily well-designed and sturdily built permanent population centers. This section deals with these cliff dwellings and pueblos, and modern man will do well to study them carefully, for they are probably the models that his successors in this land will have to emulate.

In a general evaluation of solar energy use, a consideration of primitive settlements and activities must be included, for the adaptation to solar and other natural energies by low- and non-technological cultures provides a basis for a contemporary, low-technology passive systems approach to the satisfaction of human energy needs. The inclusion of primitive settlement patterns in this discussion also gives a contextual and philosophical continuity to the concept of environmental amelioration. All present-day actions thus link with both past and future attempts to provide for human comfort. Unfortunately, the clues and lessons of the past seem to have been ignored and devalued, in both present actions and future plans. The old population centers cited in this section are representative of a great number of sites and settlements which provide the best existing examples of arid environmental adaptation. The selected sites are located within the heart of the arid region and represent varied settings, resources, and human actions.

Fifteen thousand years ago the Four Corners area, a zone that is now Colorado, Utah, Arizona, and New Mexico, was the site of a number of settlements. Primitive cultures, which had earlier crossed the Bering Strait, moved slowly from the cold northlands into the warmer areas, always settling near the natural springs and rivers necessary for survival. Three centers developed, each taking advantage of the small concentrations of water. As human activity became more sedentary and agricultural, sites with water became natural areas of population concentration and social activity. With agriculture also came comprehension of seasonal and daily climatic cycles and changes, a recognition that had a social impact.

The agricultural people typified by the settlement at Mesa Verde, in the first center, the southwest quadrant of Colorado (circled no. 1 in Figure 1), required three things: arable land, a permanent supply of water, and shelter from the elements. The caves of Mesa Verde, formed by the interface of seeping water and the sandstone cliffs, provided a natural, if somewhat damp and dank, shelter. Shallow open pits constituted an individual's dwelling space. These pits did little, however, to enhance environmental protection. As agriculture developed, the people moved out of the caves onto the mesa to be nearer the fields and found themselves nearer also to the natural elements. More sophisticated pit houses were constructed, all facing in a southerly direction, perhaps because of the climate, but probably because of the belief that "evil spirits come from the North."[5] Approximately AD 800 pit construction was abandoned in favor of the pueblo structure, an expression of community living and solidarity. Pit construction was refined and used only for the development of subterranean *kivas*, which became the religious center for each house block. The Mesa Verde story ends about AD 1300, after a return to the caves and the development of the great cave pueblos. These caves, bitterly cold and damp, provided a secure and safe position for the last Mesa Verde inhabitants. Structures of stone, adobe, and wood were built and nestled into the great stone openings. The cave's rock shelf provided a strong overhang that kept out the intense summer sun and allowed the winter sun's rays to enter. Structures evolved into a sophisticated massing of interacting,

living units, each with its own sun terrace or outdoor area. The structures grew by accretion rather than by fixed plan and, for the most part, were dark and poorly ventilated, a feature that probably prompted people to spend most of their time outside, except in extremely adverse weather.

These shelters were primitive thermal control devices. Since a primitive, preindustrial society lacks the technology to "ignore" the climate and to escape its effects, these people's early human response was to collaborate with nature. The construction of environmentally sound control units evolved as rigorous building methods developed which achieved tight masonry joinery for thermal control, as well as structural massing where units protected each other.

Chaco Canyon, a settlement in the second center—northwestern New Mexico (circled no. 3 in Figure 1), represents the epitome of open-ground pueblo construction. The profusion of pueblo structures is best characterized there by Pueblo Bonito, a five-story "apartment house" with 800 rooms. Recent analysis has revealed a sophisticated orientation toward the sun's cycles, leading some to believe that the structures were carefully designed to optimize human comfort. The intricately fitted stone and plaster walls and the interlocking units represented the close-knit community life-style. Although the rock massings were indeed oriented to the sun, the probable reason was the culture's "spiritual" life, making the settlement an Indian Stonehenge. According to Dr. Jonathan Reyman, the great pueblo was designed to monitor "astronomical events," and the architecture clearly served functions beyond the provision of shelter.[6] His hypothesis emphasizes the important relationship between architecture and other cultural features—astronomy, agriculture, and ritual.

The ability to accurately establish a solar calendar, reflected by the architecture of the Pueblo Bonito, increased the chances for successful farming. It can be further speculated that this knowledge of solar activity and patterns could also have led to the creation of a more comfortable environment, but, as mentioned earlier vis-à-vis Mesa Verde, much of the pueblo's core was uncomfortable and almost intolerable for habitation. The "sun deck" areas and plazas with their subterranean *kivas*, however, provided a more direct energy relationship between sun and man. Shaded by living units and exposed to the warmth of the winter sun, these open public spaces provided the habitable communal space within which most tribal activities occurred.

Kayenta, the third center—in northeastern Arizona (circled no. 2 on Figure 1), typifies a culture using a number of adaptive environmental modes. Huge cliff dwellings, such as Betatakin, reveal a great emphasis on cave residences, where every perch, every niche, was sought out and built upon, as Figure 8 reveals. Kitsiel, also depicted in Figure 8, on the other hand, consisted of open dwellings located adjacent to a cave. Perhaps the builders of Kitsiel were seeking more comfort or a greater relationship between shelter and agriculture. Kayenta is an example of the search for permanence and stability, yet the construction of different designs at different locations within the same time period and in the same climatic zone raises a serious question as to the conscious construction of climatically determined settlements. Continuity seems to have provided the evolutionary context for all three cultural centers, a continuity in which the spiritual meaning of the sun is emphasized and a spiritual and biological ecology centered on an animate nature, a common life force existing in the water, earth, trees, animals, and man, is stressed.

A fourth center should be mentioned at this time—the Hohokam settlements (circled no. 4 in Figure 1). Although much smaller in population, the Hohokam succeeded in achieving fantastic feats of irrigation engineering with very little technology but with a high degree of organization. Settlements consisted of single-unit structures, sometimes arranged in compound groupings, with depressed floors, side entrances (usually oriented toward the east for morning light and summer cooling), and walls made of poles and branches packed with an adobe mud. There were two types of shelter, one for winter and one for summer. Winter shelters were more massive with little or no openings and enough thermal mass to contain heat and exclude cold. The summer shelter was a ramada type with a loose, open "weave" of vegetation which afforded shade from the intense desert sun and allowed for the movement of air as a cooling and ventilating medium. The adaptive modes of the Hohokam lend credence to the belief that they were a people who understood some of the basic natural systems available to man as a resource, and to the argument that human adaptation is an effective "solar energy device."

The assimilation of primitive responses can be seen today in various Indian communities. Pueblo settlements in the Southwest exist much as they did at their inception, even with the arrival of contemporary technology. Acoma Pueblo, one of the oldest existing settlements, continues to optimally use its natural

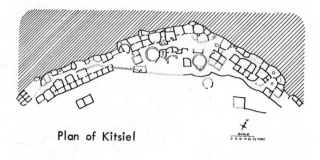

Plan of Kitsiel

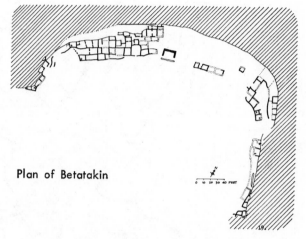

Plan of Betatakin

Figure 8. Early settlement patterns: Kitsiel and Betatakin.

resources. The "People of the White Rock," as Figure 9 reveals, settled at the easternmost point of the mesa, a location of natural cisterns that also held spiritual and religious meaning focusing on the rising sun. The alignment of the buildings and streets is east–west with higher density units occurring on the northern side of the blocks. This orientation may have been designed to provide maximum exposure to the sun. It also, however, creates a formidable "back" to the evil spirits from the north. The spacing of the streets, orientation, terracing, and unit design (which incorporates heavy massings of adobe, a good thermal material, and the minimization of openings) set a stage on which the potentials for natural heating and cooling could be realized.

The solar energy potentialities of a contemporary urban environment must be realized with maximum utilization of natural processes and systems as well as technological ones. With the inclusion of these natural systems and passive approaches, the options available to the environmental designer are significantly increased in number and in variety. We must entertain serious questions about the "romantic" portrayals of primitive settlement design. Climatic

Figure 9. Acoma pueblo.

determinism, although important, was probably not the primary form shaper of these early human settlements; cultural values and significance were the overriding factors determining settlement form. The social significance of the Navajo hogan and the Hopi pueblo cluster was far more important than considerations of comfort.

Nature prepares the site, and man organizes it to satisfy his desires and his needs. The goals, ideals, and values of a culture have a direct impact on the "appropriate" environmental response. The symbolic and cosmological meaning seem to determine the form of shelter; therefore energy should be viewed in a symbolic as well as a utilitarian context. The attitude toward nature, people, and the relationship between the two are significant form shapers. There are three ways of conceiving of this relationship between these two shapers:

1. Religious and cosmological—nature is regarded as dominant over man.
2. Symbiotic—man and nature are in balance, with man regarding himself as nature's steward.
3. Exploitative—man is the completer and modifier of nature, thus the creator and finally the destroyer of the environment.

The analysis of contemporary culture and values is, however, obviously complex and time consuming. More importantly, it is also obvious that nature contains the potential to satisfy a great percentage of human requirements directly. The question of primitive cultures and climatic determinism is not as important as the present realization of the solar potential that existed in the past and still exists today. The concepts of solar orientation, direct solar gain, thermal mass, thermal storage, the thermal flywheel effect, and seasonal adaptation through changing patterns; the laws of thermodynamics and energy transfer; the existence of life cycles and other patterns; and the availability of direct, natural sources of energy (sun, wind, earth, water, man, animals, plants) are the basis for satisfying needs. The materials once used have inherent characteristics for moderating the impact of nature. The adobe and stone used by primitive man required substantial width in order to stand. The thermal characteristics of this mass were then an ancillary benefit: we should take advantage of it now. Cliff settlements had the potential for climatic modulation, especially in the case of south-facing caves. This potential, as well as the material mass of the ancient walls, provides a simple contemporary approach to solar-responsive living.

Adaptation. Adaptation, considered in the solar energy context, holds great promise as an environmental design approach. It gives planners another option in scale of possible solar uses. Current technology and development are focused on adoption of the sun's energy into a mechanized system; adaptation, on the other hand, calls for responsiveness to existing solar conditions. The former is typified by collectors functioning as comfort-providing mechanisms; the latter, by living units serving as collectors. The spectrum that is available thus ranges from the adoption of devices to the adaptation to

conditions. Biological studies discuss three types of adaptations: evasion, avoidance, and tolerance.

Perceptual and conceptual arid-region principles should have as their basis natural environmental systems abstracted and applied to the human-built environment. Natural cycles and rhythms must have a direct relationship to human habitats, rural and urban. From the beginning, man has struggled to adapt to a world that he perceived as harsh and inhuman. Human growth—or progress—has been marked by increased control over the elements which continually impinge on the organism. More often than not, adaptability has taken the form of manipulation—either altering the effects of impinging forces or altering other elements to act as a barrier between man and nature. Control manifests itself today mainly in the form of energy, the primary abstract symbol of human domination over nature. The high costs of this domination are now being felt economically and environmentally. The search for new alternatives has focused on new resources and/or more efficient exploitation. Instead, modern man should turn to natural systems and processes, which provide a sound basis for design and problem solving. The use of basic "natural technology" augmented by more technical systems—if needed—can satisfy man's needs. Consideration of natural approaches necessarily includes the modification of human living patterns to more closely approximate the rhythms and cycles of nature, of which man is a part.

Adaptation to arid regions relies on both the internal and the external functions of the organism. Tolerance is affected by the internal operations and usually exists within very well defined limits; if these are exceeded, damage to the biological unit results. Evasion, on the other hand, deals with orientation, daily cycles, activity patterning, the extent of nocturnality, and the use of natural shading, burrowing, and passivity during times of maximized climatological conflict—all dealing with external functions. Avoidance is similarly an external adjustment by the organism which creates a secondary environment that denies the fact and the impact of the primary environment, even at its extreme limits.

CONCLUSION

The camel's fluctuating body temperature enables the animal to store excess heat during the day and then to give it up in the evening. The built environmental shell, an extension of the human body, can assume the same function of absorbing, storing, and radiating heat in order to protect its interior organ, man. Instead of being simply a barrier, a shelter can become an adaptive membrane responsive to changing conditions.

The avoidance characteristics of plants need to be emulated—their highly reflective surfaces which dissipate light, and their boundary layers composed of air and textured surfaces such as spines and rough bark, which enable a fine "skin" of air to be trapped and to act as an insulating barrier, a transition zone, which modifies intense temperature. The fluted stems of desert plants also scatter light because of the refractive plant shape and light incident angles. The feather and hair layers of animals and birds exhibit characteristics similar to these. Human habitats can reflect the same principles—white reflective surfaces and dark absorptive surfaces; faceted, textured surfaces for air film layering and light dispersion; the creation of "decompression" zones so that the human body can adjust itself through more gentle temperature transitions; and the use of building forms that break up light impact or gather it in (whichever is appropriate) or do both, depending on the seasonal and daily cycles.

Such orientation and patterning are evasion modes of all life forms. The contemporary grid pattern refuses to recognize such vital modes. Shading devices and burrowing into the earth (features of the early cliff dwellings, *kivas*, and pit houses) utilize both these evasion modes and the fact that physical screens, thermal mass, and the inherent coolness of the earth can serve to absorb excess heat.

The adaptation mechanisms presented and recommended here are independent of each other and of other important factors such as social and cultural values. An arid region, however, does not consist of a series of unrelated, isolated elements coexisting in the same area, but represents a complex interaction of life forms and patterns. Large plants shelter small plants; animals live at the plant's root level, benefiting from its ability to stabilize the soil and in return supplying the plant with fertilizer and constructing water canals.

Arid-region adaptation must focus on two primary concepts: one is life cycles, and the other is interactive patterns. It is simply not enough to imitate other life forms. Superficial imitation rejects the recognition of how and why man relates to the other elements in nature. The desert—the arid region, any region—functions in the context of total energy conservation. Only in the activities of the human organism can we find examples that attempt to deny this truism. But the human organism can exist comfortably and gently, matching internal needs and external resources, if it understands cycles (growth, seasonal, daily, etc.) and interactive patterns. The human environment must be perceived in the total context of an arid region, for the question of human survival is simply the choice between assuming a role as a part of the natural desert system or departing from the desert.

NOTES

1. Environmental Science Services Administration, *Climatic Atlas of the U.S.* (Washington: U.S. Government Printing Office, 1968), p. 43.
2. The California cities are all included in the "arid" classification because, despite their lush green appearance, all of them live by importing water—some, like Los Angeles, from great distances and at prodigious expense. None receives as much as 20 in. of rainfall annually.
3. See *Climatic Atlas of the U.S.* for such data.
4. See *Energy Conservation in New Building Design* (New York: American Society of Heating, Refrigerating, and Air-Conditioning Engineers, 1975) for a discussion of this particular design standard.
5. Thomas M. Moher, *Mesa Verde* (n.p., 1966).
6. Jonathan Reyman, "Astronomy, Architecture and Adaptation at Pueblo Bonito," *Science,* **193** (September 10, 1976), 957–962.

SUGGESTED READINGS

Environmental Services Administration. *Climatic Atlas of the U.S.* Washington: U.S. Government Printing Office, 1968.

Givoni, B. *Man, Climate and Architecture.* Amsterdam: Elsevier Publishing Company, 1969.

Knowles, R. *Energy and Form.* Cambridge: The Massachusetts Institute of Technology Press, 1974.

Life Pictorial Atlas of the World. New York: Time, Incorporated, 1961.

McGinnies, W. J., Goldman, B. J., and Paylore, P., eds. *Deserts of the World.* Tucson: University of Arizona Press, 1968.

Solar-Oriented Architecture. Washington: American Institute of Architects Research Corporation, 1974.

The World Almanac. New York: Newspaper Enterprises Association, 1976.

CHAPTER 5

Environmental Psychology and Housing Design in Arid Urban Areas

R. B. BECHTEL, W. H. ITTELSON, L. WHEELER

Many chapters in this book reflect a concern for people—indirectly. The authors consider solar energy, water resources, transportation, landscaping, heat exchange systems, and even the physiological responses of human beings to the environmental conditions imposed by arid regions. All these are essentially physical matters related only implicitly to the perceptions, needs, values, goals, and behavior of people. In this chapter we discuss more directly certain questions associated with human psychology. Such questioning may yield answers differing solely as the environmental stimuli associated with arid and with temperate regions differ. Can it be said with any confidence that people differ in their needs, goals, and perceptions, depending on whether or not the environment is arid? If so, are these differences relevant in the planning and designing of human settlements in such regions? Case histories, anecdotal evidence, and a small number of experiments and field studies lead us to suppose that the answers to these two questions may turn out to be affirmative.

At the University of Arizona, the graduate program in environmental psychology is ideally located for behavioral research on arid regions. Situated within the Sonoran Desert and close to the Great Basin, the Mohave, and the Chihuahuan deserts, we have an immense laboratory at our doorstep. Psychological research in natural and constructed environments has been a central interest of the staff for many years.[1] The university is, moreover, strongly dedicated to an interdisciplinary program for the study of arid lands. Many of its faculty members are engaged in this work on a worldwide basis, and unanswered questions are in the process of being answered, or are scheduled for examination in the near future.

For the moment, however, there are restrictions upon what we can usefully discuss in this chapter. We can explore some anecdotal materials, we can describe some research data, we can consider research plans and methods that will help to close the gaps in our knowledge, and we can define theoretical or conceptual issues that we believe are important in approaching the problems of behavior in arid regions. We cannot, however, present a series of neat, explicit formulae that will wholly satisfy the current needs of designers and planners.

THE BASIC ISSUES

Wealth.   Even though we lack some of the necessary data, we are virtually certain that a few important human behaviors have clear implications for the design of arid-region environments. The first of these is the accumulation of wealth. Whenever sufficient affluence is attained, it is possible to buy technology and energy for the creation of any desired level of environmental control. Just as the rich are said never to be insane, so they also need never succumb to heatstroke or dehydration. Designing for the wealthy, in arid regions as elsewhere, principally involves stylistic choices, and the problems encountered, therefore, are essentially trivial.

But money accumulation is a dimensional or scaled behavior, positively related to the control of energy and resources. As we move down from the top of the scale, design problems become less trivial and conservative solutions become increasingly important. At the bottom of the scale, conditions sometimes arise that cause the wealth of an entire community or nation to be partially redistributed, in order to prevent deaths—or even impoverished life-styles—that some portion of the population does not care to have on its collective conscience. In such situations, design ingenuity of the highest order is necessary, because the redistributed money is never sufficient to provide truly humane solutions, especially when the cost of administration is subtracted from the sum originally allocated.

Consider the businessmen and politicians who control the local ordinances and codes that determine design choices, limitations, materials, and processes. These figures in the community rarely develop building codes that optimize housing conditions for the poor. There would be little profit in doing so. If they did, the more affluent—let alone the poor—might then actually build homes in which expenses for labor, materials, maintenance, and long-term power consumption were all minimized. To the successful accumulators of wealth, this might appear to be a major catastrophe. (The implied criticism here is made with full awareness that these are the same people whose energy makes possible the technology that sustains human communities in difficult environments. Though we may not always approve of their methods, these people do get things done.)

Today, in Tucson, where mud adobe construction could still be attempted by individuals at low cost and with highly favorable outcomes in terms of creating low-energy, high-comfort environments, such construction is virtually outlawed by codes that demand an exceptionally large initial investment. A hundred years ago we were saner: the *Arizona Citizen* for June 23, 1877, stated: "'Love in a cottage' is all right in cooler climes, but if you wish to enjoy the real article in Tucson, you need to get inside adobe walls to start with. . . ." Post and beam buildings, with walls made of adobe dug on the site, are still being constructed by Indians and others at locations not far from Tucson, but these inexpensive structures are illegal within the city limits. Baked adobe (a handmade, low-fired block equal in size to four conventional bricks) is, however, permitted as a construction material in Tucson. This lovely block is imported from Mexico, but it is being driven off the market by an egregiously pink, machine-fabricated, concrete imitation made in the United States. Thus the building trades really have nothing to fear from any sort of adobe any more. Possibly we should recall, however, something that Douglas Lee said in 1969: "In those communities where the dream of air conditioning is becoming reality, attention to thermal protection in *house design* is of decreasing importance, but for the less fortunate it should still be given major consideration."[2] Lee, then and 6 years earlier, showed himself to be one of the very few investigators directly concerned about the psychological aspects of life in arid regions. He believed that attitudes about the desert can truly affect adaptation to the desert.[3]

Aesthetics.   If wealth gathering is a human behavior of first importance in our efforts to cope with arid environments, then surely aesthetic perceptions and responses constitute a second major psychological category that has important consequences for desert living. Joseph Wood Krutch, an intensely sensitive observer of the emotional impacts of the desert, has written:

What one finds, after one has come to take for granted the grand general simplicity, will be what one takes the trouble to look for—the brilliant little flower springing improbably out of the bare, packed sand, the lizard scuttling with incredible speed from cactus clump to spiny bush, the sudden flash of a bright-colored bird. This dry world . . . is their paradise. . . . Can you, like them, not merely look, but live spiritually here? Can this seemingly difficult land, which nevertheless flourishes vigorously and lives joyously, come to seem to you not merely strange and interesting but . . . normal . . . ?[4]

Ralph Parachek, another thoughtful observer, in speaking of the rapid growth of desert cities, has also shown strong aesthetic reactions:

And the population is exploding! Scarcely settled for 10,000 years, the desert now blossoms with cities. . . . Now, as before, over it all is the infinite turquoise sky, the sense of great distances, and the spell of the desert. . . . The desert, at once hard, sharp, fierce; and at the same time strangely beautiful, infinitely subtle, and of compelling fascination.[5]

The aesthetic situation created by living in an arid region can be one of shattering contrasts. A hiker who dies of heatstroke or dehydration in the mountains that we can see from our patios in Tucson does not, perhaps, care at the end about the flowers, lizards, and birds, though these may have been the reason for the hike. As Leopold has noted:

Stand a healthy human adult in the middle of the desert, without water, on the morning of a hot summer day, and he will experience no instant discomfort. . . . By nightfall, if it has been a 120-degree day, he may well be dead, but if the temperature has gone only to 110 in the shade he has a life expectancy of one more such day.[6]

The bulldozer operator who provides a good living for his family may never see or understand the fabulous, intricate, natural design in the mesquite, paloverde, ocotillo, and agave that he strips from the land to make room for houses, shopping centers, or factories. The real estate agent or the building contractor, who hopes by his own work to accumulate the money for college educations for his children, may find beauty in the homes constructed on the highly visible mountain slopes surrounding the city. The active, vigorous drivers of off-the-road sports vehicles probably never realize that in the fragile ecology of the desert any mark made by man may endure, not a year or two, but a century or two. Even if they did know this, the idea would not disturb them. Their desert is a place for motion, challenge, and danger.

The desert is, indeed, many things to many people. Our folklore has it that, if someone lives in the Tucson area for as long as 2 years and likes it, no other place will ever satisfy him: the desert will always draw him back. There is much truth in this. The desert exerts a tremendous psychological grip on its devotees, who are often the people most distressed by the inroads that man makes on the ecological fabric of the land and also the most resistant to population growth in "their desert." These protective and possessive behaviors may be based to a large extent on aesthetic perception or attitudes.

A desert, as many have noted, is a deserted place, and this must surely be one of its most compelling qualities. If it becomes instead merely a hot, dry, crowded place, what happens to the aesthetic values associated with solitude, open and untouched vistas, and natural grandeur? If an arid region merely provides new living space, replete with imported energy, interior spaces that have temperate-zone characteristics, and imported water, is it any longer in an aesthetic sense the desert?[7] A common saying among desert lovers is, "Now that we're here, let's keep everyone else out." But it is already too late in some places. Predictions have been made that the Phoenix–Tucson–Nogales corridor will have a population of approximately 2 million by about the year 2000.[8] If this comes to pass, we will have an arid-region linear city, but not a desert. For many people this will represent an aesthetic loss never to be regained.

We must continue our efforts to obtain a detailed understanding of people's aesthetic reactions to arid environments. The research tools for gaining this knowledge exist, but modern communities in the desert are, for the most part, dreadful examples of our ignorance concerning the beauty of arid regions and the ways in which we can preserve it.[9]

Changes in Behavior. Changing behavior patterns constitute a third psychological issue that has important consequences for habitation design in desert areas. Reitan and Green have stated, "One of the main climatological problems of arid lands is the lack of a satisfactory system for determining water need and water use, and for expressing aridity in those terms."[10] It is important to remember that these needs and uses, though poorly defined, have been subject to immense change over the years, and that the rate of change is apparently increasing rapidly.

With these shifts in water use and water needs have come equally large changes in the behavior of groups and of individuals. As Splinter reports, population pressures are causing more arid and semiarid land to be used for farming, but these same pressures may, as Goodland and Irwin note, be turning certain lushly vegetated areas into deserts.[11] The habitability of the arid regions of the world is thus in a state of flux, and so is the social life of their peoples. Lerner describes how the traditional societies of these areas have been moving increasingly toward western values and customs.[12] This change has recently been accelerated among the members of the Organization of Petroleum Exporting Countries (OPEC), as Abercrombie tells us, by a surge of new construction and planning.[13] Even in the United States the arid lands are the fastest growing areas.[14] Chapanis describes part of this change as a new cosmopolitanism, a new sophistication of demands that is accompanied by rising expectations.[15] Lerner found in 1958 that the newer urban residents in arid regions are happier than the more traditional rural people.[16] Seven years later Cantril discovered high expectations for the future both in Egypt and in Israel, when both nation-states were young.[17] There is little reason to believe that this optimism has faded.[18]

Our problem with these recent changes in the population pressures on arid regions is not knowing how Western technology suits the people of these regions and how it should be applied. Completely prefabricated California ranch houses are being freighted to the Arabian desert, but pouring concrete foundations in the equatorial sun can be disastrous, unless special cooling methods, such as ice chips, are used. Supply problems, alone, are often so great that the ports of Iran, Saudi Arabia, Egypt, and other countries are stacked with unloaded ships for months, sometimes for more than a year.

These houses, and even whole cities created by Western designers, have been developed in response to the needs of residents of Western, temperate regions. Two broad problems emerge from this attempt to transfer Western technology without adapting it to arid regions. The first is due to a misunderstanding of design requirements in arid lands, in terms of climate and terrain. The second is due to a failure to respond to the cultural and social requirements of the particular area. Indeed, the same two mistakes are regularly made in the arid regions of the United States; we are, thus, simply exporting our local errors.

BASIC COMPLICATIONS

The Climate. Modern, ranch-type houses with their large windows are not satisfactory in hot, arid lands. Picture windows let in heat and reduce cooling efficiency. The desert sun can be so strong that air conditioners cannot usefully be placed on roofs. Water towers must have their tanks shielded by sun screens. Many roof types have been tried unsuccessfully; concrete roofs usually crack and leak, and asphalt shingles quickly disintegrate. To add to these problems, condensation within the cool interiors of houses can cause severe water damage, especially along the coasts of arid regions.

Persian rugs, one of the most delightful products of the Middle East, quickly fade if left in sunlight, and many modern curtain and drapery fabrics deteriorate even faster. For this reason—and others of even greater importance—the orientation of the house to sunlight is much more critical in most arid lands than it is in temperate climates. The main open area must face away from the sun, and roof overhangs must keep windows shaded.

It is not, perhaps, trivial to notice that another problem in using rugs is their constant abrading from sand. Ordinary wear and tear results in shorter rug life in arid lands than in temperature zones. The sand penetrates everywhere, and it is the constant complaint of homeowners that ordinary sealing and caulking materials do not last in arid conditions. Special rugs must be used if one hopes to retain the wall-to-wall luxury of a Western-style dwelling for several years.

Ranch-type houses typically do not have basements; indeed, the excavation of basements can represent an expensive addition to the already high cost of arid-land construction. To compound the difficulty, the attics of arid-land houses become so hot (120°F and up) that their use for storage is not practical. Much more storage space ought, therefore, to be built into the house proper. Inadequate storage space is another mistake we often make in our temperate areas and then export.

The Culture. Physical design problems in arid regions are difficult, but the problems created by failing to design for the indigenous culture can be even more severe. Perhaps the best—or worst—example of failing to consider indigenous culture is Le Corbusier's city of Chandigarh in India.[19] This city was an attempt by the government to be unfettered by the traditions of the past. The result was an entirely Western city that had to be reclaimed by Indian culture. Kitchen counters are now used for storage space, while cooking is done outside on the veranda or on the floor (where everyone knows it should be). The irreligious Westerners did not think of including an interior nook suitable for an altar, so a closet has to do. Clothes then must be hung on hooks, instead of in the closets, while bedding is stored in trunks safe from rats, not on open, vulnerable shelves. No provisions were made for the ubiquitious outdoor shops that characterize Indian life, so these flourish now in illegal areas.

In the United States similar cultural error has marred the designs for American Indian communities. In an effort to supply American Indians with "decent" homes, the ranch-type house was built without thought for the cultural needs of the tribes or the peculiar requirements of desert life. By contrast, a traditional house, the Navajo hogan, represented a successful adaptation to desert living. With its octagonal shape and orientation to the east, it provided minimum exposure to sun.

The ranch-type houses were at first constructed without regard to orientation to the sun and with a great deal more space than Indian families needed. Also, among some tribes it was the custom to burn a dwelling where someone had died, so that the spirit would not linger. With the new houses this proved to be too expensive a custom. Finally, a series of programs began in which architects consulted directly with tribal members. Compromises were worked out in which the design approached a more Western style than the native habitats and for which certain customs were suspended. Among some tribes, however, there could be no compromises, for example, on the matter of bringing such abominations as the toilet indoors.

The Western house design is based on the needs of the nuclear family, and difficulties occur when the Western architect assumes that the single-family house is universally desired. But it is entirely possible that the main social configuration of people living in most arid lands is the extended family. It acts as the chief conveyor of values to the young, as the enforcer of law, as a welfare service for its poorer members, as babysitter, as marriage broker, as chief entertainer, as hospital, an an extension of the church and school, as a place of honor and usefulness for the elderly, as the builder of houses, as the arbiter of disputes, and as the main source of social rewards for the majority of people living in non-Western countries.

When there are no Western architects to interfere, we find that a house quite different from the California ranch style is typical in Iran, India, and other places in the Middle East and Asia, not to mention countries such as Peru.[20] It has an outer wall without windows, and its rooms face an interior courtyard. The ancient Romans and Greeks often built their houses in this same style, as Coulanges notes, and the basic type is repeated in many cultures.[21] It is especially appropriate for arid lands. There are exceptions, such as the cylindrical houses of the Dogon with their accompanying granaries, but even these dwellings can keep the extended family in close proximity within the larger village. Even when urban migration takes place, there is evidence that extended-family relationships are retained in the move from village to city.[22]

When nuclear family habitations, such as apartments or Western-style houses, are the only homes available, adaptation to the forced family separation usually occurs. Poorer families crowd three or more nuclear families into one dwelling, while the more wealthy can satisfy their needs either by locating houses close together or by visiting as frequently as possible with relatives. In a recent study in Iran, visiting among relatives was found, in fact, to be the most important single form of recreation.[23] This study took place in Tehran, where the most acculturated families live, but it can be assumed that visiting is even more important in the small villages that contain the majority of the population.

The importance of visiting has several other facets, for in another study it was discovered that families living on an Army base in Alaska also exhibited a high frequency of visiting as a major part of their entertainment.[24] We may ask whether people in the two foregoing kinds of remote or isolated environments are forced into the same entertainment pattern by similar environmental forces. One way to test this is to determine whether the residents of both types of environment perceive their surroundings as similar. Another way is to discover whether this response occurs when people of the same culture experience both environments.

Data collected in 1970 in Alaska by Matthiasson and in 1975 in Saudi Arabia by Bechtel make possible a partial test of such perceptions. We can compare the ranking of 12 descriptive adjectives describing the environment in Fort McMurray, Alberta, Canada, and the ranking of the same adjectives describing Dhahran, Saudi Arabia.

Fort McMurray is located 260 mi northeast of Edmonton and is a new mining town of approximately 6000 persons. Its temperature sometimes drops to 60°F below zero, but can reach the high 80s in summer. Dhahran is located near the east coast of Saudi Arabia and has a high average temperature of 108°F during July and August, with a low in the 40s during January and February. The "European" population is about equal in both places, but Dhahran also has a population of Saudi Arabians. Data on the Arabian American Oil Company (ARAMCO) employees, shown in Table 1, were collected by Bechtel under contract with ARAMCO's Community Services Division.

Each community rated itself as primarily friendly and expansive. "Lonely" was ranked near (or at) the bottom of the list by both. It seems, therefore, that both locations had highly sociable groups. The largest disparity in the data is between the ranking of "cold" by the Canadians (eighth) and the ranking of "hot" by the ARAMCO employees (fourth). The

Table 1   Ranking of Environments by Two Communities

Adjective	Ranking by Canadians (N = 850)	Ranking by ARAMCO Employees (N = 147)
Friendly	1	1
Expansive	2	2
Challenging	3	6
Isolated	4	3
Gossipy	5	5
Normal	6	7
Boring	7	10
Cold (Hot for ARAMCO)	8	4
Exciting	9	8
Lonely	10	12
Intimate	11	11
Barren	12	9

Source: Robert B. Bechtel, *Profile of Housing Needs of ARAMCO Employees*, report presented to the Arabian American Oil Company, November 1975, appendix, p. C-1. The Canadian data were first presented in J. S. Matthiasson, *Resident Perceptions of Quality of Life in Resource Frontier Communities* (Winnipeg: Center for Settlement Studies, The University of Manitoba, 1970), p. 21.

Canadian cold is extremely debilitating to the Canadians, in terms of physical pain and the preparations necessary before going out in it, but perhaps the ARAMCO employees, who came from a temperate climate, notice the heat of Arabia more than the Canadians notice the cold to which they have adapted over a lifetime.

Other disparities are the differences in the ranking of "challenging," "boring," and "barren." The Canadians see their community as more challenging, but also as more boring. To the ARAMCO employees their community appears more barren. The latter finding is probably a reflection of the lack of trees in the regions surrounding the residential areas and plantations on the Saudi Arabian east coast.

The correlation between the two rank orders is +.825, reasonably high considering the difference in location. Yet each community is isolated at the end of a long supply line and is subject to climatic extremes that tend to keep residents indoors for several months of the year. This frontier quality may be a major factor contributing to the nature of the social recreation in each place.

The visiting pattern at Fort McMurray is not known, but the visiting patterns of families at climatically similar Fort Wainwright, Alaska, and of ARAMCO families show similarly high ratios, compared to other activities. Adults among the Alaskan families reported 696 hr of visiting per year; the ARAMCO families, 660 hr. Visiting, including family visiting, has been a notable and frequent recreation in many cultures (at many times in our own), but reliable baseline data cannot be found. Do people spend an average of almost 2 hours a day visiting in the continental United States?

Another interesting similarity occurred in recreational patterns. When men living in the barracks at Fort Wainwright were asked to name their single, most important activity, except sleeping, the majority (55.6 percent) said they spent most of their time reading. ARAMCO employees also indicated that reading was their most time-consuming activity. This was true for both single and married males.

Although these few examples do not constitute a definitive study, they suggest that current living conditions in arid lands (cold or hot) cause people of Western culture to experience isolation, compensated for by large amounts of recreation, chief among which are visiting with friends and reading. Where television is available (e.g., the Alaskan study), this activity becomes a rival to reading.

In contrast to many of our modern, Western subcultures, members of some Eastern cultures appear to spend most of their recreational time visiting relatives. This behavior may be strongly influenced by isolation factors, or it may be a general imperative of the culture. Only the vaguest inferences can be drawn, given the present data, but life-styles in Iran provide a vivid example of differences in cultural imperatives, differences that it behooves Western designers to notice.

Iranian architects have informed Bechtel that in Moslem countries the orientation of the house has religious significance. The main entrance should face north, and the house should have a north–south orientation. In the bedrooms sleeping facilities should be designed so that the head can face north. The bathroom, however, should feature toilets oriented east and west so that the person relieving himself does not face north. (It is not known whether the religious significance is Muslim or a carryover from the earlier Zoroastrian religion.) Other design features of the oriental toilet are worth mentioning. This toilet is an enameled, ceramic fixture in the floor of the bathroom, and one squats to use it. It is thought that this position is a healthier one than sitting, especially for defecation, though Moslem men often squat also when urinating.

A flexible water tube for cleansing oneself is provided in modern oriental toilets, and a long-necked jar in older facilities. According to Kira, the Western authority on bathrooms, this method is more hygienic than the use of toilet paper.[25] In modern and wealthier homes, the oriental toilet is giving way, not to the American standard of tub, shower, and stool, but to the European standard of tub, shower, stool, and bidet.

Another custom in Moslem countries is to cleanse with the left hand and to eat with the right. At Arab meals it is a gross social error to reach for food with the left hand. Left-handed Arabs presumably must be ambidextrous when it comes to certain behaviors dictated by their culture.

In even the poorest house the living room typically has its Persian carpet or, at least, the most expensive carpet the family can afford. The custom is to display what wealth there is in the carpets of the home. Carpets are also a form of savings account, and only a tragic financial crisis forces a family to sell its carpets. One of the expressions of severe disapproval heard concerning poorer families who have gone Western is "They sold their carpets to buy a television." The American middle-class standard of wall-to-wall carpeting has, indeed, been emulated in many middle-class homes throughout the Middle East, but this new symbol of affluence is proudly covered with the treasured Persian carpets that now last longer because of the support given them by the underlying wall-to-wall nylon.

Shelving in Iranian homes has both a utilitarian and a religious significance. There is a desire in most fundamentalist homes to have a small altar, preferably in a niche in the wall. Older homes have many of these niches throughout the walls of the house, and they satisfy a prevalent custom of display. Moslem Iranians like to display objects of art and antiquity in these niches, along with other memorabilia, including pictures of relatives. Many modern houses have been designed in ways that ignore these desires, so the few shelves are pathetically overcrowded with belongings. The modern, open room-divider with shelves is, however, quickly catching on in middle-class and wealthier homes.

Sleeping on the floors in winter and on the roof when weather permits is traditional. Bedding is kept in trunks, which are large and take up a great deal of space, because storing bedding in linen closets would carelessly expose it to insects and mice. It is much better sealed off in the heavy trunks. Here is evident another design error: the closets should have been made verminproof.

The Iranian house is quite similar in arrangement to houses in India, Egypt, and South American countries, but the Iranians especially emphasize air and light. Bechtel has observed that, even in the most crowded squatter settlements, there is usually an attempt to build a skylight over the most central part of the house. This may be related to another traditional design in which the center of the house is a courtyard, open to the sky so that air and sunlight can enter. In the center of the courtyard is a fountain; and, if the owner can afford it, a garden with trees surrounds the fountain. The center is considered the symbolic heart of the house, and to this center the visitor is admitted gradually. The living quarters are traditionally considered too private for casual visitors.

Before entering the house, the visitor stands outside and notices the highly individualized doors that admit him to a foyer, called a *hashti*, or a place of preparation. There the visitor leaves his shoes, and there, through a wooden or stone screen, he catches a glimpse of the center of the house, the fountain and garden. He is greeted in the *hashti* and is then ushered down a hallway into the courtyard.

A quotation from the Koran is placed in the transom of the house to ward off danger and accidents. As soon as a house is completed, a Koran is brought in and set in a place of honor with a mirror behind it. This is an example of the general fascination that mirrors exert on the Moslem people. The interiors of many Mosques are studded with thousands of reflecting surfaces that curve into great sloping arches and are considered the epitome of beauty in Moslem architecture.

Modern, Western kitchens can frequently be seen in Iranian homes. These are complete with the latest appliances and cabinets. Often accompanying this display, however, is a little kerosene stove where the "real" cooking is done or, preferably, a charcoal brazier. In Iran charcoal is the first choice among cooking fuels because of the flavor it imparts to the national dish, *chelo kabob*—broiled lamb and rice. One frequently sees both traditional and modern cooking facilities juxtaposed in even the most modern homes, but cooking and washing outdoors are preferred above all. It is commonplace to see women washing clothes in the ever-present drainage ditches of Iranian towns and villages.

The *koursi* is a custom centered around the charcoal brazier. In a separate room the brazier is placed beneath a low wooden table. It is important to wait until the coals are just right and are not using too much oxygen; in older, draftier houses, the *koursi* did not result in asphyxiation as often as it does in newer, more airtight ones. At the proper moment the family gathers around the table, with everyone's feet extended toward the brazier underneath. Finally, a quilt or blanket is placed over the table and over the legs of the people surrounding it. In this way the family can spend an entire day of communal eating, sleeping, or conversing, all the while warmed by the hot coals and the blankets. Although this custom is disappearing, some wealthy families are still building homes in which one room is set aside for the *koursi.*

In the midst of these traditional behaviors, urbanization and westernization go on, even though the carrying capacity of Tehran has already been reached. Migration to Tehran is being discouraged; instead, migration to the provincial centers of Shiraz, Isfahan, Messhad, and other centers is being planned for. Whether this will work remains to be seen, but the ingenuity of Iranians in coping with these changing demands is boundless. For example, whereas other countries have squatter settlements of bamboo, wood, palm leaves, tin, or paper, nearly all the squatter settlements of Iran feature solid brick, which is the traditional building material. The government should, however, keep economic realities in mind when it builds housing. A recent project for squatters was mistakenly erected far from city jobs, with the result that 60 percent of the new home owners promptly sold their houses at a sizable profit. Many of those who remained rented their already cramped quarters to two or three other families. Others converted parts of their homes to shops, grocery stores, bakeries, and boutiques. The business zeal of the residents was not dampened by government regulations.

Although Iran may seem a far cry from the areas of the great American desert, many of the problems are similar: the attempt to use houses that were really meant for a wetter, more temperate climate; the loss of older building techniques that were actually more efficient for arid lands; and the rapid approach of the day when limited water resources will impose limits on city populations. To meet these forthcoming challenges, each culture will have to adapt greatly. And yet both, because of their relative levels of wealth, seem to feel that serious adjustments are not needed.

THE ADVANTAGES OF OLDER DESIGNS

While the older house style served the extended family well, certain traditional methods of construction were also useful in other ways, in enhancing life in arid lands. The domed roof, for example, is an architectural structure that allows the minimum possible exposure to the sun, regardless of solar position. Given a brick exterior, the domed roof provides, according to Rapoport, the coolest interior that is possible without artificial air conditioning.[26]

Houses in the hotter climates of all parts of Africa, the Middle East, and India traditionally have had a cool basement for use in the summer months. Where these still exist, they are typically deeper than the basements of Western houses in order to take advantage of the earth's natural coolness (about 58°F) at depths where the sun's warmth cannot penetrate. Residents leave the street level of the house and descend into the basement before noon, remaining there until just before sunset. Many of these basements can still be seen in southern Iran at Dezful and Bandurabbes. Rooftop air scoops are another old method of keeping cool in Iran, but these are largely being replaced by the ubiquitous air conditioner.[27]

Many of the older methods of adapting habitations to arid lands that have been successful down through the ages are now losing out because of their labor-intensive qualities. For example, the construction of *qanats* (underground irrigation tunnels) is an extremely labor-intensive undertaking, one that might be impossible in a country like the United States where labor costs are very high. Another example is the hand-made adobe brick, used extensively in early settlements of the American Southwest, but now too costly, at present labor prices, for the average house. Yet, in a world that must eventually come to terms with dwindling energy supplies, the older techniques may become the methods of last resort. Some of the so-called new methods now being tried in arid lands were either inspired by, or are copies of, older methods. Fathy, for example, pleads for a return to simpler, more easily available materials such as mud bricks and to the practical domed roofs of the ancient villages.[28] There is some debate about the effectiveness of the methods he advocates, but an apparently safe judgment is that they have not yet been given a fair test.[29]

The Australian desert provides an ample proving ground for both new and old methods. New communities are being built in the heart of the Australian desert, and in some of these an attempt is being made to take advantage of the earth's coolness by going underground.[30] In another case the Australian architect Lawrence Howroyd has designed a new kind of community for desert living above ground. At Shay Gap (population 862) in the Pilbara District of northwestern Australia, he has crowded the houses closely together in a semicircle, to cast shadows on one another or on the children's play areas. Cars are parked along the perimeter of the town, and there are narrow walks between houses. The proximity reportedly also works to create a closer sense of community. Howroyd is said to have developed his concepts by looking at the medieval walled desert cities of the Middle East.[31]

Any discussion of housing or building in underdeveloped arid countries should include some comment on the recommendations of E. F. Schumacher.[32] Although his proposals do not deal with housing directly, his analysis of Western technology (of which the housing industry is a major part) makes his theories relevant to habitability in arid lands. His basic message is that Western technology is too expensive, in terms of capital investment and the ultimate cost of energy, for countries not already industrialized. He proposes the development of a middle-level technology that would be more advanced than the existing traditional one, but not nearly as capital intensive as current Western technology. His conclusions tend to support those of Fathy concerning the use of available materials, but Schumacher's theories also support the self-help movement in housing proposed by Turner and Fichter, Opat, and others.[33] In any case, Schumacher's theories and the self-help movement are of interest to an increasingly wide audience in the arid lands of the world.

THE NEED FOR CONTINUING RESEARCH

It would be emotionally satisfying to announce in this chapter that we are moving toward solutions for many of the arid-land problems discussed above. To some extent this is true, for we see that research is taking useful directions, but we also see continuing application of advanced, Western temperate-zone technology, both at home and abroad, without consideration of the human consequences. Too few attempts are being made to examine the best of the old techniques and to decide where these can be applied to current human conditions, and a comprehensive approach to the behavioral problems of living in arid lands is still lacking. Textbooks have been written (e.g., Fry and Drew's *Tropical Architecture*), but immensely important psychological and cultural elements have been totally ignored.[34] No one has collected the psychological literature on life and

social behavior in arid lands. Although several building research stations throughout the world are studying the physical problems, the question of human acceptance of the proposed solutions has not been fully explored.[35]

Our present goal is an extended program of study and research on arid lands, similar to the fruitful programs that have been conducted for the polar regions (e.g., Cold Regions Research and Engineering Laboratory of the Army Corps of Engineers, the National Science Foundation Polar Studies Program, the Arctic Medical Research Laboratory of the U.S. Army, and Operation Deep Freeze of the U.S. Navy). Scientists in these excellent programs have collected the research literature concerning a particular geographical area, have centered research programs on the problems of the region, and have developed a corps of experts who can pursue the knowledge necessary to improve living conditions there. As mentioned previously, similar activitives relative to arid regions are now taking place at the University of Arizona.

CRUCIAL CONCEPTS FOR DESIGN AND RESEARCH

Studies addressed to specific problems of arid-land living, along the lines suggested, are an essential step toward a full understanding of how to deal with human activities in these areas. It is at least as important, however, to recognize that people in arid lands are not a species apart and that studies in these lands can both contribute to and be helped by findings related to broader conceptual issues that go beyond specific settings and are generally related to the science of environmental psychology.

Habitability. The habitability of dwellings is one such issue that has recurred repeatedly throughout the preceding discussion. Habitability, as we have seen, includes such physical problems as maintaining suitable climates within dwellings, the relationship between internal and external climates, and the durability of building materials. But, perhaps more importantly, it also includes the question of what constitutes psychological habitability and how the answers to this question can be reflected in the design of housing. Here the overriding unresolved issue seems to be whether to aim for uniformity or for diversity. Is psychological habitability the same for all peoples at all times and in all places, and, therefore, can it be achieved by a uniform set of housing designs? Or is habitability so influenced by situational, cultural, and personal variables that it acquires essentially different meanings and requires specific and unique housing provisions? Those who transplant a housing form bodily from one setting to another, as has been done with the suburban, ranch-style house and the urban high-rise apartment building, implicitly answer in favor of uniformity. The same belief is quite explicitly stated, for example, by those who would design uniform, monolithic cities, whether glass enclosed or not, that presumably can be dropped with equal effectiveness anywhere on the face of the globe. Yet the evidence we have developed with regard to arid lands, together with findings from other regions, suggests quite the opposite conclusion, namely, that psychological habitability is heavily affected by cultural and personal differences. The greatest design enemies of habitability would then seem to be uniformity, which inhibits the development and expression by a particular group of its own unique living patterns, and overdesign of the individual unit, which inhibits the development and expression of personal uniqueness.

Environmental Experience.   Closely related to the conceptual issue of habitability is that of the nature and range of environmental experience. One generalization seems to be emerging: people do not universally experience the environment as a single, unitary, monolithic, external thing.[36] Rather, different people at different times under different circumstances experience the environment in a variety of different ways. There are, then, multiple realities that must be understood and accounted for in any particular design or policy decision. With regard to arid lands, we have noted that the environment is variously experienced as an external hazard or threat, as an arena in which certain actions can or cannot be carried out, as an object to be conquered, manipulated, or adjusted to, and as a source of aesthetic inspiration and appreciation. We have not treated other important aspects of the environmental experience, such as the role of the environment in constituting part of one's sense of self or personal identity. While the range of environmental experiences may well be universal for all people, it is probable that the relative importance of each of these experiences and its specific manifestations vary from setting to setting. We suggest as a general design consideration that the full range of environmental experiences be recognized and that opportunities for such experiences be built in rather than designed out.

Environmental Change.   Nothing in human life, however, is static, and this is especially true in today's arid lands. We have repeatedly emphasized their changing character. The land itself is changing—desert areas are becoming fertile, and fertile areas are becoming deserts. The people too are changing, through both the influx of new immigrants and the changing ways of native populations. Moreover, the relationship between people and places, as reflected in cultural, social, and individual patterns of behavior, is also changing. All of these are manifestations of the general process of environmental change. Here again is a conceptual issue that extends far beyond arid lands. Certainly one of the major theoretical problems facing environmental psychology involves the processes of environmental change and continuity. The rapid and at times cataclysmic changes taking place in arid lands must be studied if we are to act effectively in these areas. At the same time, such study affords us an opportunity to increase our understanding of the general phenomena involved in environmental change.

Technological Impact.   One particular aspect of environmental change, the role of technology, was singled out earlier for special attention. The central part played by technology in bringing about environmental change is nowhere questioned. Certainly most—and perhaps all—environmental changes of significance today (with the possible exception of long-term climatic changes) are recognizably the consequences of large-scale technological interventions. And yet, while significant steps are being taken to understand the physical, ecological, and biological effects of technological innovations, study of their psychological and behavioral impact is virtually nonexistent. Nevertheless, this is—or should be—a principal concern when considering technology transfer, a question of overriding importance in arid lands today. As we have pointed out for other areas of research, the study of what constitutes appropriate technology for arid lands can at the same time add to our general understanding of the behavioral consequences of technological innovation. And this, in turn, can be of value to those charged with the responsibility of formulating social policy for the future directions of both science and technology.

One generalization seems to stand out in the application of technology to arid lands. The findings of energy research and animal studies converge: it is seldom a single dramatic factor that allows animals to survive or that permits energy savings to accumulate significantly, but rather a series of small adaptations acting in concert.[37] It is this principle, the seeking out of a series of small adaptations, as opposed to searching for the single dramatic factor, that should govern future research.

SUMMARY

In this chapter we have tried to pull together most of what is known about the psychological aspects of living in arid lands. Many of our observations rest on a rather shaky empirical base, and we have often suggested the need for further research directly related to arid lands. Finally, we have pointed out that any and all *ad hoc* findings addressed to immediate practical issues can be fitted into a larger conceptual framework and can both contribute to and be augmented by the broader theoretical understandings that are beginning to emerge in the field of environmental psychology.

In the United States today, we have virtually no environmental psychology of arid lands. This research field remains for us to explore. To it we can apply concepts and methods that have been shown to be useful in other regions, and we can discuss our observations of other arid lands. We hope that a similar chapter, written 5 or 10 years from now, can be based on research material obtained here at home. Many of us are working toward this goal.

NOTES

1. See Robert B. Bechtel, "Experimental Methods in Environmental Design Research," in *Designing for Human Behavior: Architecture and the Behavioral Sciences,* J. Lang et al., eds. (Stroudsburg, Pa.: Halstead Press, 1974), pp. 286–292; William H. Ittelson, Harold M. Proshansky, and Leanne G. Rivlin, "The Influence of the Physical Environment on Behavior: Some Basic Assumptions," in *Environmental Psychology: Man and His Physical Setting,* H. Proshansky, W. Ittelson, and L. Rivlin, eds. (New York: Holt, Rinehart, and Winston, 1970), pp. 27–36; William H. Ittelson, Karen A. Franck, and Timothy J. O'Hanlon, "The Nature of Environmental Experience," in *Experiencing the Environment,* S. Wapner, S. B. Cohen, and B. Kaplan, eds. (New York: Plenum Press, 1976) pp. 187–206; Lawrence Wheeler, *Behavioral Research for Architectural Planning and Design* (Terre Haute, Ind.: Ewing Miller Associates, 1969); and *idem,* "The Design Function, a Negative-Feedback Control System," in *Theoretical Models of Human-Environment Relations,* C. C. Frazier, ed. (Lawrence: University of Kansas School of Architecture and Urban Design, 1975), pp. 16–24.

2. Douglas H. K. Lee, "Variability in Human Response to Arid Environments," in *Arid Lands in Perspective,* W. G. McGinnies and B. J. Goldman, eds. (Tucson: University of Arizona Press, 1969), p. 240.

3. See Douglas H. K. Lee, "Human Factors in Desert Develop-

ment," in *Aridity and Man, the Challenge of Arid Lands in the United States,* C. Hodge, ed. (Washington: American Association for the Advancement of Science, 1963), pp. 339–367.

4. Joseph Wood Krutch, *The Desert Year* (New York: Viking Press, 1952), p. 20.

5. Ralph E. Parachek, *Desert Architecture* (Phoenix: Parr of Arizona, 1967), p. iii.

6. A. S. Leopold, *The Desert* (New York: Time–Life, 1962), p. 127.

7. See W. D. Lipe, "Man and the Plateau, an Archaeologist's View," *Plateau, the Magazine of the Museum of Northern Arizona,* **49,** no. 1 (Summer, 1976), 27–32.

8. See J. Hernandez et al., "Toward the Year 2000: How Fast Is Tucson's Population Growing?" *Arizona Review,* **21,** nos. 8–9 (August–September, 1972), 1–9.

9. See T. C. Daniel et al., "Quantitative Evaluation of Landscapes: A Preliminary Application of Signal Detection Analysis to Selected Forest Management Alternatives," *Man-Environment Systems,* **3,** no. 5 (September, 1973), 330–344; T. C. Daniel and R. S. Boster, "Measuring Landscape Esthetics: The Scenic Beauty Estimation Method," U.S. Department of Agriculture Forest Service Research Paper no. 167 (Washington, 1976).

10. C. R. Reitan and C. R. Green, "Weather and Climate of Desert Environments," in *Deserts of the World,* W. G. McGinnies, B. J. Goldman, and P. Paylore, eds. (Tucson: University of Arizona Press, 1968), p. 60.

11. See W. E. Splinter, "Center-Pivot Irrigation," *Scientific American,* **234,** no. 6 (1976), 90–99; R. Goodland and H. Irwin, *Amazon Jungle: Green Hell to Red Desert* (New York: Elsevier Press, 1975).

12. See D. Lerner, *The Passing of Traditional Society* (New York: Free Press, 1968).

13. See S. Abercrombie, "The Middle East: Design, Politics, and Policy," *Design and Environment,* **6,** no. 4 (1975), 10–39.

14. See *Time,* March 15, 1976, p. 55; *U.S. News and World Report,* April 12, 1976, p. 58.

15. See A. Chapanis, "Cosmopolitanism: A New Era in the Evolution of Human Factors Engineering," in *Ethnic Variables in Human Factors Engineering,* Alphonse Chapanis, ed. (Baltimore: Johns Hopkins University Press, 1975), pp. 1–10.

16. See Lerner.

17. See H. Cantril, *The Pattern of Human Concerns* (New Brunswick, N.J.: Rutgers University Press, 1965).

18. See *National Geographic,* January 1975, pp. 2–47, and October 1975, pp. 494–533.

19. See B. Brolin, "What Went Wrong at Chandigarh?" *Smithsonian,* **3,** no. 3 (1972), 56–63.

20. See A. Rapoport, *House Form and Culture* (Englewood Cliffs, N.J.: Prentice-Hall, 1969); and B. Rudofsky, *Architecture without Architects* (Garden City, N.Y.: Doubleday and Company, 1964).

21. See F. de Coulanges, *The Ancient City* (Garden City, N.Y.: Doubleday and Company, 1955).

22. See P. Doughty, "The Culture of Regionalism and the Acculturation of Peasants into the Urban Life of Lima, Peru," paper delivered at the 66th annual meeting of the American Anthropological Association, December 3, 1967; Robert B. Bechtel, *Studies and Planning Services to Develop and Apply Performance Specifications in Procurement and Evaluations of Housing* (Silver Spring, Md.: Tadjer, Cohen, Shefferman, and Bigelson, 1975).

23. See Bechtel, *Studies and Planning Services.*

24. See Robert B. Bechtel and C. B. Ledbetter, *The Temporary Environment* (Hanover, N.H.: U.S. Army Cold Regions Research and Engineering Laboratory, 1976).

25. See A. Kira, *The Bathroom* (New York: Viking Press, 1976).

26. See Rapoport.

27. See A. Ferebee, "Air Scoops or Air Conditioners?" *Design and Environment,* **6,** no. 4 (1975), 9.

28. See H. Fathy, *Architecture for the Poor* (Chicago: University of Chicago Press, 1973).

29. See U. Cliff, "Designers of Human Settlements: Hassan Fathy," *Design and Environment,* **7,** no. 1 (1976), 22–25.

30. See J. Gorman, "The Earth's the Ceiling," *The Sciences,* **16,** no. 2 (March–April 1976), 16–20.

31. See "Hostile as Anywhere," *Time,* June 9, 1975, p. 67.

32. See E. F. Schumacher, *Small Is Beautiful* (New York: Harper and Row, 1973).

33. See J. Turner and R. Fichter, *Freedom to Build: Dweller Control in the Housing Process* (New York: The Macmillan Company, 1972); and E. J. Opat, "Better Housing through Self Help," *Design and Environment,* **7,** no. 1 (1976), 36–41.

34. See M. Fry and J. Drew, *Tropical Architecture* (New York: Reinhold, 1964).

35. See P. Paylore, *Arid Lands Research Institutions: A World Directory* (Tucson: University of Arizona Press, 1967).

36. See S. Wapner, S. B. Cohen, and B. Kaplan, eds., *Experiencing the Environment* (New York: Plenum Publishing Corporation, 1976).

37. See G. N. Louw, "Water Economy of Certain Namib Desert Animals," *South African Journal of Science,* **67,** no. 3 (1971), 119–123.

SUGGESTED READINGS

Fathy, H. *Architecture for the Poor.* Chicago: University of Chicago Press, 1973.

McGinnies, W. J., Goldman, B. J., and Paylore, P., eds. *Deserts of the World.* Tucson: University of Arizona Press, 1968.

Saini, B. S. *Building Environment—An Illustrated Analysis of Problems in Hot Dry Lands.* Sydney: Angus and Robertson, 1973.

Social and Economic Problems and Prospects 3

CHAPTER 6

Community Organization and Problems in the American Arid-Zone City

COURTNEY B. CLELAND

This chapter describes how communities organize themselves to provide what are defined broadly as social services. Partly as a result of this process, each community tends to develop a social character. We will particularly explore whether or not aridity plays a part in this process.

In the deserts of the American Southwest there are new large communities—"new" in the sense that most of their population growth has been relatively recent. Examples include the cities of Phoenix and Tucson in Arizona, Albuquerque in New Mexico, El Paso in Texas, and Las Vegas in Nevada.

Most of the data reported here are based on observations made in Tucson. Although Tucson, like other southwestern cities, has its military, industrial, tourist, and border-related commerce, Meinig comments that "the most pervasive impression is of people seeking recreation and relaxed living in a desert setting." He also notes that the family home is characteristically oriented inward toward a wall-enclosed patio featuring gravel lawns and native shrubs. The residences, he notes, are "a combination of Anglo, Mexican, and desert elements which creates the distinctive regional style that can be found through much of this border country, but it is nowhere as common or as fully elaborated as in Tucson."[1]

Several southwestern cities, such as Tucson, are old (Santa Fe and El Paso date back to the seventeenth century; Albuquerque and Tucson to the eighteenth century), but as metropolitan communities they actually are new. After years of stable, small size, they grew to metropolitan status only after World War II. In 1940 Tucson and Albuquerque, for example, each had a population of approximately 35,000. Phoenix was substantially larger, as it continues to be, but was still under the 100,000 mark in 1940. Then came the great influx of migrants. By the mid-1970s the city population of Phoenix approached 800,000 (metropolitan population close to $1\frac{1}{3}$ million), the Tucson metropolitan area had 450,000 people, and the counties containing Albuquerque, Las Vegas, and El Paso were each in the 300,000 to 400,000 range. (Contiguous to El Paso is much larger, fast growing Cuidad Juarez in Mexico.) From 1970 to 1974 these metropolitan areas registered population increases of 14 to 24 percent. Not until 1975 was there any indication of a slowdown in the rate of growth.

In his book *The Great American Desert, Then and Now*, Hollon states, "Of all these desert cities, none more closely resembles the ideal of a large oasis than Tucson." Significantly, Hollon also asserts that Tucson "stands the best chance of running out of water in the next ten years of any major city of the Great American Desert."[2] Hollon's book was published in 1966, and, although a decade later Tucson has not yet run out of water, its rising cost, its anticipated rationing, and the legal contests over its control dramatize the water problem and have intensified "controlled growth" controversies there. Taking place in early 1977, for example, was a recall election of city council members who had instituted sharp increases in the price of water, partly as a conservation measure. The incident is symbolic of the way in which matters once routinely considered "technical" have become social and political problems.

THE THEORY OF COMMUNITY ORGANIZATION

To comprehend such events in a community organization context, it is necessary to discuss several basic concepts. Although the focus is ostensibly on the development of communities, the typical vehicles used to reach this developmental aim are themselves formal organizations. It is not always recognized that there is a difference between the latter and communal organizations, such as the neighborhood (when it is a true social entity) and the community.

Often communities are a by-product of activities that are largely the result of formal organizations.[3] American history provides many examples. After settlers came to a locality and founded farms or ranches, they decided they needed a church for their families or a school for their children. Soon these social services were formally organized. Someone else came and started a store at the crossroads, providing the nucleus of a trading center; next a local government was formed. Thus the "community" emerged as a secondary result of these and other efforts. There is, of course, also the phenomenon of the "intentional" or planned community where such is the formal goal from the start, but most traditional communities have been essentially unplanned results of other planned activities.

An important question, therefore, is how one uses formal organizations deliberately to plan, change, or try to control the development of a different type of social organization, the community. This is not an insurmountable problem, but we should be aware that the community as it has existed in history has not often been initially the result of a formal, conscious effort to develop a community as such. There were and will be variables that the planners and others who would try to rationalize processes of community building probably will not be entirely able either to anticipate or to control.

A community may be defined as a group of people who interact to meet their recurring physical and psychological needs and thereby acquire some degree of relative self-sufficiency and institutional coherence which enables them to be perceived by themselves and others as a community. All the parts of this definition are important: the idea of interaction; that of recurring needs which are psychological as well as physical; that of relative self-sufficiency, at least for items needed on a day-to-day basis; and certainly that of institutional coherence. In fact, one way of looking at a community is as a constellation of institutions—familial, economic, political, recreational, religious, educational, and so on—most of which involve formal organization. (We cannot overlook the fact that these are also national institutions, but our concern here is with the local versions that help to determine a given community's social character.)

For deliberate community organization, the residents' perception of themselves as a community is critically important: if they do not know that they are a community and do not feel and act accordingly, then neither internal nor external groups are going to relate to them as a community. This feeling underscores the psychology of the community, the "consciousness of kind" or a feeling of consensus; thus, periodic communitywide occasions to remind the people of their identity as a community—elections of community leaders, local festivals, parades, the annual rodeo, or camel races—are symbolically important. These more obvious manifestations of a shared local life hardly have an effect—or even take place—without community organization. Years ago this phrase was employed in the United States mostly by social workers to refer to such efforts as the organizing of "community chests" (united funds) and councils of social work agencies. Today it has acquired a broader meaning. Community organization is an umbrella term that refers to a variety of methods used by citizens to instigate, implement, or resist local changes, sometimes through government, sometimes through private groups, often through both.

The more specific modes of community organization are given names such as community development, social planning, and social action (those forms of it that take place at the local level). Rothman distinguishes among these three modes on twelve different points.[4] For example, in community development, the goal is "process" oriented—more precisely, self-help or the educating of people to try to handle their own problems. In social planning, supposedly the concern is more with specific problem solving, a task-oriented approach. In social action, the emphasis is on a shift of power among groups in the community.

Naturally, different strategies are implied. In community development, it is "people involvement" and the effort to gain consensus; in social planning, the analysis of facts in order to make the most rational decisions; in social action, confrontation and negotiation. No wonder, then, that the community developer tends to regard himself as an encourager or enabler, the planner as an analyst or implementer of programs, and the social action agent as an activist or advocate for an oppressed group.

These are conceptual distinctions; in actual life, there is a blending among these three modes of community organization. An innovation in community services may begin as social action to call attention to a problem. It is then typically consigned to social planners, and the planners in seeking a representative input from consumers may turn to community developers in order to stimulate citizen participation. In this example, it is clear that the term "community development" refers not to the physical infrastructure of the community but to its social underpinnings. In "doing" community development, one tries to constitute or sometimes to renovate local initiative, which involves developing the citizen skills of both individuals and groups. Community organization thus may be perceived as guided community change in which local people become involved in the initiating, planning, legitimizing, diffusing, carrying out, and evaluating of local programs. If needed, enough outside help is provided to encourage development, but not so much as to smother initiative. The aim is more confident and competent people and better functioning groups, able not only to enact physical improvements but also to cope successfully with other types of community problems. Usually the goal is not merely to maintain the community as it is, but also to guide it toward what it may become. On occasion these organizing skills may be used to resist change and to reorient community attitudes as to the direction or speed of changes.

As illustrated above in the case of Tucson, the last possibility became apparent during the mid-1970s in the new large cities of the American desert. Many citizens became disillusioned with constant change. Apparently they had experienced too many changes and desired a period of stability, at least in some areas of community life. Leaders of a new "cactus politics" talked about the value of "controlled growth" and the need to halt "urban sprawl." Politicians were turned out of office, new freeways

and other formerly cherished projects were voted down, prime desert areas were protected from residential subdivision, and pressures were exerted to put "human" needs first. In no sense was community change halted, but its substance was challenged and redirected, largely through the application of community organization techniques. (Recent election results, however, may represent a drawing back of this thrust.) Presumably such shifts can be expected in the life history of a viable community, in response to changing regional and national contexts as well as to new conditions on the local scene.

THE AMERICAN ARID-ZONE CITY AND ITS PROBLEMS

In the work of community organization, to what extent does an arid environment make a difference? In some ways, perhaps none at all; presumably the techniques used would be about the same as those for a humid-area community. What clearly may differ are some of the problems to which the techniques are addressed. Aridity may affect directly the substance of certain community development efforts and, at least, provide a most pervasive presence. The desert has an impact on the city, but the city also has an impact on the desert, a reciprocal relationship that becomes the special concern of particular community groups. People in deserts must deal, for example, with characteristic technical problems, such as the provision of water, the cooling of air in buildings, and the control of paradoxical desert floods—pursuits that often imply community organization and its implementation under the rubric of "social services."

Desertification. Of major concern is desertification, the deleterious influence of man on the fragile physical environment.[5] As the desert becomes populated, man and his imported animals affect vulnerable desert vegetation. Imported trees and grass lawns devour scarce water and disperse unwanted pollen in the air. Mechanical vehicles cause eroded land, which is not quickly overgrown in a desert and thus partly repaired as it would be in a humid area. The extent of local efforts to confront such arid-related issues can be considered one measure of community organization in the desert. That there is diversity among cities in their motivation or capacity to do just this is an aspect of the varying social natures of communities.

Population Growth. In these new large cities the numerically greater social problems of crime and suicide are not so much directly related to the aridity as they are to what the aridity in part has led to—the staggering rate of population growth. The dryness, the warmth, and the scenery of desert and mountain ("amenity resources," as they are sometimes called) attracted people for reasons varying from a hoped-for alleviation of a health problem such as arthritis to a desire simply to live close to the wilderness. (Figure

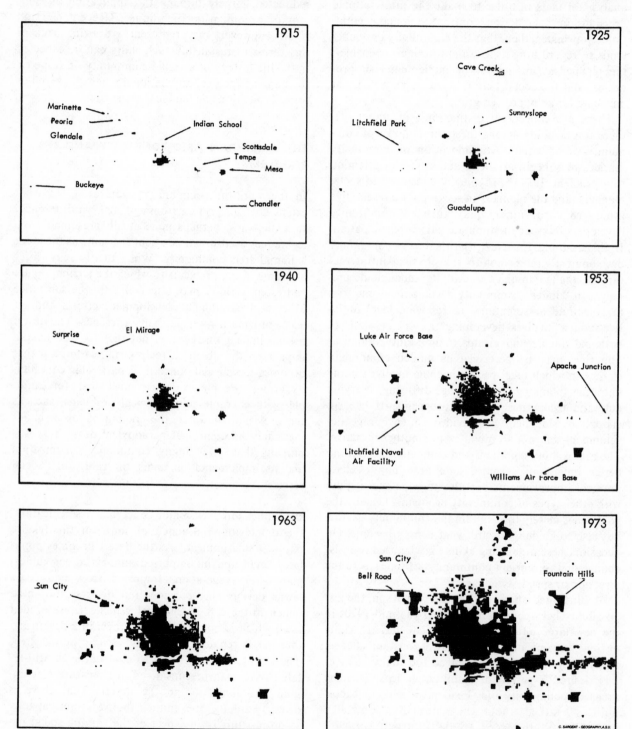

Figure 1. The growth of Phoenix, Arizona, 1915–1973. Redrawn from "The Blob That Ate Sunnyslope," *Arizona,* February 17, 1974, pp. 52–53. Maps by Dr. Charles Sargent.

1 traces the expansion of the Phoenix area since 1915.) Light manufacturing, mining, the construction industry, military bases, services for tourists and residents, higher education, research enterprises, the savings of retired migrants—somehow the economic props needed to support a rapidly increasing population were found. Nevertheless, such a high growth rate is bound to strain the social capacity of any community and to overload the public facilities needed to absorb a diversity of strangers, including some seeking escape from personal problems which, however, they tend to bring with them.

Population Composition. Years ago, people from the eastern United States began to migrate to the Southwest for varied reasons such as the desire for economic or health advantages. Many Americans saw the area for the first time during World War II. Much of the in-migration since then has been of young people, and it would be even greater if there were more economic opportunities. (The picture of Arizona's population as topheavy with older people is a stereotype, unsupported by fact except in highly visible enclaves such as Sun City.)

The result of in-migration is that, in cities like Tucson, at least two thirds of the population is not native to the state. Of the total Arizona population in 1970 of about 1,773,000, only 605,000 were native born with 1,165,000 born outside of Arizona. Most of them came from areas some distance away, particularly the midwestern states of Illinois, Ohio, Michigan, Missouri, Indiana, and Iowa. Significant numbers also came, however, from Texas, California, New York, Oklahoma, and Pennsylvania. The adjacent states of New Mexico, Utah, and Nevada contributed relatively few. Thus the arid cities are made up largely of populations who came from humid areas. (The Indians and Mexican-Americans represent a notable exception; most of them grew up in arid regions, including the estimated 5 percent of the migrants who were born in Mexico.)

This population composition is a contextual variable of great weight in community organization. Someone who has just arrived from Pennsylvania, for example, does not have an arid-region mentality. He does not conserve water as though it were a scarce resource. It is only among the old residents or those in isolated places where water supply is erratic and inferior that one finds behavior approaching Zimmerman's concept of water-use personality.[6] It is, however, a concept that may take hold more and more as water becomes expensive; in cities like Tucson residents are converting their grass lawns to

gravel, and some of the more adventuresome even paint the gravel green. On the other hand, in a seemingly spontaneous "grass roots" reaction, thousands of Tucsonans in 1976 signed petitions to protest the increased cost of water, indicating a resistance to a forced change in water-use habits.

Population Flux. Population statistics may understate what has happened. Many people are not counted as citizens of these arid states because they maintain their primary residences elsewhere, yet live up to 6 or 7 months of the year in places like Apache Junction (east of Phoenix). A fluctuating population, not revealed by the statistics, is still important from the standpoint of community organization. One can observe the temporary residents in Apache Junction, together with the year-round inhabitants, struggling with various community problems; they work on the problems all winter and then go away. Perhaps little is accomplished until they return in the fall. Some people, however, do not come back. New ones arrive in their stead, and they begin debating the same problems again. And so the cycle continues.

Land Use Planning. Many of the community debates revolve around questions of land use and thus the distribution of new population. Arizona, as a state, has been slow to plan land use. It is only now at a point where it may be able to head off some of the land frauds that have plagued remote-site developments. Land use planning can also be a tool used by county commissioners (e.g., in the Tucson area) to curb outward metropolitan growth, for it is evident that the population density within the city is relatively low and could be much higher. It is so low, in fact, that it exacerbates problems such as the provision of mass transit.

Tucson and Pima County must work together in land use planning, a test they appear to have failed in the case of water management. There is a movement, in fact, to change to a metropolitan form of government, in which local governments might be merged into one smoother operating entity. Tucson is fortunate in that it is not fringed by numerous separately incorporated suburbs, yet, despite this absence of obstacles, in 1976 the movement for a "metro" county government seemed unlikely to succeed.

Dewesternization. Geographically, Tucson was once an elongated community along a north–south axis, but after 1945, as Figure 2 reveals, the new population spread mostly to the east. One result is

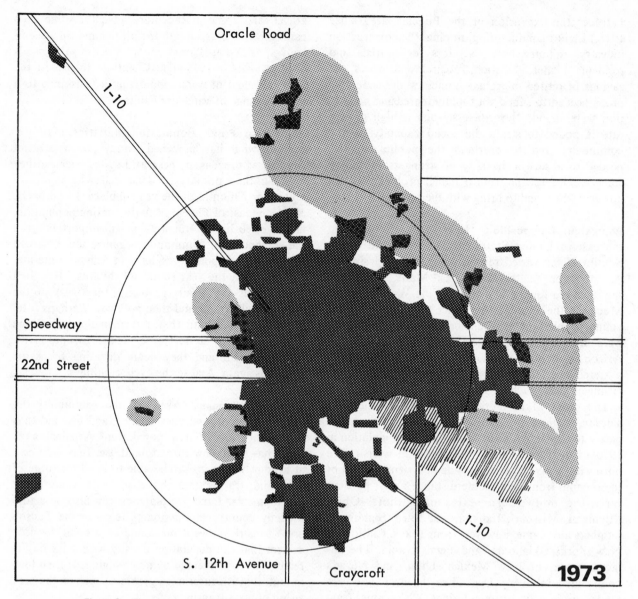

Figure 2. The eastward expansion of Tucson, Arizona, with recent growth areas noted in gray. Redrawn from *Tucson: The Shrinking Desert* (Tucson: *The Arizona Daily Star*, 1973), p. 5.

that Tucson is like many other cities in displaying an "old town–new town" phenomenon.[7] The old "Mexican" core of the city stands out in striking contrast to the newer subdivisions. In the case of Tucson the old pueblo was once the very heart of the community until an urban renewal project in the 1960s replaced part of it with a modern civic center complex. Some residents have decried this type of development: they call it the dewesternization of Tucson, and they believe it is "spoiling" Tucson by making it look more like Des Moines.

However, the newcomer (bringing us back to problems inherent to the region's population composition) may not have that impression, because probably Tucson still looks like a different kind of city from the one he came from. One similarity may be Tucson's downtown area, fighting deterioration and the competition from regional shopping centers, such as El Con and Park Mall, which provide completely enclosed, air-conditioned places to shop. Despite their convenience they may be greeted with some ambivalence in view of the apparent fate of the "old town" core.

Ethnicity. In the Southwest, there is a tendency for minority ethnic groups to retain their identities perhaps more tenaciously than in some regions. Indians and Spanish speaking people occupied the area long before the arrival of Anglo-Americans. Programs of bilingualism and bicultural education are growing, not receding. Thus, on the Navajo Indian reservation, there are schools where instruction is given in both the Navajo and the English languages; and cultural education reflects the "American" (Anglo version) as well as the important Navajo values. Roughly, the same can be said of the Mexican-Americans, who constitute about 20 percent of the Tucson population. Ethnic advocacy thus becomes an expected part of community organization.

Assimilation, in terms of the classic idea of a "melting pot," has been rejected in the region since the days of the early Spaniards.[8] Community integration, therefore, must come about through other mechanisms, not exclusively through individuals learning English, intermarrying, and becoming "Americanized." It is a multicultural society, and integration will occur through activities like community development, in which representatives of various groups work out problems that are of interest to the community as a whole—obtaining a new county hospital, for example. It does not matter in such an instance which language is spoken or what nationality background one has, for a hospital is of collective importance. As elsewhere, residents must discover what kind of community they can forge for the future, in which the necessary changes will be guided, debated, and understood, rather than imposed by the majority on the minorities.

Social Stratification. The rapid growth, then, has produced in Tucson a population that is heterogeneous in various senses, including not only ethnic composition, but also social class. Of course, there are variations within the city. It is predictable that one neighborhood will be in favor of bike paths, while another area is more concerned about housing rehabilitation. These differences reflect social stratification, of which the type of air conditioning can serve as an appropriate index. The more affluent homes possess electric refrigeration, costing typically $200 a month in the summer for electric current (1976 prices). Other segments of the community use evaporative water coolers, which are much less expensive and quite satisfactory for cooling as long as the atmosphere stays dry. A third stratum, the poorest one, has no type of mechanical air cooling at all. (Inflation and the energy crisis may have lessened the reliability of this indicator, but not greatly.)

Social Pathology. Other measures of the social character of Tucson reflect relative social pathology compared to stabler communities. Levels of crime, divorce, suicide, drug addiction, and alcohol abuse in some recent years were said to have been among the highest in the country. Some observers attributed a high rate of burglaries to the number of drug users in the population and Tucson's closeness to the source of supply, channeled through the international border with Mexico. Unemployment and particularly underemployment are problems for some new residents. Not uncommon is the "overqualified" employee working for less compensation than he or she was accustomed to earning elsewhere.

Controlled Growth Movement. Community controversies with regard to floodplain building, water conservation, desert preservation, historical preservation, rebuilding the inner city, or spending money on human services rather than physical improvements may seem to involve separate issues, but they are interrelated. Most of them can be subsumed under the concept of controlled growth.

Carpenter's 1975 study on Arizona residents' attitudes toward the size of their communities found that in Phoenix about 95 percent of the people, if they had their preference, would rather live in a smaller community.[9] As he surveyed smaller communities, the percentages expressing this view declined. In Tucson about 75 percent of the residents would prefer a smaller community; in small cities like Yuma and Prescott, people are satisfied with the community as it is. Most people in large centers elsewhere also assert a preference for a smaller city, but the percentages are not as high as in Phoenix or Tucson. A related sentiment is seen in Tucsonans' opposition to construction on surrounding mountain peaks and high slopes, their dislike of high-rise buildings, and their general disapproval of anything that damages the view of the mountains or, perhaps, simply reminds them of larger cities.

An increasing amount of community organization effort arises in response to such growth issues or environmental concerns, broadly defined, in both public and private organizations. A main vehicle in Tucson during the 1970s has been the local government-sponsored Comprehensive Planning Process (CPP). Predictably, such public planning efforts tended to stimulate an assortment of *ad hoc* organizations:

Citizens United in Favor of the Plan, Citizens Organized to Oppose the Plan, Citizens Opposed to the Plan but for Slightly Different Reasons, and so on. (These are fictitious names, of course.) Business and construction industry leaders opposed a "no growth" policy—hardly the correct term because even the planners talked only about controlling growth and not about stopping it (which they considered an impossibility). But, as in any governmental plan, they encountered problems in gauging public opinion and earning public acceptance.

Social and Human Service Needs. In the private sphere, a leading force for social and human services in Tucson is the United Way. Its work supports about 30 private organizations, but their makeup changes somewhat from year to year as priorities shift. The aridity of the region is reflected in the relative importance of groups such as the Arthritis Foundation with its service and educational programs. Many people seek Arizona's dry climate because of arthritis; thus the community support is substantial. The Information and Referral Service, in a community encompassing many new residents, is especially important because problems exist in connecting the services of agencies with the people who need them.

There has been an explosion not only of population but also of variety of services: many simply were not offered 10 years ago. Portable Practical Education Preparation (PPEP) is a self-help project assisting low-income people with housing, health, youth, transportation, and other basic problems. It focuses especially on the rural areas near Tucson, because they have been almost forgotten in the rush to develop the metropolitan center. The Voluntary Action Center, a volunteer bureau, illustrates that not all migrants have only problems; some bring great skills, which they contribute to the community. Not all community development resources, however, are located in formal associations, as illustrated by the directory called the *Tucson's People's Yellow Pages.*[10] It lists individuals as well as groups who are willing to assist with a specific problem. For example, Larry Armstrong built his own house with solar forced air heating (using rock storage under the house) and is willing to help with or give advice on similar projects. Another man has no technical experience but volunteers his time to help build alternative energy devices.

The Citizens Participation Council, sponsored by the city government, is a deliberate effort to motivate citizen input into such programs. It is perhaps one heritage of the 1960 War on Poverty with its stress on "maximum feasible participation," followed by the "model cities" experience, during which an effort was made to stimulate citizens to specify their priorities and, in turn, to persuade the experts to be more responsive to rank-and-file citizens.

Without systematic directed research, it is difficult to evaluate the rapidly developing range of new social service programs, of which only a few examples have been mentioned. In 1976 the Citizens Participation Council asked the Tucson city officials for 48 social service programs, many of which represented expansions of familiar projects such as home health care for the elderly, adult basic education, neighborhood recreation centers, legal aid, and child abuse prevention. Some of these were started under private auspices in the past and, as they succeeded, were taken over by government. The citizen group also asked funding for new programs such as a handyman service to make minor home repairs at reduced prices, a proposal aimed especially at retired citizens' needs. Although the city cannot finance every request, there does seem to be a willingness to consider new types of social services. Meanwhile, in the traditional areas such as health, welfare, employment, rehabilitation, probation, and parole, the city and county governments continue to struggle with needs that are typically greater than the capacity of the available staffs.

One interesting aspect of the Southwest region is that, in the past, its communities have been slow to adopt social programs. To do so would have contradicted the old pioneer tradition of self-reliance. Tucson took advantage of the federal government's urban renewal program 10 years after it could have done so because of a widely shared local feeling throughout the 1950s that urban development was a task for private enterprise. Another example of this conservative approach is that Arizona was the last of the 50 states to embrace Medicaid (accepted in principle, but still not in effect as of 1976).

Environmental Protection. Among current environmental groups in Tucson, there are old established organizations such as the Audubon Society and newer ones such as the Arizona Clean Energy Coalition and the Arizonans for Water without Waste. Many private groups come together initially as a small nucleus of people, focus on a problem, draw adherents, and develop plans for action. A group called Stop Mining around Residential Tucson

(SMART) was formed at a time when the people in a particular foothills neighborhood were startled to find a mineral company beginning to drill near their homesites. (Some new residents did not even realize that in the American West it is common for mineral rights to be separated from the land surface title.) The SMART organization mobilized public opinion, and the company finally ceased its operations, although probably it was legally in the right. Citizen action that is competently directed and effectively publicized had shown its power.

COMMUNITY ORGANIZATION IN PRACTICE

Numerous recent cases in Tucson can be cited to illustrate the blend of social planning, citizen action, and locality development that comprises community organization. In a new residential subdivision on Tucson's east side, the developer pursued the usual practice of clearing off most of the desert vegetation and building houses designed for families of middle income. The people who bought these homes claimed that the developer did not keep all of his promises; for example, he did not preserve certain areas for recreational purposes. They formed a neighborhood residents' association and received help from another formal organization, the Tucson East Community Mental Health Center. The residents formulated a plan for the neighborhood that they said better represented their own ideas and tried to put pressure on the developer to keep his alleged promises. They also attempted to influence various levels of government.

In the Rancho Romero case the developer announced plans for creating a new community of 15,000 to the northwest of Tucson. It would have been located on the very edge of the Catalina mountain range, reaching to the national forest, an area rich in desert vegetation and valuable scenery that also happens to be the habitat of a few elusive mountain sheep. The general public became aroused, and a coalition of environmental organizations took aim at the proposition. It was turned down unanimously by the county commissioners, who made the ultimate decision after public hearings were held and the recommendations of the planning and zoning commission were received. Now Rancho Romero is in the process of being made into a state park. The developer meanwhile has traded some of his original land for other property in the area and probably will do well economically in the long run. Obviously the

outcome was the result of a concerted campaign that included community organization techniques.

Another voluntary association, Tucson Public Power, comes closer to the social action model, at least thus far. This incipient movement has arisen in response to the high cost of electricity and gas provided by the Tucson Gas and Electric Company and the fact that large users of energy, for example, the copper mines, receive a lower rate while small users pay a higher rate. Tucson Public Power advocates a "lifeline" rate schedule (as already exists in some cities) to benefit the small user needing a minimal amount of power to run a household. According to Tucson Public Power, the more electricity or gas used, the higher the rates should be—just the opposite of the present situation. The group's organizers have not seemed to receive much response from the general public (unlike the later vigorous reaction to the city's water-rate increases), but, as the cost of utilities rises, there may be more support.

The University of Arizona is the target for a group called the University Area Neighborhood Coalition. As the university grew rather quickly to approximately 30,000 enrollment, it built a few high-rise structures, but it is also gradually expanding outward, clearing away older homes of modest but still sound construction. The residents are not pleased about this situation. Little state money has been forthcoming to buy the doomed homes, nor is anybody else very much interested in buying a house that may be toppled by a bulldozer in a few years. The neighbors have organized to have the whole matter of university planning reconsidered, and the indication is that their efforts will have some impact.

The examples cited above represent a small selection from among literally hundreds of activities that could be considered part of the community organization of Tucson as of the mid-1970s. Furthermore, underlying the manifest community organization are changing and intricate processes whose exposition would be part of a fuller account. No claim is made that the sampling given here is even representative, nor does this chapter constitute a highly objective study of an arid city so complex and undergoing such transition that a decade from now its sociological portrait may be substantially altered.

CONCLUSION

A need exists for systematic research in order to evaluate more fully the nature of America's fast

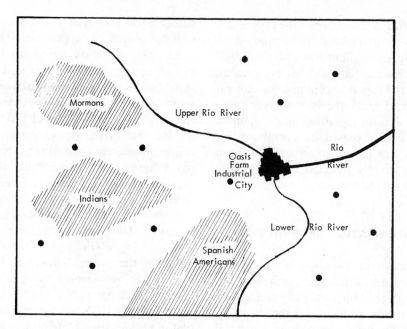

Figure 3. Arid-Western-mentality oasis–farm–industrial city. Redrawn from Carle C. Zimmerman and Richard E. Du Wors, *Graphic Regional Sociology* Cambridge, Mass.: The Phillips Book Store, 1952), p. 205.

growing desert cities: dilemmas that are created for the provision of social services, proper ways to view the rate of growth and related issues, and some typical responses of community organization, public and private. Our approach here has been that of a partial case study, a method suited to exploratory research but limited in its generalizing power.

Perhaps when enough cases have accumulated, it will be possible to see certain patterns and thus to make generalizations that encompass other arid regions of the world as well as the American deserts.[11] Newspaper reports of places such as Dubai in the Persian Gulf depict a town expanding from 20,000 population to 300,000 in a few decades; this sounds like Tucson. Dubai is said to have a boom atmosphere where the sidewalks are few and far between; this also could be said of Tucson, especially in its newer sections. Kraenzel, who tried to extend his sociological studies of the semiarid Great Plains of the United States to countries like Iran, pointed to metropolitan-based, oasis-centered social organization, similar to that in Figure 3 as a concept that spans different arid cultures.[12] He discussed a population in Middle East cities composed of civil servants, army people, oil refining personnel, landlords, retailers, and importers of wholesale goods. This description seems reminiscent of the occupational profile that might be found in some of the

lightly industrialized American southwestern cities. The latter cities also typically began as oases: water was available, and a rather modest agricultural effort started, but it is only recently that they have grown into metropolitan complexes. In countries such as Iran, however, there were metropolitan oases in the fourth and fifth centuries BC or earlier.

The closest historical parallel to this in Arizona is the Hohokam Indians about the year AD 1000. They built elaborate irrigation complexes drawing water from the Salt and Gila rivers and supporting possibly 50,000 people at that time. We cannot be altogether certain why they disappeared around the year 1400, but quite possibly they began to have problems of water supply, as did Mesopotamian society about the same time. Such international observations, although fragmentary, hold out the eventual prospect of longitudinal, cross-cultural generalizations that will help us better to understand how urban man has adapted to aridity wherever deserts, which constitute no less than one fifth of the earth's surface, are found.

NOTES

1. D. W. Meinig, *Southwest: Three Peoples in Geographical Change, 1600–1970* (London: Oxford University Press, 1971), p. 114.

2. W. Eugene Hollon, *The Great American Desert: Then and Now* (London: Oxford University Press, 1966), p. 223.

3. See George A. Hillery, Jr., *Communal Organizations: A Study of Local Societies* (Chicago: University of Chicago Press, 1968).

4. See Jack Rothman, "Three Models of Community Organization Practice," in *Strategies of Community Organization,* 2nd ed., Fred M. Cox, John L. Erlich, Jack Rothman, and John E. Tropman, eds. (Ithaca, Ill.: F. E. Peacock Publishers, 1974), pp. 22–39.

5. See Patricia Paylore, ed., *Desertification: A World Bibliography* (Tucson: Office of Arid Lands Studies, University of Arizona, 1976).

6. Carle C. Zimmerman and Richard E. Du Wors, *Graphic Regional Sociology* (Cambridge, Mass.: Phillips Book Store, 1952), p. 112.

7. See Meinig, pp. 48–50.

8. See Edward H. Spicer, *Cycles of Conquest: The Impact of Spain, Mexico, and the United States on the Indians of the Southwest, 1533–1960* (Tucson: University of Arizona Press, 1962).

9. See Edwin H. Carpenter, "The Day They Invaded Prescott . . . or, Where in Arizona Would You Like to Live If You Could Live Anywhere You Wanted?" *Progressive Agriculture in Arizona,* **26,** no. 6 (November–December 1975), 6–11.

10. See *New West Trails: Tucson's People's Yellow Pages, 1975–76, Bicentennial Edition* (Tucson, Ariz., 1975).

11. See Courtney B. Cleland, "Do We Need a Sociology of Arid Regions?" in *Social Research in North American Moisture Deficient Regions,* John W. Bennett, ed., Contribution No. 9, Committee on Desert and Arid Zones Research, American Association for the Advancement of Sciences (Las Cruces: New Mexico State University Press, 1966), pp. 1–12.

12. See Carl F. Kraenzel, "Great Plains Concepts as Applied to Other Arid and Semi-Arid Lands," in *Great Plains Sociology: A Symposium,* Courtney B. Cleland, ed., Social Science Report No. 7, North Dakota Institute for Regional Studies (Fargo: North Dakota State University, 1962), pp. 4–11.

CHAPTER 7

Social Issues in the Arid City

LEONARD GORDON

The interest in social issues and problems in the arid city is a reflection of the global concern with urban living. Worldwide, 30 times as many people live in cities with populations of 100,000 or more as in 1800, although the total world population has only quadrupled in that time.[1] The rapidity with which this global urbanization process has occurred has caused major adjustment problems at every level of the social system and has resulted in an age in which social solidarity of the type existing in small communal settings with strong intergenerational kinship ties is declining or even nonexistent. This shift to cities initially produced a widespread sense of marginality, which Everett Stonequist described as a situation in which one "does not quite 'belong' or feel at home."[2] Stonequist's observation was based on the findings of Robert Park and other urbanologists in the "Chicago School" and came less than two decades after the U.S. Census of 1920, which first reported that most Americans lived in urban areas.[3] By midcentury, however, Axelrod (1956), Komarovsky (1946), Rogers (1961), and other urban analysts were finding that a second and third generation of American urban dwellers were exhibiting fewer signs of marginality and stronger primary and more stable secondary relations.[4]

Since midcentury two trends have emerged. The first is the massive shift in population concentration from the large, old cities of the society—located primarily on the northeastern seaboard and in the industrial Midwest—into the surrounding suburbs. The second has been the development and growth of large cities in previously rural or sparsely settled areas in the South and the arid Southwest.

These new urbanizing trends have generated new and complex problems. Renewed anomie is now evident, the symptomatic signs of which include divorce rates growing twice as fast as marriage rates, pockets of chronic, intergenerational ghetto area underemployment and poverty, and increasing *de facto* residential and educational segregation on the basis of race and social class.[5] To overcome these and other signs of anomic alienation, a new planning ethic is needed on a metropolitan-wide basis. The problems in the old industrialized cities, the expanding small communities in the rural South, and the new cities in the arid southwest share some features as well as having some distinct characteristics. It is the purpose here to focus on the American arid-area cities and their general (i.e., shared with all urban areas) and specific developmental problems.

An analysis of any urban area directs itself to the whole complex of problems facing human beings in the modern world as it now exists and as it is rapidly developing. In such a context there are so many problems that it is difficult to get an analytical "handle" on them from any single disciplinary point of view, whether it be that of political science, economics, sociology, architecture, or any other field. It is therefore necessary to employ an interdisciplinary point of view in order to assess the urban condition in arid areas. Although this analysis is primarily sociological, many references are made to urban research in other disciplines. The aim is to develop the kind of perspective that can lead to consideration of new social policies and planning strategies. Such policies and strategies are necessary to generate community environments that meet the numerous and diverse interests of the wide variety of individuals and cultural groups living in arid cities.

This writer's research has been done predominantly in the old city of Detroit, Michigan, and in the new arid city of Phoenix, Arizona. Consequently, many of the contrasts of old and new (arid) cities illustrating general findings are drawn between Detroit and Phoenix.

HISTORICAL CONSIDERATIONS

The Emergence of Urban Society. In the days of the early demographer Thomas Malthus at the beginning of the nineteenth century, there were approximately 1 billion people on Earth. The world population has grown fourfold since that time, with the United Nations' population bureau recording a world population base of 4 billion.[6] The fourfold increase fulfills the part of the Malthusian prediction concerning the rapid growth of global population. Of all the people who have ever lived in the world since the beginning of human time, the majority are living now.

Whereas world population has quadrupled in a century and a half, the portion of the population living in communities of 100,000 or more, as we already noted, has grown 30 times since the early 1800s. Thus we have not only a population explosion but also a geometric explosion in urban areas. And it is not simply the size of the explosion, but also the rapidity with which it is occurring, that is having a tremendous impact on all levels of social life. All institutions—familial, educational, economic, governmental, and others—are trying to adapt to and cope with this inordinate population concentration in urban areas.

American society, and global society generally, is now in what John Gunther calls "the Age of Cities." In a book entitled *Twelve Cities,* Mr. Gunther, after examining the cities, writes, "Today is the age *par excellence* of great cities—huge and voracious cities, proliferating all over the place, seeping like inkblots into the countryside. . . . The growth, density, and seminal energy of these human muligatowanies is one of the overriding phenomena of this exacerbated century."[7] Of the 12 cities Gunther visited and analyzed, 9 were old, established cities like London, Paris, and Rome, and 3 were arid-area cities:

Jerusalem, Beirut, and Ammon. These three are old cities too in one sense, but they are old cities like Atlanta, Georgia, or Tucson, Arizona: cities with a heritage now dynamically and rapidly expanding. They are actually new cities on top of old cities, and a complex set of problems has surfaced there similar to those of the recently emergent new cities in the arid southwestern United States, such as Houston, Texas, or Phoenix, Arizona. This arid urban explosion is a reflection, on a global basis, of emergent market capabilities that have been generated out of the old urban setting, partly as a consequence of the old industrialization processes and partly because of new cybernetic capabilities.

The Emergence of Urban Sociology. The early-century urbanologists, particularly the sociologists at the Chicago School, the first great center of sociology in the United States, came into prominence just as the country was urbanizing and Chicago was becoming one of the great urban centers. These early analysts noted, viewing their city as a social laboratory, the problem of uprooting oneself from a former cultural condition. The uprooting process occurred there among both those already present in the society and the immigrants. With both groups there was at that time a severing of former intergenerational roots, resulting in a sense of rootlessness since they had broken their old social ties and were now in a new setting which either had not solidified or had solidified for only a limited group. Thus the city residents, particularly the immigrants, very often were marginal both to their past and to their present social existence. The adjustment problems were most severe in the 1930s, when Stonequist wrote his book on marginality in modern urban society and popularized the term "marginal man."[8]

These early urbanologists were trying to analyze what the urban condition does to human beings. A theoretical problem with their analysis is that it actually was descriptive of a particular time and setting. By midcentury, urban analysts noted that the situation had changed, that in the older urban developments, particularly those east of the Mississippi and north of the Mason-Dixon line, the sense of anomie and marginality was no longer general.[9] Except for minority and low-income groups, the people within the urban area had established a widespread network of both personal and strong secondary relationships. Thus the question of the general effect of urban living on people was not as clear at midcentury as it was once thought to be, for it was evident that viable social relationships could indeed be established at the primary through the secondary institutional levels within an urban context.

Urban sociologists are now attempting to assess the effects of the massive population shift from the old cities into the surrounding suburbs and the emergence of new cities out of both old, small cities (primarily in the South) and localities with no prior community structure, as is happening in the arid Southwest of the United States. New problems have emerged because of these trends. For example, the development of suburbia has had a deleterious effect on the old cities, because the people who have moved into suburbia are the ones who have most of the resources in the metropolitan regions. Thus the people left in the cities are members of social minorities and relatively low-income residents. In the newer cities, residents have had problems establishing social roots in a new kind of urban context.

In the old cities, for example, Detroit, we see the first problem. The U.S. Census Bureau reports indicate that there are approximately 1.5 million people now in Detroit, the same number as during the 1920s. Thus the total city population has not changed in over 50 years. But, whereas in the 1920s there were fewer than 50,000 people in Detroit's suburbs, there are now over 3 million, and the composition of the population in the city is very different. In the 1920s blacks and whites and every income level group were found within city limits. By the 1970s most whites, particularly middle-class young adults, were in surrounding suburbs, while Detroit retained a high proportion of aged, low-income residents and racial minorities. The resulting deteriorating city tax base caused a dilemma. Growing city-based services declined in quality in such fundamental areas as schools, job opportunities, and police and fire protection. This decline was a basic, underlying factor behind Detroit's 1967 race riots, the most damaging in American urban history. *The Report of the National Advisory Commission on Civil Disorders* noted that the community factors resulting from the racial and class cleavages in Detroit are markedly similar to those opearating in other older cities that experienced disorders, such as Philadelphia (Kensington riot of 1964), Cleveland (Hough riot of 1966), and Newark (inner city riot of 1967).[10]

In the new arid cities, for example, Phoenix, we see the second problem—that of adjusting to great and continuing city population expansion. In 1940 the Phoenix standard metropolitan statistical area (SMSA), including the city and its surrounding suburbs, had fewer than 200,000 people with fewer than 70,000 in Phoenix itself. By the mid-1970s there were over 1.3 million in the SMSA with over half of them in the city. About half of the people in the Phoenix metropolitan area, in addition, did not live there a decade ago.[11] As a consequence of this population explosion, the new arid cities are experiencing some of the old urban problems, with new variations, of anomic rootlessness and alienation.

A number of indices demonstrate a widespread sense of anomie in arid cities. For example, the divorce rate is over twice as high in the new cities in the arid Southwest as in urban areas elsewhere in the country. The crime rate is popularized in the mass media as being very high in the older big cities of New York, Philadelphia, and Newark, but a check of the *Uniform Crime Reports* of the FBI shows a relatively higher crime rate in new arid cities, with Phoenix registering the highest national rate in 1975. Furthermore, the traffic fatality rate is about a third higher in Phoenix than in Detroit. Detroit is known as "murder city" because more murders are committed there *per capita* than in any other city in the Western world. Yet, when the lower murder rate in Phoenix is combined with the higher traffic fatality rate, its *per capita* unnatural death rate is approximately the same as Detroit's.[12]

In both the old metropolitan settings of Detroit, Philadelphia, Boston, New York, and St. Louis and the new arid cities of Albuquerque, El Paso, Tucson, and Phoenix, what has developed is a general need, now becoming more widely recognized, to harness and direct social forces in order to create city environments conducive to maximal human growth and development. There is a growing consensus among urbanologists such as Greer, Jacobs, and Wood that, to make modern city living viable, a planning ethic is required on a city and metropolitan basis if widespread economic, social, and political dislocations are to be avoided.[13] The stakes are high. At issue in old cities and perhaps most poignantly in new arid cities, where hope is high, is the ability of the American democratic system to function in this urban age.

The Emergence of Arid Urban Society in America. In America new market capabilities can be graphically shown as growing out of the market expansion of the older cities. The old cities on the northeastern seaboard, including New York,

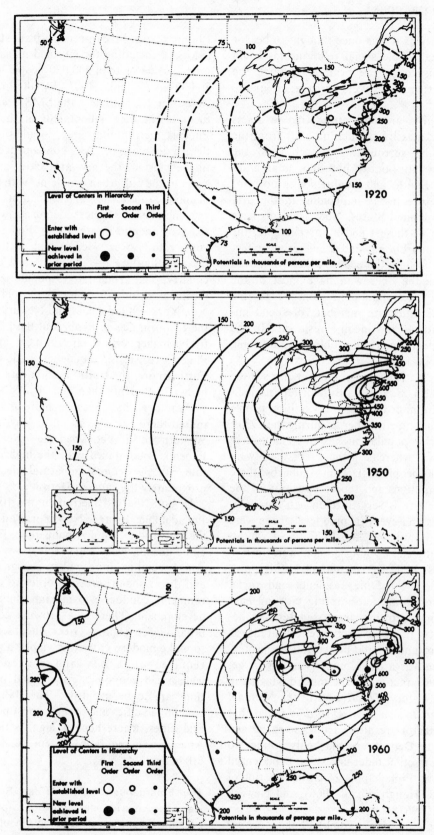

Figure 1. Market potential, 1920–1960. From Brian L. Berry, *Theories of Urban Location* (Washington: Association of American Geographers, 1968), pp. 11–12). Reproduced by permission from the Association of American Geographers' Commission on College Geography Resource Papers Series, no. 1, 1968, B. J. L. Berry.

Philadelphia, Baltimore, and Boston, were generated by the industrialization and urbanization of Western European society. Similarly, the arid Southwest urban communities are a consequence of the expanding market resource potential of urban locales long established in the Midwest and Northeast. Figure 1A shows the urban centers in the United States in 1920 located along the northeastern seaboard and expanding into the Midwest. The figure shows how each urban center developed a hinterland of market capabilities which in itself produced new urban areas. This hinterland's measurement, a coefficient relationship between the urban population concentration and spatial distance, is a positive correlation: the greater the population, the greater the distance. In 1920 there was further expansion as the Midwest began to develop its own centers—Detroit, Chicago, St. Louis—and they started to spread market capabilities into the Southwest, just barely touching New Mexico. Also in 1920 there was some urban development on the West Coast (Los Angeles and San Francisco), but these developments, a consequence of the Panama Canal, did not affect the hinterland at this point in time. Technological and market capabilities were not sufficient to push the hinterland into the Southwest in the first quarter of the century.

With the expansion of highways by 1950, however, as Figure 1B reveals, there was a continued expansion of market capabilities from Midwest urban areas into the arid Southwest, further into New Mexico. In California the developments in Los Angeles, San Diego, and San Francisco also began to affect some of the arid Southwest (i.e., Nevada). By 1960, just 10 years later and into the "cybernetic age" discussed below, there was, as Figure 1C shows, a great shift westward. It was not just the eastern seaboard and Midwest urbanization processes that affected new market regions, but also the concentration on the West Coast and the expanding and intensifying conditions in the Northwest, Denver, Dallas, and Houston. The stage was now set for the current major growth of urban arid areas because of their proximity to market regions of both the Midwest and the Far West. Thus, within the last quarter century, it is no accident that each year Tucson and Phoenix have been among the nation's top five cities in population growth.[14] It is, furthermore, no accident that the three states leading in population growth over the last decade are Florida (the recipient of retirees from the Northeast), Arizona, and Nevada.[15] Those three states are regularly among the

annual top three; New Mexico is closely behind. In fact, in 1973, California, for the first time in its history, appeared to have lost population, and many of those persons moved to arid Arizona, Nevada, and New Mexico.[16]

In terms of market capability, the arid Southwest area now is situated in an ideal economic position. (This would be true on a global basis of cities in the Middle East such as Cairo, Tel Aviv, and Beirut should peace ever break out in that arid region.) One can see this plainly over the last 15 years or so. For example, between 1950 and 1960, Phoenix grew by 332,000, more than any other city in the United States.[17] As can be seen in Figure 2, every state in the arid Southwest—Arizona, New Mexico, Nevada, and Texas—has now established urbanized areas.

BASIC SOCIAL FORCES AFFECTING ARID CITIES: THE CYBERNETIC AND HUMAN RIGHTS REVOLUTIONS

Certain global developments must be noted to understand what has happened and is continuing to happen in the arid cities of the Southwest. In 1964 a group of 32 analysts from a variety of disciplines identified what has come to be called "the triple revolution," a term popularized by Perucci and Pilisuk in their best selling social problems book by that name.[18] The three revolutions cited were the military technology revolution, the cybernetic revolution, and the human rights revolution. The analysts contended that these developments were of revolutionary magnitude, that society's current responses to them were proving inadequate, and that major radical, new measures were needed to control and direct the changes in beneficial directions. The last two of those revolutionary developments, cybernetics and human rights, are important in understanding why cities are developing in arid regions and what social dynamics and problems have emerged within those cities. We first should consider the military technological revolution, however, in order to understand how some arid communities began.

Military technology was transformed with the emergence of nuclear weaponry, because, until nuclear weapons were first used at the end of World War II, military technology had always been tied to diplomacy: war was simply a form of diplomacy like negotiation or discussion, since it was very unlikely then that war would destroy any society. The emergence of nuclear weaponry and the techno-

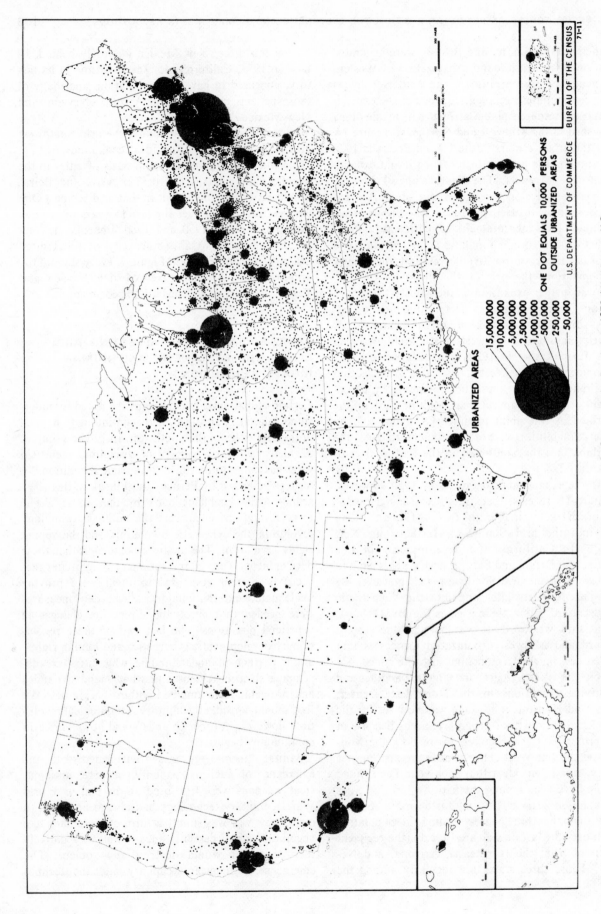

Figure 2. Population distribution, 1970. From *U.S. Census of the Population, 1970* (Washington: U.S. Government Printing Office, 1973). Vol. 1, part 1, section 1, p. 15.

logical capability of bringing war into the arena of any combatant or noncombatant society, on a moment's notice, necessitated a strategic dispersement of defense installations. These installations are no longer concentrated along the periphery of a society, as was the case at the onset of World War II when the United States had its entire Pacific fleet stationed at Pearl Harbor. For strategic safety major nuclear nations now deploy globally and throughout their society. As a result of this new military reality, a major part of the first urban economic nucleus in the arid Southwest came as a result of—and was stimulated by—the installation of military establishments. One of the largest Air Force bases in the country, Luke Air Force Base outside of Phoenix, has been developing and growing since the late 1930s. Since World War II it has been a major facility, one that brings approximately $300 million into the state of Arizona.[19] This installation, as a consequence of the revolution in military technology, became the nucleus for the development of small businesses, schools, and settlements, as thousands of Air Force and support personnel came to be stationed there and provided a market base. Once the growth was generated—and this is why the military technological revolution is of secondary importance in the development of urban society in the Southwest—a set of inner dynamics occurred. For example, Motorola and General Electric located in the Phoenix area as part of the ancillary industrial network that supplied the military. Now, most of their business is domestic (e.g., television sets, refrigerators). Once their domestic business began growing in the region, it took on a life of its own, independent of the military and aided by the emergence of industry and urban development on the Pacific coast, since such arid cities as Phoenix, Tucson, and Albuquerque were directly on the Midwest–Pacific routes.

At a given point of development, military technology became less important to arid-area cities. Now, for example, metropolitan Phoenix is growing so rapidly that it is squeezing close to Luke Air Force Base. Air Force spokesmen have said that if the city comes any closer the base will be forced to move. Simultaneously, some local planners in the Phoenix area noted regretfully that the military may well have to relocate because the land has become too valuable: if developed, it could produce more than the $300 million generated by Luke Air Force Base. Thus there is a tradeoff after a while, a point at which the economic role of the military establishment is no longer significant to urbanization in the arid region.

The two other revolutions, however, are still very important to the nature and rapidity of urban growth in arid regions. First, there are the effects of "cybernation." The term itself is only about 20 years old, but cybernation (i.e., the combination of automated techniques and computerized technology) is as important a development in modern society as industrialization was in the nineteenth century.[20] It is a quantum leap over the older industrial processes. Thus new urban communities that have developed over the last quarter century during the cybernetic revolution have emerged into a social context which bypasses the century and a half of economic development that the older cities went through in the aftermath of the industrial revolution. As a result there is a crucial difference in policy implications and prognostications. The cybernetic revolution increases production capabilities while reducing the previously massive need for unskilled labor. The result is a new level of economic capability, energy restrictions notwithstanding, with a concurrent set of complications for planners in the new arid cities.

To some extent the problem of predicting society's ability to adjust to rapid population growth in arid-area cities is the problem Thomas Malthus faced in the early 1800s in assessing population and food production growth. Malthus examined the fertility and mortality rates of his day, did some quantitative analysis, and forecasted on the basis of control of mortality as a result of early medical breakthroughs and the rising standard of living in the expanding economy of Western European and British society, a tremendous population expansion. He was correct about that, but he was not correct about the other side of the picture—food production. Malthus predicted a geometric growth of population, but he also predicted an arithmetic growth of food production.[21] What he could not foresee were the effects of the industrial revolution. For example, within approximately 20 years after his death, a whole series of early power developments and farm technological innovations produced a quantum increase in food production that was even greater than the population growth. One example of a technological advance that Malthus could not predict was the invention of the wheelless hayrake. With this device (introduced in American agriculture after 1820) each farmer was able to increase production 6 to 10 times.[22] Malthus did not factor this kind of development into his prediction of a population crisis and mass starvation.

In predicting future human capability to adapt to new conditions, we are in an analogous position today, particularly in regard to the newest of communities—the arid city. As Malthus stood in advance of the industrial revolution unable to accurately predict its impact, we stand before the cybernetics revolution able only to estimate its effects on urban life. What it may mean for the current urban context can be suggested by an example. In one plant of the Ford Motor Company outside of Detroit in River Rouge, a work force of approximately 30,000 produces several hundred thousand cars per year. In the 1960s the Ford Motor Company opened a new facility in Cleveland which produces the same number. At the Cleveland plant, however, computerized technology was instituted that has the capability of analyzing breakdowns in the production process and being self-corrective with only minimal technical assistance from relatively few personnel. The work force in the Cleveland plant is thus approximately one-third the size of that in the Detroit plant. In other words 10,000 workers using cybernetic technology are producing the same number of units as the 30,000 member work force in Detroit.[23] The Ford Motor Company was able to do that in Cleveland because it was opening a new facility. It cannot do it in the Detroit area plant because the United Auto Workers (UAW) would strike to protect its workers. But new industries in new cities are developing within the context of the cybernetic revolution. They are not going to hire as many semiskilled and nonskilled personnel in the first place. A hint of what is happening nationwide can be seen in the membership statistics of basic semiskilled unions such as the UAW, which hit its membership peak of somewhat over 1.5 million members in the mid-1950s on the eve of the cybernetic revolution. The union now has approximately the same number of members. It has not grown during a time when the economy (up until 1972) was expanding at a tremendous rate and the American population grew from approximately 150 million in the 1950s to over 200 million in the 1970s.

As a consequence of the cybernetic revolution, the new cities in the arid Southwest do not experience the push–pull pattern that characterized the growth and development of the older cities. With the advent of the industrial revolution, people were pushed off the farms and pulled into the cities because the industrial revolution was dependent on huge numbers of semiskilled workers. The big cause was the mass assembly line, not only in the automotive industry, where it began, but also in all industrial production. The mass assembly line meant that a large number of semiskilled workers was needed along an assembly line in order to perform one limited manual function in the production process. This represented a shift in production needs. Because of the cybernetic or "quiet" revolution, the average worker is now much more highly skilled. We are, therefore, now in a situation where the push is still off the farms for semiskilled workers, but the pull from the cities is no longer present. This is a global development, and it can be seen in United Nations statistics. In France, for example, in the early industrial period in the mid-nineteenth century, more workers were needed in industry (approximately 15 percent of the population) than there were in the cities (less than 10 percent).[24] Thus the industries had the capability of absorbing workers coming off the farms. In the former French colony of Tunisia, the opposite pattern holds. In Tunisia in 1950, just at the beginning of the cybernetic revolution, there were more people in the cities (over 15 percent) than in industry (approximately 7.5 percent).[25] This means that modern industry has a declining ability, due to the cybernetic revolution, to absorb people who do not have technical skills. The indigenous and inmigrant population mix in arid cities has been heavily influenced by these cybernetic-induced circumstances.

The third revolutionary development, the human rights revolution, is a dynamic factor that affects everything that goes on in urban areas, whether they be new or old. This revolution is related to the global decline of colonial empires since the end of World War II. The end of global colonial empires has meant the emergence of nations whose peoples, on an international basis, have historically been minorities. The growth of such nations can be seen in the United Nations membership. When the U.N. was formed out of the old League of Nations in 1945, there were fewer than 50 independent nations in the world; now there are over 150: a threefold increase in less than a generation, with most of the new nations carved out of the old European colonial empires in Africa, the Middle East, and Southeast Asia.

This worldwide human rights revolution is paralleled within American society by the multiple social movements of minorities (e.g., blacks, Chicanos, native Americans, and women) aimed at achieving equal rights and opportunities. In light of these movements, the term "minority relations" no longer communicates the nature of ongoing interaction in contemporary global or domestic society. "Intergroup relations" is a more appropriate term, because people who are technically in the minority no longer view themselves as such. As a consequence, in an urban context minorities can and do organize and politically challenge the system at every level, including the municipal one. Coleman Young, the first black mayor of the old city of Detroit, and Raul Castro, the first Arizona governor of Mexican ethnicity, elected with strong support from Chicanos in the arid cities of Tucson and Phoenix, are symptomatic of the ongoing human rights revolution.

As a consequence of the multiple human rights movements, American society is increasingly pluralistic in nature. Cultural groups other than the historically dominant Anglo white Protestant are increasingly visible and culturally autonomous participants in the heterogeneous American society. This is reflected in the new arid cities. For example, in the Phoenix metropolitan area, where over half of Arizona's approximately 2 million people reside, there are many culturally different peoples with several thousands in their ranks. In addition to the minority groups of blacks, Chicanos, and Native Americans, there is considerable cultural pluralism within the dominant "Anglo" category. In the Phoenix area almost one quarter of the population is Catholic (most of whom are not of Mexican heritage), another 7 percent are Mormon, and another 2 percent are Jewish. Additionally, there is wide denominational and economic class variation among white Protestants.[26]

American blacks have been influenced by developments in Africa, and Chicanos by those not only in Mexico but in all of Latin America as well, just as American Irish Catholics identify with their coreligionists in Northern Ireland in the civil conflict there and American Jews and Moslems identify with the Israeli and Arab disputants, respectively, in the Middle East. Not only are there cultural ties but also the effects of international developments are actually felt within the indigenous American groupings. Thus it is now generally recognized that Black Power movements in the Southwest are influenced by, if not a part of, independent developments of black peoples in Africa. Similarly, the growing economic and international political influences of Mexico and other Latin American societies have their impact on persons of Latin descent in arid cities of the American Southwest. Within society, including that of the arid Southwest, this has meant that the racial and ethnic groups coming into the urban context have a growing sense of group self and an ability to organize to challenge the status quo.

As a result of the human rights revolution, we are in the midst of a series of social movements—global and national—that build upon each other. The black civil rights movement of the 1950s and 1960s clearly influenced the Chicano migrant laborers' movement led by Cesar Chavez, for example, and both had an effect on the emergence of the women's movement in the late 1960s. In fact, the first leaders of the women's movement were often heavily involved in these earlier civil rights movements. Thus there is often even a personnel overlap.[27] Whether the movements are cohesive or disorganized, such as those leading to the civil disorders of the mid and late 1960s, and whether they are or are not immediately evident on the surface, these human rights revolutionary movements are a dynamic factor in the evolving urban area. It is a potentially stabilizing factor leading to new cooperative intergroup relations. It is, however, also a potentially dangerous and destabilizing factor if ignored. As James Baldwin noted in *Another Country,* minorities, even though they may not be able to gain opportunities within the structure of the society, can still fundamentally disrupt it because they are situated strategically in the nation's urban areas.[28] Those in positions of power in arid cities, as elsewhere, need to come to terms with the effects of human rights movements on whatever developmental problems may exist in the city.

THE ARID URBAN AREA TODAY

Urban Organization. The analyses of the Chicago School in the 1920s, including those of Ernest Burgess and Robert Park, helped to develop a number of urban theories. The most generic was Burgess' concentric zone theory of urban growth.[29] According to this theory, depicted in Figure 3A, wherever the seaport was (and all cities in the United States of a million or more population are seaports) would be the early downtown area—what Burgess identified as "zone 1." From that, growth would occur in concentric circles: first, a rooming house area; second, an immigrant settlement area; then, a working-class residential area; next, a middle-class housing and apartment area; and finally, the higher income suburbs. The old industrial cities did indeed tend to develop according to this concentric model into the 1930s. This analytic model turned out, however, to be a reflection of what was happening at a given stage of urban development rather than a universal modern growth model.

Another theory advanced in the late 1930s was the sector theory of Homer Hoyt, who noted that

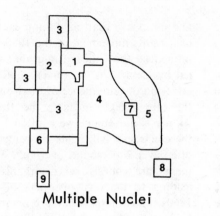

Multiple Nuclei

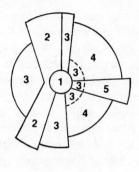

Sector Theory

DISTRICT

1. Central Business District
2. Wholesale Light Manufacturing
3. Low-class Residential
4. Medium-class Residential
5. High-class Residential

6. Heavy Manufacturing
7. Outlying Business District
8. Residential Suburb
9. Industrial Suburb
10. Commuters' Zone

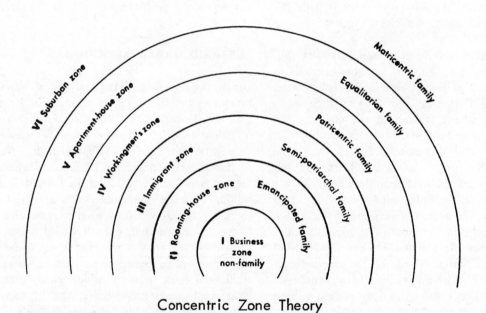

Concentric Zone Theory

Figure 3. Theories of urban development. Redrawn from Ernest W. Burgess and Harvey J. Locke, *The Family* (New York: American Book Company, 1953), p. 117, and C. D. Harris and E. L. Ullman, "The Nature of Cities," *The Annals of the American Academy of Political and Social Science,* **242** (1945), 13.

concentric circles no longer conceptually described the way in which urban areas were actually developing.[30] By the late 1930s Hoyt observed that cities were indeed developing the inner core described by Burgess, but, then, with the emergence of mass automobile usage and the growth of highway arteries, the development, as Figure 3B shows, was along sectors, wherever the transportation routes were within the city and in the suburban areas. In the sector theory the same general pattern of the concentric theory, with the low-income groups concentrated in the central city and the higher income groups in the outer city and suburbs, held.

By the 1940s the more complex nuclei theory was developed by Chauncey Harris and Edward Ullman.[31] This model, depicted in Figure 3C, reflects the complexities that have existed since the beginning of major urbanization in the arid areas. This theory holds that an urban area in modern society no longer necessarily has just one central business "downtown" area but can have a number of such areas spatially separated within the city and in several suburbs with a concomitant dispersal of housing and industrial parks.

The old eastern seaboard and midwestern cities tend to reflect the concentric zone and sector theories of urban growth. In cities like Baltimore, Detroit, and Chicago, there is a positive correlation between distance from the city center and educational level and income of residents. Arid-area cities, as a consequence of their emergence when cybernetic economic development was more technically efficient and widespread, reflected at very early stages the multiple nuclei pattern within the central city and in the concurrently developing suburbs. (The suburbs are often no newer than many parts of the central city.) For example, in Phoenix, as Figures 4 and 5 show, there is wide spatial distribution of low, middle, and high educational and income groups. Unlike the situation in older cities, there are approximately as many persons with a college education within the city as in the suburbs. As Figure 5 reveals, areas whose per capita average earnings are $15,000 or more are located both in suburban Scottsdale and in large tracts of northern Phoenix. Those who earn between $12,500 and $15,000 are also widely distributed. Neither do the new arid cities exhibit a rigid spatial separation of ethnic groups. In Phoenix, as Figure 6 shows, over half of the metropolitan area has a 10 to 15 percent or more black and/or Chicano popula-

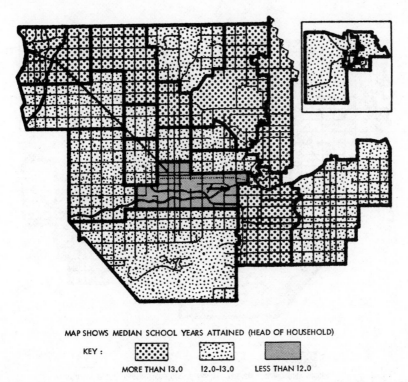

MAP SHOWS MEDIAN SCHOOL YEARS ATTAINED (HEAD OF HOUSEHOLD)

KEY :

MORE THAN 13.0   12.0–13.0   LESS THAN 12.0

Figure 4. Educational attainment of Phoenix, Arizona, population. From *Inside Phoenix* (Phoenix: Phoenix Newspapers, 1976), p. 18.

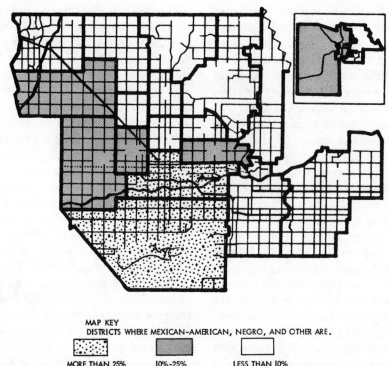

MAP KEY
DISTRICTS WHERE MEXICAN-AMERICAN, NEGRO, AND OTHER ARE.

MORE THAN 25%   10%-25%   LESS THAN 10%

Figure 5. Income level of Phoenix, Arizona, population. From *Inside Phoenix* (Phoenix: Phoenix Newspapers, 1976), p. 26.

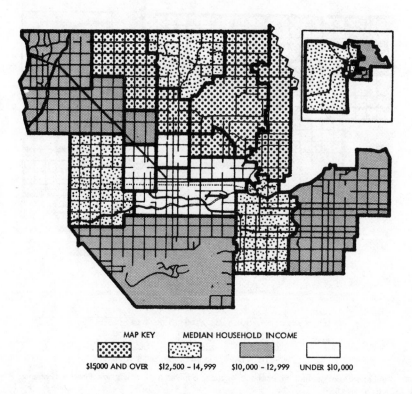

MAP KEY   MEDIAN HOUSEHOLD INCOME

$15,000 AND OVER $12,500 - 14,999 $10,000 - 12,999   UNDER $10,000

Figure 6. Racial composition of Phoenix, Arizona, population. From *Inside Phoenix* (Phoenix: Phoenix Newspapers, 1976), p. 14.

tion, even as the central city retains a majority of middle- and high-income Anglos. Unlike the situation in most old cities, where the suburbs house the overwhelming proportion of Caucasian and higher income residents, all major income and ethnic groups continue to interact politically and economically within all areas of the new arid cities.

Community Characteristics. Among the factors affecting the stability of arid urban development are intracommunity issues of both a general and a particular nature. Those of a general nature involve ecological processes such as those just reviewed. The particular arid-area problems are to a considerable extent based on the recent nature of urban development in this region. One useful way of considering these particular problems is to examine what Philip Hauser lists as the five main hindrances to successful economic and community development in less developed areas.[32] Such an examination provides some useful insights, not only into the problems of developing societies, but also into the problems of new arid-area cities contrasted with those of older cities.

Hauser notes, first, that there typically exists among long-established dwellers a set of traditional spiritual values rather than the modern materialistic values operating in less developed areas. In American industrialized urban society the more traditional values, insofar as they exist in an urban context, are more evident in older cities than in newer ones. The people who came *en masse* to the arid region over the last quarter century identify relatively highly with material development. Such identification was, in fact, one of the reasons they went there in the first place. Gerhard Lenski, when at the University of Michigan, tested Max Weber's Protestant ethic theory in the Detroit area, and it held up.[33] The original theory held that Protestants shift their theological focus from other-worldly rewards to worldly material achievements and therein give religious sanction to such rewards, including those that are economic.[34] What Lenski found in the Detroit area was that Protestants tended to be more materialistic than Catholics, just as the theory suggests. When Fred Whitam of Arizona State University tested the same hypothesis in the Phoenix metropolitan area, however, it did not hold up there; Catholics were as materialistic as Protestants.[35] Whitam appears to have tapped a different cultural orientation in new arid cities.

Second, Hauser notes that underdeveloped areas tend to be highly stratified in terms of social classes.

However, in comparing social rigidity and mobility between old cities and new arid cities, it is the older cities that appear to have the sharper social class differentiation. This can be seen in a variety of ways. One way is to consider the racial and ethnic residential patterns of the new arid cities such as Albuquerque, Phoenix, or Tucson. As noted above, there is a greater mix of people economically and ethnically over larger tracts of the metropolitan arid-city area than can be found in the older cities. For example, an analysis of black–white residential patterns in old cities like Detroit, Philadelphia, and St. Louis since the 1920s shows a growing distance between blacks and whites, with blacks (and low-income groups generally) being located primarily within the central city and middle- and upper-class whites being concentrated in the suburbs.[36] Sharp economic class, racial, and ethnic differences do exist in new arid cities. However, the massive inmigration of residents with generally compatible skills for the growing job opportunities has made for less rigid social stratification in arid cities.

Hauser notes, third, that less developed areas are characterized by wide age differentials. Contrary to what is popularly imagined, it is not the arid Southwest that has above-average age differentials. Rather, it is the older urban Northeast and Midwest that are characterized by particularly wide ranges. For example, U.S. Census data reveal that 10 percent of the American population is 65 years of age or older. Several of the areas with an above-average aged group are located in such heavily urbanized older states as Massachusetts, New York, and Pennsylvania. In contrast, the census indicates that arid Arizona—with its Sun City, Leisure World, and other retirement communities—has an over-65 age population that represents only approximately 7 percent of its total population, well below the national average.[37] As a consequence, arid cities like Tucson and Phoenix have a narrower and younger range of ages than do the older developed cities in American society.

The fourth point that Hauser notes about less developed areas is their characteristic nonscientific mentality. By this, Hauser means a value-laden orientation resistant to modern technological innovation. In American society older cities appear more resistant to new scientific technology than new arid cities. It is not that the older cities are of advanced scientific technology, but these cities do exhibit signs of William Ogburn's cultural lag concept.[38] The older cities have developed over the years in such a way that many people there now depend on the economic and social structure as it has developed, even though it may no longer be functional in terms of competitive market capability. For example, recall the two Ford plants discussed earlier in terms of economic efficiency for the company and for the consumer. The Ford plant in River Rouge near Detroit is employing approximately 20,000 more workers than would be needed for the same production capability if the plant could use cybernetic technology.

Detroit area industry (i.e., older city industry) is, of course, not nonscientific; the industrial base, however, developed in line with the technological knowledge available a half century ago. Now, the people—many of them in well-established labor unions—who are dependent on the system do not want to change it because the older methods of production give them job security. The situation is similar to that illustrated in a movie of the 1950s, at the beginning of the cybernetic age, entitled "The Man in the White Suit." What the main character (played by Alec Guinness) did, operating in some nook or cranny of a university, was to develop the perfect material which never wrinkled, never got dirty, and never wore out. Once the local textile workers found out about it, they almost lynched him, because his technical advance would have destroyed a substantial part of the labor market in the area quite quickly. Without a clearly viable alternative source of jobs and steady income, the fictional textile workers reacted in very much the same way real-life union workers would react—they protected themselves. This kind of worker resistance to new technology is more evident in older American cities than in new arid cities. Industry being new in arid cities, there is more business and labor flexibility and willingness to adopt new technological innovations. Consequently, arid-area industries are positioned to compete effectively.

A fifth factor that Hauser cites as characteristic of less developed areas is anomistic, loosely knit social ties. On this count it is the arid-area city that exhibits a greater degree of a destabilizing factor. The older cities manifest stronger primary and secondary relationships, since familial, neighborhood, and occupational ties are long established. The general strength or weakness of such community-based relationships has strong supportive or inhibitive implications for community organization and development and is therefore a major consideration in policy formation and planning efforts. In new arid cities there are many symptoms of loose social ties. Problems of

social adjustment and adaptation are not only faced by the hundreds of thousands of inmigrants to each arid city over the past two decades; old residents of new arid cities confront a changing social world as well. This situation is similar to what happened during the early history of the old cities. An example of the fundamental change that faced old residents is the case of a farmer during the early-century urbanization in Chicago. This family founded its farm in the nineteenth century in what is now part of the downtown loop area. When Chicago's urban expansion began, as described by Burgess' concentric zone theory, the farmer was asked by city officials to sell his old farmhouse, as he had most of the surrounding land. For a period of years the farmer successfully refused to sell. In the 1920s a picture showed huge skyscrapers and traffic congestion all around the farmhouse, which soon came down.[39]

What happened to the Chicago farmer is happening constantly to people in arid cities with their new residents, new construction, and new industry. New social worlds are constantly being generated. In this context a loose, anomistic community structure is inevitable for a period during which symptoms are evident.[40] One such symptom of a lack of social cohesion is lower then average contributions to the community's United Fund. In voluntary work this author found the *per capita* contributions in the new urban area of Phoenix to be less than half those of the old urban area of Detroit. Another index, of loose social ties, noted earlier, is a high divorce rate. Nationally, the divorce rate is one for every three marriages contracted. In the new arid cities of the Southwest, on the other hand, the rate is approximately two divorces for every five marriages.[41] Just as Axelrod, Komarovsky, Rogers, and others have found increasingly stable social ties in older cities, it is likely that, after a generation of population settlement, the arid cities will begin to exhibit more signs of the social cohesion which is an important condition for planning.

Open-Space Heritage. The arid area's open-space heritage is a further factor inhibiting the organized planning of arid cities. The open-space heritage has influenced overall American values but is now more evident in the arid region with its late urban development. This heritage, which has its origin in the idolization of the West throughout most of American history, is not only non-planning-oriented but is also negative toward big cities. It is a value-laden factor that is only beginning to change in the older urban areas of the society.

The meaning of the western open space to the entire society is explained by historian Frederick Jackson Turner's "safety-valve" thesis.[42] European society, according to Turner, was spatially confined and, before overseas colonization, was forced to continually redevelop its cities because it was not in a position to abandon them for new settlements. Thus there developed an urban heritage, a heritage revealed by the importance of Rome to Italy, or Paris to France, or London to Great Britain. In the United States, on the other hand, there existed by mid-nineteenth century a transcontinental land space with a constantly expanding westward market capability. From the colonial period down into the twentieth century, as developmental problems occurred in the established settlements in the East, urban or otherwise, there was always new land in the West to be developed. Americans were not pressured, as were the Europeans, to preserve or to redevelop their cities until well into the twentieth century. Either Americans abandoned entire urban areas, the residents of the earliest cities such as New York, Boston, and Philadelphia relocating in newer cities like Cleveland, Detroit, and Chicago; or, as has happened more recently, Americans abandoned the city *per se* and went into the suburbs. Americans are so situated now that the arid Southwest is the last vast open space to be urbanized in the continental area of the 48 contiguous states. This is the reason why arid cities such as Albuquerque, Las Vegas, Phoenix, and Tucson have the fastest growth rates in the nation. Yet, even in the arid Southwest, the major growth is beginning to occur in the suburbs rather than the central cities. Consequently, the arid city is rapidly facing the reality of needing to take preservation and redevelopment steps to ensure its viability. This objective reality notwithstanding, the way of thinking is still influenced by the open-space, "safety-valve" theme.

The tenacity of this individualistic ethic that opposes community planning is deepseated, for the open-space heritage has been rooted in the ideals of the American republic from its inception. Thomas Jefferson noted that cities were suspect in terms of democracy because mobs are more likely to form and there is less likelihood of national rule. Jefferson said, "I view great cities as pestilence to the morals, the health and the liberties of man. True, they nourish some of the elegant arts, but the useful ones can thrive elsewhere, and less perfection in the others, with more health, virtue and freedom, would be my choice."[43] Even though the major independence movements occurred in the large colonial cities like Boston, New York, and Philadelphia, Jefferson and other American revolutionary leaders maintained a critical attitude toward cities and idealized agrarian small-town life. Consequently, there has not been in American society what is evident in European society, that is, a deep-rooted urban heritage. When one thinks of Paris or Rome or London, it is possible to go back centuries and recite the great events that occurred within the city, and even to define French, Italian, and English culture largely in terms of the cities. In contrast, the central American experience is tied to an agrarian community life, and the effects of this are felt in the urbanized present. The English idealize London, the French Paris, and the Italians Rome, as the most preferred places to live in their societies.[44] In contrast, when Americans are asked where they prefer to live, whether they then live in cities or in small towns, most express a preference for the latter. A national sampling by the National Public Opinion Survey Center in 1971 found that, while 55 percent of the American people live in cities or suburbs of 100,000 or more, 64 percent expressed a desire to live in the open country or in a small town, and only 14 percent listed residency in a "larger city or suburb" as their first choice.[45] This small-town preference is another factor that has many implications for what can be done in terms of community organization and developmental planning in new arid cities. It is, furthermore, a preference that is exaggerated in the arid Southwest, for the arid region has not only a small-town heritage but also an open-space heritage more recent than exists anywhere else in the society.

Arizona's arid cities of Tucson and Phoenix show the effects of this spatial heritage. Few residences have basements or attics. Until the last few years, acre lots for home construction were common, and the land was cheaper than old city lots one-eighth the size. Now, however, land is no longer as cheap, smaller lots tend to be used, and there is a rapid growth of apartments. Another indication that land is becoming dear is a growing movement to discourage continued mass inmigration. Elizabeth Huttman has noted that the "no growth" community movement is evident not only in older city suburbs but in the Southwest as well. As Huttman observed, "actions of the 'no growth' or 'limited growth' movement in communities across the United States are taking land out of development in many desirable . . . [new] communities."[46]

The emergence of such movements in arid-area cities is a strategy that appears to counter the dominant laissez-faire, open-space values. Thus these movements provide an impetus toward urban planning. At the same time, movements to limit growth raise another issue, one dealing with the stable or conflict-prone interaction between ethnic and economic groups in the arid city. As Huttman inquires, "To what degree does it [the no growth movement] further deter moderate and low income groups from receiving a measure of equality with the middle class in the type of residential environment they live in?"[47] This question brings us to the more general issues raised by the human rights revolution, as it manifests itself in the new arid city.

Intergroup Conflict. The people who are moving into the cities of the arid Southwest come from all over the country—mostly from the Midwest, but from over half the states *in toto*.[48] Most of them have come within the past decade. In our society's oldest cities the minority groups either moved in concurrently with the higher income, more dominant group members, or they came into the area later. Thus racial and ethnic minority members usually were inmigrants who became subordinate to those who either came in with them or were there before they arrived. Thus, for example, blacks coming out the South and moving into old cities like Cleveland or Pittsburgh found themselves to be a new low-income minority, not only in terms of the big cities, but also in terms of the entire region.

A somewhat different pattern, however, has developed in the arid areas. The urban emergence in the arid Southwest occurred so rapidly that there was not, as in the Northeast and Midwest, a prior decimation of the native populations.[49] The Native American Navajos, Hopis, Apaches, and several other tribes were indigenous to the area for a century or longer before the first major Anglo settlement. Their reservation system, with all its problems, was intact in the Southwest at the time of mid-twentieth century urban explosion. Similarly, the cultural roots of the thousands of arid-area inhabitants of Mexican heritage extend back to the colonial period. It has been more than a century since the Treaty of Guadalupe Hidalgo in 1848, before which the region was in fact Mexican territory. Thus, whereas most Anglos have recently moved thousands of miles from older midwestern or northeastern cities to the arid cities, indigenous Chicanos and Native Americans have made only short sojourns within the arid region that is their cultural base.

Because of these historical factors, intergroup relations are different in new arid cities than in old cities.

Typically, the technologically superior inmigrant group—the Anglos—established dominant migrant superordination.[50] However, the indigenous Chicanos and native Americans have maintained some degree of tightly organized kinship and community organization. In the older cities both blacks and whites arrived having some family and other ties but not a cohesively organized community. The long-established cultural roots of indigenous minorities in the new arid cities have social–psychological implications in terms of community intergroup relations. In the old cities of the Midwest and Northeast, until the white blacklash of the late 1960s and the Black Power movement, the black-led civil rights efforts aimed at integration and assimilation.[51] In contrast, most indigenous Southwest area minorities have always placed a heavier emphasis on cultural autonomy, if not separation. The challenging nature of this emphasis was noted by Meinig, who observed:

The basic internal strength of these local cultures has long been displayed in the simple fact of their persistence in the face of powerful pressures for assimilation into dominant national patterns. What is new in the Southwest among these groups is a change in attitudes about the nature and possibilities of their position, a change from seeing themselves as a besieged remnant desperately hanging on to the hard core of their culture, to a feeling of pride in seeing themselves as creative and expansive peoples with something special to contribute to the life of America.[52]

The basic internal strength of the Chicano culture was symbolized by the election of the first individual of Mexican descent, Raul Castro, as governor of Arizona in 1974. The underlying discontent with minority status was evident in the south Phoenix Chicano rioting in July 1967, the same time as the more widely publicized black rioting in Detroit.[53]

Problems for urban minorities generally are likely to intensify in the short future. As a consequence of the cybernetic revolution, there is now structural exclusion of low-income groups. This is an inherent problem in modern society which is sharply seen in the urban context. It is particularly vivid in the older metropolitan areas with their widening divisions between the old, economically declining major cities and their growing and developing suburban areas. The lower income people who remain in the cities are structurally excluded by the governmental structure there, by the job structure, which no longer needs unskilled labor, and by the educational structure, which features widely different qualities of schooling from city to suburb.

In discussing these structural problems in the context of the human rights revolution and its effect on arid cities, what becomes evident is a somewhat different, perhaps more complex, set of intergroup relations. There is, within south Phoenix, south Tucson, and sections of other arid cities, a black population which faces all the problems of minority status that exist in the society's older cities. And, as in these older cities, blacks organize and challenge the status quo. As such, they are a significant group that has to be taken into account. Yet the larger minorities are the Mexican ethnic group and the growing number of Native Americans coming off the reservations and into the urban context. These peoples, as groups that are indigenous to the area, constitute a more cohesive minority group challenge to Anglo dominance in the arid city.

Advantages over Old Cities.   Arid cities have some stabilizing characteristics that will enhance developmental prospects. Arid-city pressures for extensive social welfare services are not as intensive as those in old cities. Evolving in the cybernetic age of the last quarter century, the new arid cities have not attracted as large a number of unskilled, low-income residents as happened in the early stages of older city development. Hence the arid-city population has had from the start a higher proportion of inmigrants attuned to the modern technological economy. Additionally, the major arid cities, not only their suburbs, are still expanding. They are therefore more able, in terms of land and other resources, to meet minority and low-income groups pressures for reform and increasing opportunities within the city.

Older cities like Chicago, Detroit, and Philadelphia have had their boundaries frozen for a long time, partly because of the power that their more numerous and affluent suburbs have attained. The suburban communities surrounding the old cities have not only most of the metropolitan population, but, along with it, most of the political power within the state. Therefore, if an old city wants to enlarge its geographical boundaries, it cannot do so: since the rapid expansion of suburbs after World War II, old cities have faced too much opposition from the suburbs to successfully expand. In contrast, the new arid cities have grown so rapidly in the recent historical time span that most of the people in the metropolitan area still live within the central city. Until recent years the city retained the power to annex. Between 1950 and 1960, most of the 103 cities of 25,000 or more that annexed territory were in the Southwest. During this period Phoenix's annexations resulted in adding a total of 332,000 people to the city population.[54] Typical of other arid cities, Phoenix cannot continue to annex because a suburban population base has now been built up in Scottsdale, Tempe, Glendale, Mesa, and other suburbs. Still, the recent nature of annexations in arid cities and the continuing intracity growth mean that the fundamental tax base of the central city is not in a deteriorating situation, as it is in older cities. The new arid city does not have a preponderance of old structures with depreciating values from which it gets less taxes each year to pay for schools, roads, and fire and police services. Thus the arid cities are advantageously situated to cope with the complex of city problems.

Arid cities still have some time to formulate plans and programs that can ameliorate many of the issues and intense conflicts that exist within the older cities. Unless local organization and leadership develop, however, planning is not necessarily going to occur, whatever the objective need. In this connection it is pertinent that the new arid-area cities have a smaller amount of social solidarity than do older cities, although the arid cities have the economic resources to develop an effective planning process.

SOCIAL POLICY FOR ARID URBAN AREAS: NEEDS AND PROSPECTS

Urban planning issues are inherent in any large city, new or old. Whether involving jobs, schools, housing, police, traffic, class and ethnic divisions, or other areas, the problems generated are massive ones simply by virtue of the large, concentrated population in the urban area. Although such issues are generic, there are some consequential differences in policy formation between the American society's old cities and new arid cities. In essence, the new cities face more dynamic problems.

Over the past quarter of a century, the old cities have confronted a situation that can be described as static in terms of their populations and business and residential expansion. In contrast, over the same period, the new arid cities have experienced dynamic city population growth and extensive expansion of all types. The consequences of these differences appear less in the definition of particular problems than in their intensity and the internal city's resources to cope with them. In all significant ways, with the significant exception of cohesive community organization, the new arid cities are positioned to cope with their problems more effectively.

In view of this circumstance, what can be done to solve the problems now evolving and to take advantage of the arid cities' potentialities? This question necessarily leads to a consideration of the social policies and planning issues that have arisen in the cities of the nation generically, since the urban planning efforts in such cities as Phoenix, Tucson, Albuquerque, and El Paso affect most of the people in the entire arid region. As the historian Bradford Luckingham observes about the urban centers of the arid Southwest, "They have represented the driving force behind the growth and development of the area. In Arizona, for instance, over 75 percent of the population lives in metropolitan Phoenix and Tucson."[55]

The arid cities of the American Southwest exhibit an exaggerated form of the American emphasis on individualism, which has perceived any form of "collective" planning as damaging to, rather than protective of, individual freedom and independence. Yet, as the economist Kenneth Boulding observes, effective planning of cities is a key element in maintaining the economic and social stability of all societies and, indeed, of the international system.[56] Thus it is increasingly clear that individual rights and options are related to community organization, planning, and the implementation of such plans. The arid Southwest is rapidly catching up with the rest of America—and the world—in the decreasing amount of new space available for urban development. The arid area is perhaps the last region in which to develop great cities. These facts led to an unusual consensus among urban analysts concerning the need for planning that is akin to the consensus among demographers about the need for population control, an issue closely related to urban policy and planning. Ralph Thomlinson observes in regard to this population planning consensus among demographers:

Professional demographers almost unanimously favor controlling fertility by whatever techniques science can offer. This unanimity has reached the point where, when a television network wants to stage a pro–con discussion of birth control, it is easy to find debaters for the affirmative but extremely difficult to locate qualified experts willing to take the negative.[57]

Similarly, urban analysts may disagree on the principles and processes of urban planning, but they do not argue about the need *per se* to plan for directing city growth and development. Andreus Faludi's definition of urban planning summarizes the professional planner's perspective and his limited role in the process. He states, "Planning is the application of scientific method—however crude—to policy-making. What this means is that conscious efforts are made to increase the validity of policies in terms of the present and anticipated future of the environment. What it does not mean is that planners take over in the field of politics."[58]

The planning problem in the typically American nonplanned environment is how to coordinate the many fragmented efforts at planning on the part of professionals with those of various individuals and groups in the city. In response to multiple public pressures at the city, state, and federal levels, planning efforts have multiplied and become uncoordinated. There have been studies on educational needs (e.g., Coleman), on job needs (e.g., Ferman), and on housing and urban renewal (e.g., Greer).[59] A series of plans and projects has been generated because of widespread public pressure to, in effect, "do something." The problem with this approach in a complex urban environment is that it can intensify rather than alleviate the existing problems. For example, a basic urban planning issue is "urban renewal," focusing on housing needs in deteriorated parts of various cities. Scott Greer has made the following observation concerning the implementation of the federal Housing Act of 1949, designed to stimulate new-city housing projects (without the necessary concurrent plans for jobs, efficient transit, schools, and other city needs):

At a cost of more than three billion dollars the Urban Renewal Agency (URA) has succeeded in materially reducing the supply of low-cost housing in American cities. Like highways and streets, the program has ripped through the neighborhoods of the poor, powered by the right of eminent domain. From Boston to San Francisco, from Portland, Oregon, to Portland, Maine, hundreds of American cities and their citizens are involved.[60]

In contrast to this fragmented approach, the federal Demonstrations City Act of 1963 is symptomatic of the growing public recognition that coordinated, comprehensive urban planning is needed if stable city life is to be achieved. This Act encourages city planning that involves all the city's multiple interests, for example, business and labor, minorities, parents, and the aged.

Arid cities have, of course, the least experience in bringing together the many individual and group interests into a planning process. On the other hand, they have more resources than older cities to do so successfully.

As arid cities begin to plan, what should they take into account? Although there is no generally accepted definition of what city planning should include, Ray Northam denotes seven components that need to be available to planning groups or commissions in cities:[61]

1. *Population studies.* The rapidly changing population total and composition of arid cities is a consequence of their inordinate growth in recent decades. Without determining on a regular, perhaps annual, basis the demographic characteristics (such as age and sex ratios and income and educational levels) of the city population, it will not be possible to develop short- and long-range plans for schools, business markets, and other city needs.

2. *Housing studies.* When compared to population analyses, housing studies help pinpoint shifts in demand for different types of housing such as single, single family, and multifamily. Such studies can also show the extent to which public housing may be feasible and desirable for low-income groups and act as a stabilizing factor in their efforts to grow and develop within the city.

3. *Economic studies.* Economic studies can delineate the assets of the ongoing economy of the city and suggest directions for improving the city's economic environment through zoning, taxation, and other policies.

4. *Land use studies.* Inventories and summaries of how the urban space is being used can help planners to formulate and reformulate land needs that can minimize conflicts between residential, commercial, and recreational needs in the city.

5. *Transportation studies.* New arid cities tend to have more space and less dense settlement patterns than older cities—and, therefore, to lack an established mass transit system. To avoid the disjointed Los Angeles freeway-type development, road planning and an efficient private–public transportation mix need to be developed.

6. *Open space and recreation studies.* The arid city still has the spatial capability of ensuring sufficiently dispersed recreational facilities as it continues to grow. Without open-space planning, this advantage can be rapidly lost in the burgeoning residential and commercial construction processes.

7. *Governmental and community facilities.* Private commercial development in new arid cities is so rapid that, unless strong planning efforts are made, there will be insufficient public facilities for such fundamental needs as administrative structures, schools, medical centers, fire and police stations, and water systems.

How do these and other city planning issues become translated into social policies, urban plans, and implemented actions? The general approach, as envisioned by the Demonstrations City Act, has been the establishment of planning commissions or boards by local governments. Ideally, such city planning boards would represent the entire spectrum of individual and group interests. Included would be representatives of big and small businesses, labor unions, and various voluntary associations, among others. The planning issues would be so varied that an interdisciplinary approach would be necessary. A typical interdisciplinary effort for urban planning purposes can be seen in the 1975 new community plan report for Lackawanna County in Pennsylvania.[62] The population, housing, economic, and other studies were prepared for the Lackawanna Planning Commission by specialists in the fields of architecture, civil engineering, economics, geography, public administration, and sociology. For a large arid city other specialists could usefully be added from such disciplines as anthropology, geology, history, the biological and physical sciences, and the humanities.

A central problem in such city planning processes is ensuring that all community interests are represented at every stage from policy formation to implementation. A warning for new arid cities can be found in the planning experiences of many old cities. For example, in Detroit, in the years before the civil disorders of 1967, a comprehensive city plan was drawn up with representative input from many different components within the city. The "model city plan," according to a city councilman, included low-, middle-, and high-cost new apartments and housing, new expressway links between the city and the suburbs, new schools and medical facilities in old neighborhoods, job training and retraining programs for the unskilled, new city-county governmental structures, and new downtown hotels and businesses.[63] Ideally, this model city plan was to be implemented totally, that is, at the same time with mutual benefit to all within the city. In fact, limited financial capabilities to implement the total plan led to sharp competition among local interest groups for implementation of their parts of the plan. The result was that the more powerful groups in business and in government secured the implementation of their parts of the project. Thus there was expressway expansion in the city, reducing the availability of low-cost housing, development of high-cost and high-rental high-rise apartments, again at the expense of low-cost housing, and downtown business investment, rather than job training for those in need of it. The results were summarized in the *Report of the National Advisory Commission on Civil Disorders:*

Current trends in muncipal administration had the effect of reducing the capacity of local government to respond effectively to these needs. The pressures for administrative efficiency and cost-cutting have brought about the withdrawal of many operations of city government from direct contact with neighborhood and citizen. Red tape and administrative complexity have filled the vacuum created by the centralization of local government. The introduction of a merit system and a professionalized civil service has made management of the cities more businesslike, but is has also tended to depersonalize and isolate government. The rigid patterns of segregation prevalent within the central city have widened the distance between Negro citizens and city hall.[64]

Although perfectly understandable in terms of the traditional power-structure realities, the dozens of civil disorders in the nation's older cities make it clear that short-range advantages for only the powerful groups in a city promote long-range destabilization, to the disadvantage of all. The new arid cities with their still expanding economic bases, their intracity development, and their less rigid group and class lines are positioned to develop effective city planning processes and programs. Unfortunately, they have hardly begun to do so, leading one to label at least the short-run planning prospects of arid cities as pessimistic. Their advantageous urban position in the society, combined with the growing national recognition of the need to harness and preserve spatial and other resources, however, suggests a basis for long-range optimism, should arid cities now begin to produce the requisite private and public leadership that city planning requires.

SUMMARY AND CONCLUSION

Three topics pertinent to "social issues in the arid city" have been discussed here: (1) the historically recent emergence of metropolitan urban development in arid areas within American and world society, (2) selected social factors that will affect stable urban development in arid areas, and (3) social policy implications for urban planning in arid areas.

The first topic was discussed in terms of the cybernetic and human rights revolutions and the social impact of the rapid population expansion and concentration that occurred within the context of these dynamic developments. The rapid economic expansion was fueled by cybernetic technology, and this has been taken into account by urban location theorists to explain urban growth in the American arid Southwest. The national black and women's human rights movements of the past two decades were similarly significant, for they have influenced and been reflected by indigenous arid-area minority movements within the Chicano and Native American communities. Metropolitan Phoenix, with a population explosion from less than 200,000 in 1940 to over 1 million by 1970, was cited throughout this discussion as an example.

The second topic was discussed in terms of four factors that appear to particularly affect the stability of urban development in arid areas. The first factor is the nature of internal community development. The arid cities exhibit characteristics different from those of older urban areas as they developed initially in a multiple nucleii settlement pattern like that observed by Harris and Ullman by the 1940s and different from Burgess' concentric zone and Hoyt's sector model observed earlier in older cities. Internally, new arid cities have some different problems as a consequence of their different locale and their emergence in the modern, post-midcentury cybernetic period. The second factor affecting urban stability is the continuing influence of an open-space heritage. A deleterious consequence of this heritage is the inhibition of comprehensive urban planning. The third problematic factor is the nature of intergroup relations. The pattern in newly emerging arid cities is unlike that in older cities, where dominant and minority groups entered the developing urban region concurrently. In arid cities a typical pattern is for the indigenous groups, such as Chicanos and various Native American tribes, to become subordinate to the Anglo inmigrants. The consequent migrant superordination has resulted in intergroup conflict of a somewhat different nature from that found in the industrial Northeast or Midwest of the nation. A related fourth factor is the consequences of the distribution of higher income groups throughout arid urban communities, a pattern that cannot be found in the older cities of society.

The third topic, social policy and planning implications for arid cities, was discussed in terms of three major points of analysis: first, the emerging public concern with urban planning needs, as indicated by the federal Housing Act of 1949 and the federal Demonstrations Cities Act of 1963; second, the operationalization of community power as arid cities develop (examples of old-city local power conflicts were cited as warnings to the new arid cities as they begin to plan and to implement their planning efforts); and, third, the increasingly evident need for comprehensive metropolitan community planning in arid cities, planning which, to be effective, must incorporate the interests of all community members. This need exists in a nonplanning environment. The latter factor notwithstanding, a combination of complex city problems has led to a growing emphasis on coordinated analysis and urban planning implementation.

NOTES

1. Alexander Semenoick, population chart prepared for *Fortune*, June 1966, p. 110; "World Population Facts," *The CBS News Almanac—1976* (Maplewood, N.J.: Hammond Almanac, 1975), p. 223.

2. Everett Stonequist, "The Marginal Character of the Jews," in *Jews in a Gentile World*, I. Graber and S. Britt, eds. (New York: The Macmillan Company, 1942), p. 297; also see *idem, The Marginal Man* (New York: Charles Scribner's Sons, 1937).

3. For a typical and significant example of the "Chicago School"'s urban analysis, see Robert Park and Ernest Burgess, *The City* (Chicago: The University of Chicago Press, 1925); for the historical pattern of urban and rural population settlement in the United States since 1790, see U.S. Census Bureau, *U.S. Census of the Population, 1970* (Washington: U.S. Government Printing Office, 1971).

4. Morris Axelrod, "Urban Structure and Social Participation," *American Sociological Review,* **21** (1956), 13–18; Mirra Komarovsky, "The Voluntary Associations of Urban Dwellers," *American Sociological Review,* **11** (1946), 686–698; and William Rogers, "Voluntary Associations and Urban Community Development," *International Review of Community Development,* no. 7 (1961), 140–41.

5. For example, see William Kephart, *The Family, Society and the Individual* (Boston: Houghton Mifflin Company, 1972), pp. 566–567; Herbert Gans, "The White Exodus to Suburbia Steps Up," in *Cities in Change: Studies in the Urban Condition*, J. Walter Carns and D. Carns, eds. (Boston: Allyn and Bacon, 1973), pp. 292–303.

6. "World Population Facts," p. 223.

7. John Gunther, *Twelve Cities* (New York: Harper and Row, 1969), p. 10.

8. See Stonequist.

9. See Axelrod, Komarovsky, and Rogers.

10. *Report of the National Advisory Commission on Civil Disorders* (New York: Bantam Books, 1968), pp. 115–16, 358, and 611–659.

11. *Inside Phoenix* (Phoenix Newspapers, 1975), p. 4.

12. Kephart, p. 568; *Uniform Crime Reports* (Washington: U.S.

Government Printing Office, 1976); F. A. Whitlock, *Death on the Road: A Study in Social Violence* (London: Tavistock Publications, 1971), Table 2.

13. See Scott Greer, *The Emerging City* (New York: Free Press, 1962); Jane Jacobs, *The Life and Death of American Cities* (New York: Random House, 1961); and Robert Wood, *Metropolis against Itself* (New York: Committee for Economic Development, 1959).

14. United States Census Bureau, *U.S. Census of the Population, 1950; 1960; 1970* (Washington: U.S. Government Printing Office, 1951; 1961; 1971).

15. *Ibid.*

16. *The CBS News Almanac—1976,* p. 221. See also the 1975 reports of the U.S. Census Bureau.

17. Noel Gist and Sylvia Fava, *Urban Society* (New York: Thomas Y. Crowell, 1969), p. 54.

18. Ad Hoc Committee, "The Triple Revolution," *Liberation,* April 1974, pp. 1–7.

19. Donald Warren, "County Loses Appeal on Houses near Luke," *The Phoenix Gazette,* April 26, 1976, p. 1.

20. See Donald Michael, *Cybernation: The Silent Conquest* (Santa Barbara, Calif.: Center for the Study of Democratic Institutions, 1962).

21. Thomas Malthus, *An Essay on the Principle of Population* (1798; reprint, Ann Arbor: The University of Michigan Press, 1963), p. 6.

22. Harry Carman and Harold Syrett, "Improved Tools and Techniques," *A History of the American People,* 2 vols. (New York: Alfred A. Knopf, 1952), 1:397–401.

23. Based on an interview with a Ford Motor Company executive, Dearborn, Michigan, June 12, 1971. For a general perspective see John Owen, "The U.S. Labor Movement: Its History and Problems," *Rivista Internazionale di Science Economiche e Commerciali,* **23** (1976), 33–43.

24. Johnathan Power, "The City in Africa," in *Social Problems in the World Today,* J. Kinch, ed. (Reading, Mass.: Addison-Wesley Company, 1974), pp. 320–323.

25. *Ibid.*

26. Leonard Gordon, "Progress in Phoenix: A Multicutural Analysis," in *The Multi-Ethnic Society,* W. Noyes, ed. (Tucson: University of Arizona Press, 1973), pp. 3–5.

27. Jo Freeman, "The Origins of the Women's Liberation Movement," *American Journal of Sociology,* **78** (1973), 792–811.

28. James Baldwin, *Another Country* (New York: Bantam Books, 1963).

29. Ernest Burgess, "The Growth of the City," in *The City,* R. Park and E. Burgess, ed. (Chicago: University of Chicago Press, 1925), pp. 47–62.

30. Homer Hoyt, *The Structure and Growth of Residential Neighborhoods in American Cities,* for the Federal Housing Administration (Washington: U.S. Government Printing Office, 1939).

31. Chauncey Harris and Edward Ullman, "The Nature of Cities," *The Annals of the American Academy of Political and Social Science,* **245** (1945), 7–17.

32. Philip Hauser, "Cultural and Personal Obstacles to Economic Development in Less Developed Areas," *Human Organization,* **18** (1959), 78–84.

33. See Gerhard Lenski, *The Religious Factor* (Garden City, N.Y.: Doubleday and Company, 1963).

34. See Max Weber, *The Protestant Ethic and the Spirit of Capitalism* (New York: Charles Scribner's Sons, 1930).

35. Fred Whitam, "Religion and Response to Urban Problems," in *Essays in Urban Affairs* (Tempe: Arizona State University Center for the Study of Urban Systems, 1967), pp. 13–23.

36. Karl Taeuber and Alma Taeuber, "Negro Residential Seg-

regation in the United States Cities," in *Negros in Cities,* K. Tauber and A. Tauber, eds. (New York: Atheneum Publishers, 1969), pp. 28–68.

37. *U.S. Census of the Population, 1970.*

38. William Ogburn, *Social Change* (New York: Viking Press, 1938), p. 201.

39. John Biesanz, introductory sociology class lecture based on Chicago area experience, Wayne State University, Detroit, Mich., Fall 1953.

40. See Steven Tragash, "Crime Rate Soars as Police Force Grows," *The Arizona Republic,* February 26, 1974, pp. B-1 and B-2.

41. Kephart, p. 568.

42. Harvey Wish, "Turner and the Moving Frontier," *The American Historian* (London: Oxford University Press, 1960), pp. 181–208.

43. Thomas Jefferson, quoted in Warner Bloomberg, "Community Organization," in *Social Problems,* H. Becker, ed. (New York: John Wiley and Sons, 1967), p. 359.

44. Scott Greer, *Governing the Metropolis* (New York: John Wiley and Sons, 1962), p. 17.

45. Commission on Population Growth and the American Future, *Population and the American Future* (New York: New American Library, 1972), p. 36.

46. Elizabeth Huttman, "Social Inequality and the 'No Growth' Movement," unpublished paper presented at the annual meeting of the Pacific Sociological Association, 1974, p. 1. The paper is available from the Department of Sociology, California State University at Hayward.

47. *Ibid.*

48. *Inside Phoenix,* p. 15.

49. Donald Meinig, "Demographic and Political Patterns: 1900–1970," in *Southwest: Three Peoples in Geographic Change, 1600–1970* (London: Oxford University Press, 1971), pp. 82–94.

50. Stanley Leiberson, "A Societal Theory of Race and Ethnic Relations," *American Sociological Review,* 26 (1961), 902–910.

51. James Vander Zanden, "The Black Protest: 1955–1965; Aggression-Assimilation," in *American Minority Relations* (New York: Ronald Press, 1972), pp. 361–374.

52. Meinig, p. 131.

53. *Report of the National Advisory Commission on Civil Disorders,* pp. 84–108, 117, and 165.

54. Gist and Fava, p. 54.

55. Bradford Luckingham, "The City in the Westward Movement—A Bibliographic Note," *The Western Historical Quarterly,* 5 (1974), 305.

56. Kenneth Boulding, "The City as an Element in the International System," *Daedalus,* 97 (1968), 1111–1123.

57. Ralph Thomlinson, *Demographic Problems* (Belmont, Calif.: Dickenson Publishing Company, 1967), p. 112.

58. Andreas Faludi, *A Reader in Planning Theory* (New York: Pergamon Press, 1973), p. 1.

59. See James Coleman, *Equal Educational Opportunity* (Washington: U.S. Government Printing Office, 1966); Louis Ferman, *The Negro and Equal Employment Opportunity* (New York: Frederick A. Praeger, 1968); Scott Greer, *Urban Renewal and American Cities* (New York: Bobbs-Merrill, 1965).

60. Greer, *Urban Renewal and American Cities,* p. 3.

61. Ray Northam, *Urban Geography* (New York: John Wiley and Sons, 1975), pp. 395–396.

62. See Gideon Golany, *New Community for Lackawanna County, Pennsylvania* (University Park: The Pennsylvania State University, 1975). For other comprehensive urban planning designs see Paolo Solari, *The Sketchbooks of Paolo Solari* (Cambridge: The Massachusetts Institute of Technology Press, 1971) and Harvey Perloff and Neil Sandberg, *New Towns: Why—and for Whom?* (New York: Frederick A. Praeger, 1973).

63. Mel Ravitz, "The Crisis in Our Cities," in *A City in Racial Crisis,* L. Gordon, ed., (Dubuque, Iowa: Wm. C Brown Publishers, 1971), pp. 152–162.

64. *Report of the National Advisory Commission on Civil Disorders,* pp. 285–286.

SUGGESTED READINGS

Gist, N., and Fava, S. *Urban Society.* New York: Thomas Y. Crowell, 1969.

Gunther, J. *Twelve Cities.* New York: Harper and Row, 1969.

Hauser, P. "Cultural and Personal Obstacles to Economic Development in the Less Developed Areas." *Human Organization,* 18 (1959), 78–84.

Luckingham, B. "The City in the Westward Movement." *The Western Historical Quarterly,* 5 (1974), 295–306.

Meinig, D. *Southwest: Three Peoples in Geographic Change, 1600-1970.* London: Oxford University Press, 1971.

Perloff, H., and Sandberg, N. *New Towns: Why—and for Whom?* New York: Frederick A. Praeger, 1973.

CHAPTER 8

The Economic and Economically Related
Aspects of New Towns in Arid Areas

ALLEN V. KNEESE

A logical opening question is, what, if anything, is unique about new cities in arid areas, that is, about communities that either are totally new or have experienced extremely rapid rates of expansion in the recent past? There seem to be a number of features that, although individually not peculiar to these new cities in arid zones, together characterize them so frequently as to make it appropriate to place such cities in a separate and distinct category for purposes of economic analysis.

In the first place cities in arid areas that possess some major natural advantage, such as a strategic location near or on major trade routes, or fine harbors, or easily developed water resources for irrigation, are typically quite old or, at least, well established. The creation of entirely new cities in an arid area—or the massive expansion of existing ones—is today ordinarily the result of some major discrete development: Gillette, Wyoming, because of coal mining; Page, Arizona, because of the construction of a giant dam; the proposed new town of Burnham, New Mexico, because of energy and agricultural development there; and Eilat, Israel, because of national strategic reasons. Because these cities are the results of such developments, their growth is usually rapid (for economic and/or strategic reasons) and, more often than not, characterized by a sharp peak of activity and, later, a rapid decline. Thus these cities are usually thought of as "boomtowns" and quite frequently are boom-and-bust towns.[1] This situation presents the planner with a wide range of specific and broad economic and financial problems, as well as social problems. Some of these are examined in detail later in this chapter.

Second, because many of the types of development mentioned in the preceding paragraph take place in remote areas with austere landscapes and harsh climates, the creation of a suitable human environment is difficult. Remoteness and problems in filling labor needs result in a tendency to skimp in providing even basic public and private services—housing, public utilities, streets, and education. What might be termed the "environmental public services" are usually not provided at all. These include parks, community centers, adult education extension services, and cable television. However, because of the environmental circumstances of new cities in arid areas, the latter group of services take on unusual importance, and their absence contributes to the many severely adverse social and economic characteristics of these settlements. How to evaluate and arrange for the provision of both the public utility and the environmental types of urban public services at an appropriate level is an important economic question.

Third, almost by definition, a problem facing new cities in arid areas is how to obtain water. It is not true that providing municipal and industrial water in arid areas is always a difficult and costly proposition. Albuquerque, New Mexico, for example, is able to draw water from wells of shallow to moderate depth and provide it at a cost as low as, or lower than, that of municipal water in humid regions. But the location of these additional new cities, as already indicated, makes the frequent recurrence of such a favorable situation unlikely. Thus the result may be recourse to expensive water from deep wells, as in the case of water drawn from the limestone aquifer in Israel; to costly desalinated water, as in Buckeye, Arizona, and Eilat; and sometimes to water that is both costly and poor in quality. A number of questions grow out of such a situation. Should water always be priced at its full cost, or do certain water uses—irrigating trees and lawns, for example—carry with them social (external) benefits that would justify a subsidy? What value is to be placed on improving water quality in terms of the effects on human health and on objects that human beings value such as live plants and water conveyance and processing systems? In Israel and in several other countries as well, these types of questions are further complicated by a national objective of developing agriculture as an economic base for towns in these remote areas.

Fourth, arid environments, despite their rugged appearance, are, incongruously, usually very delicate and sensitive. Plant and animal ecological systems are easily disrupted. The landscape is blemished by any unsightly objects left or constructed on it, and such objects tend to neither hide amidst growing plants nor degrade in a dry climate. Erosion is easy to start and hard to stop. Blowing dust, as well as dust stirred up by traffic, often becomes a major problem when the natural soil cover is removed. In general, arid regions tend to easily fall victim to air pollution. They frequently experience long periods of poor ventilation with very little large-scale air motion—a characteristic associated with aridity. On a smaller scale, because of cold nights, the rapid warming of higher layers of the atmosphere in the morning, and the rapid cooling of the land in the evening, arid regions suffer from frequent atmospheric inversions. Furthermore, plenty of solar energy is available to drive chemical reactions in the atmosphere. As far as pollution supply, so to speak, is concerned, new cities in arid regions are characterized by high rates of emission of atmospheric pollutants per unit of economic activity. There are three reasons for this. First, the economic base of the town often is the extraction and processing of minerals (copper, coal). In these instances the basic economic activities usually generate large amounts of atmospheric emissions (sulfur dioxide,

particulates, trace metals). Second, in the United States, unlike some other countries, the typical urban settlement pattern is a dispersed one based on the automobile as the sole means of transportation. This means a high degree of very energy-inefficient travel, as can be seen when the number of origins departed from and the number of destinations reached are compared, and, hence, high levels of emissions. Third, the new cities are frequently located at high elevations where the atmosphere is thin and engines therefore run inefficiently. The second and third reasons are perhaps of relatively little importance when the development is small and remote, although arid cities of 10,000 to 20,000 persons have been known to experience significant smog from these sources. However, when all the factors indicated are combined, the situation may become very severe. For example, projected near the proposed town of Burnham are a number of new power plants (even though the existing ones are already degrading air quality seriously), several coal gasification facilities (producing 0.25 million cubic feet of gas per day), large additional mining operations, and a new irrigation project covering 110,000 acres. If all this resource-based economic development comes to pass and environmental management is not more successful than has heretofore been typical, the air in the area will resemble a witches' brew of smoke, chemicals, and aerosols. The economics, as well as other aspects, of environmental management acquires a special significance in the development of new cities in an arid zone.

Fifth, many areas in which new towns in arid regions are likely to develop have, for reasons of climate and remote location, been outside the mainstream of modern technological society. Accordingly, they are often the home of at least remnants of traditional cultures, sometimes of ancient origin, within the boundaries of otherwise technologically advanced nations. The Indians of the American Southwest, especially the Navajos and the Pueblos, are good examples. The Bedouins in Israel are a comparable group, as are several peoples in the Soviet Union. Whether new development in their traditional regions is a benefit or a hindrance to such folk is a matter of deeply divided opinion, even within the traditional groups themselves. On the one hand, such groups always have low monetary incomes according to the standards of the mainstream community, and new development can offer financial benefits. On the other hand, industrial development may destroy the traditional society, causing not only a cultural loss but much misery to many members of the old society as well, at least through a long transitional period. A subsidiary problem, but one more pertinent to the topic of this chapter, is how to design a settlement for such people, who may be nomadic, whose community life no doubt differs profoundly from that of the mainstream society, and for whom the pattern of the European or American town may be entirely inappropriate.

If this account of the dimensions of the requisite social–economic analysis of cities in arid areas is correct, then such analysis is a complex matter with many problems of conceptual and empirical estimation that have not yet been solved or, in many cases, even thought about at any length. Instead of trying to address this whole range of issues, the discussion here is focused on several types of pertinent studies being conducted by the Resource Economics Group at the University of New Mexico. These studies are components of the Southwest Region Under Stress project, of which I am director. A general review of the project, given first, attempts to provide a broad analysis of the development–environment conflict in the Southwest (which, for the purposes of the project, consists of the states of Arizona, Colorado, New Mexico, and Utah). This furnishes a context for a fuller discussion of two urban problems being studied by the project: (1) the boomtown phenomenon and the problems of planning and policy formulation it presents, and (2) the relationship of urban form to some environmental problems (especially air pollution) typical of arid-land cities and the policy tools available to influence this urban form.

THE SOUTHWEST STUDY

The problems of interest to the Southwest Region Under Stress study revolve around conflicts between development and environment in a region that is environmentally, ecologically, and culturally delicate. On the one hand, the amenities of the region—clean air, expansive vistas, sunshine, mountain wilderness, and cultural diversity—are a great attraction to people and industry. On the other hand, promiscuous housing and subdivision development and the exploitation of natural resources, especially energy resources, threaten to further degrade and perhaps destroy many of the amenities that are so highly regarded now and that, no doubt, will grow rapidly in value in the years ahead.

In terms of resources, the region is a (and, in some cases, the) major repository for conventional fuels—oil, gas, coal, and uranium, and some proposals for the development of these resources border on the incredible. Only the first units of the Four Corners electric power plant are in operation in the region bearing the same name, but the presence of this unfinished plant and several others in the region hint at what may be in store. The proposed Kaiparowitz plant was not approved by former Interior Secretary Morton on environmental grounds, but the decision is being contested by the utilities. Furthermore, it has been stated that 10 parallel sets of high-voltage lines are needed to carry the produced power to markets, primarily in southern California, if all the plans for coal-based electric power generation are realized. In addition, electrical generation and the exploitation of other energy resources require large-scale expansion of other transportation facilities—highways, pipelines, and railroads. This development could result in the first boom in railroad construction in many years, in addition to the construction of numerous transportation facilities in areas of great natural beauty and ecological delicacy.

For several unconventional energy sources, the region is also clearly the major repository. These include oil shale and geothermal and solar energy. Some of these look very promising already, and the growing stress on the goal of national energy self-sufficiency may lead to their early and rapid development in addition to increased coal gasification and liquefaction. Oil shale represents a vast resource, and some recent statements about its economics and the possibility of *in situ* land recovery have been optimistic. In addition, the Energy Research and Development Administration (ERDA) now views New Mexico as the most likely permanent storage site for its high-level nuclear wastes, which have to be isolated from the biosphere virtually forever.

Although the energy and associated resources of the Southwest are clearly a great asset for the nation and are absolutely basic to any effort to gain energy self-sufficiency, their exploitation carries with it a massive potential for environmental disruption. What could happen to the air, the water, and the landscape is apparent or, at least, can be inferred from what has happened already.

Although not attracting nearly as much attention as energy development, the situation with respect to nonfuel minerals features many parallels. The Southwest is one of the world's most highly mineralized regions. As with energy, we have become heavily dependent on foreign sources for many nonfuel minerals. Any attempt to change this situation or even to stabilize it would have to focus on the abundant but generally low-grade sources remaining in the Southwest. Any such attempts would mean that very large amounts of materials would have to be processed with attendant energy demands, landscape disruption, and environmental pollution.

The indirect effects of such developments may be fully as destructive as the direct ones. The pressure that enlarged populations in remote areas could exert on the natural physical and biological environment through second-home developments, recreation activities involving motorized vehicles, and the use of wilderness areas could be enormous. This is especially so since large, new efforts to develop the land's resources are superimposed on other forces leading to population increase. Nearly all of the new resource developments will occur in remote areas where there is little or no existing capacity to absorb a further increase in population.

The studies that compose the Southwest Project are shown in Figure 1. It is not necessary to go through these components individually: the reader can obtain a reasonably good impression of the project's scope by examining the chart. The Perspectives and Trends project (top) merits some additional discussion, however, because it is the key integrative device for linking the component studies into a regional analysis and gaining information on the economic, demographic, and environmental developments which provide the context for urban growth in the region.

A linear programming model of the fossil fuel industry allows economic and environmental assessment of this industry in its own right, apart from its role as a principal driving force behind regional economic, demographic, and environmental events. A similar model of the copper and molybdenum industry fulfills a corresponding need in that area. Outputs from these industry models, as well as projections for other industries treated with less sophistication, are disseminated throughout the region by means of an economic model (a Leontief–Strout gravity model), a demographic model (a modified Cohort–Survival routine), and environmental models (atmospheric diffusion and water quality models). Any regional constraints such as water availability and environmental regulation are managed through various constraint resolution models. The model is constructed for the state and regional level and for each of 10 planning districts in the Southwest.

The combination of this economic model and the industrial, demographic, and environmental models can yield estimates of the direct and indirect effects of a proposed development on the economy and population of the area where it occurs and on other areas that it affects. In addition, it can project the implications for the water demands, the water quality, and the atmospheric quality of alternative sets of such developments. Scenarios can be run, for example, based on massive developments in San Juan County, New Mexico, or on the Colorado Plateau. This is a basic tool for anticipating urban developments and the environmental and resource circumstances surrounding them.

THE BOOMTOWN PHENOMENON

The Perspectives and Trends model is able to project the economic, population, resource, and environmental consequences of various growth scenarios at a regional or larger level. This provides a context for considering the phenomenon of rapid urban growth in the arid Southwest. For closer examination of the major economic and public policy issues involved, however, it is necessary to examine the nature of the boomtown phenomenon in some detail.

The leading student of the boomtown phenomenon is John S. Gilmore of the Denver Research Institute. He has epitomized the contemporary boomtown phenomenon by describing the hypothetical town of Pistol Shot. His account is so well done and so concise that it is worth quoting at some length.

Pistol Shot is 100 miles from a town of as many as 10,000 or 15,000 people; it is more than 200 miles from a metropolitan area. Thus it has to depend on its own resources and cannot borrow consumer services from other places. Pistol Shot is a county seat in sparsely settled ranching country, although there was some mining in the past. Its population in 1970 was 1200, down from two or three times that number in the mining days.

Suddenly, this has changed. Coal mining started up again in 1973 and the industry will probably continue to grow. Construction began four months ago on the first 700-megawatt unit of an electric power plant. Plans were announced last year for a $900 million coal gasification plant, but the starting date for construction has already been postponed twice. Confusion about the future as well as about dealing with present growth problems is widespread. It is the same sort of confusion that exists in the Powder River Basin, the Four Corners, central Utah, northwest Colorado, western North Dakota, and much of the rest of the West. . . .

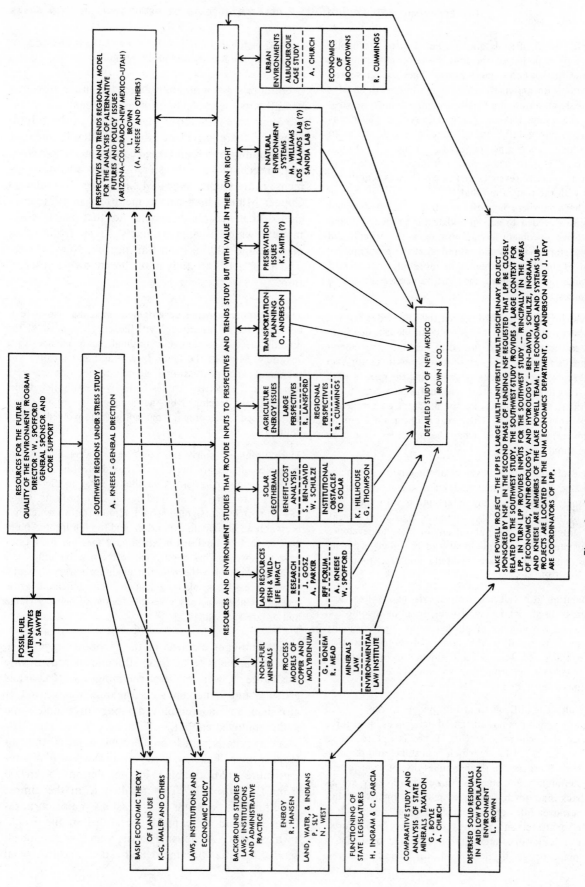

Figure 1. Southwest Regions Under Stress study: project organization.

The local elected officials and a good deal of the public have already experienced the four common phases of attitude toward this boom development. The first phase was enthusiasm, with anticipation of economic growth satisfying a classic ambition of a small, declining country town—keeping the young folks at home. The second phase was uncertainty, particularly among the elected officals, as to what the demands for public services to meet the growth might be. The third phase was near panic over the gap between prospective revenues and prospective expenditures, coupled with the realization that Pistol Shot and its school district have nowhere near the bonding capacity to build the facilities needed to accommodate the growth. Finally, there evolves a problem-solving attitude as the officals and the public start trying to understand what the problems are and how to find help for them. The more information that is available on prospective change, the sooner the fourth phase comes.

Upon realizing that they had neither the knowledge nor the resources to deal with the town's problems, decision-makers in Pistol Shot first turned to the state and federal governments for help. The response was unsatisfactory, so money grants from the industry generating the growth were sought. This led to competition and confusion among town, school district, and county, all the different governmental agencies seeking support. This created uncertainty among the firms, which wondered what the priorities should be and who should set them.

The local officials are ambivalent about land use planning and zoning. Their ranching and landowning constituents are strongly opposed to any intervention with their sole control of their property. State planning legislation is weak (a safe statement to make about any of these undeveloped western states). Many of the local leaders—in government, business, and banking—are wishfully doubtful about the continuity of Pistol Shot's boom. . . .

As population grows at boom rates, existing local services fall short of need. School classrooms, retailing inventories, housing, and the number of physicians in the community do not grow as rapidly as the number of people increases. Many people's recreational requirements are not satisfied by the available opportunities. The quality of life in the community is degraded.

As a result, it is difficult to attract people to this isolated community which has no substantial indigenous labor force to service the economic growth. There is apt to be an inadequate supply of labor, which is unstable and dissatisfied at best. Workers and their families do not want to stay in the community and some of those who do stay are pirated back and forth among employers. Industrial employee turnover rates and absenteeism go up rapidly. It is difficult to attract and retain a satisfactory work force, whether it is a work force for building and operating a power plant or gasification plant, for operating a res-

taurant, or for maintaining the county's roads and bridges. Industrial productivity and profits drop.[2]

Gilmore's account summarizes the situation which has afflicted several boomtowns in recent years and threatens to characterize many others in the future. However, there is evidence that rapid development of a community based on large-scale resources development need not be a disaster. A study of a development near Cuba, New Mexico, the Nacimiento Copper Mine, which began operations in 1971, concluded that it was beneficial to that small community, which is approximately 60 mi from Albuquerque and 100 mi from Farmington, New Mexico. The authors of the study make the following observation:

The Nacimiento Mine development in Cuba had a textbook quality of orderliness with benefits for most of the directly affected parties and minimal inconvenience for a very few. Most of the labor force was hired locally. The technical and professional people who came in were capable and effective. An aesthetically pleasing new housing area was developed by the company in response to a critical need. The company has not gotten involved in local politics.

The community spirit and cohesiveness were high. Good examples of this are the Checkerboard Health Clinic and the new swimming pool.[3] A number of local people worked very hard to help obtain funding for both projects. Cuba has supported a farsighted school administration which has been able to anticipate expansion, and to plan for and build new up-to-date facilities in an orderly fashion. Businesses have prospered. This is reflected in the new buildings and facades which give the new thoroughfare a very dynamic appearance. It is also evident in the increased gross receipts. Cuba generally gives the feeling of being a viable and progressive village.[4]

A significant element in the favorable experience of Cuba appears to be that, although its growth rate was large, it was not overwhelmingly so. Cuba has grown about 55 percent since the mine was started. It also had an underemployed labor force and some underemployed capital.

A frequently cited contrasting case is that of Rocksprings. This small city in southwestern Wyoming more than doubled its population to 26,000 from 1970 to 1974. This resulted from the almost simultaneous decisions of at least six major corporations to build or expand operations in the Rocksprings area. A housing crisis quickly developed, service facilities became overcrowded, and the social

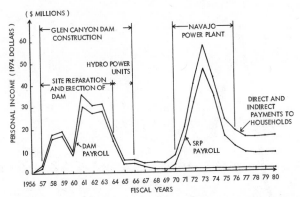

Figure 2. Page, Arizona, area personal income, FY 1956–FY 1980 (projected).

fabric began to unravel, as indicated by increased prostitution and alcoholism. The city was unable to cope with the explosive growth, and the service facilities were expanded only after the system was in chaos. This was a true "Pistol Shot" situation.

There are many and complex differences between Cuba and Rocksprings. The examples do suggest, however, that there are some upper limits of growth beyond which a given community cannot cope.[5]

A still different case is represented by the economy of the town of Page, Arizona. Data collected and projections made by the Resource Economics Group at the University of New Mexico (in a project directed by Professor William Schulze) are summarized in Figures 2 through 5 and Table 1. The income data are derived from known payrolls, as well

as from a survey of recreation expenditures and an input–output model constructed for the Page area economy. Such models have not previously been available for boomtowns, and they should prove valuable for anticipating incomes, expenditures, and tax receipts. A study is now being prepared by the Resource Economics Group of a possible new town at the site of the proposed Kaiparowitz power plant. The situation there is sufficiently similar to that of Page for the same interrelations to be applicable.

Page has had two booms and two busts in the past 20 years. The first boom occurred during the construction of Glen Canyon Dam, and the second during the construction of the Navajo power plant. The population of Page, a new town, went from 0 in 1956 to about 6000 in 1961. It dropped back to about 2000 by the late 1960s and peaked at about 8000 in 1973. The projected stable population, based primarily on the level of recreational activity at the reservoir, is about 4000.

Page had many of the same problems as other boomtowns, but these were mitigated somewhat by two factors. First, it was built and operated by the U.S. Bureau of Reclamation. Accordingly, it was possible to plan for boomtown conditions somewhat more effectively than is typical in most such cases; and, perhaps more importantly, money for public services was both more abundant and more readily available in a timely fashion than is typical. When private development is the source of the boom, not only do tax receipts lag behind needed expenditures,

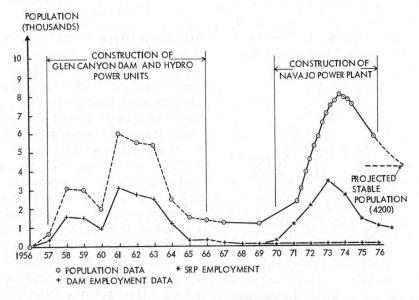

Figure 3. Page, Arizona, area population, 1957–1976.

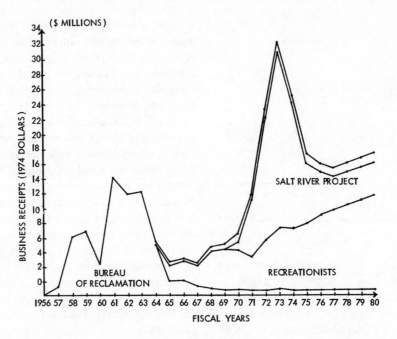

Figure 4. Page, Arizona, area business receipts by incidence, FY 1956–FY 1980 (projected).

but also it often happens that the tax producing developments occur in one political jurisdiction and the impacts of population growth are felt heavily in others.

Second, especially after Glen Canyon Reservoir (Lake Powell) filled, the Page area was in some ways a rather attractive place to live. This contrasts with other arid rapid-development areas such as the Feather River Basin in Wyoming, which is harsh and uninviting. The Page area is scenic; and, once Lake Powell filled, it became a major recreational resource, aided by the fact that the climate is reasonably comfortable. As is frequently the case,

the brunt of the boomtown hardships fell on the women, who had to tolerate skimpy housing and low levels of urban services and amenities. Thus, despite its relatively favorable circumstances, the appearance of Page and its living conditions are sufficiently raw that a recent national television program was able to portray it as an urban horror story. This fact says volumes about the conditions in less favored boomtowns.

THE BOOMTOWN PUBLIC INVESTMENT PROBLEM

Gilmore correctly pointed out that one of the major problems facing boomtowns is uncertainty about the future. But even if it proved possible to develop a regional model and local-area models in the arid Southwest that could yield perfect forecasts, some difficult questions would still remain for economic analysis and policy to answer. In actuality, such models only begin to establish the framework for the real economic decision-making analysis that must take place. One such analysis must help to determine the rate of investment in social infrastructure. Cummings and Mehr of the Resource Economics Group at the University of New Mexico are working on this problem.[6] This section further explains the problem and their approach to it.

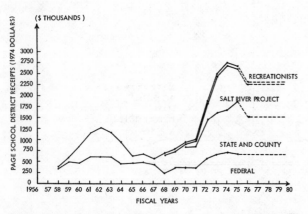

Figure 5. Page, Arizona, school district funding by incidence, FY 1956–FY 1980 (projected).

Table 1   Page, Arizona, Area Personal Income by Incidence, 1973 (Actual) and 1978 (Projected)

Incidence	Personal Income	Percent of Total
1973		
Salt River Project	52,049,000	90.7
Recreation[a]	2,591,000	4.5
U.S. Bureau of Reclamation	1,720,000	3.0
Other federal	421,000	0.7
State/county	582,000	1.0
Total	57,363,000	100.0
1978		
Salt River Project	9,757,000	61.7
Recreation[a]	3,524,000	22.3
U.S. Bureau of Reclamation	1,556,000	9.9
Other federal	450,000	2.8
State/county	516,000	3.3
Total	15,804,000	100.0

[a] Includes National Park Service.

In connection with a development like Page's or even a single boom development, a question that any planner—whether a company town planner, a U.S. Bureau of Reclamation planner, a state planner, or a municipal planner—has to face involves the optimal timing for and the amount of investment under these circumstances. One possible standard can be obtained by saying that at all times the level of public services must be maintained at some expected norm, regardless of the movement of employment, population, income, and so forth. Such a standard is a possibility, but it means that during the times when population and income are not at their peak, there will be excess capacity, and it may not be desirable to invest and have so much excess capacity. It may be optimal, rather, to accept some deterioration in the provision of public services as the area expands. The dimensions of this problem become clearer when we recall that the peak population of Page was twice that of the expected stable population. In principle, then, this is an optimum control theory. The research group hopes to actually perform a dynamic optimization of a problem of this nature, but two problems are encountered before any such powerful methodology or even a less sophisticated one is applied.

The first problem deals with identifying a criterion for a normal level of public services. There are no universally accepted standards for what a community should provide for its citizens in the way of trans-portation facilities, educational opportunities, recreational areas, and so on. The people working on this study decided that they would adopt, as a norm, the average level of public services of like nature presently provided by municipalities in the region. This appears to be a plausible approach.

The second problem that underlies the quantitative analysis of the investment problem is that, if a given community does not meet the particular public service norm in question, it will be necessary for employers in that community to pay higher wages. In other words, if a community provides little in the way of recreation services, it will be necessary to pay the worker more in order to induce him to work in that community. The extra payment is taken as a quantitative measure of the loss in well-being imposed on the worker and his family by the deficient level of public services. In a benefit–cost analysis of investment in social infrastructure, this loss (the increased wage bill) can be compared with the cost of making such investments.

Having made those assumptions, the research team gathered data concerning the capital investments that had been made in a number of different types of public services in municipalities scattered throughout the region, emphasizing the *per capita* levels of investment for education, public safety, water, sewage, and recreational facilities. They then used a multiple regression analysis to attempt to quantify the relationship between any departures from *per capita* investment and the wage levels paid in the particular communities. Some highly preliminary, but illustrative, results of this analysis will be presented shortly, but first it will be useful to review the salient decision-making process in a little more detail.

Figure 6 is what is sometimes called a "decision tree," and it lays out well the type of decisions that have to be confronted by a community that is facing a large increase in its population or by a new community where new investments have to be made. Following the chart's flow, one sees that the input is the increased population and that population is compared to the goals, that is, the norms derived from the average practice in all the communities of the region. Whether or not the norms are met for the new population depends on the existing capital stocks (which may be nonexistent in a purely new-town situation): if these capital stocks are sufficient to meet the goals, the decision tree indicates "yes," and that is the end of the line—no problem; if they are not sufficient to meet the goals, the decision-making process becomes more complicated. Then the ques-

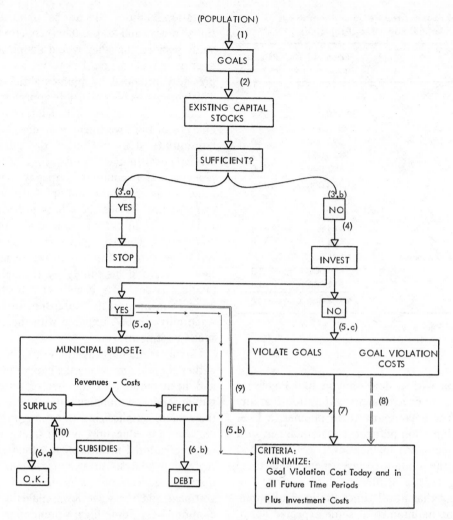

Figure 6.   Investment strategy flowchart.

tion is, Should one invest in additional facilities? If the answer is "no," then, by the nature of what has been established already in the decision tree, the goals will not be achieved. Then this violation of the norms must be evaluated in terms of the criterion which dictates minimization of the sum of the investment and goal-violation costs today and in all future time periods discounted to the present. To quantify these latter costs, one must, as already indicated, engage in some sort of analysis. In the Cummings–Mehr analysis, this cost is translated as the premium in wages that must be paid to get people to tolerate the violation of goals to some particular specified degree. If, on the basis of a comparison of goal-violation costs and investment costs, the decision is made to increase investment, one turns to the middle branch of Figure 6, where the various considerations concerning municipal budgets come into play. If the

revenues are not equal to the costs in some timely fashion, there is a deficit; if there is a deficit, either a debt or an external source of funds must be created.

Figure 6 is a schematic depiction of the types of decisions that have to be made in order to determine the optimal level of public services. This figure also shows where the Cummings–Mehr analysis of goal-violation costs is applicable.

Table 2 presents some very tentative estimates of these violation costs, determined by the regression runs. The figures are in terms of the costs per family for each dollar that boomtown stocks (*per capita*) are below the norm. The table indicates, for example, that, if in a contemplated boomtown situation the stocks (*per capita*) of educational capital are $1 less than the norm, the average weekly wage per family must be 20 cents higher. These are preliminary runs based on the available data: they are not to be taken

Table 2 Goal-Violation Costs for Capital Items Implied by Regression Results
(approximate *per capita* costs for each dollar by which *per capita* boomtown stocks
are less than those in base town)

Capital Item	For Small Towns	All Towns
Total capital	$0.10	$0.05
Education	0.20	$0.20 - \$0.001 \text{ (difference)}^2$
Public safety	$0.02 - \$0.01 \text{ (difference)}^2$	0.17
Water/sewage	$0.10 - 0.01 \text{ (difference)}^2$	$-0.23 + 0.001 \text{ (difference)}^2$
Recreation	$0.10 - 0.01 \text{ (difference)}^2$	$-0.05 + 0.01 \text{ (difference)}^2$
All other	$-0.12 + 0.004 \text{ (difference)}^2$	$0.15 - 0.001 \text{ (difference)}^2$

too seriously; they could be wrong. But, if they are right, they suggest that there could be an enormous return on investments in communities that are below the norm in services provided.

Research is continuing on the question of optimal investment in boomtown situations. Estimates of goal-violation costs are being improved, the theoretical aspects of the problem are being examined, and the pieces in the decision-making process are being fitted together. It is hoped that, along with the other regional and area economic models discussed earlier, this will be a useful economic tool for coping with any boomtown situations that occur in the arid Southwest and elsewhere in the future.

OTHER PROBLEMS

Many other thorny conceptual and empirical economic problems are associated with boomtown situations. Their exact nature will no doubt be considerably affected by the institutional setting within which the boomtown occurs. There are at least three types of settings that may exist: the town may be a private or a government "company town"; the town may be planned and constructed by a private, noncompany developer; or the town may just grow with scattered property ownership. The worst, and most frequent, case appears to be the last—Pistol Shot. The second, however, is often problematic. A private noncompany developer would, if the usual economic incentives operated, seek to maximize his own profit, and this would mean providing an economically attractive (less costly) community, ordinarily composed of manufactured housing, out in the raw countryside. The social and economic aspects of the situation that might lead to low productivity in company operations would not con-

cern him. A company town would internalize these external effects, and this should result in a more efficient operation. However, this case is complicated by the fact that a company town contains elements of both monopoly and monopsony. Whether their adverse effects would outweigh the advantages of the internalization of externalities is an open question. The area of boomtown economics is just now being explored, and there are many open questions. However, we can offer some suggestions concerning policy, based on our interpretation of what is now known.

POLICY SUGGESTIONS FOR BOOMTOWNS

The arid regions of the United States may see the development of many boomtowns as a result of rapid energy and other mineral developments. Research and logic tell us that such towns are frequently undesirable, if not disastrous, places in which to live and that their existence is of little or no benefit to the regional community at large. The following paragraphs review the main elements of the situation and outline some things that can be done.

First of all, the need for basic public services—sewers, roads, utility lines, school facilities—arises, except in unusual situations like Page, before the public funding available at the local level is even remotely adequate to provide for them. In addition, little or no advance planning normally occurs. "Front-end" money and advance planning, using the economic tools and data now being developed, are needed to cope with this situation.

Second, what we have called the public environmental services are frequently even more neglected. As a result, boomtowns are usually dreadful in appearance, and urban recreational opportunities outside the home are virtually nonexistent. A suitable urban environment requires landscaping, parks, playgrounds, and community centers. The statistical analysis reported earlier, preliminary though it is, suggests that large premiums in the form of increased wages must be paid to compensate for the absence of these types of services, perhaps much larger than would be required to improve or provide them. Doing so, of course, would also require planning and timely money.

Third, the worst quality of life is usually experienced by the women in boomtowns. They ordinarily must live in physically confining mobile homes, the upkeep of which does not occupy much of their time. They suffer most from the poor utilities and amenities in such towns. In addition, these towns, since they are economically based on a heavy extractive industry or construction, usually provide very few opportunities for women to work outside the home. A boomtown is a single-industry town whose economic activity is usually directed from a distant location and so provides few local white collar jobs. It is possible to improve this situation. A systematic effort could be mounted to identify employment opportunities in the form of work that could be done at home. In addition, use could be made of the extension activities of universities to provide continuing educational opportunities. Even something as prosaic as the mandatory provision of cable television could be very useful. But, once again, providing such things in a timely manner requires planned collective action.

Finally, the indigenous labor force in the Rocky Mountain States, more often than not Indians, is usually lacking in the training which would qualify its members for the types of jobs that become available. Therefore they either do not participate at all in the benefits that the economic development would otherwise offer or are consigned to the most menial types of work. The experience of Cuba, New Mexico, described earlier, suggests that this need not happen, however, if appropriate skills can be developed in advance and a suitable arrangement can be made with industry. A systematic and timely program of manpower training can accomplish two important things: it can make better use of indigenous populations, thereby necessitating less movement into the area, and it can therefore help some of the most economically disadvantaged parts of our population.

Clearly, then, mitigating the bad effects of boomtown development is dependent on advanced planning based on improved means of regional and area economic forecasting and investment planning;

proper institutional arrangements for the implementation of such plans; and—certainly not least important—a large amount of front-end money. These are the essential ingredients which have been lacking in virtually every boomtown development in the nation's history. The federal government, in cooperation with the states, must take a leading role in dealing with this situation. It appears to be beyond the means—or at least beyond the will—of the states to deal with the situation by themselves or to successfully impose the full responsibility on the industries exploiting the resources and thereby causing the problems. Moreover, federal involvement is appropriate because the costs and benefits of the developments that give rise to boomtowns usually extend beyond the region or even the state in which they occur.

Consequently, I would propose that, as part of the nation's energy policy, which contemplates such heavy use of the Southwest's resources, the federal government take the lead in addressing the boomtown problem. It could do this by making loans available to the states at moderate interest rates, thereby providing the front-end money required where large natural resource developments that will give rise to a boom situation are contemplated. These loans could be used to provide for funding for the development of improved planning methods, for basic public services, for environmental public services, for useful and satisfying activities for women and young people, and for manpower training. Under present capital market conditions, it appears that the federal government would have to provide the loans directly rather than guaranteeing loans made by private sources. The loan would be repaid in two ways. First, the money for the basic public services—the schools, the public utilities, the electric lines, and the sewers—would be repaid from levies or normal taxes charged the people using these public services. Second, where the life of the capital was long relative to the period of the boom, part of the loan for environmental services, for establishing activities for women, and for manpower training would be repaid by severance-type levies on the extracted mineral. This not only would provide a method for repaying the loan but also would do so in a manner whereby at least some of the social costs of the extraction would be reflected in the private costs of the development companies and then in product prices.

The first element in a strategy to mitigate the ill effects of boomtown development would, then, be the provision by the federal government of repayable front-end money for specified purposes. The second element would be the planning of livable communities and the implementing of such plans. The actual process of planning for basic public services and environmental public services, although a challenging task, should be quite manageable, especially as planning methodology is further developed through research. Some capabilities already exist in state planning departments and in the planning department of the Navajo nation, and they could probably be augmented very readily if money were available and a serious intention to implement plans were evident. In making such plans, the location of the town as well as its character should be considered. It might be possible to situate a town in such a way that it could serve mining operations at several deposits sequentially, thus extending its life and making capital investments in it more worthwhile. The more sociological aspects of planning (e.g., coping with the plight of women in these communities) are more subtle, but, as I have indicated, it is not too difficult to think of promising possibilities. Experience suggests that the most difficult thing would be seeing that the plans were actually implemented. Indeed, successful implementation of urban planning in the United States is a rare event. Here, again, the federal government would be in a position to play a leading role by imposing requirements on the states that every public or private development in areas designated as boomtowns (rapid-growth areas) would have to proceed in accordance with the plan for it or else the state would become ineligible for the federally provided front-end money.

A program of the sort sketched briefly here could make the boomtown at least tolerable. To a large extent, it could prevent the unhappiness, alcoholism, high divorce rates, and low productivity characteristic of such situations—insofar, of course, as these problems are caused by the living conditions. In addition to the mitigation of adverse effects, some positive effects could accrue from the program, especially in the areas of education and manpower training.

Finally, where it was extremely difficult and costly to establish a decent community close to the operation, and where both boom and bust were likely to take place within a relatively short time, it might be better not to try to establish a community at all. In such cases, it would probably be preferable to provide barracks for the workmen, with long work days while they are on the job and extended periods of time off at home. A ferrying service, using buses where distances were not great or an aircraft shuttle where they were, would be a necessary part of such an approach. Except where clearly inappropriate, this alternative should always be considered in planning. Benefit–cost analysis would be very helpful in determining the desirability of this option.

SOCIAL COSTS AND URBAN FORM

So far the focus has been on relatively small boomtowns. If, however, one regards cities that have multiplied in size in the last few decades as "new towns," nearly all the major cities in the arid Southwest can be classified as such. Denver, Phoenix, Tucson, and Albuquerque are prime examples. One characteristic that all these towns have in common is that they have exhibited not only rapid growth but also urban sprawl, of which they are probably the outstanding examples in the United States. There are, no doubt, many reasons for this, among them the ready availability of very cheap land and inexpensive fuel for automobiles. In addition, a number of public policies may have contributed significantly to the sprawl. The tax assessment of undeveloped land at very low rates has made holding such land for speculative purposes relatively inexpensive and development of it relatively costly. Public utility pricing practices which establish base rates on the average rather than on the marginal costs of service have also contributed to this sprawl, especially in service areas characterized by substantial differences in elevation. In Albuquerque, for example, the elevation difference between public utility customers may be more than 1000 ft. Clearly, providing water to the higher elevations is much more costly than bringing it to the lower ones. Roads to outlying developments, which are usually provided by the public rather than the developer, have also contributed, and zoning practices have not been effective in shaping urban form in a planned manner.

One may hypothesize that the way in which urban form has developed in these arid regions has entailed substantial social costs, which are not borne by either the developers or the residents of the scattered new developments. Some of these social costs are higher in arid regions than in more humid ones. Certainly the costs of providing public utility and transportation services are much higher for a dispersed than for a compact city. Furthermore, a large amount of travel is needed relative to the number of origins departed from and the number of destinations reached.

This, in addition to the fact that many of these cities are at high elevations, where engines tend not to run efficiently, and the fact that they have a higher than usual number of old and often poorly maintained cars, means that emissions to the atmosphere are abnormally high *per capita*. As indicated at the beginning of this chapter, atmospheric assimilative capacity is at the same time low. Moreover, since many miles of roads must be provided, they are often not constructed and paved in the best way. In an arid area this means there will be dust from both traffic and wind in the air. This particulate matter is one of the most important atmospheric pollutants in arid areas.

It should also be noted that the "open spaces" left by scattered development are not beneficial in arid areas. As a sidelight, it is interesting to note that planners, city councilmen, and others who for the most part grew up in humid environments continue to stress the need for open space in the cities of the Southwest. Unfortunately, desert and steppe vegetation cannot sustain itself well in urban environments because the assault of trucks, cars, motorcycles, and even pedestrians is deadly. What remains is not an attractive open space but, rather, a repository for newspapers, napkins, paper cups, and plastic objects—all the flotsam and jetsam of a throw-away society. This vacant land is the main factor contributing to the raw and perpetually unfinished appearance of the cities in the arid Southwest.

A project under the leadership of Professor Albert Church of the Resource Economics Group at the University of New Mexico is investigating the relationship between local government policies, such as those indicated above, and urban form and the resultant impact on social costs of various kinds in arid regions. The aspect presently under study is air pollution. Ambient standards of air quality cannot be met and/or maintained in most large and rapidly growing municipalities in the arid regions of the United States just by imposing emissions controls. To evaluate the ability of local governments to plan for pollution abatement and to try to understand the extent to which local government policy tools can be used to achieve this end, a land use simulation model is being designed and data are being collected for it. Albuquerque, New Mexico, is being used as a case area.

The first stage of the Albuquerque case study is now partially complete. The purposes of this effort are to create quantitative indicators of the sensitivity of land use patterns to policy alternatives available to local governments and to identify the emissions and environmental quality indicators associated with various land use patterns. This simulation model is a prerequisite to the second stage of the project, which is the playing out of alternative 30 year development scenarios. These projections are designed to provide comparisons of the possible effects of alternative policy packages on environmental quality over a 30 year span. Such scenarios are expected to provide insights into the impact of urban form on environmental quality which have not before been possible.

Land Use–Environmental Quality Simulator. The Land Use–Environmental Quality Simulator consists of a set of linkages that are used to estimate the effects of policy tools on the operation of land, housing, and dependent commercial structure markets; the impact of these markets on land use patterns; and, finally, the kinds and quantities of emissions that are engendered by various land uses. These linkages are summarized in Figure 7. The sequence of policy-initiated effects begins with exogenously determined instruments which can be used by local governments. These are zoning, the timing and location of utility systems and transportation networks, user charges for these services, and property tax rates. In the model, physical site characteristics affect the land and construction markets, as do the governmental policies just listed. The pertinent physical attributes include distances to employment and shopping centers, as well as the suitability of slope, soils, and water table for building, using septic tanks, and developing independent water supply systems.

Land prices and new construction are specified recursively. It is assumed that all vacant land is held or transferred solely for investment motives until it is developed. The development of vacant land is constrained by its zoning classification, but other policy variables also affect choice through market or hedonic index prices. An econometric model has been designed to determine the prices of land parcels zoned for single-family, multifamily, and mobile home use, as well as for commercial uses serving the local population (dependent commercial land) as they are affected by government policies and site attributes. Changes in housing stock and dependent commercial employment are determined in the model by the availability and price of the land zoned for each purpose, as well as directly by the policy variables and exogenous site characteristics already described. This particular sequence presupposes that

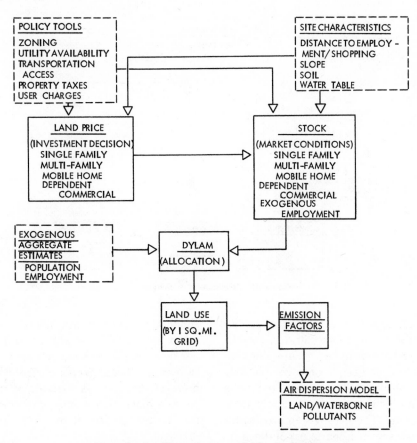

Figure 7. Land Use—Environmental Quality Simulator.

developers and consumers of housing are price takers with respect to land prices. It also assumes that the demand for housing and dependent commercial structures is satisfied within each time increment specified by the simulator.

After a simulation of land use and intensity is available, the next step is to estimate residual discharges for each square mile grid. The residuals included are carbon monoxide and particulates emitted into the air, as well as waterborne and solid residuals. Emission figures are based on the available published and unpublished literature, adapted to the outputs of the simulation model. The spatial distribution of trip origins and destinations is noted in order to estimate automobile exhaust emissions for zones that act as transportation corridors. Total residuals (in mg/liter and lb/year) are estimated for storm water discharges and solid wastes generated in each zone. In the case of atmospheric emissions, a simple air dispersion model is used to estimate emission concentrations and air quality in each zone, given the exogenous parameters of wind direction and speed, air turbulence, and mixing heights.

Alternative Development Scenarios. Once the pieces of the Land Use–Environmental Quality Simulator are estimated, are assembled, and are functioning together, the model will be employed to project alternative development scenarios. The first possibility is designed so that land use changes will enhance air quality, since air pollution is one of Albuquerque's problems and is likely to be most sensitive to land use changes. Existing and potential "hot spot" concentrations of carbon monoxide will be identified to the extent possible, since this city, like many others, maintains only a handful of air quality sampling locations. Adjacent and upwind land uses will then be modified over the 30 year simulation period so as to reduce sources of emissions contributing to these concentrations. A feasible policy package to achieve this end will be simulated in order to see the amount of equilibrium and other effects of these specific policies. The general equilibrium model will be reapplied until the population and employment control totals are accommodated. Once the simulations are consistent from this standpoint, emission criteria will be applied to each grid square,

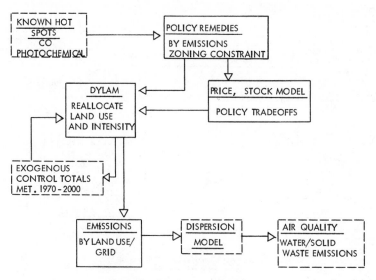

Figure 8. Development scenarios.

dispersion simulated, and final atmospheric quality estimated. Calculated residual concentrations in the atmosphere are expected not to be "accurate" on an absolute scale, but only indicative on a comparative scale. Thus these results will be compared to a "trend" scenario in which no policy alterations from the 1970 ones are made. The step-by-step process for simulating the "hot spot" scenario is outlined in Figure 8. Several other possible scenarios involving major land use changes are envisioned. These include simulating the effects of a limited-access circumferential highway and the right-of-way acquisition or easement that for several years has been planned for it, and those of a narrow east–west strip city orientation featuring alternating intensive and open land use and two satellite cities.

CONCLUSION

The economic study of new towns in arid areas is just getting under way, motivated largely by the existence of boomtown situations concentrated in these regions, the special environmental problems that seem unwilling to yield to traditional engineering solutions, and the need to take a new look at settlement policies. Accordingly, the literature is thin, a fact that is reflected in this chapter. Nevertheless, an attempt has been made here to indicate some special

economic and economically related features of developing new towns in arid areas and to give at least a sampling of the research now in progress with respect to them. We can afford to be optimistic, however, because, as a result of this research, in 5 years a much richer and more complete chapter on this subject can be written.

NOTES

1. This phenomenon has happened often and for a variety of reasons, especially in the United States. What is new is the widespread notion that human and environmental costs are so large that this phenomenon should no longer be permitted to happen in the free-wheeling manner of the past but should be the objective of analysis and management.

2. John S. Gilmore, "Boomtowns May Hinder Energy Resource Development," *Science,* February 13, 1976, p. 535. Copyright 1976 by The American Association for the Advancement of Science.

3. The Navajo Indian Reservation extends nearly to Cuba but is not continuous. Rather, in this area, Indian lands are interspersed with non-Indian lands. Hence the area is called "The Checkerboard."

4. Berry Ives and Clyde Eastman, *Impact of Mining Development on an Isolated Rural Community,* New Mexico State University Agricultural Experiment Station Report No. 301 (Las Cruces: New Mexico State University, August 1975).

5. Gilmore puts the limit at 15 percent annually, but, in view of the complexity of the factors that may come into play in the different cases outlined here, the limit must be quite variable depending on the circumstances.

6. Ronald G. Cummings and Arthur F. Mehr, "Municipal Investments for Social Infrastructure in Boomtowns," *Natural Resource Journal,* in press.

Designing Life-Support Systems 4

CHAPTER 9

Planning Heating, Ventilating, and Air-Conditioning Systems for Structures within an Arid-Region City

STANLEY F. GILMAN

DEFINING THE PROBLEM

The climate of a particular region has considerable impact on the design of a heating, ventilating, and air-conditioning system. Thus it is necessary to define the climate in an arid region. The climate is characterized, first of all, by a high maximum outdoor dry-bulb temperature of 100 to 115°F. In air-conditioning technology, we speak of 115°F as "desert" conditions. Second, this climate is characterized by a high daily dry-bulb temperature range of 25 to 35° from its daytime high to its nighttime low. Thus in arid regions we find very hot days, and—because, as the sun goes down, the arid soil radiates very well and very quickly to the clear sky— cool nights. The third characteristic of this climate is the large amount of sunshine, 80 to 95 percent of the maximum amount possible. Associated with this is a fourth climatic characteristic, low relative humidity, which is more properly expressed as low absolute moisture content, that is, pounds of moisture per pound of dry air. As an example of these climatic characteristics, we can, in the American Society of Heating, Refrigerating, and Air-Conditioning Engineers (ASHRAE) *Handbook of Fundamentals,* look at the data for Tucson, Arizona.[1] There we find a design outdoor dry-bulb temperature of 105°F and

a low corresponding relative humidity of approximately 23 percent (humidity ratio of 0.011 lb of moisture per pound of dry air). Thus there is little moisture in the hot air. A large area of the western United States has this hot, arid climate.

Contrasted to this is a large, heavily populated area of our nation—the South. The typical design dry-bulb temperature of 95°F is significantly lower than the arid-region design temperature range of 100 to 115°F. However, the design wet-bulb temperature range of 78 to 80° is higher. Thus the amount of moisture in the air is substantially greater. For example, at a 95° dry-bulb and 78° wet-bulb temperature, the humidity ratio is 0.019 lb of moisture per pound of dry air, and the relative humidity is nearly 59 percent, almost twice that in typical arid regions. This contrasting area is thus defined as a hot, humid region. Furthermore, the daily dry-bulb temperature range is small—about 20°, as contrasted with 25 to 35° in arid regions. With a daytime high of 95°F, the nighttime low will be 75°F (approximately the desired indoor temperature); hence no nighttime cooling can be accomplished by ventilation. However, a dry-bulb temperature of even 80° is comfortable in arid regions because of the low relative humidity, and, therefore, nighttime cooling is not absolutely necessary.

141

PLANNING FOR THE SITUATION

The planner's object must be to take advantage of the high daily temperature range and the low moisture content in arid regions. Thus the plan should be to keep heat from getting into the building during the day so as not to have uncomfortably high indoor temperatures and then to remove during the cool night whatever heat has entered. There are a number of ways of accomplishing this twofold task.

Shading. First, we should look to shading. Many devices based on rather simple principles are available.

The *ASHRAE Handbook of Fundamentals* includes tables that list the solar altitudes for several times of the day for the 12 months of the year. Solar altitude is the angle between the horizontal and the sun. Looking at these tables for 32°N latitude, at noon at the winter and summer solstices (the yearly extremes), we find that the solar altitudes are 34.6° and 81.5°, respectively. Knowing this, we can take advantage of overhangs and similar shading devices in order to keep the solar energy from entering an interior space through a transparent surface in the summertime, and use the sun as a heat source in the winter, allowing it then, when the sun is low in the sky, to enter the transparent surfaces of the building. Figure 1 illustrates both the summer and the winter orientations.

This principle is further illustrated by both primitive and modern examples. In the settlement of Mesa Verde, Colorado, the Indians located their dwellings under cliffs for summertime shading and still received the winter sun for heating because their southern-facing dwellings were open to the low-altitude winter sun. In present-day Morocco apartment buildings often use semienclosed porches to shade the dwellings located behind them. The designs are fairly complex since the architect is trying to fully control the climatic situation. The Indians in Colorado used what the terrain made available to them and, therefore, did not attain a comparable level of control.

Building Materials. The Morocco designs usually use white building materials since white is a very good reflector of solar energy and also a very good emitter of low-temperature (100°F) infrared energy. Thus, when the surface warms up, it very efficiently radiates long-wave radiation and hence keeps itself cool.

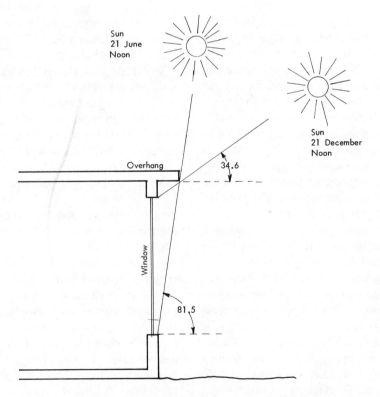

Figure 1.   Design using an overhang to regulate the solar radiation entering a structure (32°N Latitude).

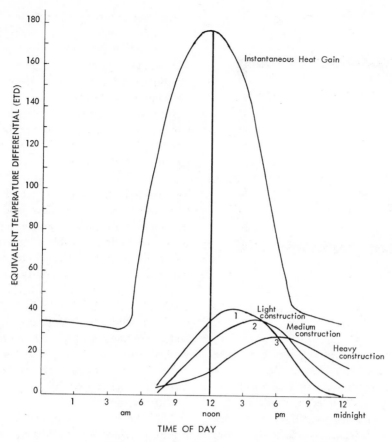

Figure 2. Heat gains in interior when different wall construction materials are used.

In addition to color, we should be concerned with the material *per se,* since we do control the construction of the opaque walls and roofs. In determining what materials to use, we should consider two points: the material's thermal resistance and its thermal capacitance. The former is the ability to resist heat transfer from exterior to interior and can be increased by, for example, adding insulation; the latter is the ability to absorb, store, and then release heat. The thermal capacitance is important because, if it is high, a lot of the heat that strikes the exterior surface may be stored in the wall or roof for a period of time and then, in the cool nights, flow back into the exterior environment without ever having reached the interior.

Thermal capacitance is the specific heat of the material [measured in $Btu/(lb)(°F)$] times its weight in pounds. The specific heat of most building materials is about $0.20\ Btu/(lb)(°F)$, as compared to 1.00 for water. Therefore the thermal capacitance depends largely on the weight. If we are building a wall, the higher the weight per square feet of frontal area, the greater the thermal storage and the lower the heat flow into the interior. Thus a massive wall is ideal for hot, arid climates because much of the heat entering the exterior surface during the day will be temporarily stored and flow back at night without ever getting into the interior. This is the principle, for example, behind the adobe huts in the American Southwest, where thick walls of clay, which has a high mass, were used because of their high thermal capacitance.

Figure 2 shows a typical relationship between instantaneous heat gain (energy striking the building envelope) and the actual heat flow into the interior through a flat roof. We note that for heavy construction materials the peak interior gain is much less than the peak instantaneous heat gain. Also, we note that the former peak occurs several hours later. Thus high thermal capacitance reduces the peak load and also shifts it to a later hour, as can be seen by comparing the curves in Figure 2.

Ventilation. We can also minimize interior heat in arid areas by using a ventilation system that takes advantage of the low outdoor dry-bulb temperatures

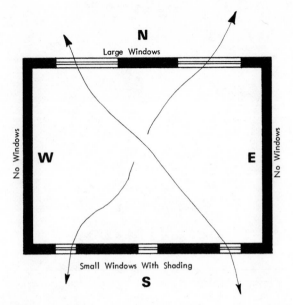

Figure 3. Design for natural ventilation and minimum solar penetration.

which characterize the region at night. We can use natural ventilation or forced ventilation to circulate outside air through the house and cool it down. Then, after the structure has been cooled down during the night, it can be closed up during the day, taking advantage of the thermal capacitance of its walls and roof to maintain the interior temperature within a comfortable range the next day.

Another planning principle is to take advantage of prevailing winds. To do this, an opening, some egress, and an air path connecting them are required. The design depicted in Figure 3 combines natural ventilation with protection from the sun by placing no windows on either east or west walls (where exposure to the sun is the most direct); small, shaded windows on the south wall; and large windows on the north walls, thus creating direct, through-flow ventilation paths.

Evaporative Cooling. If shading, high-thermal-capacitance walls and roofs, and ventilation do not provide comfortable conditions, evaporative cooling is one alternative possible in an arid region, if enough water is available. Evaporative cooling takes advantage of the low humidity ratio and lowers the relatively high dry-bulb temperature by evaporatively cooling air which will then be higher in humidity but lower in dry-bulb temperature. If we take a tank of water equipped with a recirculating pump and spray water into the air, some of the water will evaporate. When it evaporates, heat is taken from the air. Therefore the air cools, and at the same time the moisture content increases.

The skeleton psychometric chart presented in Figure 4 relates dry-bulb temperature and humidity ratio. Figure 4 represents the situation for typical American arid regions with 100° design outdoor dry-

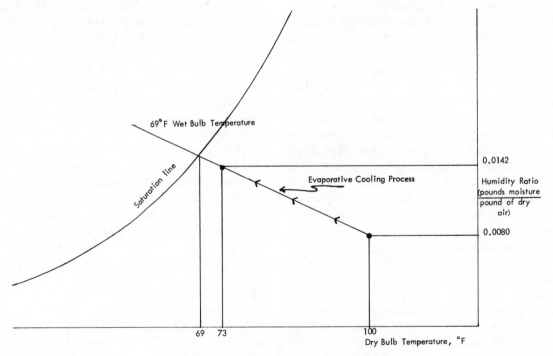

Figure 4.   Evaporative cooling prospects in Arizona.

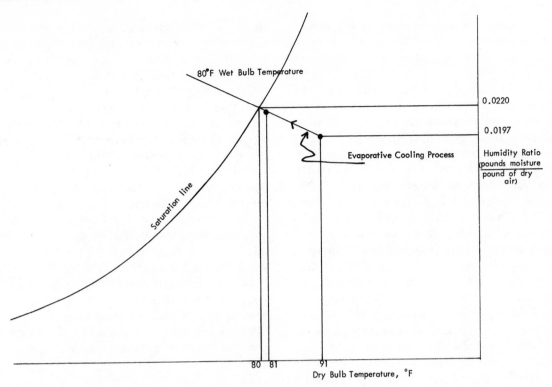

Figure 5.   Evaporative cooling prospects in southern Louisiana.

bulb and 69° wet-bulb themperatures. Evaporative cooling is along the diagonal 69° wet-bulb line. If we move up toward the saturation curve to the point of maximum efficiency (90 percent for most equipment), we will obtain a lower dry-bulb temperature with more humid air. Since the effect of the increased relative humidity here on comfort is small compared to the reduction in dry-bulb temperature, we end up with an acceptable situation—73°F air entering into the structure. This example is, of course, for the hottest part of the day. When the outdoor temperature falls to 80°F, the air leaving the evaporative cooler will be 66°F and hence will very effectively cool the building. Not surprisingly, therefore, we find evaporative coolers, also called "swamp coolers," all over Arizona, New Mexico, northern Texas, and California. In an arid region we can definitely cool a building by taking advantage of evaporative cooling principles.

This method is not nearly as effective in southern Louisiana, for example, where the design dry-bulb temperature is 91° and the wet-bulb temperature is 80°F, since the air is significantly moister to begin with. As Figure 5 reveals, there is very little potential for evaporative cooling, since attempts to evaporatively cool the outdoor air in a humid climate

produce little reduction in the outdoor dry-bulb temperature even at 90 percent saturation efficiency.

There are other matters to consider before choosing an evaporative cooling system. First, when we evaporatively cool a structure, we waste air: we bring in outside air, put it through a saturator, push it into the house, and then emit it therefrom, completely changing the house air. There are advantages to this, but if such waste is undesirable, we may have to resort to electrically driven, mechanical refrigeration systems which recirculate most of the air they use. Second, when we evaporatively cool, we use water. If there is a water shortage, recourse to an air-cooled refrigeration system may again be necessary. Third, when we evaporatively cool, we raise the relative humidity. If high relative humidity is undesirable, for example if we are storing metal parts, rare books, or government documents, or running a pharmaceutical laboratory, we will have to turn to a refrigeration system to avoid rusting or material degradation problems.

Fourth, when we evaporatively cool, we cool inexpensively. Of course, with increased costs usually go increased conditions of comfort. An evaporative cooling system will keep a structure at a comfortable dry-bulb temperature, but there will be a high relative humidity, to the point of possibly having mildew form on the furniture. An air-conditioning system, on the other hand, controls both the temperature and the humidity, giving us 75° temperature and 50 percent relative humidity—more for our money. Finally, when we evaporatively cool, we pump not chilled or hot water, as we do with mechanical or centralized solar energy equipment, but air. Since we could not possibly afford to pump air from place to place, each structure has to be cooled separately. Thus, in New Mexico or Arizona, we see boxes 2 or 3 ft square on top of houses: these are evaporative coolers. They have fans in them which draw in outside air, run it through a filter over which the water trickles, and then pump it into the house. If designed properly, they operate quietly: noise is not a problem. The filter eventually gets saturated with salts, but another can be bought for a few dollars: operating expense is not a problem. The problem, if it is one, is that we are tied to separate units for separate structures. If this is desirable, we have no problem; but if a single system serving many structures is preferred, we will have to turn to a mechanical air-conditioning system.

Mechanical Cooling.   When we mention mechanical cooling, we are referring to a refrigeration system. What we are trying to do when we mechanically cool is to take heat out of an interior and reject it into the atmosphere, which is what a household refrigerator essentially does: it absorbs heat from the food in the cabinet and rejects it into the kitchen, thereby keeping the interior space cool. To do this in a structure, we push air with a fan across a heat exchanger (evaporator) with a liquid refrigerant in it, as Figure 6 shows. The refrigerant circulating through this exchanger is just like a pot of water boiling on the

stove: as the refrigerant boils, it absorbs heat. The liquid refrigerant absorbs heat from the room air because this air is about 75°F and the refrigerant 40°F. The refrigerant boils, vaporizes, travels to an electrically driven compressor, and is then passed through a heat exchanger (condenser) exposed to outside air of (in arid regions) 100°F. The temperature of the gas entering this exchanger is 140°; therefore, when the heat is exchanged, the outside air becomes warmer and the refrigerant cools, condenses, and is returned to the first heat exchanger. Thus heat is removed from the house.

Figure 7 depicts a typical heating, ventilating, and air-conditioning system. The air entering the unit is a mixture of air being returned from the conditioned space and fresh outdoor air required for ventilation. It is then cleaned by the filters. During the cooling season, either chilled water or refrigerant cools and dehumidifies the air, which is then supplied to the space to overcome the external and internal loads and thus maintain the desired space temperature and humidity.

The hot vaporized refrigerant can also be condensed and cooled by water. Typically, the water comes into the system registering 85° from some source and leaves registering 95°. Generally we do not simply dump the 95° water into the sewer; we transfer it to what is called a "cooling tower." In this tower 95° water is sprayed over a large surface area while air is forced through it by large fans. Evaporation occurs, and the 95° water is cooled to 85° and sent back to the water-cooled condenser. The heat is rejected from the cooling tower into the atmosphere, which, as in the air-cooled system, is the final heat sink. Since the only water used in the cooling tower is that which is evaporated into the air, a cooling tower is a "water conservation" device.

Water-cooled units come in all sizes, but the larger the structure, the more likely it is that we will have to depend exclusively on such a system. This poses a problem in a hot, arid region with a definite water scarcity. In such a case we are going to be hard pressed, because (again) with large installations water cooling is essential.

Furthermore, when we use a mechanical refrigeration system, whether air cooled or water cooled, we have to consider energy. It takes energy to operate these devices, and we may be faced with a scarcity of energy or, as in many arid-region countries, prohibitively expensive energy. Therefore, when we elect a mechanical refrigeration system, we should also select the most energy conserving type. For example,

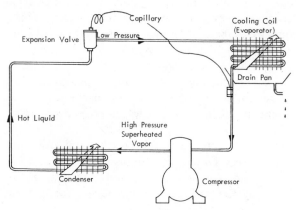

Figure 6.   Refrigeration cycle.

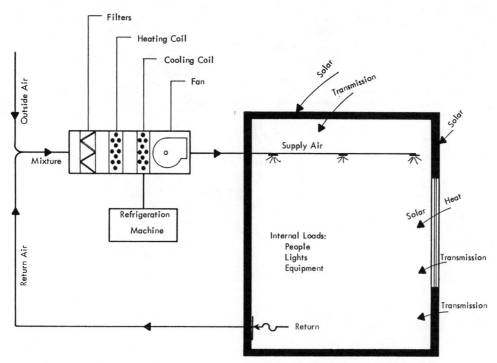

Figure 7. Basic air-conditioning system.

an office building facing north gets a good amount of sun on its south wall in wintertime and no sun on its north. Therefore it is not unusual to find systems supplying heat to the north zone and at the same time (using an air-conditioning system) extracting heat from the south zone and rejecting it into the atmosphere. This may sound silly, but it is a very simple, straightforward way of designing systems. We should try to take the heat that we are removing from the south side and use it on the north side. A heat pump provides a very sound way of doing this.

The heat we have expelled from a structure using a mechanical air-conditioning system—plus the heat equivalent of the energy put into the system by the compressor, which also shows up in the condenser— is rejected into the environment. In the wintertime, we want to heat the structure. If we could reverse this refrigeration cycle, we could take heat from the outdoor air and reject it into the structure. Indeed, we can do this, and again we do it with a heat pump.

An air-to-air heat pump cycle is depicted in Figure 8. The upper diagram illustrates the cooling cycle; it is the same cycle as that depicted in Figure 6. The lower diagram shows the heating cycle. The reversing valve now directs the refrigerant discharged from the compressor to the indoor coil, where it condenses and gives up its heat to the 70°F room air. The heated air is then distributed to the space to over-

come the winter heat loss. Meanwhile, the refrigerant evaporates in the outdoor coil, thus absorbing heat from the outdoor air. This heat, plus the heat equivalent of the electrical power consumed by the compressor, shows up in the indoor coil (condenser) and is delivered to the space to be heated.

Several types of heat pumps are available. One is the water-to-air heat pump. In the cooling cycle, the refrigerant, after leaving the compressor, goes to a water-cooled condenser, where the heat is rejected. The refrigerant cools to 40° in the evaporator and hence cools the air being pushed through a refrigerant-to-air heat exchanger. A person who wants heating simply reverses the flow of refrigerant, and condensing (heat rejection) takes place in the structure to be heated. If we have one system cooling and one heating, taking heat from one area of the structure and putting it into another, we have an ideal energy conservation system.

Another type of heat pump is a water-to-water pump. The principle is illustrated in Figure 9. In the cooling cycle (left portion of the figure), water is pumped through the evaporator (cooler) and circulated to the air-handling unit, where chilled air is distributed. In the heating cycle (right portion of the figure), water warmed by the refrigerant in the condenser is circulated to the air-handling unit so that heated air is distributed to the interior space. As

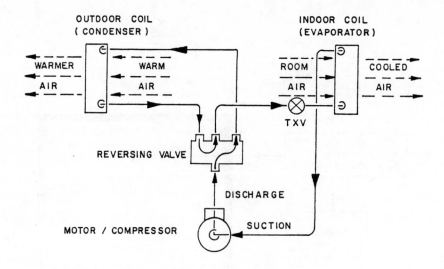

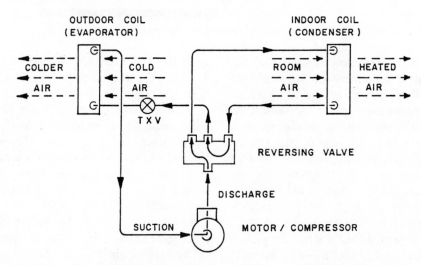

Figure 8. Air-to-air cooling and heat pump system. From "Heat Pumps—What They Are and What They Do," in *Solar Energy Heat Pump Systems for Heating and Cooling Buildings,* Stanley F. Gilman, ed., ERDA Technical Information Center Document, Conference 7506130 (University Park, Pa.: The Pennsylvania State University Press, 1975), p. 5.

we can see, the water circuits, rather than the refrigerant flow, are switched in a water-to-water heat pump. As a consequence, this type is more efficient than a water-to-air heat pump because the evaporator and condenser functions are not switched; that is, the evaporator always performs as an evaporator and the condenser as a condenser.

Heat pump systems save energy because some energy is taken from the environment, whether it be in air or water or some other medium. Air-to-air heat pumps have heating seasonal performance factors of 2 to 2.5, which means they use 40 to 50 percent of the amount of energy consumed by an electric resistance heating system. Much documentation for this exists in the literature and in ARI-certified manufacturers' data.

Another way to cool or heat while conserving energy and minimizing energy costs is to introduce a

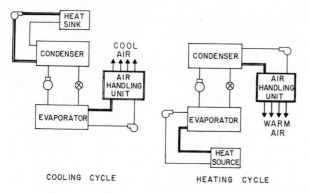

Figure 9. Water-to-water cooling and heat pump system.

storage system and to heat or cool this system at night during nonpeak energy-use hours, when power is not so expensive and is readily available.

Whatever mechanical system we choose, we need not worry excessively about strain on the equipment due to climate, for the hottest, most arid climate is not hard on mechanical equipment. The most severe climate is that on the seacoast, where there is salt spray in the air. Since salt, water, and aluminum do not mix very well, the aluminum fins on cooling coils tend to disappear in time. Rusting is also a problem in seacoast areas. The periodic dust storms in places like Arizona and New Mexico do not pose any particular problem. The extremely high altitude and dry-bulb temperatures require the machines to operate at higher pressures and temperatures, but the penalty here is simply higher operating costs because of the reduced efficiency.

SOLAR HEATING AND COOLING

Since arid regions are characterized by high-intensity sunlight and clear days, we should think in terms of solar energy systems for either heating or cooling, although the technology for solar cooling is not nearly as well developed as that for solar heating. Solar energy is less feasible outside these regions; it is particularly well suited to hot, arid areas.

Solar energy systems are basically of two types. First, there are passive systems which take advantage of natural processes (free convection, e.g.) and use little or no fan power. Second, there are active systems using water pumps, fans, and other devices that require relatively large quantities of mechanical energy.

Passive Systems. An example of a passive system is the Hay system,[2] which is depicted in Figure 10. On top of a metal roof are polyethylene bags filled with water with a black surface underneath them and an insulated roof on top during the summer day. As the sun strikes the roof surface, the interior is kept cool; the heat is being absorbed by the water. At night the roof slides back, and the heat in the water with the black surface beneath it radiates to the clear cold sky. The water thus cools until sunrise, when the roof is replaced and the cool water beneath it is again ready to absorb heat from the rooms and keep them cool.

Conversely, in the winter sliding back the roof allows the daytime solar energy to be absorbed by the water. Then, at night, the roof is slid forward to cover the rooms and provide warm, radiant heat.

A French design of a passive system is depicted in Figure 11.[3] One wall is composed of glass with a high-mass wall behind it. During the day, solar energy is absorbed by the high-mass wall, causing a rise in its surface temperature. This creates a gravity

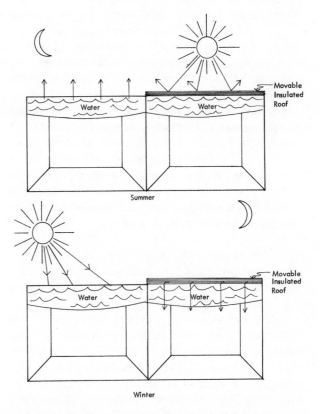

Figure 10. The Hay system. Redrawn from H. R. Hay and J. I. Yellott, "A Naturally Air-Conditioned Building," *Mechanical Engineering*, **92**, no. 1 (1970), 19.

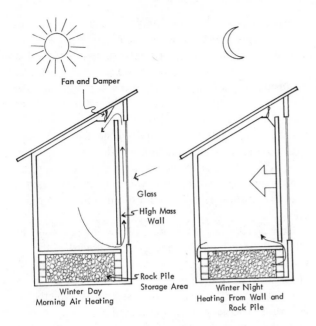

Figure 11. A passive solar heating system by Trombe with storage capacity.

circulation of air that warms the room. When the room becomes comfortably warm, excess thermal energy can be directed to a rock-pile storage area by the small fan and damper. Nighttime heating is from the high-mass wall, which has stored solar energy. If required, additional heat can be obtained from the rock-pile storage area.

Another simple passive system is a solar hot water heater, thousands of which were sold (in Florida primarily) until natural gas became available. The collector and a storage tank are located on the top of a structure. Water circulated through the solar collector–storage tank by using a thermosiphon warms the interior. It is a type of natural circulation; the system does not demand a pump.

Active Systems. The basic types of active solar energy systems are winter heating with air or water, solar-energy-assisted heat pumps, and combined solar heating and cooling.

In the winter heating air system depicted in Figure 12, fans are used to circulate air through the solar collector when solar energy is available for collection.[4] This heated air is then distributed to the conditioned space directly or diverted to a rock storage unit if the space thermostat so dictates. When solar energy is not available, dampers divert the circulating air in a path through the storage bed to extract heat for the space. An auxiliary heating system of the conventional type (gas, oil, electricity) supplies

needed heat when the stored thermal energy is depleted, as will occur, for example, during a long, cloudy period.

The water system for winter heating operates in essentially the same manner with pumps, piping, valves, and heat exchangers handling water instead of air. The air system has the advantage of not freezing up. Freeze protection is needed in most American climates. This is obtained by circulating an antifreeze solution in the collector circuit and exchanging the heat gathered here with the pure water storage and distributing system by use of a heat exchanger.

A solar-energy-assisted heat pump system is depicted in Figure 13. It is a water type, which is usual, and has all of the components mentioned above plus a water-to-water heat pump. Such systems are feasible only if summer cooling is required, for a heat pump would not be used for winter heating only. The system has two basic modes of operation: direct heating and heat pump heating. When the temperature of the water in the storage tank is at a useful level, say above 90°F, the water is diverted to the air-handling unit to supply heat to the interior space. When the storage water is below a useful temperature, for example, 60°F, the heat pump operates and "lifts" the temperature to a useful level, leaving the condenser at approximately 120°F. This hot water is then circulated through the air-handling unit and hence heats the interior space. The system depicted schematically represents an actual solar-energy-assisted heat pump system in Albuquerque, New Mexico, that is being field tested through a U.S. Energy and Development Administration (ERDA) contract with The Pennsylvania State University, of which the author is Principal Investigator.[5]

Combined solar heating and cooling systems are not as advanced as the others described above. The technical problems of solar cooling are much more difficult to overcome than those encountered in solar

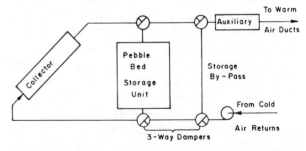

Figure 12. Solar energy heating system. Redrawn from John A. Duffie and William A. Beckman, *Solar Energy Thermal Processes* (New York: Wiley–Interscience, 1974), p. 274.

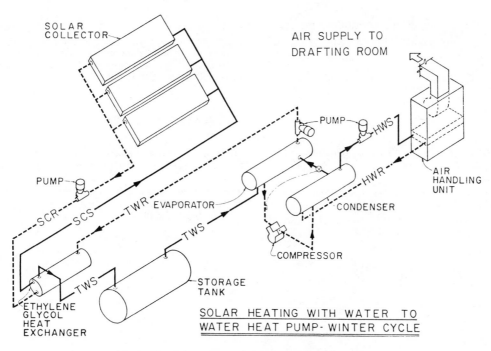

SOLAR COLLECTOR

AIR SUPPLY TO DRAFTING ROOM

PUMP

HWS

PUMP

AIR HANDLING UNIT

SCR SCS TWR EVAPORATOR

HWR

CONDENSER

TWS

COMPRESSOR

TWS

STORAGE TANK

ETHYLENE GLYCOL HEAT EXCHANGER

SOLAR HEATING WITH WATER TO WATER HEAT PUMP-WINTER CYCLE

Figure 13.   Solar-energy-assisted water-to-water heat pump.

heating. The basic reason is that water temperatures of at least 180°F are required to run absorption cooling machines, the only type yet developed. Furthermore, since the efficiency of flat plate, water-type collectors decreases as the water temperature rises, a large collector area is necessary. At about $15/ft² this becomes very expensive, and the amount of time required to recoup the investment by obtaining free energy from the sun is often greater than the life of the system.

Much research remains to be done in the field of solar heating and cooling, and a great variety of projects are currently being sponsored by ERDA. Experience thus far has taught us at least two things. First, if solar energy systems are used, structures will typically face south, giving a community an east–west orientation. Second, it may be better to have a large, central, efficient collector that will supply hot or chilled water to a number of structures. For example, in a community with a school as a central focal point, we could put one solar collector on the roof of the school and feed the gathered energy out to various businesses and homes.

CONCLUSION

We must keep in mind that special weather conditions are characteristic of hot arid areas and try to ex-

ploit these conditions. One approach is to prevent the intense heat from solar radiation from entering a structure by using shading devices, either added to the building or designed as an integral part of it. Another is to take advantage of the thermal capacitance of the opaque building structure. In addition to these measures, natural ventilation can be used effectively under the proper conditions. If mechanical systems are also required, the use of evaporative cooling in arid climates can be effective, if an adequate source of water exists. If water is scarce or unavailable, however, recourse must be made to mechanical systems of the electric-drive type with (probably) air-cooled condensing. Finally, the potential of solar energy for winter heating, and possibly summer cooling, must not be overlooked.

There are of course, economic considerations too. With an evaporative cooling system, a person pays for the water and the pumping and fan power, whereas with a mechanical heating and air-conditioning system costs range anywhere from $600 to $3000/ton of refrigeration. The additional cost of an active solar energy heating (only) system for a 2000 ft² residence can easily be $10,000 or more. A combined solar heating and cooling system may cost $13,000 or more. The Hay system previously described, on the other hand, consists of water in polyethylene bags, a structurally sound roof, and movable insulation panels. It may, therefore, not be prohibitive in cost. These economic considerations must be weighted carefully against the specific needs of each arid-region community and the specific uses to which a given structure will be put.

NOTES

1. See the *ASHRAE Handbook of Fundamentals* (New York: American Society of Heating, Refrigerating, and Air-Conditioning Engineers, 1972).

2. See H. R. Hay and J. I. Yellott, "A Naturally Air-Conditioned Building," *Mechanical Engineering*, **92** no. 1 (1970), 19–25.

3. See J. A. Duffie and W. A. Beckman, *Solar Energy Thermal Processes* (New York: Wiley-Interscience, 1974), p. 232.

4. *Ibid.*, p. 274.

5. Information on this project and many other solar energy projects on the heating and cooling of buildings can be obtained from the Heating and Cooling Branch, Division of Solar Energy, ERDA, Washington, D.C., 20545.

SUGGESTED READINGS

ASHRAE Handbook of Fundamentals. New York: American Society of Heating, Refrigerating, and Air-Conditioning Engineers, 1972.

ASHRAE Handbook and Product Directory, 1976 Systems. New York: American Society of Heating, Refrigerating, and Air-Conditioning Engineers, 1976.

CHAPTER 10

The Use of Solar Energy in Arid-Zone Houses

RICHARD L. CROWTHER

As the populations of arid settlements expand, it becomes increasingly difficult to satisfy the energy and resource requirements resulting from the impact of winter housing and built environmental support facilities within the arid zone. In residential architecture, opportunities exist for both indirect and direct solar uses. Variations in arid-region solar radiation, including the effect of latitude on seasonal sun positions and the effect of solar radiation's interaction with the prevailing topography and built environment, provide both advantages and constraints on the range of possible solar uses. Once the variants of solar radiation, temperature, humidity, and latitude are defined and correlated to topographical, environmental, and human needs, a full range of solar energy uses in arid-zone architecture can be clearly defined.

John Yellott, eminent scholar and solar energy pioneer, describes our American arid region as the specific areas west of the 100th meridian that receive less than 20 in. of rainfall each year. This area includes parts—if not all—of the western continental states of Arizona, New Mexico, Utah, Colorado, Idaho, Wyoming, Nevada, North Dakota, South Dakota, Nebraska, Kansas, Oklahoma, Texas, Montana, California, Oregon, and Washington. Particularly excluded from this designation as arid are the high-elevation mountain morass areas and the mountain coastal regions, such as the Pacific Northwest, that receive heavy rain and snowfall.

Most of this arid region of the United States receives above-average amounts of solar radiation, which can be translated into cost-effective space heating during the winter months or used for domestic hot water heating as well as other purposes throughout all seasons. At midsummer in an unshaded arid environment the sun at first appears to be a merciless furnace. Nevertheless, as we learn to design passive and active uses for the sun, the wind, water, and earth as energy reservoirs, arid regions can increase their human carrying capacity and even be made suitable for food production, since, as long as there is an adequate initial water supply and evaporation can be controlled, the sun can be used for the conservation of water, assisting in the processes of filtration, reconditioning, and recycling.

As the preceding paragraph indicates, solar radiation can be used in many ways to satisfy human requirements, such as the constant need for clear, fresh water, a need that increases with permanent settlement and the design of areas attractive to sun-seeking visitors. The distillation of water is, as we noted, readily accomplished with solar energy, as are space heating, domestic water heating, evaporative cooling, humidification, air tempering, ventilation, food drying, daylighting, climate control and plant growth in greenhouses, power generation, device actuation, and cooking.

The design of arid-zone solar architecture should be based on holistic evaluations of and conceptual developments in all internal, biophysical, behavioral, and occupational activities, interfacing the design response to the external elements of the microclimate and environment and including appropriate specific solar applications. In doing this, developers and new-community planners, as well as individual architectural designers, should consider the complete range of solar uses. Table 1 suggests the range of possibilities, all of which could be directly or indirectly applicable to arid residential architecture. In addition to these tasks, planners and designers must remember that the fragile environment of arid areas needs to be gently treated. Overall, a solar central power source, solar architecture, and solar community planning are urgently needed and must be primary considerations in the human settlement of arid lands.

In line with this large need, Aden and Marjorie Meinel of the University of New Mexico have proposed large-scale arid-region solar farms to generate electric power. Their concept envisions an extensive arrangement of solar collectors, steam generators, and storage facilities in the open desert for the production and delivery of electric energy, as well as for solar thermal storage. A shaded field would be provided by the arrangement of collectors, and under its protection agriculture and cattle raising would flourish. This regenerative concept would be a direct benefit in the pumping of irrigation water, as well as in the heating, cooling, and lighting of homes and other buildings. Transportation systems could

Table 1   Solar Uses

Space heating	Hydrotemperature energy
Humidification	Thermal storage
Space cooling	Thermal inertia
Air tempering	Thermal lag
Convection	Thermal radiation
Evaporation	Reflection
Sterilization	Refraction
Bioconversion	Phototropism
Photosynthesis	Bleaching
Drying	Purification
Distillation	Biophysical effects
Daylighting	Sundials
Power generation	Operating equipment
Polarization	Photography
Spectral use	Vision
Heating fluids	Image projection
Controlling devices	Chemical effect
Aquatood production	Agrifood production

also be designed to derive their energy from this form of solar electric power.

This concept is, of course, ambitious. It also reflects an awareness of solar energy's potentialities that is rarely matched, for in the arid regions and elsewhere in the United States progress has been painfully slow in either the realization or the development of beneficial solar systems. Little understanding has been reached, and few defined analyses or practical efforts have been made toward designing communities and architecture that effectively use solar radiation and realize its broad range of possibilities. Surprisingly few examples of either planned passive or active solar architecture exist in the arid regions of the United States, and the holistic implications of solar and direct natural energy use remain virtually untouched.

It is difficult to define clearly the difference between "passive" and "active" solar systems. Nevertheless, these terms have come into being and serve the purpose of general identification and differentiation. A passive system is one that can sustain its functional capability by the use of natural energy. The application of man-assisted external power, however, may be necessary in some cases to initiate or to intervene in the passive energy process. Sun, wind, water, and earth are the natural energy sources used, with the movement of air and the thermal properties of water and earth directly or indirectly activated by the power of the sun. In contrast, active systems need a sustained input or man-assisted external energy in order to fulfill their designed functions. Largely because of this need, experience and scientific comparative analysis have confirmed the primary practical and economic wisdom of using passive solar and other natural energy systems in arid-zone residential architecture.[1]

PASSIVE SYSTEMS

Although all land formations and buildings are solar collectors, almost all of the existing built environment would be ineffectual and inefficient if required to passively provide for 100 percent of human comfort needs. A worthy objective, however, is that a home or building itself should effectively and autonomously respond to diurnal variations and seasonal changes to provide as much human comfort, natural daylight, and other desirable conditions for human activities and occupations as possible. This passive, responsive architecture may be best achieved by using contemporary construction techniques with the integration of low-energy-demand control systems.

Past and Present. Infusions of sixteenth to eighteenth century Spanish culture into early American Southwest architecture and planning pleasantly addressed the harsh, bare character of the arid region and its imperious solar intensity. Delightful isolation from the prevailing arid climate was obtained by the enclosure of outdoor courtyards with massive walls, rooms of earth construction, shaded archways, ventilated roof eaves, and the grace of quiet gardens. The central open courtyard was both the center of life and the modifier of solar intensity and other adverse natural forces. Rooms remained cool throughout the hot afternoons and sustained acceptable internal room temperatures during cold periods with minimal supplemental heat from the burning of brush and wood. The residential courtyard with rooms surrounding it was a successful passive system. Pools of water and fountains often helped to cool the courtyard and the surrounding living quarters.

The concept of the central verdant courtyard as a focal point remains as a cultural vestige in some recent and near-recent architecture. Unfortunately, the Southwest cultural practices of today generally manifest a lack of awareness of the arid climate and of solar energy potential. The comfort of buildings or rooms is maintained through the applied energy of conventional fossil fuel heating and air conditioning, since the earlier massive adobe and earth structures, which maintained comfort conditions, have disappeared as light-frame construction has become prevalent. The climate-responsive, earth-constructed hogan of the Southwest Indians has similarly succumbed to light, uninsulated framing. The arid West and Southwest have a rich tradition of earth construction that has faded and needs to be again brought back into focus.

Parallel to the advent of lighter construction materials is a serious decline in levels of human awareness of climatological design responses during the past 100 years. Almost all speculative builders have consistently failed to recognize the distinct energy and climatic advantages of appropriate architecture as the prime ingredient in solar economics. Furthermore, the average builder–developer has not demonstrated adequate concern for ecological preservation or a proper understanding of how energy can be conserved through architecture or of how cli-

matically responsive architecture can be fully developed with the use of sun, wind, earth, and water energies.

General Recommendations. Daylighting by direct or diffuse solar radiation must be carefully planned to avoid thermal overloading. Reflective surfaces appropriately located, formed, and shaped and having proper surface qualities may be used both to produce desirable amounts of internal daylight and to reflect indirect solar radiation into the residential interior. Interior surfaces should be selected for the reflective and absorptive qualities that best fit with the occupant's needs in regard to color, shape, texture, and form. Skylight and clerestory windows can be used to produce internal daylight directly, but must be carefully applied to avoid an exaggerated interior thermal impact. Diffuse daylight from the vault of the northern sky can serve quite successfully to provide a uniform cool infusion of natural light. Diffuse amplification of this daylight can be pleasantly achieved by reflection from roof, wall, and ground surfaces that employ a light to medium color, depending on the internal needs for light. Light, however, is never free of thermal gain, and, with temperature differences among air, fluids, and solid materials, heat is provided to interior spaces by means of thermal convection, conduction, and radiation.

In arid regions, earth subsurface temperatures, clear sky temperatures, and nocturnal air temperatures can all be used as cooling agents and as agreeable foils to the dominant power of the sun. Underground and partially underground dwellings are particularly suitable for the storage of solar energy and the provision of summertime cooling. Landscaping and land contouring can also have a profound influence on the sun's effect on habitat.

Unfortunately, very few of these fundamental natural energy and energy conserving concepts are used or even considered today in arid-zone architecture. To the author's knowledge, very few examples of residential architecture have been designed or constructed that use even a portion of the possible solar and natural climatic energy or employ fluid or solid mass construction to maximize solar thermal storage, solar inductive ventilation and air tempering, solar domestic hot water heating and solar water distillation, optimized daylighting, solar power generation, solar-actuated controls, adequate solar shading, or attached energy conserving solar greenhouses. In contrast, solar evaporative cooling in the form of the common "swamp cooler" is widespread in houses and modular and mobile homes located in arid zones. Other forms of evaporative cooling, such as the Australian rock-bed regenerative cooling system, patio gravel trenches, and other diverse evaporative methods using porous, fibrous, or capillary action, need to be further developed and used as practical low-cost means of cooling.

Examples of Passive Systems. The following brief descriptions illustrate several basic passive solar systems that either have been used in arid areas or are directly adaptable to such a climate.

First of all, viable residential design direction is evident in the American Southwest. It features the transparent enclosure of central atriums with room spaces opening onto an indoor court area. Pools and fountains located in these enclosed environments avoid the large evaporative loss characteristic of outdoor pools and fountains. Further advantages would result from an ability to regulate the amount of exposure of the enclosed atrium to the night sky for desired nocturnal cooling and to impose control, attenuation, and insulation as needed to regulate solar penetration, solar shading, and internal thermal losses. Such control could be attained by the use of two Steve Baer trademarked designs: Skylids, a series of large, overlapping, movable aluminum louvers that are solar actuated using a Freon control cannister, and Beadwall, a system that selectively impels small Styrofoam pellets between two parallel sheets of clear glass, and removes them. Both allow for the direct use and the insulative exclusion of solar radiation.[2]

David Wright, another Southwest architect, has designed and built for himself and for clients homes that passively utilize solar energy. He employs adobe walls covered with an outer layer of polyurethane for insulation and surfaced with a stucco coating for protection to make the whole house a thermal mass. In his own home he has a large, vertical, southern-facing glass area at the front. Hinged, insulating panels fold upward here to expose the interior of massive adobe walls to direct winter solar radiation. The rear interior walls are curved to better receive the winter solar radiation. To prevent internal heat losses during cold periods, day or night, the insulative panels are manually dropped in place by a pulley system. Another home of his design rises in four angular tiers of southern-facing glass. The construction and the solar controls are similar to those used in his own home. The provided environment, complete with growing plants, is like living in a greenhouse.

Greenhouses themselves, providing food production as well as aesthetic and creative enjoyment, can (just as atriums, sunrooms, window bays, and conventional windows) be fitted with Skylids, Beadwalls, movable insulative panels, and insulative draperies and blinds for the purpose of solar attenuation and exclusion. These additions, when properly designed with respect to latitude, the environment, and the architectural envelope, can allow solar gains and internal thermal retention during external cool and cold periods, in addition to shading and thermally induced ventilation and cooling during warm and hot periods. Inasmuch as most growing plants are able to tolerate a greater range of temperatures than can human beings, greenhouse so equipped can provide a welcome climatic buffer between interior residential living spaces and the external climate.

Theodore Von Dresser of the Southwest has modified the traditional adobe construction of homes to include passive solar collection and thermal storage systems. His systems and adaptations are relatively simple. In one project a southern-facing greenhouse with a vertical glass face attenuates summer thermal gains and collects winter solar radiation. A gravel heat storage area located between the northern adobe walls provides further heat to the interior during cool and cold periods.

William Lumpkins, a Southwest architect, has developed a number of residential designs using peripheral greenhouses, central atriums, and large internal thermal masses that gain energy during the winter months. Solar radiation is allowed to enter either through southern-facing glass walls or from overhead through skylighted areas, and solar gains are captured in either massive adobe or concrete-filled block walls. Lumpkins' architectural solutions often include partially underground residential construction to reduce energy losses and gains from changes in the external climate.

One of the more inventive passive systems, featuring passive solar heating and natural cooling, was invented by Harold Hay. This system uses plastic water mattresses placed on a metal roof that is also the ceiling of the dwelling space. During the cooler winter months, solar radiation is allowed to heat up the dark-colored plastic exposed to the sky, and heat is transferred by conduction to the water and the interior. When adequate solar radiation is not available, sliding insulating panels are moved across the roof. This insulating roof cover greatly reduces thermal heat losses to the cooler outdoor air. The solar-heated water in the components then radiates its heat energy through the metal ceiling to heat the interior of the house. During periods when it is desirable to cool the interior, the water-filled roof components are exposed to the night sky and the cool night air temperatures, thereby cooling the water. The movable insulating panels are then moved across the roof, and the daily accumulation of heat energy from the interior is absorbed by conduction through the metal ceiling roof into the cooler water mass, from which it is then later reradiated to the night sky. Although man-assisted energy is used to move the insulating panels across the top of the water storage mattresses, the Hay system is classified as passive. If desired, the plastic enclosure may be adapted for use as an open pond, which will accelerate the process of cooling through evaporation. Loss of water volume due to evaporation, as well as dirt and insect contamination from such an open roof pond, must, however, be considered.

Albuquerque, New Mexico, is the location of a home designed by Steve Baer which uses the southern exterior's glazed walls for solar collection. Water-filled 55 gal drums horizontally mounted across the full wall area are supported by a metal frame and have their exposed ends painted black. These ends are heated during cool winter months by direct solar radiation and by indirect solar radiation reflected from a large, hinged insulating panel in front of the glazed area. Convective internal thermal heat currents are activated into focus within the water in the drums, and heat is subsequently transferred to the interior. Inasmuch as reradiation of thermal heat from the water in the drums occurs over an extended period, the home's interior is heated on a delayed basis. The hinged outdoor reflective insulating panels are closed at night and at other times during cold or cool weather to preserve the stored solar heat for use within the interior of the house. Many adaptations of this system are possible. Although external man-assisted energy is needed, as in the Hay system, to raise and lower the exterior reflective insulating panels, the system is again essentially passive.

Felix Trombe of France has developed a somewhat similar system that uses large southern-facing glazed areas with an interior black-painted concrete wall. The wall receives direct solar radiation during colder periods and reradiates thermal energy to the interior by thermal lag through the wall and also by reradiation through convection currents that are designed to pass between the outer glass and the surface of the concrete wall. This heat rises upward and passes through slits in the concrete wall near the ceiling. As

it gives off its thermal energy, the convective interior moving air mass descends from the ceiling and toward the north wall of the interior, thereby warming the house. This system can be adapted to arid-zone uses. It is simple and efficient and can be designed to permit southern penetration and many hybrid system solutions.

The author is the architect–owner of a passive solar home, designed in 1972 for direct solar heat trapping in winter. It also ventilates and cools by inductive solar ventilation when external night or day temperatures are between 55 and 75°F. In the very cold winter season of 1974, the *per annum* total supplemental heating cost with natural gas was $72 at a thermostat setting of 70 to 72°F. During cold months the external air pollution of Denver is generally high because of temperature inversions. During these months internal air is recycled, using carbon dioxide absorption and humidity respired by large green plants, as well as filtered by electronic, charcoal, and fiber filters. Solar radiation increases this winter humidification and carbon dioxide absorption by increasing plant growth.

Other architects and individuals in the Southwest arid region, as well as our own Crowther Architects Group and Crowther/Solar Group, are working on designs and plans using passive solar or passive solar hybrid systems. We have been developing some architectural arrangements that employ solar radiation and pools or cylinders of water in combination with thermal masonry and earth masses for space heating and humidification in arid zones. The advantage of these elements is the high capability of water to store and then to release heat at a slow rate. Since the climate in arid zones may feature very cold peaks or even periods of sustained cold, movable insulation for internal winter energy retention becomes increasingly important to these designs. This need can be fulfilled with insulated movable panels, heavy insulative draperies, or movable blinds. Reflective roof and wall surfaces can either be selectively reflective or be mobile to reflect, when in place, the hot rays of solar radiation away from the home during late spring, summer, and early fall. These designs reflect such solar heat back to the sky or toward open space, rather than onto one's neighbor.

The Economics of Passive Systems. The holistic interdependency of all the variants in the residential design process determines the configuration, orientation, shape, form, mass, buffering, openings, entries, color, texture, and operational features required to reduce energy demand, optimize the use of solar and other natural energies, and eliminate or minimize the need for and use of supplemental conventional fuels. In line with these goals, cost-effective, life-cycle costs of solar passive architecture and related systems are practical: operational costs are usually minimal or nonexistent, and maintenance requirements are low. The lack of adequate thermal storage and the lack of adequate thermal control can, however, be partially offsetting disadvantages. Passive systems are often actual parts of the architecture and therefore economically serve an architectural, as well as a systems function—a further advantage. In virtually all cases, we should note, active solar collection, solar storage, and thermal energy distribution systems of the flat plate or concentrating variety are more expensive and require greater operational expenditure of external energy than do passive systems. Thus, generally speaking, passive, energy-optimized, cost-effective energy conserving designs produce the greatest economic return at the lowest life-cycle costs.

Furthermore, when energy conservation and passive solar functions are optimized, supplementary active solar collection systems can be smaller in size than would be customarily used for a specific size and type of residence. With such a hybrid system, in most arid regions there should be no problem in providing total heating for a home without the aid of supplemental fuels.

The use of on-site or local massive materials and earth-handling techniques in construction will not only avoid the cost incurred in the importation and transportation of building materials but will provide a thermal mass very suitable for arid-zone residential design and construction. The sun can also be used in total life-support systems and the recycling of wastes and water, as well as in food production and the provision of power independent of public utilities, thus making the solar system still more economical.

ACTIVE SYSTEMS

Active solar collection systems have been pioneered in the arid regions of the United States. The list of pioneers includes A. G. Eneas, Dr. Charles Greeley Abbot, Frank Lloyd Wright, Dr. John I. Yellott, Dr. George O. G. Löf and Drs. Aden and Marjorie Meinel, plus numerous other contemporaries. Corporate interest in this endeavor, however, has been virtually nonexistent.

Dr. George Löf, the internationally recognized solar pioneer, has lived in a solar home with an active air-type system of his own design since 1958 and was engaged in research on solar energy implementation before that date. He is presently director of the Solar Energy Applications Laboratory of Colorado State University in Fort Collins and was involved with the systems engineering of three homes using solar collection systems of three different generic types at this location. Assistant directors of this laboratory are Drs. Dan S. Ward and Susumu Karaki.

This author and his former associate, Charles E. McWilliams, AIA, were the architects of the Fort Collins Colorado State University solar homes, made possible by a National Science Foundation grant. Solar House I is equipped with a liquid-type Roll-bond aluminum collector, water storage for thermal retention, and a lithium bromide absorption system for mechanical solar cooling; Solar House II is, in contrast, fitted with an air-type system similar in design to the Solaron flat plate collector and a gravel bin for solar thermal storage. A third home, Solar House III, was recently equipped with an evacuated tube collector—a liquid-type system—employing water thermal storage and a lithium bromide absorption system for cooling.

The Solaron Corporation, for which Dr. Löf is the technical director, is involved with a growing number of air-type solar collection systems in arid regions. Our own Crowther/Solar Group has completed in western states 15 solar homes with energy-optimized, cost-effective, energy conserving systems and has numerous other projects in which active systems will be employed. Some of these residences are under construction, and others are in the planning and development phases. In all cases our projects have been economically designed to fit our clients' limited budgets. The cost-effective use of active solar energy systems has required us to first optimize the topographic, landscaping, and building energy conservation factors and then to design the shape, form, and other details of the building itself to perform well as a solar collector during the winter months and a rejector of heat through the warm and hot seasons of the year. During the holistic design process a carefully efficient system is established to lessen the problems and costs of the total installation of the active solar collection system and the associated thermal storage system. In solar residences we have been able to reduce energy requirements by 60 to 70 percent, as compared to conventional structures, through architectural design, including in our designs more than

120 items that affect energy losses and gains. Some of our homes, for example, use the sun to initiate ventilation and aid in internal cooling either through western-facing solar plenums, heat chambers, or air-type solar collectors utilizing wind turbine assistance. This latter process cools the solar collector panels, which directly experience the impact of the summer sun, thereby increasing the longevity of the panels. In some cases the combined natural heat gains of the home and of the collector are used to heat the domestic hot water supply.

More detailed information on total systems concepts using solar and other natural energies for homes and other buildings is contained in the Crowther/Solar Group publication *Sun/Earth*.[3] Important basic publications on the relationship between climate and solar energy use include Victor Olgyay's *Design with Climate* and Jeffrey Aronin's *Climate and Architecture*.[4] Arid-zone conditions are considered in all these publications. Other active system solar homes by other architects and designers for the most part consider solar orientation, increased amounts of insulation, and double glazing, but very few include the design sophistications that are inherently practical, cost effective, and possible with conventional or nonconventional construction techniques.

Active system solar homes of both air and water types are either completed or under construction in all of this nation's arid-zone states. These range from properly engineered and carefully evaluated systems to the do-it-yourself varieties. All solar collection systems will gather some solar energy for use, but the non- to less-engineered, poorly conceived, improperly fabricated, or grossly undersized systems waste material and labor and reduce solar credibility. Unfortunately, many of the systems being designed are of this kind.

A more expensive kind of design is typified by one of the largest solar installations, sponsored by the Copper Development Association for a show home in Tucson. Because of its scale and luxury, it does not represent what the average consumer would be able to buy, but it is an impressive project. Unfortunately, it is not readily applicable to the ordinary demand encountered in the growing Southwest.

Other active prototypes should be mentioned. The city of Colorado Springs, Colorado, sponsored a solar home that uses a water-type system with a heat pump serving as a backup. Peter Wood designed and built a solar home across the street from it, using the Thomason system. This is a trickle water system in which water descends over black-coated corrugated sheetmetal under the protection of a glass cover. Thermal storage is provided by a water tank surrounded by a rock bed. Air blown through this rock bed is heated and subsequently distributed through the home. The Thomason system may lack some of the thermal advantages of a closed fluid system, but it could be adapted to provide for solar humidification of arid-zone homes.

CONCLUSION

The future of arid-zone architecture lies in intensive holistic community and urban planning for the use of natural systems. Under virtually no other world situations, except those in the Arctic, are the energy interdependencies and the social and cultural factors so in need of an ongoing, total, dynamic balance. The primary social and cultural restraints on the use of solar and optimal energy conservation lie mostly within the ingrained habits of those who design, build, and occupy new homes in arid communities. The aesthetic fantasy that a home should look and function as a home always has, coupled with the American frontier belief in personal independent decisions, is the destructive factor running counter to the delicate interdependencies needed in an arid community. To overcome this counterproductive force, education must be applied at all levels to bring about the meaningful development of the arid environment. In such education, the strong identification of solar energy with arid regions should be stressed. This is a positive association in conjunction with which the multifold purposes of solar use can be extolled.

Beyond this education to solar energy, the author advocates the following procedures, which are critical to the life-support capabilities of arid lands:

1. The comparative inventory of arid regional building and energy resources that have low energy demands and low environmental impacts.
2. Arid regional and community planning that holistically considers regenerative systems in terms of projected population densities and deployment.
3. The planning and design of a built environment that uses direct natural energies of sun, wind, water, and earth and is in dynamic balance with the prevailing ecology.
4. The analysis of and design provisions for the biophysical and the behavioral environmental effects of human settlement.

5. The development of a system of controls and balances to regulate inequities in the planned dynamic systems by political, cultural, social, and economic policy and implementation.
6. The study of facilities and organizational entities in terms of their time frame, multiuse functions, and programming.

The one central objective in architecture will remain the provision of shelter, but the architect and building designer in the arid environment must, in order to do this properly, learn to handle the delicate balances and sensitivities of the climate and effectively employ the natural energy rewards available through his design processes and his ability to correlate and integrate the great range of large and small factors that produce a successful arid passive or active solar habitat.

NOTES

1. This analysis was conducted by Doug Balcomb at the Los Alamos Laboratories.
2. These Baer designs, as well as those by Wright, Von Dresser, Lumpkins, Hay, Baer again, and Trombe described below, were discussed in 1976 at an albuquerque conference on passive solar systems. The papers presented at that conference will be published by Los Alamos Laboratories under Doug Balcomb's editorship.
3. See Richard L. Crowther, *Sun/Earth* (Denver, Colo.: Crowther/Solar Group, 1976).
4. See Victor Olgyay, *Design with Climate: Bioclimatic Approach to Architectural Regionalism* (Princeton, N.J.: Princeton University Press, 1963); and Jeffrey Aronin, *Climate and Architecture* (New York: Reinhold, 1953).

CHAPTER 11

Water Supply Systems for an Arid-Zone City

DANIEL HILLEL

In addition to the natural growth of the existing population in the arid regions, there seems little doubt that the growing tendency to establish new cities in these regions will increase the population still further in the foreseeable future. The reason for this new impetus to settle in arid regions probably arises from the fact that these regions have what more densely settled regions lack: the valuable resource of space. Beyond that, the arid regions afford man a rather pleasant climate for habitation. Many people wrongly believe that arid regions are unbearably hot; they are, rather, pleasant because they are seldom excessively hot and the air is dry and usually clear. Romance is associated with the arid regions because they are attractive. Furthermore, arid regions, which are still by and large undeveloped, contain huge potential reserves of various mineral and energy resources. Much of the world's oil is in arid regions, as well as coal, metals, and all sorts of mineral deposits that need to be developed over the next generation or two. Development will occur there because of the available space, the resources, and, finally, the abundance of solar energy. Many people predict that in the future, as fossil fuel energy becomes increasingly prohibitive in cost, more energy will be derived from the sun. Solar energy exists in the greatest abundance, obviously, in the arid regions. For all these reasons, therefore, it seems almost a certainty that mankind, already overcrowding certain parts of the world, will want to colonize the arid regions. These regions are, in a sense, the latest, if not the last, frontier for settlement and development.

Unfortunately, whereas certain areas of the globe are endowed with a sufficient supply—and sometimes a superabundance—of water, other areas are afflicted with a shortage. The latter areas are caught in a dilemma because the supply of water in an arid region is limited and, at the same time, the demand for water is unusually high. That demand is caused by the dry climate: there are a greater number of bright days than occur in nonarid areas; the radiation from the sun is stronger in arid than in nonarid regions; the skies are clearer than those in nonarid areas; and the air is exceptionally dry and hot. A discrepancy between supply and demand occurs occasionally even in what are called the humid regions, but in the arid zones it is a fact of life and the crux of the water shortage problem. In principle, we can solve it by maximizing supply and minimizing demand. These are two tasks that must be pursued in tandem by urban planners, agriculture developers, and, ultimately, arid-zone settlers themselves.

The water supply in arid regions is limited primarily because the precipitation is limited. Yet precipitation is not negligible in arid regions. In most cases, even in the desert, precipitation is appreciable. It seems negligible only in comparison to the extremely high water demand imposed by the evaporative climate on all plants, animals, and human beings. In nature we find many interesting examples of plant and animal species adapting to life in the arid zone. How different species contrive to exist in the arid zone and reproduce despite the shortage of water—how they manage to balance their water supply against their demand—is a fascinating subject in itself. Survival is an age-old problem, not merely one that we have suddenly become aware of; it has always been faced by many forms of life and specifically by human beings who for one reason or another have had to live in the desert or in a semiarid zone. In fact, because of some strange combination of historical and geographical circumstances, a very considerable part—about one third—of mankind now lives in the world's arid and semiarid regions. Thus, when we discuss the problems of water supply in arid regions, we are not simply discussing a theoretical or hypothetical possibility of developing and establishing new towns. What we are discussing is, to begin with, a very imminent problem of how to supply water to an already existing population.

SOURCES OF WATER

The problem of water supply is different in different arid regions, for arid zones in various parts of the world differ in many important respects. Some arid regions have been endowed with water resources that do not originate in the arid regions themselves but are brought quite naturally into these regions by, for example, rivers and underground aquifers carrying water from a neighboring humid region. For instance, the Indo–Gangetic Plain in northern India is a very arid region but happens to have passing through it two very large rivers, the Ganges and the Indus, both of which receive their headwaters from the melting snows of the Himalayas, a humid region. Wherever this natural "importation" occurs, the problem of development in an arid region is simplified. It becomes merely a matter of harnessing these water resources and then regulating their use in proportion to their supply. There is danger, of course, if the demand is in excess of the supply and use becomes abuse. But water can be used efficiently in proportion to its supply, and, when it is, there are tremendous possibilities for development in these fortunate arid regions of the world. For instance, the Sahel region of sub-Sahara Africa is now suffering from a terrible drought, and literally hundreds of thousands of people are starving. This region has, however, good aquifers and rivers that could be harnessed for irrigation.

Other arid regions have usable fossil water deposits. Such deposits date back to some previous geological age in which the climatic conditions were more humid than they are now. This water has remained since then in the bedrock in aquifers. In North Africa, for instance, there are large water deposits in certain parts of the Sahara, and similar resources have been found in the Sinai Desert. This water cannot be renewed; therefore pumping cannot be sustained. A deposit may be sufficiently large, however, to be tapped over a long period of time, in the same way that nonrenewable petroleum deposits are mined.

In still other cases, an arid region is sufficiently close to a humid region with an excess of water which can be transported by pipeline or open channel into the arid region. There are numerous examples of this fortuitous arrangement. Southern California imports its water from the Colorado River and from northern California, and is even considering the importation of water from Oregon, Washington, and perhaps even from Canada, a distance of 2000 miles or more. These are not merely pipe dreams—or visions of the future—but the sort of projects that are under way even now.

These are the easier cases to handle. In many instances, however, there are no such advantages, and the arid region, if it is to be developed, must depend on its own renewable water resources. In these arid regions the use of natural precipitation must be considered. Under natural conditions most of the precipitation that reaches the ground in arid regions is unusable. Most is lost directly by evaporation from the surface, which is generally bare, within just a few days. The water that does not evaporate directly is generally absorbed and then transpired by the sparse natural, economically useless vegetation existing in the arid region. Some of the rainwater fails, however, to penetrate and may tickle downslope. This water, called "runoff" or "overland flow," can sometimes be collected and used.

A major potential source of water in the arid regions, therefore, is runoff water, that is, precipitated water that, after reaching the surface, is not soaked into the ground, but trickles off the surface and collects in depressions and stream beds. Such runoff does occur. Even though rainstorms are infrequent in the desert, sometimes they are very strong and cause flash floods—torrential flows of water through the dry river beds. Unfortunately, this water is lost because it runs downstream uncontrollably.

ANCIENT USES OF RUNOFF

How to capture naturally occurring runoff water is an age-old problem. Since runoff happens to be the only water source for many arid regions, people for thousands of years have been grappling with this problem and have found partial solutions to it. For instance, some native Americans in the southwestern United States and in Mexico have found ways of checking the flow of water in small streams and of damming and diverting the flow of water in larger streams into cisterns and storing the runoff there for subsequent use by human beings and animals. They have also found ways of diverting this water to irrigate their crops. People in the Middle East 3000 years ago learned about runoff use. In the Negev in Israel, for example, evidence abounds of ancient cities with populations in the tens of thousands which subsisted entirely on runoff water. There was no groundwater storage to speak of in the Negev, and no perennial rivers. Moreover, there was certainly not, at least at that time, any way to bring water in from the outside. But there was runoff, and that runoff was somehow harnessed to serve the needs of a population larger than ever before or after (except for the last few years). Perhaps the climate has changed and it was more humid then, but all the available evidence suggests that the climate has not changed in the last 1500 to 2000 years. In fact, the most striking difference is between the nature of the dense population which existed in the Negev then and that of the thin population which existed there subsequently. Until very recently only nomadic Bedouins lived where previously there were luxurious cities. The people living in that region have simply lost the ability and social organization needed to control runoff water.

The people living in the Negev during the Israelite, Nabatean, Roman, and Byzantine periods did more than simply trap the natural runoff, they went so far as to induce additional runoff artifically, that is, to "milk" more water off the hillsides and to use that water for drinking purposes and for agriculture. To do this, they would rake off the surface gravel, called the "desert pavement," and expose the fine material under the surface stones. Then, when the rain came, the beating of the raindrops would partly seal the surface by forming a crust over the soil, reducing the absorption of water and increasing the runoff. The desert dwellers of ancient times would collect this runoff in channels leading into hollow cisterns in the rock or leading down the fields to irrigate trees. Hundreds of square miles of arid land were thus developed. About 2 to 3 percent of the land surface was cultivated, and the rest was set aside to supply runoff. The ratio of runoff-contributing area to

runoff-receiving area was thus of the order of 20 or 30 to 1. Written legal records from this period in the Negev's history deal not only with the number of acres of cropland that a man could bequeath to his heirs but also with the amount of hilly land he should have to collect water, because obviously he could not grow anything down in the valley unless he had a hill from which he could collect water and channel it into the valley. The hills featured very shallow, stony, usually saline soil where nothing could grow. Water, however, could be collected there and brought down to the valley to irrigate crops.

The Negev region receives approximately 3 to 6 in. of rainfall per year. Even though that sparse rainfall occurs almost entirely in the five months between November and April, the ancient people still were able to develop and sustain a continuous civilization that lasted hundreds of years, only to be destroyed by war, not by climate or by inefficiency. In this area different specific systems resulted from different social arrangements and levels of technology. As the association grew from one of individual families through one of tribal units to a city stage, a larger area of land could be controlled and the hydraulics of the water supply system could be centrally planned and regulated. As part of the Roman or Byzantine Empire, people were able to plan regionally to provide a water supply. The tribal people were not always successful, for they worked by trial and error, and they did not have much science at their disposal, but were dependent on experience, patience, and diligence.

USING RUNOFF TODAY

To use runoff in the desert today, we should rely not only on its natural occurrence, but also on the possibility of inducing runoff artifically. Although we do not have the human slaves that the ancient people had, we have our own slaves in the form of tractors and land-moving machines. With these, the land can be shaped and smoothed to yield a greater supply of runoff. Furthermore, we have another slave called chemistry. Many chemical substances can do a job for us that we working with our hands cannot. We have chemicals with which we can treat the surface so that it repels more water; and, if we put machines and chemistry together to work for us, we can increase the yield of runoff from sloping ground from about 10 to 15 percent to a maximum yield of 80 to 90 percent of the annual rainfall. The desert surface can thus supply a great deal of water for the development and expansion of our civilization.

Rainfall in the desert is scarce but not negligible. A typical desert region may receive 200 mm of rain a year (approximately 8 in.). Assuming an impervious surface, all of that water can be collected: 200 liters/ m^2, or 2000 m^3/ha. Conservatively, it is possible to have a family subsist on 100 gal/day (approximately 400 liters). This amount can be reduced still further if their water use habits can be changed (e.g., if people can be educated to enjoy gardens with xerophytic plants, such as cacti and other succulents, instead of hydrophylic plants). If, for example, a family needs 200 m^3 of water a year, how much land does it need? If our system is only 50 percent effective, we can collect in a typical desert 1000 m^3/(ha)(year). A hectare can thus supply five families for a year. We would need 200 ha to support 1000 families, and that is only approximately 1 mi^2. Although this calculation is not really accurate, it gives a reasonable order of magnitude. If a city is to be established in the desert, therefore, the land surface necessary to collect the water must be provided, in proportion to the projected population and industry.

We still have to store the water, however, because the rainfall does not occur every day or even every week. It occurs, instead, about 4 or 5 or maybe 10 times a year. Water, moreover, has to be stored from year to year, because some years are very wet whereas others are very dry. This storage problem can be solved. Water is, in principle, available if the land is correctly allocated and treated to collect water. It can supply even a medium-size city, and it can supply industry and agriculture—not open-field agriculture, perhaps, which wastes water, but certainly greenhouse agriculture, which is much more efficient in terms of water use. Planning, however, is essential. What may happen to a city in an arid region without a planned adequate supply of water is exemplified spectacularly by Fatehpur Sikri, the magnificent city built in northern India by the Moghul King Akbar the Great. That city of palaces had to be abandoned just a few years after it was completed, simply for lack of water. What a terrible failure of planning!

Environmental Effects. There are some adverse effects on the environment or ecology of a region every time anything is built, and these consequences must be weighed against the advantages of the construction. Do we prefer to maintain the existing ecological system or to build a city for the benefit of mankind?

There is, however, no danger to the ecological system of the total desert from building a few cities on a very small fraction of its land. The deserts are still very extensive, and for the time being we are in no danger of building cities on anything exceeding 1 percent of the land area.

Soil erosion is a problem affecting both the environment and the effectiveness of runoff collection. Some soils are naturally stable, but others are very unstable and tend to scour easily. The more vulnerable soils must be protected. To prevent erosion the soil surface can be impregnated with asphalt emulsions, which will bind the soil grains together. In some cases a thin solution of cement sprayed on the soil surface can help to hold it in place.

Soil Treatment. Related treatments are used to solve another problem, one caused by the fact that soil particles, in their natural state, are hydrophylic, that is to say, they have an affinity for water, so that an assemblage of soil particles exercises a capillary attraction for water, like a blotter. To induce runoff, we would like to prevent the desert soil from absorbing the water, so that it will run off the surface and be collected downslope. There are, in principle, two ways of doing this. One way is to plug the pores (the spaces between the individual particles) by impregnating the soil with a viscous material that will solidify and form a physical barrier between the soil and the water—a kind of skin or crust. Examples of such materials are asphalt, concrete, rubber, and different synthetic polymers which can be added to the soil in either solution or emulsion form, either poured or sprayed over the surface. Unfortunately, the quantity of such material needed is large; therefore these treatments are likely to be expensive. Furthermore, it is very difficult to find materials that will stand up under the sun and wind, be resistant to ultraviolet radiation, and survive changes of heating, cooling, wetting, and drying. In many cases these materials begin to deteriorate after a short time, cracking and peeling off the surface. Then they become useless because they no longer form a continuous seal over the surface. Nevertheless these methods are likely to be more economical than spreading sheets of plastic or rubber over the entire ground surface.

The other way to force the surface to reject water is not to plug the pores but to treat the particles themselves so as to change their physicochemical behavior. They are thus transformed from hydrophylic into hydrophobic surfaces. (This is commonly done in the textile industry, as, for example, with rain-coats.) Capillary attraction is thereby changed into capillary repulsion. Silicones can be used, for they are organic polymers that have the property of water repellency. Before spraying such substances on the soil, the land surface has to be smoothed. If this is not done, little pockets will form into which the water will run off and eventually evaporate into the air or soak into the ground. Then, after the water-proofing, the surface must be stabilized because, as water runs off the surface, it can scour away the soil and lead to erosion. There are many different chemical formulations that can be used to waterproof the soil. The choice depends on the type of soil and on economic considerations, that is, on the original price of the material and the longevity of the effect of the treatment. Many experiments have been done to determine which products are best. Many of these were carried out in Arizona by the U.S. Water Conservation Laboratory in Phoenix and by the University of Arizona in Tucson. The promising results reveal that no one method will work under all conditions. There are, however, different methods for different soils (depending on the clay content) which will result in increased runoff. Moreover, what is economical in one case may not be economical in another. Thus it is impossible to say that any one treatment is the best under all conditions. For example, if the soil contains clay, we can disperse the clay. Clay consists of the small colloidal particles in the soil, which in most cases are clustered in little flocks. If we add certain chemicals to deflocculate or disperse the clay, it will swell, hydrate, and clog the pores of the soil, forming a natural crust. We can also treat the soil with diluted sodium salts, a commonly used method of sealing the bottoms of reservoirs and channels.

Water Storage. The simplest way to store water is to dam a stream and thereby establish a pond or lake in which to store the water. There are some disadvantages, however. Because of evaporation into the air and seepage into the soil bottom, much of the water will be lost.

The best place to store water, then, is underground. Sometimes natural geological deposits are suitable for water storage, such as gravel beds, if under the gravel bed there is a clay layer which will contain the water. In other cases we have to create artificial reservoirs. One way to do this is to dig a basin, line it with plastic sheeting, and fill it with gravel, which will prevent the water from evaporat-ing. Then the water can be drawn out by a siphon, pump, or drainage pipe.

Many types of cisterns have been developed. In ancient times whole cities were supplied by runoff through local, not central, storage. For example, in Jerusalem, every house had a gutter system to collect water from the roof and cisterns to store it in the yard. These cisterns would be excavated, and the walls plastered. There the family's water would be stored. This was, however, inadequate for whole cities, so the kings built large cisterns (reservoirs) and conveyed the water over distances of 10 or more miles. Concrete silos or reservoirs can also be built and covered with concrete roofs, small floating parti-cles like Styrofoam or chemical agents such as certain fatty acids being used to reduce evaporation. Such treatments may be expensive, but sometimes the needs of the settlement will justify the expense.

THE DISADVANTAGES OF OTHER SOLUTIONS

Animals and plants require more water in the desert than in humid regions. Human beings evaporate a great deal of water to maintain bodily heat balance. It is interesting that, in Israel, people were taught at first not to drink much water in order to reduce perspiration; they were, in other words, taught to solve the problem by conserving water. Soon, how-ever, the country's doctors began to notice a very substantial increase in the incidence of kidney stones and urinary tract troubles, because people were not drinking enough to maintain their water balance. Their urine was becoming increasingly concentrated to the point where it began to precipitate and form kidney and bladder stones. Therefore the conserva-tion recommendation was withdrawn. In southern Is-rael, which is more arid than the northern part, the demand for water is much greater. People who be-come conditioned to life in the north and then move south often do not adjust their drinking habits quickly enough; hence there is a much higher inci-dence of kidney stones in the southern than in the northern part of the country.

Plants transpire, and so, if crops are to be grown in a desert, they must be irrigated with a larger amount of water than would be required in a humid region. As a solution, some have pointed to the fact that a certain amount of water can be recycled, for ex-ample, the water used in closed systems such as some industrial and domestic ones. Once used, the water is generally of lower quality; therefore the economics of recovering, recycling, and reusing the water should be compared to the economics of making new water available. One of the advantages of runoff water is that it is of very high quality. Moreover, it is generally available where needed, and not much energy has to be invested in the transportation of water.

For a long time the public has been led to expect that the desalination of sea water will provide an answer to water shortages, but that is a very energy-intensive process. As the cost of energy has increased, the economics of desalination have become worse today than they seemed just a few years ago. A breakthrough in this area appears very doubtful because the energy derived from fossil fuel is now more expensive and that derived from nuclear power plants is now also understood to be more problematic, and ultimately more expensive, than was thought a decade ago. This situation may change in the future, but for the time being the desalinization process is not the universal answer. Also, in many cases, water made available by desalination along the seacoast must be conveyed inland and upland to supply the needs of a settlement in the middle of a desert, a process that greatly increases costs.

CONCLUSION

A desert settlement is more likely to be urban than rural. It is more likely to be industrial than agricultural, because a certain inefficiency is inherent in agriculture in the desert because of the greater de-

mand for water. The development of agriculture in arid regions will probably be limited unless water is abundant, as where there are large rivers or underground resources. Such agriculture as may be developed in the desert is more likely to be in greenhouses (a controlled environment) than in the open field. The industrial development must be of a type that depends on local raw materials—minerals, fossil fuels, and so forth; a type that can make use of the abundant solar energy; or a labor-intensive type such as electronics industries.

The quality of rainfall in the desert is variable and in some years may be very low, but the lack of per area quantity can be compensated for by setting aside a sufficiently large area of land for water collection. Furthermore, sufficient storage is required to compensate for the fluctuation in amounts of rainfall. Perennial storage is essential to help overcome drought and should be an integral part of the system.

SUGGESTED READINGS

Cluff, C. B. "Water Harvesting Plan for Livestock or Home." *Progressive Agriculture in Arizona,* **19,** (1967), 3.

Hillel, D., et al. "Laboratory Tests of Sprayable Materials for Runoff Inducement on a Loessial Soil." *Israel Journal of Agricultural Research,* **19,** (1969), 3–9.

Hillel, D. et al. *Runoff Inducement in Arid Lands,* final research report presented to the U.S. Department of Agriculture. Jerusalem: The Hebrew University of Jerusalem, 1967.

Myers, L. E. "Waterproofing Soil to Collect Precipitation." *Journal of Soil and Water Conservation,* **16,** (1961), 6, 281–282.

Myers, L. E., et al. "Sprayed Asphalt Pavements for Water Harvesting." *Journal of Irrigation and Drainage,* **93,** no. 3 (1967), 79–97.

CHAPTER 12

The Integrated Design of Utilities for a New City in an Arid Zone

JEROME H. ROTHENBERG

When a new city is initiated, a coordinated sequence of planning and construction is necessary to insure the availability of utility systems to the buildings of the town and to the town center when occupancy occurs. An adequate electrical capacity, operational heating and cooling, a supply of potable water, and facilities for liquid waste treatment and solid waste disposal are needed in any community, whether in a normal or an arid region. In an arid region there is, however, often a complete lack of shared infrastructure with any other region, so that all these facilities there must be completely independent. Also, in an arid area the planner must certainly place an increased emphasis on the careful use of water.

The site preparation, the cleaning and grading, the utility installation, and so on must be staged, timed, and coordinated. After the grading is complete, the storm and sanitary sewers, the power lines, the fuel lines, and the hot and cold water distribution lines must be installed in sequence before building construction begins. In a conventional city all of the trunk lines and distribution centers must be planned in advance so that they can be installed in the area in stages.

The existence of sufficient resources to support the service needs of the city is the first major factor to consider in determining the location and/or growth potential of the city. Should other factors dictate a city location with insufficient resources to satisfy the demand for public utility services, a utilities system design that reduces the resource requirements will lower or even eliminate the cost of obtaining the resources from a distant location. One approach that would probably be taken is the construction of decentralized conversion and treatment facilities— what may be called integrated facilities, placed in a small site on a schedule consistent with the construction of just the immediately planned portion of the city, even though a larger city is planned eventually. This concept makes the fullest use of the resource potential of the processes by which utility services are provided.

MODULAR INTEGRATED UTILITIES SYSTEMS

Utility systems for new cities in arid regions require large-capacity central electric-generating power plants, projected to become operational at once or incrementally during the term of the new city's projected growth, with corresponding high-capacity distribution systems. Today, with the high cost of fuel and the increased dependence on imported fuel, the emphasis is on nuclear plants; currently, with all the environmental considerations, it has been taking 12 to 15 years to set up a normal nuclear plant of 1000 to 2000 MW or 1 to 2 million kW capacity. The principal sources of power generation in our society, however, are fossil fuels, such as oil, gas, and coal (in that order); nuclear fuel and hydroelectric power are still secondary.

Decentralized conversion depends on the concept called "total energy." Total energy uses the heat from the generation of electricity (which is normally wasted or rejected into a river or the atmosphere from cooling towers) to heat and cool buildings, to treat wastes, to treat the water supply, and to heat the potable water. Total energy is a concept that first became attractive and has received increased attention in the United States during the last 20 years. It has been emphasized in western Europe, particularly Scadinavia, Germany, and France, in the last 10 years.

In the United States about 700 total energy plants have been built, and approximately 400 are currently in operation. In the late 1960s the federal government, through the Department of Housing and Urban Development (HUD), became increasingly interested in the concept of integrated utility systems for decentralized conversion and their use in planning for growth in an effort to respond to the national goal of a decent living environment for every American family, concomitantly with a reduction in the use of our natural resources. Even before the cost of fossil fuel increased, however, HUD research on utilities concerned with community growth tried to discover ways to use energy and fuel most efficiently. Extensive studies, were carried on between the Atomic Energy Commission (ORN C) and HUD to find a way to use the heat wasted in generating electricity, since even the most efficient central station rejects over 60 percent of the energy in fossil fuel. Two major studies were conducted on the use of waste heat from central stations for the heating and cooling of buildings.[1]

In other societies, central stations are being built to use waste heat from fossil fuels. This is happening in Germany, and in Sweden plans call for the use of waste heat in a combined cycle from a nuclear plant in order to permit industrial and then residential areas to be built around the nuclear complex. Such a plan, however, does not lend itself to the way we build and finance development in the United States, where construction is carried out for the most part by the private sector, seldom with federal incentives unless there is some sort of special program such as the New Communities Program. Only then, and necessarily in line with the type of society envisioned to take place within development concepts at that time, did the prospect of decentralized conversion for a community ranging from 300 or 400 or 500

residential units in a small town up to almost any size at all become practical. The Integrated Utility Systems Program was then initiated; in an experimental industrial housing site in Jersey City, New Jersey, with 500 units on a 6½ acre site, a total energy plant was installed. The heat the energy plant rejects from the five diesels is used to heat, cool, and condition the buildings and heat the water. The waste is not integrated as in a fully integrated utilities system, simply because this first effort was undertaken to gather data and evaluate the economic, technical, and institutional problems associated with the total energy concept. The Department of Housing and Urban Development calls the program the Modular Integrated Utilities Systems (MIUS) Program.

The MIUS is basically an on-site combined-package plant, smaller than "conventional" utility plants, designed to provide communities of varying size with electricity, heating and air conditioning, potable water treatment, and waste treatment and disposal. All major components and subsystems are usually located within or adjacent to a central equipment building on the development site. Electric and thermal energy are distributed from the equipment building, using district hot and chilled water piping systems to provide space heating and cooling and domestic water heating (see Figure 1); and liquid and solid wastes are delivered to the MIUS for processing and disposal.

Each MIUS can be increased in size to accommodate from several hundred to thousands of multifamily dwelling units, a reasonable number of single-family dwelling units, and associated commercial facilities. The MIUS program anticipates a complex of small, on-site combined-package plants, each sized to meet the demands of the development in its grid. The MIUS is termed modular because it can be installed near its users in phase with the actual demands of community development or redevelopment, according to a schedule consistent with the construction of the community. It uses an integrated systems approach in which some resource requirements of one service are met by using the effluent of another. For example, heat rejected from electric power generation might be used for residential heating, and the effluent from liquid waste treatment for fire protection and/or as cooling tower water.

A series of evaluations of the major components and subsystems of utility technology applicable to MIUS has been completed as part of HUD's MIUS Program.[2] The criteria for evaluation included envi-

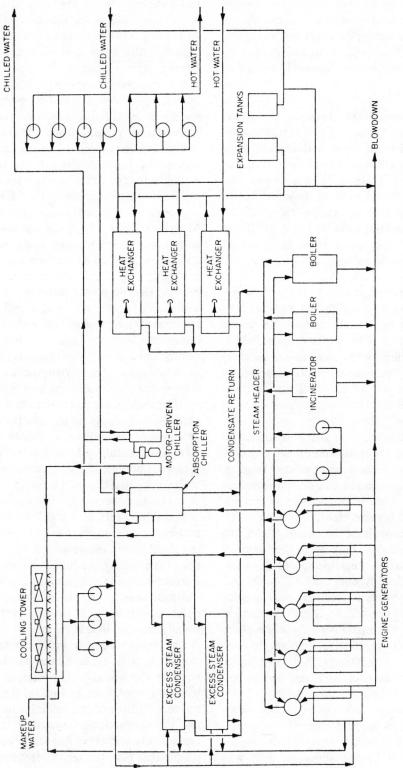

Figure 1. Schematic flowsheet for MIUS thermal–electric subsystem. Redrawn from *MIUS Technology Evaluation*, no. 6 (Washington: U.S. Department of Housing and Urban Development, 1976), p. 22.

ronmental impact, use of fuel and other natural resources, economics, and availability. These studies included systems analyses of hypothetical MIUS installations in comparison with projected models of the conventional utility systems that would otherwise be used.

Electric Power; Cooling and Heating. To avoid possible limitations on the use of the MIUS due to shortages of oil and natural gas and to contribute more postively to the conservation of these premium fuels, the Department of Housing and Urban Development and the Department of Interior jointly sponsored the development of a coal-burning MIUS. This model, under development at the Oak Ridge National Laboratory, uses a coal-fired, fluidized-bed combustion chamber coupled with a closed-cycle gas turbine to generate electricity. A fluidized bed is a chemical engineering concept which employs a large, vertical, cylindrical tank, usually filled with sand, to crack petroleum fuel catalytically and also to reduce ores. In the MIUS, coal is fed to the cylinder, which is raised in temperature by the combustion, as air is bubbled through it. The system maintains a certain temperature, and it looks just like boiling water. The heat is transferred to the turbine-generated cycle to create electricity.

This fluidized-bed concept is being tried out in many ways. Its big advantage is that almost any type of fuel with any type of contamination can be used, and the effluent contamination can be controlled almost perfectly, just as ore is reduced. In our experiments we are using 2 percent high-sulfur coal, which is readily available throughout the United States. (In fact, all Pennsylvania coal is high-sulfur coal, none of which is environmentally acceptable according to Environmental Protection Agency (EPA) guidelines, creating coal-use problems in electric power generation by conventional systems.) By using limestone in the bed, sulfur dioxide emissions to the atmosphere are almost completely eliminated and an environmentally acceptable system is created. The waste heat could then be recovered and utilized for residential heating and cooling.

Increased utilization of fuel energy causes a corresponding reduction in the heat released to the environment. In the MIUS models analyzed the overall thermal efficiency of engine–generator sets was between 60 and 70 percent for annual operation in all climates except that of Dallas, but more nearly optimum installations, or an improved match between electrical and thermal loads, could increase this value

to 80 percent. When the thermal efficiencies of different systems are compared, a MIUS operating at 70 percent is found to reject into the environment less than half the waste heat of a large, modern steam-electric plant operating at 36 percent. In addition, the heat rejected by a MIUS is generally accompanied by exhaust gases at temperatures not exceeding about 300°F; a conventional system can produce temperatures ranging from 1200 to 1700°F. Cooling towers would normally be required for use with absorption and compression chillers, but operation would be limited to the summer season.

The latest application of the MIUS is planned for a portion of the new community of St. Charles in Maryland. The MIUS-served town will probably comprise 725 multifamily units and approximately 200,000 or 300,000 ft^2 for commercial, religious, and town center use. An integrated utilities system will provide electric power, heating and cooling, potable water, fire protection, and liquid and solid waste treatment. Integrating the system in this way is consistent with the goals of reducing the use of critical natural resources, such as fuel and water, and of protecting the environment. Furthermore, it reduces the solid waste disposal problem by about 85 to 95 percent, increases the reuse of water by 60 to 80 percent, and equals or reduces the construction cost of conventional utilities. Certainly all the burdens of large interceptor systems and regional systems are removed, because the grid served by a decentralized utility system is dependent for the most part only on distribution systems within its boundaries.

The advantages of integrating electrical and thermal subsystems in any new city or new town include the significantly increased use of the fuel energy and the sufficiently reduced energy consumption. Furthermore, the integrated utilities concept lends itself especially to the development of new towns or cities devoid of any existing infrastructure, as is usually the case in arid regions.

The major problem with an integrated facility is that it has to be set up and engineered in such a manner that it can be reliably operated, with the responsibility for operations resting on the people using the products. Much of the incentive behind construction and the concomitant disposal of real estate involves tax benefits and other financial issues. Therefore the people that plan the facility frequently take their tax benefits and leave, and the people who take it over either do not understand the facility or feel no responsibility for its successful use. As a result the facility is permitted to run without maintenance until breakdown occurs, and then the capital cost of repairs is passed on.

Potable Water. A potable water supply is very important in the development of an arid region, for potable water is needed not only for drinking but also for bathing and cooking. Water comes from two sources: from the surface or from underground. Either way, in arid areas it is difficult to obtain, and therefore water conservation is important. Sometimes the available water is not in a fresh state, as that from the surface, and requires some treatment. In arid regions desalination may be necessary to reduce dissolved solids, and equipment the size required by a MIUS is currently available. In general, integration with other MIUS subsystems will be minimized if ground water is the source and maximized if desalinization technology is required. Desalinization technology may be integrated into a MIUS using low-grade heat, however.

The advantages of the integration of potable water systems, including on-site treatment facilities, into a MIUS are numerous. There is, first of all, no dependence on outside sources since water does not have to be piped or brought in. Second, the need for additional land for constructing costly pipelines or transmission systems, which require energy, is eliminated. Third, the fact that power is available on-site usually enhances the possibility of using groundwater which requires only minimal treatment. Certainly in arid regions, if the power is made available and the need for water has been reduced, the value and growth capabilities of the region will be increased, because more water will then be available per unit of land and *per capita*.

WASTE DISPOSAL AND TREATMENT

Just as important as the need for water and power is the ability to collect, treat, and dispose of liquid wastes. In an arid region a properly designed system, with water conservation and reuse and a corresponding minimum of underground lines, affords substantial savings over an improperly and wastefully designed system. Every gallon of water that is conserved by recycling is one less to be supplied, transported, and disposed of after treatment. The treatment facility capital cost is thus optimized.

Liquid waste treatment plants are normally sized to meet the calculated demand of users, which is based on the anticipated future growth of the popula-

tion, and they are usually limited by the available capital. Such estimates are extremely difficult to make, and as a result plants are often built that are too small to meet the demand and therefore soon become overloaded. Much of this overloading is due to unexpected industrial growth, as well as to inferior installation of collection sewers, resulting in excessive infiltration. Because of the large capital investment required for treatment facilities, there is also a tendency to build a plant of only the size needed at the time of construction.

In the United States at the present time, the most common form of treatment is biological. However, many communities still either do not treat their wastes or provide only primary treatment that removes large solids. A few physical–chemical treatment plants exist at this time, and a number of communities are considering the use of this type of treatment. The current status of liquid waste collection and treatment, illustrated in Table 1, shows that, of the sewered population, only 70 percent receive secondary treatment service; however, most of these plants do not consistently produce effluents meeting the new EPA requirements for secondary treatment.

Although the construction of treatment plants is expensive, most of the capital costs in waste collection and disposal are incurred for the collection and interceptor sewers. Interceptor sewers do not normally serve individual waste producers directly, but rather gather the waste from collection sewers serving a number of customers. Interceptor sewers are generally very large in diameter and are normally

Table 1 Changes in Sewered Population and Degree of Treatment

Item	1968	1969	1970	1971[a]	1972[a]
Sewered population (millions)	140	144	148	152	156
Total U.S. population[b] (millions)	201	203	205	207	209
Percent sewered	70	71	72	73	75
Level of treatment (percent)					
Sewered, no treatment	7	7	6	6	5
Sewered, primary	31	30	28	25	24
Sewered, secondary	62	63	66	68	70
Sewered, advanced	1	1	1	1	2

Source: *The Economics of Clean Water—Summary of Analysis,* for the U.S. Environmental Protection Agency (Washington: U.S. Government Printing Office, 1972), p. 12.
[a] Estimate based on 1962–1970 growth trends.
[b] Series D estimates of U.S. Bureau of the Census.

buried deep underground. The length of interceptor sewers required depends on the size of the area served, the topography, and whether regional systems serving a number of communities are employed.

Liquid Waste Collection and Disposal.   Liquid waste collection, treatment, and disposal can be performed within the utility framework of the MIUS, using currently available technologies. The small size and self-contained nature of the MIUS, however, create special situations with respect to the application of existing and future technologies and the integration with other subsystems in the MIUS. In general, conventional waste treatment systems are not large consumers of electricity or waste heat, but new concepts such as distillation, reverse osmosis, and elevated temperature biological processes can consume electricity or waste heat. The major advantage of integration is expected to be the use of treated effluents for irrigation, fire protection, industrial purposes, or cooling water.

Pressure or vacuum sewers for new installations, shown in Figure 2, might have advantages in arid-zone cities over conventional gravity-flow sewer systems. Since such sewers do not have to follow the hydraulic grade lines requires for gravity sewers, excavation could be reduced, a definite advantage in arid regions, where climatic conditions can lead to rapid erosion after excavation unless definite steps are taken to prevent it. In addition, capital costs might be reduced, although operation and maintenance costs would be higher than those for gravity sewers. The vacuum sewer, used in conjunction with a specially designed vacuum toilet, reduces water use in dwelling units, and other water conserving plumbing fixtures are also available. Integrated management and the importance of life-cycle costs to a MIUS owner may provide the incentives necessary for the use of water conserving systems.

Small, factory-built sewage treatment plants that could be used in a MIUS are commercially available from many manufacturers. The capacity of a MIUS (usually less than 0.5 million gal/day) makes the use of a plant that could be prefabricated and shipped to the installation site attractive. At the time of our evaluation of the available technologies applicable to the MIUS, most package plants used biological treatment processes, and only about five physical–chemical treatment units were commercially available. However, liquid waste treatment is currently undergoing rapid change. New systems using physical–chemical treatment or biological treatment supplemented by physical or chemical treatment have been developed and are being used to effect high removal of suspended solids, nutrients, and trace organics. These systems, many of which are available in packaged plants, are designed to provide effluents of sufficiently high quality to be reused for fire protection, irrigation, cooling, recreational purposes, and so forth. Direct recycling of effluents for use as potable water is also feasible but must await further study of such problems as virus control, the reliability of plant operation, and monitoring methods.

Many smaller technological advances also can aid water conservation in a community. If build into structures within the community, they save large amounts of water, thus reducing the burdens on the treatment plant and on demand. The Liljedah toilet uses only $\frac{1}{3}$ gal per flush, as opposed to the conventional flush toilet, which uses 5 to 6 gal. Another low-water-use toilet advertised today uses $3\frac{1}{2}$ gal per flush. Low-water-use devices can cut water consumption demand *per capita* considerably, perhaps by 20 percent or more.[3] Mineral oil toilets which are used in construction sites and have to be pumped out are another alternative. The U.S. Park Service last year for the first time purchased a large number of mineral oil toilets, which look the same as conventional toilets but use a very light, low-viscosity mineral oil. Residue settles to the bottom, and about once a year this type of toilet, like a septic tank, has to be flushed and recharged. It is self-cleaning, the oil never appears soiled, and the unit uses no water. Chrysler is marketing a unit called a toilet incinerator, which incinerates all the waste at a high temperature, producing no discharge whatsoever. Certainly commercially available low-flow showers, in which the user is not aware that his water flow is reduced to about 3 gal/min by means of properly designed orifices, should be used, or low-flow shower heads, which reduce shower water use by 8 to 10 percent. Another innovation, which is very popular in the Low Countries and Denmark, is an instantaneous hot water device that uses electricity right in the sink to produce hot water, thus reducing hot water storage and use. Some of the newer mechanical designs are going to have such devices right in the sink.

Other innovations can affect water supply, water distribution, and water supply lines. Insulated fiberglass pipe is available, as well as Bondstrand piping, which is preinsulated with vinyl chloride for cold water distribution. All these water supply and waste treatment innovations should be incorporated into

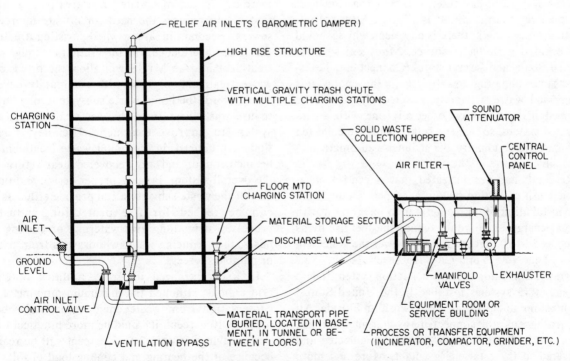

RELIEF AIR INLETS (BAROMETRIC DAMPER)

HIGH RISE STRUCTURE

VERTICAL GRAVITY TRASH CHUTE WITH MULTIPLE CHARGING STATIONS

CHARGING STATION

SOUND ATTENUATOR

SOLID WASTE COLLECTION HOPPER

CENTRAL CONTROL PANEL

AIR FILTER

FLOOR MTD CHARGING STATION

MATERIAL STORAGE SECTION

DISCHARGE VALVE

AIR INLET

GROUND LEVEL

AIR INLET CONTROL VALVE

MANIFOLD VALVES

EXHAUSTER

EQUIPMENT ROOM OR SERVICE BUILDING

MATERIAL TRANSPORT PIPE (BURIED, LOCATED IN BASEMENT, IN TUNNEL OR BETWEEN FLOORS)

PROCESS OR TRANSFER EQUIPMENT (INCINERATOR, COMPACTOR, GRINDER, ETC.)

VENTILATION BYPASS

Figure 2. Typical vacuum collection system for solid wastes. Redrawn from W. J. Boegly, Jr., et al., *MIUS Technology Evaluation,* no. 9 (Washington: U.S. Department of Housing and Urban Development, 1973), p. 16.

any new city in an arid region, especially regions where the water table is not high, where ground freezing is rarely a problem, and where a large amount of excavation is undesirable.

Solid Waste Collection and Disposal.   In general, in arid regions all over the world, the major method of solid waste disposal at this time is land disposal. Incineration constitutes only a small fraction of disposal operations. Usually solid waste is collected and carried to a place that is dedicated to refuse. For the most part it is a sanitary landfill or a partially dugout site, often adjacent to a hill or with the earth bulldozed every 3 ft. These methods are fairly inexpensive, aside from the cost of the land itself. Land disposal costs $2 to $3/ton, whereas incineration may cost as much as $5 to $10 and collection can cost anywhere from $5 to $40/ton. In highly concentrated urban areas, where solid waste has to be taken long distances and growth is taking place, landfills are not acceptable within a short distance of the living area, and the cost of the trucks, labor, and travel time that result becomes a significant factor.

Of course, landfill is a waste not only of the land, but also of all of the resources within the solid waste itself. Solid waste has about one fourth as much or more energy than coal and is cleaner. After collecting and processing it, there is no reason why it should not be used as a fuel resource. Many cities in the United States and several states (Connecticut, Texas) have statewide programs to regain the energy lost from solid waste. Certainly any new city should be planned in such a way, especially one with an integrated system, so that the solid wastes are collected in an efficient, unobtrusive manner—automatically, if possible.

Research has demonstrated that a central pneumatic trash collection system can operate quite well. The installation of an incinerator to integrate it with a total energy plant would reduce the fuel use by as much as 5 to 10 percent and also lower the collection costs. The New York City Roosevelt Island New Town has a pneumatic trash collection system. There are about 15 systems installed in the United States, the most notable being at Disneyworld in Florida. All the trash cans are connected to charging stations, from which the trash is automatically collected and delivered to the total energy plant. More and more interest will be exhibited in this method of solid waste disposal in the next decade. Costs will be reduced initially, although probably not very much because of the capitalization. However, as the number of

systems manufactured and the number of trained installers increase, and as experience with these systems becomes more extensive, they will become more like commercial or production systems, their use will become widespread, and the cost will be reduced significantly.

WASTE DISPOSAL AND MODULAR INTEGRATED UTILITIES SYSTEMS

Whether it is more economical to treat the waste at an individual MIUS or to install an interceptor sewer connected to the nearest available large waste treatment plant will depend on the size of the MIUS, the capacity of the nearest existing plant, the geological and topographical conditions affecting the cost of an interceptor sewer, and the projected growth patterns for buildings and utilities in the urban area. In addition, it might be possible for a number of MIUS complexes to use common collection or treatment facilities. Thus each MIUS and urban growth pattern projection must be evaluated separtely.

The advantages of integrating the liquid waste subsystems with the other MIUS subsystems are numerous. The use of on-site waste treatment systems, first of all, reduces the need for off-site interceptor sewers. Second, in areas where existing treatment plants are overloaded, the integration of liquid waste treatment into an MIUS will allow the provision of waste treatment in phase with community development. Third, the liquid waste subsystem may be able to use waste heat from the electrical–thermal subsystem to improve treatment efficiency. Fourth, sludges produced during liquid waste treatment can be incinerated, and any recovered heat returned to the overall system. Finally, proper design and operation of the waste subsystem can provide effluents that can be reused for fire protection, industrial processes, irrigation, lawn watering, or cooling purposes, thus reducing water withdrawals from natural or potable sources.

In a decentralized integrated utilities system in arid regions, although the maximum amount of fuel conservation from waste could theoretically be as much as 10 percent, it would be more practical to say that a savings of only 2 to 5 percent will be realized because of the heating and cooling load profiles and storage problems. In brief, the advantages of integrating solid waste subsystems are the reduction of the environmental and community impacts of these systems, the savings in fuel consumption for solid waste transportation, the reduction of the land area requirements for ultimate disposal, the reduction or elimination of health hazards and environmental effects associated with landfill operations, and the contribution of recovered waste heat to fuel needs.

The population of the MIUS-served development significantly affects the methods of solid waste disposal that should be considered. Developments in the size range of 300 to 3000 dwelling units would require the disposal of about 14 to 140 tons/week of solid waste, respectively. Disposal systems, such as incineration, would be required to operate 5 days/week and 7 hr/day to process approximately 0.4 to 4 tons/hr for this range of development size. Such capacities are considered small in the field of solid waste disposal; as a result, very little work has been done in developing systems of MIUS size and there is little field experience with them.

Disposal methods that produce effluents usable in other MIUS subsystems include incineration and pyrolysis (chemical change brought about by heat). Pyrolysis reduces waste volume and produces gases that may be of use as fuel, but pyrolysis plants are not now commercially available in sizes applicable to a MIUS. The recovery and utilization of waste heat inherent in the MIUS, together with the goal of energy conservation, make the use of incineration with heat recovery a very attractive option. An evaluation completed in 1973 indicated that incinerators which could be incorporated into a MIUS were currently available (with and without heat recovery), that new and unique designs were under development, that emissions would represent only a small contribution to air pollution, and that the economics of employing incineration with heat recovery might be acceptable. Further development, demonstration, and operating experience are necessary, however, before valid conclusions can be drawn.

Systems analyses comparing the fuel requirements of a MIUS that includes incineration with heat recovery to those of a MIUS without incineration are complex and depend on many assumptions which affect the amount of waste heat produced by the generation of electricity, the amount of auxiliary incinerator fuel required, the amount of usable heat produced by incineration, and the coincidence between the time when recovered heat is available and that when it is needed. Dwelling and MIUS heat balance calculations were completed using hourly weather data for a particular MIUS application serving 720 garden apartments. With and without solid waste incineration, the results indicated that incinera-

tion with heat recovery could reduce total fuel consumption of the MIUS model by about 2 percent with San Diego and Miami weather, 3 percent with Dallas weather, 4 percent with Philadelphia weather, and 5 percent with Minneapolis weather.[4]

COMMON TRENCHING

Since the MIUS developer is responsible for the installation of all utilities, he may benefit from the use of common trenching in installing his utility lines. Common trenching is the installation of two or more utilities in the same trench. This method of installation was first used in the United States during 1960 by Commonwealth Edison and Illinois Bell. These companies reported savings of up to 15 percent on common trench installation of telephone and power cables over installation costs using two separate trenches. The use of common trenching is gradually spreading to other utility companies. Since common trenching benefits accrue to the greatest degree to a new area, they would be applicable to new towns in arid regions, especially if the climate was not severe, because then the trench depth required to ensure protection against freezing would be rather shallow and the excavation costs low.

The major technical considerations in the use of common trenching are concerned with installation practices, systems compatibility, and the design of the trench itself. Modification of current installation practices may be required, but none of these factors represents a serious deterrent to common trenching. On the other hand, although it is clear that the technological problems associated with common trenching of utilities are, for the most part, amenable to solution, institutional constraints in the coordination, application, and administration of these systems limit their use. Many of the problems arise from confusion concerning whom the benefits accrue to. In many cases the benefit derived from common trenching is not perceived by—or does not directly accrue to—the individual who performs the work of coordinating the utilities. In the case of a MIUS the benefits accrue directly to the developer or his installation contractor.

In short, common trenching reduces the amount of land required for easements in installing utilities; may result in more rapid installation time, producing less interference with other building activities and subsequently lowering costs; reduces the amount of excavation required and the need for multiple trenching operations; and decreases the possibility of "dig-ins," since the location of all utilities is known.

CONCLUSION

Several advantages of subsystem integration are common to all subsystems or result generally from the use of the MIUS concept. The MIUS subsystems may share operating personnel, land, buildings, and other site improvements associated with utility systems. A MIUS using currently available technology can provide reliable service completely independently of conventional utilities. Thus utilities can be installed in phase with the requirements of developing communities in arid zones, eliminating the need for off-site transmission of services. Since many new utility components are first proven with units small enough for direct application to a MIUS, the potential to rapidly incorporate advanced technologies into a MIUS is considered at least equal—and perhaps superior—to that for conventional systems.

Other advantages would include the reduction of energy consumption through increase of fuel use efficiency and through waste heat use and integration. Energy savings of from 30 to 50 percent are possible. Water use, due to reuse, may be increased 65 percent. A volume reduction in solid waste disposal of 70 to 90 percent may be realized, with 5 to 10 percent energy resource recovery and a corresponding fuel saving. Environmental benefits corresponding to reduced fuel use and emissions include decreased thermal pollution and liquid waste and solid waste disposal needs.

NOTES

1. See A. S. Miller et al., *Use of Steam-Electric Power Plants to Provide Thermal Energy to Urban Areas* (Washington: U.S. Department of Housing and Urban Development, 1971).

2. See A. Samuels and W. Boegly, Jr., *MIUS Technology Evaluation*, no. 17 (Washington: U.S. Department of Housing and Urban Development, 1976).

3. See James R. Bailey et al., *A Study of Flow Reduction and Treatment of Waste Water from Households* (Washington: U.S. Department of the Interior, 1969).

4. See Hittman Associates, *Evaluation of the Refuse Management System at the Jersey City Operation Breakthrough Site*, in press.

SUGGESTED READINGS

Boegly, Jr., W. J., et al. *MIUS Technology Evaluation: Water Supply and Treatment*, no. 16. Washington: U.S. Department of Housing and Urban Development, 1974.

Boegly, Jr., W. J., et al. *MIUS Technology Evaluation: Compression Refrigeration Systems for Air Conditioning*, no. 19. Washington: U.S. Department of Housing and Urban Development, 1976.

Boegly, Jr., W. J., et al. *MIUS Technology Evaluation: Solid Waste Collection and Disposal*, no. 2. Washington: U.S. Department of Housing and Urban Development, 1973.

Compere, A. L., et al. *MIUS Technology Evaluation: Water Supply and Treatment*, no. 21. Washington: U.S. Department of Housing and Urban Development, 1976.

Gill, W. L., et al. *Technology Evaluation of Heating, Ventilation and Air Conditioning for MIUS Application.* Houston: National Aeronautics and Space Administration—Johnson Space Center, 1974.

Hise, E. C., et al. *MIUS Systems Analysis: Comparison of MIUS and Conventional Utility Systems for an Existing Development*, no. 20. Washington: U.S. Department of Housing and Urban Development, 1976.

Payne, H. R. *MIUS Technology Evaluation: Lithium Bromide-Water Absorption Refrigeration*, no. 7. Washington: U.S. Department of Housing and Urban Development, 1974.

Row, T. H., et al. *Final Environmental Statement—Application of Modular Integrated Utility Systems Technology.* Washington: U.S. Department of Housing and Urban Development, 1975.

CHAPTER 13

Transportation in Arid Areas

MATHEW J. BETZ

The world's urban populations are increasing at an unprecedented rate. This effects virtually every country, no matter what its economic status or geographical location. Countries such as Mexico, Brazil, Algeria, Egypt, Nigeria, the Sudan, Kenya, Pakistan, and Indonesia increased their urban populations at a compound growth rate exceeding 4 percent between 1970 and 1975. More developed countries such as Australia, Japan, Germany, Denmark, the United Kingdom, and the United States were, in 1970, already more than 75 percent urbanized.[1] As the preceding indicates, a number of the countries with both rapid population growth and high urbanization rates are in the arid areas of the world. In addition, within some of the major developed countries, the United States specifically, internal population shifts are causing population increases in arid areas. The fact that Arizona is the nation's second most rapidly growing state is evidence of this trend.

This chapter discusses the provision of transportation in arid regions, with an emphasis on urban areas. Much of the information cited is equally applicable to other climates, but an attempt is made to emphasize the unique characteristics caused by the lack of rainfall in arid areas with high annual temperatures, as opposed to the arctic or subarctic arid zones, since the former are the centers of much of the world's population growth. Concerning these areas, it is important to note at the outset that any kind of man-made development in these climatic conditions must be undertaken with the utmost care. The

world's hot, arid environments tend to be fragile, and therefore the flora and fauna must be carefully protected. In addition, many of the desert areas are prone to temperature inversions, which can lead to the rapid deterioration of air quality in urban areas. Furthermore, the arid zones are prone to natural phenomena such as sand or dust storms which can have detrimental effects on human development, as well as causing maintenance, deterioration, and safety problems in transportation systems.

In light of all these climatic factors, the need for careful water management in desert areas should be obvious. The survival of preindustrial human populations in these areas was, in fact, dependent on the development of community and cultural patterns that provided for exactly such management. The development of irrigated agricultural areas and cities has further emphasized this need to the point that water supply problems, in the short run, are now often less acute in desert areas than in areas where rainfall is more abundant and, therefore, taken for granted.

INTERCITY TRANSPORTATION

Before addressing some of the issues pertinent to intraurban travel, a few words should be said concerning intercity transportation facilities in arid areas. The major characteristic of most areas lying between arid cities is the basic absence of a significant rural population.

There are probably four basic patterns of rural settlement that can be identified in these areas. The first of these is virtually no population whatsoever, as in the northwest corner of the Republic of the Sudan, other parts of the Sahara, and the interior of most of the world's great deserts. In these areas there is no major permanent or even semipermanent population, although occasionally there will appear either a preindustrial or a modern caravan.

The second basic pattern is one with a significant, but not a large, nomadic population. These peoples usually change their abode on a seasonal basis and generally are involved with livestock of one sort or another. In desert areas with seasonally adequate rainfall, these seminomadic peoples may have specific locations where they raise some crops.

The third basic pattern—and the one that is probably most important as well as most common—is that of clustered, relatively permanent settlements. Obviously, these normally are located at available water sources, whether they be natural springs, water holes, rivers, or modern water resource sites. These settlements may in time become a node for urban growth, since water is available there, usually for preurban agricultural use. These clusters of villages, which may later become towns or cities, are generally widely interspersed throughout the area and are probably more self-contained than similar villages or small towns that develop in more temperate climates. A very limited study of Arizona towns with populations of approximately 50,000 indicates that the development of community spirit and the determination to complete community plans may be somewhat stronger in these clustered, water-based arid communities than in communities at higher elevations which have adequate rainfall and water. Although no analysis has been done, it could be hypothesized that this is an outgrowth of the need for cooperation between individuals, families, and small community organizations in these arid villages in the management of the irrigation systems necessary to the survival and economic health of the community.

A fourth and very rare pattern in arid areas is that of dispersed individual family units or other very small social units uniformly over a large area. Such a pattern is found in the Navaho nation in Arizona and New Mexico. It demands not only the provision of an extensive, all-weather transportation system but also extensive social and cultural institutions serving the overall community.

As the preceding patterns suggest, the need for regional transportation and the demands for facilities tend to be less in arid areas than in more temperate ones. Furthermore, they tend to reflect more intercity

travel and transport demands than hinterland-to-city travel and demands. In fact, the hierarchical pattern often identified in temperate regions, stemming from dispersed farming and livestock operations centered on a local village, which serves as the hinterland for a nearby county town that, in turn, serves as the hinterland for a major city, is not as evident in arid areas.

It is possible that as arid areas develop, as has already been seen in the southwestern United States, they will be characterized by a limited number of large urban areas, which are farther apart than those in temperate regions. The intercity transport demands of such a pattern are obvious. First of all, there will be less demand, in most cases, for a highly interconnected and thorough transportation system throughout the region, such as is necessary when the region is populated by small to moderate sized farms. In addition, since the cities will be relatively far apart (a hundred miles or more) the role of intercity air transport, both as a new technology and as one better suited to connect distant points, will become more important. This is not to say that it will supersede ground transportation for the movement of people or goods, but only that it will be relatively more important in terms of both commercial and private operations than it would be in a community of similar size in a more temperate environment. This development will be accentuated because most of the larger urban complexes now developing in arid areas are developing, not from an agricultural or similar base (although there are exceptions where large-scale irrigation projects are under way, such as the area between the White and Blue Niles in the Republic of the Sudan), but rather as centers of tourism and national and international business (such as the Middle East petroleum-based cities). These different orientations will further emphasize the role of air transportation because it is a major servant of both the businessman and the long-distance tourist. Furthermore, not only will air transportation play an increasingly important role, but also the specific location of the airport in the arid urban community and its connecting ground transportation will pose difficult and significant planning problems.

For intercity ground transportation the arid regions generally provide a more friendly environment from the engineer's perspective. Because of the lack of freeze–thaw problems and, generally speaking, moisture throughout most of the year, the investment in all types of roadway, railroad bed, and even support facilities for elevated, high-speed ground transportation will be less than in wetter climates. One cautionary note must be added, however: although subsoil moisture may be less of a problem, the provision of surface water drainage facilities cannot be neglected because many desert areas are subject to periodic flooding or flash flooding and therefore require significant drainage facilities (often appearing excessive to the lay traveler) to handle the high-intensity, short-duration flow of water.

THE STRUCTURE OF A TRIP

To understand both urban and interurban travel and to identify the functional advantages and disadvantages of different modes of transportation, it is useful to develop a conceptual framework that identifies the several components of a particular trip. One method is to divide the trip into four basic parts: collection, distribution, line haul, and transfer functions. These are depicted in Figure 1.

This framework is flexible enough to apply to virtually any trip. For example, in considering an interurban trip, the collection and distribution might be the ground transportation within the two communities; the line haul might be the air link between them; and, finally, the transfer would occur at the airport terminals. Furthermore, the ground segment at either end of this large trip can itself be analyzed by the same method. For example, the individual may have been driven to a central city terminal and

taken from there by bus or high-speed ground transportation to the airport. In this case the auto trip from the home to the downtown terminal would be the collection function, the city terminal the transfer point, the bus or other transit ride to the airport the line haul function, and the processing through the airport itself the distribution function. The application of the method to more typical intraurban trips, by automobile or mass transit, is illustrated in Figure 1.

Technological Improvement. The concept is especially helpful in identifying the portions of a trip that have been improved by advanced technology as opposed to those that still abound with adverse characteristics, from the user's point of view. Modern technology, generally speaking, as applied to transportation systems, has increased the speed, efficiency, and capacity of the line haul function. This is true in regional transportation as well as in intraurban movements. Furthermore, most of the concepts that have been recently proposed further improve the speed and capacity of this function. Although improvement in the line haul does increase the overall efficiency of the trip, there is a point of diminishing returns with regard to the improvement of this component and the neglect of all others. Supersonic transport for midrange and intracontinental travel is a prime contemporary example of this phenomenon. What good is the saving of an hour on a 1000 to 2000 mi trip when the processing time at the airport terminals and the ground transportation to these terminals remain unchanged?

The technology of urban transportation available to solve the problems will not be emphasized here. Although relatively few new forms of urban mobility have been implemented over the past quarter century, it should be noted that conceptual and component innovations during that period have broadened the choice of transit systems into a continuous spectrum of alternatives. This spectrum ranges from conventional rapid rail transit, to buses using special freeway lanes, to individualized mass transit which approaches the automobile in personalized service and flexibility. The last group would include dual-mode systems, public-supported car pools, and a number of other newly developed, personalized rapid transit concepts. Within the existing forms the possible diversification of propulsion systems is equally as broad. The prevailing internal combustion engine and electric traction motors will probably continue to

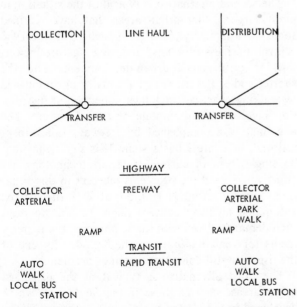

Figure 1. The structure of a trip. Redrawn from Mathew J. Betz and Judson Matthias, *Thirteenth Arizona Town Hall on Traffic and Highways* (Phoenix: Arizona Academy, 1968), p. 74.

be modified and remain dominant for some time. However, alternative propulsion systems, many with a low pollution potential, may play an increasingly important role. These use fuel cells, conventional electric batteries, solar cells, linear electric motors, mechanical flywheels, external combustion, and other more or less exotic alternatives.[2]

Improvements in the collection and distribution functions have been fewer. They do come into consideration, however, when the transportation planners talk of "flexibility." By this term they generally mean the ability to move the individual from a collection function, through a line haul, and back to a distribution function without interfering with the individual and his immediate surroundings. Of the currently popular forms of urban transportation, the automobile has the greatest flexibility, according to this definition. However, there are possibilities of developing dual modes of transportation as well as initiating more personal service on public transportation which will exhibit high flexibility.

The most difficult portion of the trip to improve through modern technology is the transfer function. In many cases improvement of the transfer situation involves problems of management and scheduling, rather than of engineering hardware. In trips using mass transit, the transfer points are the terminals, stations, and bus stops. These have long been noted to be major stumbling blocks in the development of efficient and attractive mass transit systems.[3] (The effects of these stumbling blocks will be discussed later.)

As the transfer point is traditionally the most critical and difficult to improve in regional transportation and urban transit, so it is also for trips using the automobile. In the freeway automobile trip the transfer point is the interchange and the immediately adjacent area. Recently, more attention has been given to the necessity of controlling the flow of traffic at these interchanges, and several recommendations concerning the metering of ramp traffic have been implemented. Complicating the picture is the necessity of controlling land development in the interchange area, for such land is quickly developed because of the economic desirability of efficient access to the freeway system.

Alternative Urban Trips. Both the relative and the absolute length of the various portions of a trip (collection, distribution, and line haul) are important when evaluating possible alternative transportation

modes. Three possible combinations are (1) relatively short collection and distribution compared to line haul; (2) relatively short collection or distribution with the other component longer; and (3) relatively long collection and distribution with respect to the line haul (but relatively equal with respect to one another). In other cases, where the line haul portion is short in absolute terms, the total trip is usually short and will lend itself to some form of local and very flexible transportation. In the overall analysis of urban networks, the shorter trips are not particularly significant, especially since many of these never leave the local transportation facilities such as the local streets. Currently, such trips are made either by foot, bicycle, or automobile. There will almost never be a sufficient accumulation of short trips in any one part of an urban area to justify a high-capacity system. Thus, for large-system evaluation, it is the three combinations listed above of longer trips that are of interest. Where the line haul portion is of considerable length, trips with different collections and distributions often combine, requiring a relatively high-capacity system.

In the first alternative, the long line haul is connected to very short collection and distribution functions. This pattern is usually indicative of high-density development featuring a concentration of like activities. Here the collection and distribution functions are normally accomplished by walking or possibly taking some form of minitransit or a taxi.

The second alternative is typical of the situation in many larger, older urban areas that have retained some high-intensity districts (usually in pre-1940 central business districts) but now feature newer, low-density, dispersed urban developments. Thus the shorter end of the trip may typically be accomplished by walking, whereas the longer collection or distribution involves an automobile or transit system. The line haul is accomplished by freeway, rail transit, railroad, or express bus system. It is significant that no single form of current transport technology has effectively solved the problems inherent in this situation. Some dual-mode transportation forms or the automated highway concept might be able to meet such demands. Even with these, however, the requirements for vehicle storage at the high-density end of the trip may still constitute a serious problem.

The third alternative is typical of the dispersed urban areas, such as those in the Southwest, which developed in the United States and in other countries after World War II. The problems in this situation are most effectively met by automotive transportation or rubber-tired forms of transit (e.g., the bus). They could also be solved by dual-mode systems in the future.

It should be emphasized again that the conditions at the transfer points are probably the most important and most difficult to improve. The preceding brief discussion of three alternative trips illustrates the ability (or inability) of general types of transportation to meet different kinds of urban demand. In general, the first can be solved by using technology that provides for high-speed, high-capacity line haul and relatively slow collection and distribution. The third may allow some decrease in the efficiency of the line haul function but requires more efficient and probably faster collection and distribution. The second, as we noted, is often the most difficult of all to handle, since it combines the problems of the first with those of the third.

THE INTRAURBAN TRANSPORTATION PROBLEM

Trip Purpose, Length, and Timing: Defining the Problem. In order to address the basic urban transport problem, it is necessary to understand the nature of urban transportation demand. The urbanite does not travel for the sake of travel alone. His travel is a response to demands placed upon him to do the things that are important to his social and economic well-being. Thus it is the social and economic structure of the urban area, especially as reflected in the land use pattern, which is of primary importance in determining the transportation demands and in evaluating the feasibility of alternative systems.

Residential land use is the most prevalent in all urban areas, the home being the focal point of the individual's activities. Thus the residential location is the most probable beginning and ending point of urban travel during a normal 24 hr period. (In addition, the home and its characteristics—the neighborhood density, location, economic level—are probably the best socioeconomic indicators of transportation.) These trips, often referred to as home-base trips, in fact, represent about 80 percent of all urban travel. If this percentage seems high, we must remember that the vast majority of urban trips are single purpose in nature. Thus the typical trip is from home to work with a later trip back home, or from home to shopping center with an immediate return.

If we define the purpose of a trip by the activity engaged in at the destination, the normal distribution

of trip purposes is as indicated in Table 1. These purposes include both going home plus going someplace to do such conventional activities as working, shopping, socializing, or recreating. It can be seen from the table that the trip to work represents a substantial portion (20 percent) of urban transportation. It must also be remembered that this figure represents only the trips to work and, for every trip to work within a 24 hr period, there is also a trip from work, most of which will end at the residence. Thus approximately 40 percent of urban travel is work oriented. Table 2 indicates the normal distribution of land use in American metropolitan areas. A comparison of the two tables illustrates the importance of commercial and industrial activities in transportation planning. Although 20 percent of all trips are to work locations, only 6.5 to 7 percent of total land area is industrial. Even if the 2.5 to 3.5 percent devoted to commercial use were to be included, this would still be significantly less than the 20 percent figure for trips to work, not even including the 9 percent figure for business trips. A similar statement can be made concerning shopping trips: they account for approximately 10 percent of travel, but commercial use represents only approximately 3 percent of the total land area. Thus the intensity of transportation demand depends on the land use. This is what should be expected, since there are underlying economies which result in the concentration of manufacturers or merchants in order to achieve industrial or retail efficiency.

A second important relationship, that between the average length of a trip and the trip purpose, is illustrated in Figure 2. Trip length can be measured in either time or in distance traveled. Normally, time is used for urban studies. As indicated in Figure 2, a high percentage of shopping trips and most other

Table 1   Typical Urban Trip Purposes

Activity at Destination	Percent of Trips
Residential	40
Work	20
Shop	10
Social–recreational	11
Business	9
School	3
Miscellaneous	7

Source: Mathew J. Betz and Judson Matthias, *Thirteenth Arizona Town Hall on Traffic and Highways* (Phoenix: Arizona Academy, 1968), p. 50.

Table 2   Typical Urban Land Use

Land Use	Percent of Total Developed Land
Residential	37.0–43.0
Commercial	2.5–3.5
Industrial	6.5–7.5
Railroad	4.0–5.0
Streets	27.0–30.0
Parks and playgrounds	4.0–7.0
Other	10.0–11.0

Source: Mathew J. Betz and Judson Matthias, *Thirteenth Arizona Town Hall on Traffic and Highways* (Phoenix: Arizona Academy, 1968), p. 52.

nonwork trips in urban areas are short, whereas work trips tend to be significantly longer. In fact, it is almost universally true that work trips are the longest of all urban trips. This is to be expected, for the urbanite tries to optimize his economic position. Thus, if shopping, one normally goes to the closest retail location that provides the needed goods. If this is a loaf of bread, the trip may be quite short; if it is a week's groceries, the trip may be somewhat longer; if it is a new automobile (a very unusual shopping need), the trip may be longer than the average work trip, although made only occasionally.

It is the trip to work, however, that is of extreme importance. One does not necessarily accept the job located closest to his home, since to do so may well

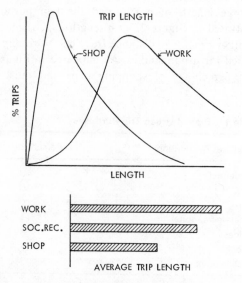

Figure 2. Typical urban trip lengths. From Mathew J. Betz and Judson Matthias, *Thirteenth Arizona Town Hall on Traffic and Highways* (Phoenix: Arizona Academy, 1968), p. 60.

mean the loss of income that could be obtained by traveling somewhat farther. Theories have been advanced that there should be a close relationship between one's place of residence and one's place of employment because of the regularity of travel between the two. However, there is little to indicate that there is a relationship that might minimize transportation cost or commuting time. A desirable place to live, determined by housing availability, educational facilities, cultural activities, and other amenities, and a job featuring the best working conditions and the highest possible income are probably the two most important goals in the life of the modern urbanite. In most cases he will attempt to obtain the best possible home location and work situation and will be willing to spend considerable time and money on transportation in order to commute between the two. Therefore it should not be surprising that the work trip is substantially longer than any other urban trip.

It should be noted that today's urban transportation problem (one that will still plague us 20 years from now) occurs 2 or 3 hr/day during two peak periods.[4] It is during these peak hours that transportation facilities are most heavily loaded. The other 20 hr of the day find most urban areas with capacity that exceeds transportation demands. It is not uncommon to find that 10 percent of the total daily transportation demand occurs in the morning peak hour and another 10 percent in the afternoon peak hour. In most urban areas midday nonpeak travel, in terms of person trips (the number of people traveling times the number of trips they make in a specific time period), is less than one half of that during the peak demand period. There are two fundamentally important characteristics of this peak period that need to be emphasized: first, the intensity of the period contrasted with the off-peak travel; and second, the substantial proportion of the peak period transportation that is composed of work-oriented trips. If the short walking and bicycle trips of students to school are not included in the data for American urban areas, trips to work will normally exceed 70 percent of the peak hour trips. Hence peak hour congestion and demands on the overall transportation system are even more acute than is indicated by the intensity of the peak as measured by person trips, because of the predominance of the work-oriented trip, which is longer than the other or average urban trips.

In the United States the difference between the peak use of public transit and the use at other hours is even more extreme than that for total urban traffic. It is not unusual for the peak hour transit use to be from 15 to 20 percent of the daily total. This is reflected in a very high lack of transit use during off-peak periods and a very low level of use during weekends. Thus transit operators currently have to answer very high demands during short periods, which seldom exceed a total of 15 to 20 hr/week.[5] At other times, because of the terms of their franchise or other legal commitments, they must provide services even though there are few passengers and little revenue. To understand the difficulty of operating under these conditions, we need only to imagine the economic disadvantages to a factory forced to produce a product on such a basis. Finally, mass transit, largely because of its peak hour load, is even more heavily oriented toward the work trip than is private transportation, for it is used almost exclusively for trips to work and school. Many people inhabiting arid areas have accommodated themselves to the climate by introducing a long midday break (the siesta, in Latin American countries). This creates four pronounced peak periods within the day, since, in many of these urban areas, a substantial number of workers return to home at midday. This improves the transit's operation and financial position, but it also substantially increases transportation costs for the worker.

In summary, it is the combination of the purpose, length, and timing of urban trips that defines the urban transportation need and causes the urban transportation problem, which is largely the peak hour problem. The systems are overloaded because trips are not evenly distributed throughout the day but are concentrated into short periods. That the trips involved at peak hours also happen to be the longest intraurban trips accentuates the problem. The situation for mass transit, as we noted, is even more acute. We might therefore suggest that a rational attack on the urban transportation problem would involve a specific analysis of peak periods, and most particularly the work trip, for it is questionable whether the transportation planners need to be too concerned with trips that occur during off-peak hours. Thus the normal procedure of examining all trips and determining peak hour factors may be somewhat in error. We might suggest that only the trips to work be analyzed: this might be both easier and more accurate. Although much of the growth in urban travel will be in off-peak trips generated because of increasing real affluence, there is no indication that the peaks will not retain their extreme importance.

The Bases of Individual Choice: Evaluating Solutions. It is the individual urban dweller's decisions that produce urban transportation demands. Thus, in planning for new facilities or in planning new areas, an understanding of that decision-making process is helpful. In regard to transportation many characteristics such as cost, speed, comfort, and privacy are important. As some of these may be difficult to evaluate in purely monetary terms, the analysis of transportation alternatives from the users' viewpoint is often complex. Only in the past few years has research—much of it borrowed from the social and the psychological sciences—been productive in this area and been substantiated by collected basic data.

A fundamental assumption underlying all these discussions is that the individual user is rational in his decisions among the urban transportation alternatives available. The problem is to identify his rationale. This requires not only a consideration of nonquantifiable items such as comfort and privacy but also a realization that the user is not equally sensitive to the expenditure of all quantifiable items such as time and money. We will touch briefly on a number of these variables to demonstrate what knowledge is currently available and to indicate the characteristics of transportation systems that both positively and negatively affect their users.

Although it is generally agreed that there are a number of nonmeasurable factors, at least two can be measured: the dollar costs of transportation and the time it takes to make a trip. Although most economic analyses rightfully indicate and compare the total cost of transportation alternatives, we must realize that the individual, in making decisions among such alternatives, generally does not decide on a total-cost basis. Economists have long contended that the effect on the public is modified by the timing of and the method used in charging the costs to the individual. The widely used credit card and the witholding feature of the national income tax are examples of such modifications. When alternatives are compared, there is a question of whether previous investments should be included or whether such earlier decisions should be neglected. When this question is brought down to the individual level, the answer is obvious, for there such previous investments have a profound effect. In fact, this factor probably has an overriding influence on the individual's view of the direct costs of alternative forms of urban transportation.

Specifically, once an automobile or any other unit of privately owned transportation has been purchased, the user very seldom includes depreciation in his decision regarding its use for a particular trip. This is especially true for relatively short urban trips. (Depreciation may become a factor when planning an extensive interurban trip of several hundred miles.) This is not to say that the individual never considers this cost. It is probably very seriously considered before the initial purchase and in relation to the availability, cost, and convenience of all other modes of transportation. It is expected that the depreciation of vehicles will be less severe in arid climates than in those having harsh winters or seacoast-related salt problems. Nonetheless, depreciation costs will represent, in any climate, a substantial portion of the total vehicle operating cost. There is, furthermore, a possibility that, because of the high rate of private car style obsolescence, the factor may be at work in reverse. This would be the case when the individual user, having purchased a vehicle, believes that he needs to "get his money out of it." He would then use this mode of transportation even when a full consideration of costs would indicate it to be an unwise alternative. Similar owner philosophies may be applied to other periodic costs such as insurance, garaging, general maintenance, and even tire replacement.

The expenditures that have the greatest impact on users are those which are collected on a cash basis each time a service is used. Typical of these costs are parking fees, tolls, and transit fares. In fact, many users, when taking a short urban trip, do not (even when asked) evaluate its cost in terms of gasoline consumed. They consider that the gasoline purchase has already been made, and, although they realize a certain amount of fuel will be burned on each trip, they think rather in terms of filling the tank every so often. They do not consider one short trip as having much of an effect on the gas level or cost. It seems, then, that, because of the methods of cost collection, individually owned or publicly supported types of transportation will tend to be favored. Any facility that collects the cost of transportation from the user as each individual trip is accomplished is at a major disadvantage.

The second quantifiable determinant of urban transportation choices is travel time. The transportation user considers this to be the total trip time, that is, the time from when he leaves an origin until he gets to his destination. The user is more sensitive to this total time than to potential time savings involving just the line haul portion of the trip.

In measuring the amount of time saved by making a trip via one mode as compared to another, at least two major items are of interest. The first is whether the actual time saved really provides an advantage, and the second is the monetary value that can be placed on the savings. In the first case it seems reasonable to assume that the individual's view of any time saved must certainly take into account the pleasantness or unpleasantness experienced during the trip. Time is said to "fly" when a person is engaged in an interesting or appealing activity. On the other hand, a very short period of time may seem quite long if spent under unpleasant or hostile conditions. Although this seems like a very real and simple concept, its application to the development of urban transit systems and to an understanding of their users' decision-making processes has not been quantified until recently. These new studies indicate that time spent in waiting (sometimes called excess travel time) during a trip is weighted between 2 and 12 times as much as the same amount of time spent in motion.[6] Thus, any waiting, such as waiting for a vehicle to move, waiting at a transfer point, or waiting at an intersection, is viewed very negatively. Although not documented, an extension of these findings may indicate that the conditions under which one waits are also of importance. Thus, in a hot, arid area, the time spent in waiting at an exposed bus stop may be an even more important deterrent to the use of bus systems than in temperate zones. Heavy arid-area community investment in modern air-conditioned buses may be of relatively small importance to the user if he must spend 15 or more min waiting in intense heat. Although it is not definitively known whether a few long waits are more offensive than a large number of shorter delays (with the same total delay and under the same conditions), it would not be unreasonable to assume that the numerous short delays would be more exasperating.

Other important characteristics of time expenditures become clear if we investigate the user's view of the monetary value of time. Since many, if not most, improvements in urban transportation are justified, not on the basis of a reduction in operating cost but rather on the basis of a reduction in travel time, transportation economists have been interested for years in establishing the value of time. First of all, it is essentially the use to which the saved time is put that is important in determining its value. Thus we should be careful of an analysis which indicates that one alternative is better than another because of very small time savings (a minute or two) on the individual trip, even though this may be multiplied thousands of times each day of the year, since this small amount of time, although accumulated by many people, probably would not be put to much productive use as far as the economy is concerned. The value of time saved is, furthermore, certainly a function of the purpose of the travel. Third, it is also related to the income (or productivity) of the individual making the trip.

Research has indicated that the urban traveler is quite sophisticated in his view of the value of time saved. The value assigned per unit saved tends to increase with the absolute amount of time saved, reflecting the first factor noted above. In simple terms, this means that a saving of 1 min on each of 10 trips is not valued nearly as much by the user as a saving of 10 min on 1 trip. Furthermore, research indicates that the user is sensitive to the fact that a small amount of time saved on many urban trips cannot be put to productive use. One study of urban travel indicates that the value placed on time savings ranges between 25 and 40 percent of the pay rate of the traveler's occupation.[7]

Beyond these two quantitative factors of money and time, numerous other factors—most of which cannot be quantified—have a direct effect on the individual's choice among urban travel alternatives. These include frequency of service, necessity of changing vehicles, reliability of service, expected delays, personal comfort, sense of freedom and safety, control of one's environment, and convenience. It can be readily seen that a number of these will be more critical in arid areas, especially in months when high temperatures prevail. One primary concern seems to be the reliability of the travel mode in reaching a destination in a proper or at an expected time. This factor is quite important for the work trip.[8]

Two general considerations that subsume many of the factors cited above are comfort and convenience. These would include the absence of waiting lines, the availability and comfort of seats, the presence of storage space for packages, privacy, the ability to listen or not to listen to the radio, the ability to smoke or to be separated from those who do, and the ability to control temperature and ventilation. The fact that these are normally more important to the individual on a work trip than on a trip for another purpose probably reflects both the length of the trip and, possibly, a desire to be free of others after hav-

ing been subjected to the stresses of the day at the place of employment. This may also be one explanation of why car occupancy is lower during peak than during off-peak hours.

From the preceding discussion it is fairly obvious that the more things are learned about urban transportation, the greater is the necessity to analyze the entire trip and its various components in both relative and absolute terms. These facts, once analyzed, must be brought to bear on decisions concerning future transport investments, for any system should be designed to minimize the discovered adverse factors.[9] Typical guidelines that might, after study, be established are the following:

1. Minimize the direct cost to the user.
2. Avoid repeated direct charges for service.
3. Minimize travel in time and distance.
4. Keep delays and waiting periods to a minimum.
5. Minimize especially any small recurring delays.
6. Decrease uncertainty either by established schedules or by frequent service.
7. Provide relatively small travel compartments or units for maximal privacy.
8. Provide the individual with the greatest amount of control possible over his environment, including ventilation, temperature, and smoking.
9. Minimize transfers and improve the conditions encountered at transfer points.
10. Maximize safety and freedom from breakdowns.

Urban Form: Minimizing the Problem. To establish the form and distribution of land use in an urban area is to determine, to a large extent, its transportation needs. The industrial cities that grew substantially before World War II were often characterized by being radial in form. Because the major form of transportation was steel rail technology (either elevated subway systems, street cars, or commuter railroads), a limited number of lines were built, and these normally radiated out from the center of the city. High-density development occurred adjacently to these rail lines, since the collection and distribution functions from the stations were normally provided by walking. Furthermore, this pattern identified and intensified the dominance of the central business district as the focus for most economic and commercial activity, including most retail trade.

After World War II, with the increased availability of automobiles, their relatively low cost, and the rising real incomes in many countries, rubber-tired technology made possible an expansion of the urban area's geographic limits. From a technological view, the automobile, unlike the railroads, which required a substantial investment in road bed and rail before any transportation could occur, was flexible enough to permit the use of narrow, poorly constructed streets and, in fact, unpaved streets and roads for access to new urban residential areas. The automobile had no directional preferences and could travel almost anywhere there was a dry surface. Thus it gave the urbanite increased accessibility to large areas. Many urban dwellers moved to these newly accessible areas and built (in low-density patterns) single-family dwelling units. Furthermore, parallel improvements in communication, management science, and freight movement resulted in the decentralization of many business and industrial activities that themselves were in a period of rapid growth. Following the same stimuli, retail sales and other central district activities were dispersed throughout the urban area.

There is a very important point to be learned from the preceding: the relationship between urban form and transportation technology. The steel wheel technology limited the number of lines that could be built and the amount of land that could be economically developed. It was the introduction of a more flexible transportation technology that ended these constraints. This made available new areas for urban development, but it did not require that this land be developed, or that it would necessarily develop, in a low-density, dispersed fashion. Obviously, other forces were at work, including increasing affluence, value scales, cultural heritage, and governmental policies, which helped determine the desirability of single-family, low-density development. Thus there is no reason to believe that the automobile caused the new pattern of development; its availability did, however, allow the low-density pattern to happen. This kind of relationship between urban form and transportation must be considered in planning any future urban development, especially in arid zones.

The terms "dispersion" and "low density" have been used repeatedly in the preceding paragraphs. It is important to define "dispersion" accurately as well as to identify some of the future problems characteristic of dispersed development which may have an impact on urban transportation but which may be avoided by adequate planning. First, dispersion is not necessarily related to density. The opposite of disper-

sion is concentration, and, in the context here, the latter term refers to both concentration and commonality. Thus "concentration" means the location of all like activities in one area. It means placing all the retail establishments in one area or all the libraries in one area or all the governmental activities in one area. Certainly a large regional shopping center represents concentrated retail activity, but is not "concentration" as the term is used here, since the center does not represent all the retail activity in the entire metropolitan area. Therefore dispersion or concentration is an areawide phenomenon, and the entire urbanized area has to be considered in evaluating whether substantial concentration or dispersion has taken place.

Dispersion is usually directly connected in many people's minds with low-density development, since, in most areas of the United States, the two have occurred together. They do not necessarily have to occur together, however. It is possible to have very high density activity, residential or other, in a dispersed pattern. High-rise office buildings dispersed throughout an urban area are one example. The large regional shopping centers mentioned above are another example of a highly intense activity, and yet the centers are dispersed. Conversely, relatively low density concentrations might be possible if one could conceive of an urban area with modern, one-story industrial plants, all collected into one section of the metropolitan area. Here the density might be no higher than in dispersed patterns, but certainly there would be concentration and the one area would be common on a regular basis to the majority of urban workers.

This distinction between dispersion and density was made because the two result in different types of transportation problems. A tendency toward concentration and the development of a point of commonality has a systemwide effect. Theoretically, trip lengths will have to increase, since a large proportion of trips taken will be to this common area. To provide for the concentration of transportation demand from the entire urban area to this point, extensive facilities will be required at the immediate point of concentration and for some distance away from it. This will be true whether the concentration is high density or low density, although the problem may be somewhat more acute for high-density concentration. On the other hand, the introduction of a high-density-use area in a dispersed pattern will generally have little effect on the overall transportation system or demand picture. It may, however, cause acute problems for the transportation facilities in the immediate area. Thus the exact location of one high-rise office building or one high-density residential complex or regional shopping center will not significantly change the overall requirements of the transportation system but will affect local design decisions.

As emphasized earlier, the urban transportation problem is mainly that of controlling the flow of traffic between home and work. Thus, although concentration and dispersion of all urban activities have definite social and political impacts, from the transportation standpoint we must especially consider the concentration and dispersion of industrial and residential land use.

Urban development in arid areas will normally occur with increasing population and probably with increasing real income. Based on the experience of the last 25 to 50 years, good advice for such areas would be to avoid concentration and thus avoid backing into the situation faced today by many large American metropolitan areas. Plans for tomorrow often reflect today's problems but unfortunately are based on yesterday's traditions. It seems that every generation looks back on the preceding one and sees it as good and secure. In reality, memory is dulled and has forgotten the troubles and tribulations that caused people of that earlier era to desire to change their condition. To identify tomorrow's problems and to solve them with innovative ideas and technologies is much more difficult, but it is critical that this be done in arid areas.

As indicated earlier, airport location is extremely important in all urban areas, especially in the newer communities developing in an arid environment. Thus, in these urban areas, the one point of concentration that is increasing in importance and seems, at this time, to defy dispersion is the airport. It may well be that in arid urban communities the airport, more than any other single location, represents a point of common experience for the population. Thus it is not inconceivable that in the future the airport may develop some of the transportation problems normally found in central business districts in older metropolitan areas. The question should be given considerable attention, and decentralization of airport activity, as currently seen in southern California, may not be an unrealistic alternative.

A recommended planning philosophy will incorporate dispersion as a basic principle and probably do much to minimize transportation demand. This will

be referred to as the concept of a community. The resulting communities would have many of the attributes of the new towns being built in Great Britain and continental Europe, except that, in many of these locations, they are geographically separated from the rest of the nation's or area's urban development. However, an urban complex of significant size could be developed by what might be called an "accumulation of communities." These communities would contain all the urban activities needed to make them substantially self supporting. Therefore they would provide not only governmental, cultural, recreational, educational, and retail activities but also, very importantly, employment opportunities for the residents. They would be based on the fundamental premise that everyone who works in the community can live there and everybody who lives there can work there. Specifically, a balance between employment and residential units, with the provision of an adequate range of residential types to accommodate families of different sizes and incomes, would be provided.

Similar communities already in existence vary considerably in size, and there has been much academic argument over the ideal size of such an urban development. However, the British experience indicates that the towns originally planned were too small, and the towns currently being planned and developed are often designed for 150,000 to 250,000 residents. The lower of these two numbers is probably more appropriate when forming a major urban complex from an accumulation of abutting communities. The important fact is that each community is planned as a unit with an internal balance. In the United States the use of the neighborhood as a basic building block has led, in some cases, to city planning without adequate consideration for industrial needs. It must be remembered that the basic *raison d'être* for an urban complex is to collect people so that they enjoy a better life and earn a better livelihood.

It is one thing to design and build isolated new towns such as those in Great Britain; it is quite another to consider the community as a basic building block for a large, continuous urban area. Communities could conceivably be designed to be adjacent to one another with no intervening open area. Such communities, furthermore, might not necessarily have rigid boundaries, although each resident would envision his own community as that in which he operated socially and economically on a regular basis. The actual boundaries, therefore, originally somewhat ill defined, might change with time or they might be different for different functions: one's social community defined by one boundary; his retail community by another. In addition, his community boundaries would be somewhat different from his neighbor's, but there would be much held in common as well.

This type of community concept can be used in dispersed urban areas and is especially relevant for rapidly developing or new cities. It is also well suited to those located in the relatively flat topography common in many arid areas. The concept decreases the number of points of commonality for urban dwellers. It reflects a dispersion of activities and it uses this dispersion to gain relief from the peak hour transportation problems by generally shortening the home-to-work trip and possibly substituting walking and bicycle trips for existing vehicular trips.[10]

CONCLUSION

This chapter has tried to identify some of the basic characteristics of problems in and relationships involved with urban transportation, specifically in connection with the development in arid areas. It has identified the fundamental problem as that of dealing with the trip between the residential location and the work site. There are a number of possible designs for new communities which can alleviate existing problems.

One option is to concentrate all employment opportunities and residences in relatively confined, clearly identifiable areas. Such concentration at both the origin and the destination of the work trip will, it is hoped, encourage the use of high-capacity, rapid transit facilities. The alternative is to disperse residential land use and, more importantly, the sites of employment throughout the urban area in order to obtain a balanced traffic flow throughout the system, and to rely principally on rubber-tire technology. For new development, especially in arid areas, realization of the crucial relationship between land use and transportation can lead to the adoption of the community concept discussed above in order to shorten the length of the work trip and encourage nonvehicular travel. Even if such an area realizes an increase in affluence and hence in car ownership, the vehicular trips not only will be shorter but also may not concentrate in specific corridors, and thus substantial investments in high-capacity automotive routes will not be required.

In both existing arid communities and future developments where the automobile tends to be the major form of transportation, every attempt should be made to achieve greater efficiency in the home-to-work movement. Many cities throughout the United States have made extensive investments in traffic engineering and traffic management systems such as computer control of traffic signals to ease the peak hour problem. It is likely, however, that the problem will be substantially reduced only by changing the fundamental causes. For 15 years or more, repeated studies have been made on the feasibility of staggering working hours in an organized fashion to minimize the load on the transportation network. Simulations of the effects on transportation networks indicate that substantial relief could be obtained with only relatively minor changes in the starting and ending times at most places of employment. However, the idea, whenever suggested, has not met with enthusiasm. In many cases it would mean restructuring family schedules; this may cause the individual some inconvenience or increased transportation costs and, at the same time, not yield any great personal benefits. The situation might be likened to the psychological concept underlying the "tragedy of the commons," where the tendency of each member of a group of cattle owners sharing a common pasture is to overgraze the pasture to everybody's short-run benefit and long-run loss.

Recently, because of fuel shortages, resulting increased fuel costs, and environmental concerns, the concept of car pooling to and from work has become more popular. It should be noted again that average car occupancy is lower during peak than off-peak hours. Thus increased car pooling may raise the efficiency no higher than it is already for nonwork trips. Some industries have provided their employees with station wagons or vans at company expense with the understanding that the employees will provide transportation to and from work for a number of their colleagues. Either company-sponsored pooling of vans or voluntary car pooling has definite advantages to the employer such as reduction in the parking space needed and, thus, financial outlays for such facilities; enhanced attractiveness of the company to potential employees; and improved public relations. The major advantage to the employee is the reduction of commuting costs. Also, since the family car is not or is not always used for the trip to work, it is available to other family members. Obviously, the major advantages are those to the general public: reduced traffic congestion on streets and highways, less air and noise pollution, and increased energy conservation.

Some consideration should be given to the possible elimination of the work trip as it is normally conceived. Considering the types of communities likely to be built within the next 20 years, this probably could be accomplished through the substitution of modern communication techniques for transportation. Little experimentation has been conducted in this area. The technology available today, using cable television and, in the near future, other techniques, would provide multichannel, audio-visual communication for use in a number of urban functions. A more immediate application might involve the retail sales and service industry and employee–client interaction (especially where information is the major commodity). A more visionary application, which would affect the urban peak hour problem, would be the identification of the employment functions that do not require physical interrelationship and the dispersal of them throughout the community. This would involve most businesses and educational facilities, but it would certainly not affect commodity production. Small work sites with modern communications then could be developed within neighborhoods or conceivably within the residential unit itself. Needless to say, such a change might require a readjustment of the attitudes of both employers and employees. Nonetheless, the technology for such dispersion of work and elimination of the work trip is available, and in many cases the job requirements would not need to be modified. Dispersion basically would involve a modification of attitudes concerning employer–employee relationships and concerning the traditional spatial concentration for employment functions based on production, not service industry, requirements. Many arid countries today have the resources to invest in such educational and business communication systems, and because of their very rapid growth they are less hindered by preexisting investments or traditions than are businesses in Europe and North America.

A more distant possibility is redesign of the basic urban physical structures to integrate vertically the functions that the community normally integrates horizontally. Paolo Soleri's Arcosanti represents one such vision. The John Hancock Building in Chicago with its integration of residential units, office units, and some service and cultural facilities offers an existing, if smaller, example of the same concept.

Finally, the chapter attempted to identify the basic phenomena resulting in urban transportation demand and the resulting urban transportation problem. It addressed some conceptual solutions to the problem but sought mainly to reinforce the concept that the transportation problem is the result of decisions concerning economic base, urban land use patterns, and other fundamental issues. The chapter suggested some conceptual alternatives to minimize transportation costs and congestion. It tried to explain how urban areas in an arid environment may have different problems, especially in relation to various modes of transportation, from those of the traditional metropolitan areas developed in temperate climates. Although the chapter touched only briefly on the question of intercity transportation, it identified this as an area where major differences could be expected in the various climatic areas.

The reader, it is hoped, now realizes that planning of the basic components of the urban area, is absolutely necessary if one is to understand future transportation demands, for specific transportation design alternatives can be developed and evaluated only when such understanding has been reached. Many of the arid areas of the world today are realizing increased populations and increased real income. Because of the fragility of their total environments, emphasis must be placed on the adequate planning of all aspects of new communities. In the ideal case such planning will emphasize tomorrow's problems and will involve the application of the latest social, technological, and management knowledge.

NOTES

1. "Survey of International Development," *Publications of Society for International Development,* **13,** no. 2 (March–April, 1976), 1–3.

2. See Mathew J. Betz and Eugene Wilson, *Transit and the Phoenix Metropolitan Area,* Valley Area Traffic and Transportation Study, no. 10 (Phoenix, 1970), pp. 21–44.

3. See *Mode-Change Facilities,* Transportation Research Board Record, no. 557 (Washington, 1975).

4. In some locations, where there is a substantial midafternoon break in commercial and other economic activities, it is possible to have four peak periods in the day. Such a pattern has been traditional in many of the world's hot, arid areas. Although the past decade has seen a decrease in this pattern, fuel and power costs for air conditioning may reverse this trend in the future.

5. Peat, Marwick, Livingston, and Company, *Evaluation of a Bus Transit System in a Selected Urban Area* (Washington: Federal Highway Administration, 1969), pp. 8–9.

6. See B. G. Hutchinson, *Principles of Urban Transport Systems Planning* (New York: McGraw-Hill, 1974), pp. 61–65; and S. Algers, S. Hanson, and G. Tegner, *Role of Waiting Time, Comfort and Convenience in Modal Choice for Work Trip,* Transportation Research Board, no. 534 (Washington, 1975), pp. 38–50.

7. See T. C. Thomas and G. I. Thompson, *The Value of Time for Commuting Motorists as a Function of Their Income Level and Amount of Time Saved,* Transportation Research Board, no. 314 (Washington, 1970), pp. 1–14.

8. See Algers, Hanson, and Tegner.

9. See P. R. Stropher et al., *Behavioral Demand Model and Valuation of Travel Time,* Transportation Research Board, no. 149 (Washington, 1973).

10. See Betz and Wilson, pp. 61–82.

SUGGESTED READINGS

Creighton, R. *Urban Transportation Planning.* Urbana: University of Illinois Press, 1970.

Dickey, J. W. *Metropolitan Transportation Planning.* Washington: Scripta Book Company, 1975.

Fromm, G., ed. *Transportation Investment and Economic Development.* Washington: Brookings Institution, Transportation Research Program, 1968.

Meyer, J. R., et al. *Techniques of Transport Planning.* Washington: Brookings Institution, [1971].

Owen, W. *Distance and Development: Transportation and Communications in India.* Washington: Brookings Institution, Transportation Research Program, 1968.

Owen, W. *Strategy for Mobility.* Washington: Brookings Institution, Transportation Research Program, 1964.

Stopher, P. R., and Meyburg, A. H. *Urban Transportation Modeling and Planning.* Lexington, Mass.: Lexington Books, 1975.

Physical Forms for Arid Zones 5

CHAPTER 14

Planning the Physical Form of an Arid-Region New Community

BRADFORD PERKINS

The planning and development of a new community involves a vast and constantly expanding array of skills. These skills have developed in response to the many factors that determine the feasibility and quality of a new community. This chapter discusses how these skills and factors come together in one area—planning the physical form of an arid-region community.

The fact that a community is located in an arid region does not immediately define its physical form. The lack of water is an important factor, but it is only one of many considerations that determine the design of such a new community. The following discussion not only analyzes the special physical design responses to the problems of an arid region but also places these design responses within the context of the many other factors that affect new-community design both here and overseas. Overall, this chapter argues that arid-region new community design should (and often does) reflect the impact of the climate, but in the United States other factors can—and usually do—determine physical form.

The resolution of all design problems involves the consideration of many often-conflicting issues, but new-community design introduces an additional level of complexity. This complexity results from four facts that differentiate community from building design.

First of all, the development process usually extends over a lengthy period of time: depending on the size of the community, it may last over 20 years. Thus the design for a new community is usually definitive only for the first phase (the only phase for which a specific building program exists) and provides a strategic framework for the many phases that follow. Definitive and rigid plans, such as those for Brasilia, are exceptions that ignore the dynamics of city building.

Second, behavioral factors become essential community design determinants. Design on a communitywide scale must respond to a broader range of needs than does an individual building, for the community can form the total living and working environment for many of its inhabitants. Failure to reflect these needs in the design can lead to sociological problems that destroy the community.

Third, there is no single client for most new communities. Typically, the organization that hires the planning and urban design team controls only approximately 15 percent of the total investment. Furthermore, most of the buildings are financed and controlled by third parties. Therefore indirect design controls such as zoning, building codes, urban design guidelines, or covenants, rather than direct design, have to serve as the basis for the controlled evolution of the community's physical form.

Finally, large-scale development is politically and financially fragile. In our recent review of 25 new towns both here and overseas, the majority faced severe problems because their development usually extended beyond the term of any one supporting government administration and beyond the peak of any economic cycle. For example, every one of the 16 federal Title VII communities experienced severe difficulties because of this exposure to major political and financial shifts.

The projects that have successfully survived these inherent difficulties have had to be particularly sensitive to the dynamic forces that shape the development of a new community. Some of the more common of these forces, as well as illustrations of their impacts on physical form, are discussed below.

THE DETERMINANTS OF PHYSICAL FORM

The Site.   The site is always a major determinant of physical form, and in arid regions sites are particularly important form determinants. Typically, they fall into one of two extremes: flat, featureless sites and dramatic mountain or hill-country locations. The former type, which is best illustrated by the sites of new communities being developed in Texas and Arizona, places the burden of creating an attractive urban environment on man-made features such as lakes or on the pattern and density of building structures. The site for Lake Havasu City, for example, has few distinguishing features except for the adjacent Lake Havasu and the specially constructed new waterway which was designed in conjunction with the relocated London Bridge. McCormick Ranch and The Lakes are other examples of new community developments where significant lake construction has taken place to relieve the harshness and sterility of the surrounding semidesert landscape.

By contrast, the hilly terrain utilized in a number of new developments in southern California or New Mexico acts as a major determinant of form and layout. Because of a high percentage of steep land and adverse geological conditions, the site of Rancho San Diego, a new community under construction in southern California, has only limited areas where conventional house construction is possible. Housing is therefore confined to relatively narrow bands on either side of the existing valley floor, which runs through the middle of the site.

The Natural Environment.   With either type of site, however, the environmental characteristics must be respected by the man-made features. In the case of federally sponsored projects, such as the Title VII

new communities, respect for the natural environment is enforced through required environmental impact analyses. In arid-region communities, however, environmental determinants and impacts have crucial developmental and economic implications, as well as administrative ones.

The environment is, of course, not the only basis for design definition. On some Llewelyn-Davies Associates projects, an environmental analysis has indeed helped to justify a complete reshaping of the project. However, it is more often an excellent tool to shape design themes. In fact, in providing a design theme to tie together a large site, the environmental analysis is far more effective than roads or other man-made project components, and it is particularly useful in helping to integrate a new project into an existing area. How this can happen can be illustrated by a few examples from several recent projects.

At the simplest end of the spectrum is the project for which an environmental analysis reveals a natural ordering system. In the development proposals for some new communities, the floodplains and drainage easements surrounding the watercourses on the site (considerations applicable even to arid regions) have provided the most logical definition of the open-space system. This in turn has determined the layout of the major road network servicing the communities.

At times, however, the search for this ordering element can be more difficult than the consideration of drainage boundaries. At Rancho San Diego a cursory analysis would probably have led to a plan that followed the land use logic of most other developments in the region. The environmental impact analysis, however, identified a number of factors that together provided a strong structuring element for the total design. Recognition of the hazard of brush fire, which is endemic to the region, and a concern for protecting native wildlife habitats, as well as the need to conserve water used in irrigating nonindigenous landscaping, all supported the creation of an open-space network which would use native vegetation and minimize the risk of fire damage. Such a network would require a minimum of irrigation and would double as a firebreak between the housing areas and the brush-covered hills beyond the development's boundaries. In addition, a careful analysis of the site's microclimate produced a set of guidelines for the design and orientation of pedestrain pathways and buildings so as to provide an extensive, comfortable walking environment and to minimize the need for air conditioning in dwellings. Not only did these proposals help to solve serious environmental impact problems, but they also contributed to the shape and pattern of the development and thereby created a uniquely designed community with enhanced marketability.

The Initial Image. Such analyses of the Rancho San Diego site and its environmental characteristics also helped to resolve another serious issue in new-community design. In a large-scale land development, it is necessary to create some feature that will establish a favorable visual image for the community in its initial years of development and sale. This image must be attractive to both the potential market and the initial residents. Therefore some of the toughest physical design tradeoffs within the developer's budgetary constraints are between an investment that achieves high early quality at great expense for relatively few residents (such as a major lake) and a slower investment that reduces risk and retains resources for later use. Stark simplicity, which can be made into a virtue in an individual building, is unacceptable in a new community. On balance, then, the wisest course would seem to be to provide an early image or hallmark for the planned community by creating in one place a concentrated but representative environment that, although limited in area, foreshadows all the qualities that, it is hoped, will characterize later stages.

In a nonarid region, for example, Reston, Virginia, is thought of as the first village at the end of Lake Anne. In an arid region, Lake Havasu, with its widely reported purchase of London Bridge, represents an attempt to meet the same need for a publicizable image. In the case of Rancho San Diego, however, the image element already existed. An underground watercourse provided one strip of intense green running through what was otherwise a typically parched southern California site. The design was oriented to focus on this attractive feature. As a continuous band running through the entire project, it served not only as an initial phase feature but also as a design element that unified the first development phase with future ones.

The Climate. What is possible in terms of image building, as well as what is appropriate in terms of physical form, is determined in large part by still another environmental factor—the climate. Although there are exceptions, arid-region communities often are characterized by severe climates. Extreme heat, radical variations between day and night temperatures, winds that suck out the limited moisture, and, of course, lack of rainfall are all typical.

Most arid-region new communities today are being developed in the Middle East. In the ones we are working on, the typical summer daytime temperature is 140°F. In some cases heat is combined with strong prevailing winds. Thus, where possible within the other constraints of new-community design, several design features should be followed and others avoided. First of all, long, broad, straight streets oriented in the same direction as the prevailing wind are to be avoided, for they give the wind the opportunity to reach ground level and accelerate. Second, berms, buildings, and other features should be used as windbreaks. Third, where feasible, shaded walkways should be created, using man-made or natural features. (In the Middle East this is done by designing attached housing forms, narrow streets, and covered passages in areas such as the central bazaar). Fourth, a combination of wind and shade should be used to create hospitable areas of private open space. (In the Middle East this is done with shaded, cross-ventilated private courts.) Finally, the rich opportunities for interconnected communal architecture presented by the low scale of climate-related housing, combined with high densities, should be realized.

In the Middle East all of these techniques are extremely well illustrated in the recent book *Landscaping the Saudi-Arabian Desert* by Kathleen Kelly and R. T. Schnadelbach.[1] More and more designers of Middle East projects are coming to the same climate-related design conclusions as are advocated in this volume. In the United States, however, climate has often proved to be much less of a design determinant. The popularity of air conditioning, relatively great wealth, and the lack of strong, historic community and housing design traditions are just three of the reasons why most American designers have let factors other than climate determine design in arid regions. However, emerging energy considerations and cost issues may alter this approach in the future.

Living Patterns. How the new-community residents prefer to live, shop, work, and use the recreational environs is also critical. These preferences account in large part for the center hall colonial houses on large lots and the high-rise glass office buildings in Tucson, rather than designs more heavily influenced by the region's Mexican–American heritage and arid climate. All of this is changing to some degree, however, as energy costs climb, environmental concerns become more general, and public design tastes change.

In the past and the present, expanding wealth and greater reliance on the private automobile have changed community as well as building form. In the Middle East and in other arid regions in developing countries, neighborhood areas are focused on local shopping facilities within convenient walking distance of homes in the area. Many recent American new towns, including, for example, Columbia, Maryland, and Reston, Virginia, assume a similar neighborhood structure as the preferred form of community organization. In even more recent new-community designs, including projects planned by Llewelyn–Davies Associates, this strict internal focus has given way to a less structured approach that reflects the goal of community facilities shared among a number of less defined neighborhoods, thereby increasing diversity and choice. Shopping and community facilities are therefore located adjacent to major roads at the edge of a neighborhood rather than in its center, where access would normally be limited to local streets. This increased accessibility by car—and by transit in the form of buses—means that each center can serve different community wide needs such as education or facilities for a specific type of recreation, in addition to local convenience shopping and other local needs. This concept has been ratified by the market. As a result, Reston and Columbia, for example, have both sharply reduced the number of neighborhood centers and moved to more specialized centers serving the full community.

Finance. Unfortunately, the most important factor in recent American new-community planning and design has been financial rather than physical sensitivity. Virtually all United States new towns, including all of the federally backed Title VII communities, started during the 1960s and 1970s have experienced severe financial difficulties. The high front-end costs incurred for land acquisition and initial infrastructure, combined with the large organization required to manage such complex operations, have led to large annual operating expenses. Unless the developer has substantial cash resources, failure to achieve the high market absorption levels (often projected to exceed 1000 units of housing per year) necessary for financial feasibility can be fatal. Unfortunately, too many factors have combined to produce shortfalls in the absorption levels: inflation, recession, environmental disputes and litigation, competition from conventional developments, the developer's inexperience, and a number of other problems.

These financial difficulties have had several serious impacts on the physical form of new communities. The first is, of course, a strongly felt need to minimize initial costs. Therefore the investment in extra design features—even if they will be important in the long term—has been sharply reduced. Many of the physical amenities planned for American new towns have, in fact, been delayed or eliminated. The second has been increased conservation consciousness. Many major new-town developers have delayed or eliminated new (and, ironically, more environmentally and socially responsive) physical designs in order to minimize the risk of poor market reception. Higher density housing concepts, such as townhouses, have been delayed, even in areas ready to accept them, for this reason. The third result has been that the new-town physical design must reflect even more the demands and preferences of the financial community. One new community in Florida, for which our firm is acting as planner and architect, has been shifted from a predominantly high-rise plan to a low-rise one because of the lack of large-scale condominium construction financing.

The Market. Many arid-region communities serve specific market segments. Retirement or adult-only communities, such as Sun City, Arizona, exhibit one physical form with an emphasis on custom-built single-family home development at relatively low densities. More recently, however, a number of communities aimed at the retired population, for example, Heritage Village in Connecticut, have emphasized attached unit development with individual lot areas combined as community wide open space maintained by the residents' association.

Nowhere, however, is the market impact on physical form more apparent than in two recently planned new communities in southern Iran. The two are on almost identical sites, but one was planned as a community primarily for lower income petroleum workers and the other was developed as an upper income community. As a luxury community its residents could afford automobiles, air conditioners, refrigerators, and a far broader range of shopping and recreational alternatives. Therefore its roads were wider; it had high-rise, double-loaded corridor apartments (which require air conditioning since they do not have through ventilation) rather than single-story units; and its shopping was more centralized, in a Western rather than an Iranian fashion. In other words, this one change—the market—led to a radical difference in physical form.

In the United States differences in market usually appear in the level of amenities, the form and quality of housing and retail structures, the types of recreational facilities, and many other features. In upper income retirement communities the recreational areas are typically for golf, shuffleboard, and other less active sports. In a more modest family-oriented community there are fewer large amenities such as golf courses and more investment in tennis courts, playgrounds, "tot lots," and other family-oriented, low-cost recreational open space. Some arid-region developments in this country are designed in response to a market oriented specifically toward recreation. Lake Havasu City, in particular, has placed major emphasis on this market. The development, as its name implies, is located adjacent to a major lake offering sailing, water-skiing, swimming, and so forth, as well as to a 13,000 acre state park; in addition, it features a variety of recreational developments, including two golf courses, tennis centers, swimming pools, and other local facilities.

Infrastructure. The utilities, roads, and other elements that make up the new town's infrastructure can have a significant design impact. This is particularly true in arid regions. The lack of water or the expense of bringing it in will determine what part of the site is developed first, what landscaping or amenities are feasible, and many other critical design determinants. In Lake Havasu City, for example, the location of major sewer lines largely dictated the location of higher density apartment areas. On the other hand, single-family housing sites were not restrained by major infrastructure routes because of reliance on individual septic tanks.

Roads, which are a major community design determinant, are similarly subject to the impact of budgetary limits. The logical transportation plan is often very different from the one that will receive maximum federal, state, county, and local funding. Since new communities in the United States are privately financed and no developer can afford an extensive road network without substantial public subsidy, the art of transportation planning lies in finding the proper balance between maximization of funding and the planning logic determined for the transportation network.

Other Factors. Still other factors such as the construction techniques available, the form of financing, and even the politics of neighboring communities can also be primary determinants of physical form. Overall, American communities must face (without significant federal support) the full range of dynamic forces that can and will shape their future. Thus it is understandable that design responses—even on similar sites in similar climates—will be extremely varied.

CONCLUSION

A project in an arid region will—if properly designed—reflect certain themes inherent in solutions to the particular design problems posed by this environment. First of all, the significance of light and heat will usually be reflected in the lighter colors, the simpler forms, and the types of construction used in arid-region structures. Second, the lack of a lush green environment and the shortage of low-cost water have made concentrated man-made landscape areas critically important design features. Third, since the desert environment is often very fragile and susceptible to problems such as brush fires or erosion, the organization of community elements must respect these unique environmental constraints in ways such as those discussed earlier in this chapter. Fourth, the creation of shaded outdoor space, the intelligent use of landscaping, a shortening or sheltering of pedestrian walkways, and other means must be used to make the outdoor environment hospitable. Finally, the escalating energy costs, combined with the severe climate of most arid regions, must be reflected in energy-conscious building design.

For all of these points there is an underlying theme: the physical design must be sensitive to the existing environment and must enhance it. An arid region—even in the United States—is a powerful design determinant. It can be ignored only at the risk of being insensitive to community environmental needs and the many other factors that are important in the shaping of a successful new town. Therefore it is probable that, as the sophistication of American design professionals and new-town developers increases, new-community planning will become more responsive to the environment. When the environment is a major factor, as it inevitably is in an arid region, one can expect the incorporation of an increasing number of the concepts discussed here and in the other chapters in this book.

No single factor, however, no matter how strong its influence, can determine the design of a properly planned American new community. As a result no physical design problem is more complex than that of designing a new town. In response to this challenge, design processes are evolving that can identify, weigh, and define unified physical forms. To do this and to properly meet the demands of an ever-growing list of design influences will be the challenge of new-community physical design in the future.

NOTES

1. See Kathleen Kelly and R. T. Schnadelbach, *Landscaping the Saudi-Arabian Desert* (Philadelphia: Delancey Press, 1976).

CHAPTER 15

Landscape and Cityscape Design in Arid Regions

GUY S. GREENE

The civilization under which people are restricted and controlled by a material environment from which they cannot escape, and under which they cannot utilize human thought and intellectual power to change [the] environment and improve conditions, is the civilization of a lazy and non-progressive people.

Hu Shih

Those who write about cities point out that the city is the people, and that the city is the genesis of civilization as we understand it. For centuries, with this in mind, men have been thoughtfully concerned with the character of the physical structure of the city and with the ways in which the designed, man-made environment interacts with human life and activity. This chapter, too, is concerned with these questions, as they apply to the special qualities of cities in the desert.

Cities in an American mode are a fairly recent phenomenon in arid lands, made possible by modern technology. Historically, a large population could settle permanently only where it was possible to develop the agricultural base that provided the necessary food, clothing, and shelter. In desert regions, however, agriculture has been virtually nonexistent on a scale that could support a major urban complex. The difficulties in moving goods rapidly over long distances, the lack of water, and the rigors of heat and aridity have left the deserts largely to nomadic groups, few in number, who have evolved a precarious but successful balance with their environment.

Modern technology, however, has made it possible for all kinds and conditions of people to establish dwellings in the desert. The dryness and clear air have become health-giving benefits rather than hardships, and, like the sea, the desert evokes a strong sense of place. The long, sunny days and clear nights dull memories of freezing winters and gray skies. The same technology, however, also tends to isolate the desert dweller from his environment:

Holing up in his city, the westerner lives a life of humid abundance. His wells tap the water resources of a vast surrounding area—and irrigate clover lawns. His air conditioners, powered by energy from Texas gas or a river five counties away, enable him to evade the discomfort of high temperatures. . . . He lives at the expense of an arid region and surrounded by it, but not with it. His technology enables him to escape its rigors without making concessions.[1]

Man must, of course, create his own environment. The often-heard comment that he cannot escape the

199

designed environment, however, implies that he would like to, presumably because it is a bad one. Escape to what? The natural environment? There does, indeed, seem to be an almost universal feeling among people that life is improved when at least some contact with nature is preserved. Tree-lined streets, private gardens, and public parks are evidence of a human need that is greater than a desire for mere cosmetics.

In discussing the cityscape, our concern is chiefly visual quality. This is difficult to define in precise terms which can be translated into actual construction techniques. It involves tangible elements such as form, color, and texture, and intangibles such as beauty or aesthetics. Our visual perception is a major source of information about the kind of place we choose to occupy, and many of our actions and reactions stem from knowledge (or apparent knowledge) derived from what we see. Much remains to be learned about this complex subject, and a body of theory is beginning to emerge from those working in the new field of environmental pyschology. In the meantime the designer, whether lay or professional, continues to make decisions based on the best available information, which he interprets in the light of his individual experience.

Good design, whatever it is, will probably never be reduced to a formula, or become totally predictable. If this were to happen, it would be a disaster. It is important, nevertheless, to attempt to define some basic principles, or at least guidelines, which can be distilled from the specific experience of designing landscape in the desert.

THE WATER PROBLEM

Attitudes toward arid lands must be reversed. The desert is viewed as wasteland: the words are often used synonymously. Since it supports no crop and little livestock, the desert, as land in the traditional sense, has almost no value. As a basis for permanent human habitation, however, arid lands must be treated as a precious commodity. Once this precious commodity is disturbed, the desert does not recover and must thereafter be treated and maintained artificially. This can be done, but only at great expense and waste. Groundwater is limited and often poor in quality, much of it being brackish. We know how to desalinize it, but the energy requirements are enormous, and no one has found a satisfactory way to dispose of the brine effluent. The irrigation of desert

land with possible drinking water must be kept to a minimum. The use of sewage effluent for this purpose offers an alternative to the general practice of pumping groundwater, making it septic, and discarding it. The reuse of sewage should be a part of the water management program of any arid land, but it will not by itself solve all of the problems. The clear fact emerges that, if water is limited in quantity and the energy needed to acquire and distribute it must be conserved, we must use less water.

The Use of Native Vegetation and Other Techniques.   Certain water conservation measures can be used in connection with landscaping. Arid lands usually support a surprising number and variety of plants which are either true natives or have become acclimated: these can be used successfully in urban landscape design. When growing naturally, these plants are generally in very low density communities; when used in higher concentrations, as in most urban situations, they require a correspondingly greater quantity of water. Thus, when used for their visual quality in an urban setting, they are typically irrigated beyond the level of mere desert survival. For these reasons the use of native plant material does not eliminate the need for irrigation, although it is certainly true that its lower transpiration reduces the amount of irrigation necessary. From the standpoint of visual quality also, there is no question that the use of native plants is more appropriate than the importation of exotic ones.

One definition of a desert—or arid land—is an area that does not support continuous vegetative ground cover. This means not only that such a cover must be artifically introduced and maintained, but also that desert land, once thus disturbed, will not recover and must thereafter be deliberately treated in some manner. Paving with materials such as asphalt or concrete is a common (and obvious) solution, but, just as obviously, it is not always an appropriate one. The use of soil cement, gravel, or rock mulch is an intermediate treatment between asphalt and vegetation that can serve effectively to stabilize disturbed soil and that preserves the quality of the natural condition to some degree.

Irrigation Using Runoff.   Irrigation techniques can be refined to conserve water. Trickle, or drip, irrigation methods tend to be much more efficient than the usual application by spraying or flooding. Probably the best method, however, will prove to be subsurface irrigation, although the techniques are not yet perfected. Irrigation procedures, particularly with water having high salt content, raise highly technical problems involving soil chemistry and plant–soil–water relationships, which are beyond the scope of this discussion. In general, however, the specific details of the methods used to provide water to plants are an important part of the success of an arid landscape design.

Small amounts of rainfall characterize desert areas, but, in most of them, rainstorms are sudden and violent. Consequently surface runoff is rapid, and because of these large quantities, which occur infrequently, most of this runoff is carried in open drainageways rather than storm sewers. This is a valuable source of water which is not generally utilized.

Through proper management techniques, surface runoff can be retained and used for irrigation. Runoff from urban areas is highly contaminated, however, and must be managed with care. Various studies have shown that grass filtration can be effective in removing typical urban contaminants. According to Searle in 1949, the city of Melbourne, Australia, has employed grass filtration for domestic sewage treatment since 1932. With an average hydraulic load of about 0.1 acre-ft/(acre)/(day), biochemical oxygen demand (BOD) was reduced during filtration from 322 to less than 20 mg/liter, and suspended solids were reduced to 20 mg/liter.[2] Wilson and Lehman found in 1966 that BOD and suspended solids were totally removed.[3] Two years later Lehman found that large quantities of iron, manganese, and copper were taken up by grass during the filtration of domestic sewage effluent from an oxidation pond.[4] Coliform organisms will, of course, also be effectively reduced.

Notable work by Stone and Garber in 1951 on test plots in Whittier and Azusa, California, using secondary sewage effluent, led to the conclusion that water of a bacterial quality suitable for drinking purposes can be obtained by passing the effluent through a minimum of 3 to 7 ft of soil.[5] At Lodi, California, secondary sewage effluent was also applied to pilot infiltration plots by the California State Water Pollution Board in 1953. Data showed that the soil-filtered water samples had less than one organism per 100 ml at the 7 ft sampling point, which is less than the level required to meet the drinking water standard of the U.S. Health Department.[6] Two years later, Orlob and Butler conducted lysimeter studies on five California soils and found a pronounced removal of organisms at both the 1 and the 60 cm soil depth.[7] Bouwer et al. in 1974 found that, with a loading rate

of 100 acre ft/year of 0.3 acre ft/(acre)/(day) of secondary sewage effluent into soil infiltration basins, the quality of the renovated water was excellent. The concentration of total nitrogen decreased from 30 to 10 mg/liter and fecal coliforms were eventually absent, except for counts of 1 to 10 organisms per 100 ml when samples were first obtained.[8] Therefore soil-filtered as well as grass-filtered secondary sewage effluent could be used for all recreational and irrigation applications and, with chlorination or ozonation, could be restored to the groundwater basin.[9] These techniques are suitable for urban runoff as well as sewage effluent.

THE LAND USE PROBLEM

It is axiomatic that water is a scarce and precious commodity in the desert and should be used with care and restraint. The basic problem in urban landscape design, however, concerns land use itself. The traditions that city dwellers and city builders bring to the desert originate in a different kind of environment. As in nineteenth century England, the plight of the early industrial cities of this country brought about an awareness of the need for light, air, and open space. These needs become codified in the form of zoning laws and subdivision regulations, and after several generations the established land use patterns achieved the status of doctrine. They were then brought without change to new cities in arid lands.

Thus, in the desert, we find front yards required, usually planted with grass. We find requirements for minimum lot size, maximum building coverage, minimum setbacks, and all of the other constraints originally designed to provide, essentially, the greatest possible amount of greenery. The thrust of these regulations, which are generally supported by public attitudes, is to ensure that, after buildings and paving have been constructed, large areas of raw earth will be left, which then, as a matter of course, are planted. Planting in the desert should never be a matter of course; rather, it should be done in a thoughtful, deliberate, carefully planned way—almost with reluctance. Large, left-over areas of land, which must then be planted because there is no other choice, should never occur incidentally.

Functioning Landscape. One of the many challenges in urban design for arid lands is to make the use of plants in the cityscape an integral part of the total design process. This challenge immediately raises questions about the direction and purpose of urban landscape design in general, and in desert cities in particular. We have previously mentioned the elusive nature of the meaning of the term "good design." It is somewhat less elusive when the design is directed to clearly functional purposes (when form follows function). In dealing with cityscapes, plants, and their visual quality, however, we come dangerously close to becoming mired in notions of cosmetic beautification.

To avoid this trap, we must recognize that plants, even when classed as ornamental, have some important functions in an urban context. They can modify the environment by providing shade and wind protection; they can define space and provide a sense of enclosure; they can control erosion; and they can perform other functions as well. Beyond these functions there is abundant evidence that people in every social and economic condition view some contact with nature and growing plants as essential to urban life. The reasons for this is not clear. It may be that a man-made environment, however well done, exerts a kind of tyranny. Some other person, usually unidentified, it is often felt, has determined where we can drive, walk, enter, look, sit, and so on. Nature, on the other hand, seems to exist simply as part of the world that has always been here—and that was not constructed specifically to direct our lives.

Beautifying Landscape. The functioning of the city depends on the involvement and participation of its citizens. Lynch and others have shown that the way in which people function in the city is influenced by their perceived image of the city (function following form).[10] Thus the cityscape should have order without regimentation, and variety without chaos. Should it have beauty? Perhaps not.

Beauty, in certain respects, can be an inhibiting force. It may be more important to create an environment in which the occupants feel at ease. An individual may feel out of place in an area of great beauty which seems to demand that he be dressed in a suit and tie (especially when he is someone who feels ill at ease in a suit and tie). A designed environment can have this effect, but not necessarily, for almost no one feels out of place in the presence of trees. Plants, furthermore, generally provide a common reference for all people and, for the most part, bring to the city an element of human scale. Thus there appears to be ample justification for including, to some degree, the natural landscape as a part of the total cityscape, even in arid regions, where a strong argument can be made in favor of excluding plants altogether.

THE ARID CITYSCAPE

Any discussion of the cityscape is largely concerned with the street scene, since the visual quality of the city is almost entirely that which is viewed from public streets. Urban street design is based primarily on the requirements of automobile traffic. Beyond this, the street right-of-way is extended to include pedestrian sidewalks and, often, planted areas. The street, in fact, continues to expand visually to the line of building setbacks. The broad, shady, tree-lined street responds to the perfectly reasonable desire for light, air, open space, and greenery which developed as a reaction against early industrial cities and which rejects the narrow, treeless street with buildings crowding in upon it.

The latter is, however, precisely what is called for in desert regions, where there is a superabundance of light and air. The light is bright, constant, and usually synonymous with heat. The quality of the light in the desert, in fact, adds a new dimension to design which can be used with great effect, but lack of light is not a problem. The desert air itself is clean, dry, and invigorating, but there are strong desert winds, and in the city the wind is inevitably dust laden. Excessive greenery is simply inappropriate, as we noted above. Our aim in arid regions must, therefore, be to reduce unneeded land area, to use plants with restraint, and to utilize the structural systems of the cityscape to provide shade, contrast, form, texture, and protection.

Parks, in the traditional sense, are something of an anomaly in arid regions. Parks in the United States descend directly from those of Victorian England, the broad sweeps of turf, clumps of trees, and occasional ponds bringing to the city dweller a relief from structural masses and a reminder of open countryside. They seem to work very well, and for many outdoor activities a turf ground cover is unsurpassed. And such facilities are undoubtedly needed even in arid regions—perhaps especially in arid regions.

There are, however, special conditions in the desert which can be turned to advantage and possibly support park areas. Desert watercourses, or *arroyos,* are typically dry most of the time, although their occasional flows may be violent. They are usually preserved in a desert city, for it is often infeasible to design storm drains for the infrequent but massive flows of surface runoff. Properly designed detention areas in the *arroyos* can capture much of the runoff, and it can be used to provide irrigation for native vegetation and at the same time reduce the peak flows of floodwaters.

CONCLUSION

The modern city in the desert offers unparalled opportunity for sensitive, disciplined design, but this opportunity cannot be realized by slavishly clinging to urban traditions and attitudes engendered by other cities in other places. There have been desert cities in the past, but modern man is just beginning to discover the desert as a place to live. Perhaps he will learn to treat it with the same respect accorded the sea. City waterfronts, the thin line dividing the city from the ocean, are places of perpetual interest and excitement. The desert front could offer the same contrast and enhance both the character of the city and the special, fragile character of the unique environment called the desert.

NOTES

1. James Rodney Hasings and Raymond H. Turner, *The Changing Mile* (Tucson: University of Arizona Press, 1965), p. 5.

2. See S. S. Searle, "The Use of Grass Filtration for Sewage Purification," paper presented to the 12th Annual Conference of Sewage Engineers and Operators, 1949.

3. See L. G. Wilson and G. S. Lehman, *Grass Filtration of Sewage Effluent for Quality Improvement Prior to Artificial Recharge,* American Society of Agricultural Engineers, Paper no. 66-716 (St. Joseph, Mich., 1966).

4. See G. S. Lehman, "Soil and Grass Filtration of Domestic Sewage Effluent for the Removal of Trace Elements," (Ph.D. dissertation, University of Arizona, 1968).

5. See R. A. Stone and W. S. Garber, "Sewage Reclamation by Spreading Basin Infiltration," *Proceedings of the American Society of Civil Engineers,* 77 (September 1951), 1–20.

6. See California State Water Pollution Board, *Waste Water Reclamation in Relation to Ground Water Pollution,* Publication no. 6 (Berkeley: Sanitary Engineering Research Laboratory, University of California, 1953).

7. See G. T. Orlob and R. G. Butler, *An Investigation of Sewage Spreading on Southern California Soils,* Technical Bulletin no. 12, IER series 37 (Berkeley: Sanitary Engineering Research Laboratory, University of California, 1955).

8. See H. Bouwer, J. C. Lance, and M. S. Riggs, "High-Rate Land Treatment II: Water Quality and Economic Aspects of Flushing Meadows Project," *Journal of Water Pollution Control Federation,* 46, no. 5 (May 1974), 844–859.

9. See Sol D. Resnick and Paul Sebenik, "Water Sources," in *Santa Cruz Riverpark Master Plan,* Guy S. Greene, ed., report for the city of Tucson, Arizona, 1976.

10. See Kevin Lynch, *The Image of the City* (Cambridge, Mass.: Technology Press, 1960).

CHAPTER 16

Patterns of Desert Urbanization:
The Evolution of Metropolitan Phoenix

JEFFREY COOK

Phoenix at night, whether viewed in sparkling winter crispness or in scorched summer heat when the temperature at midnight is still above 100°F, is a splendid man-made jewel—a scintillating breastpiece lying on a dry and wrinkled land. But the harsh light of high noon reveals flaws marring the perfection of this desert jewel. Phoenix today is definitely the newest American city and potentially the world's largest man-made oasis. The dichotomous origins of American culture and the desert cultures of the world provide at once the source of a special vitality and a particularly valuable object lesson for planners—both those dealing with arid settlements and those dealing with postindustrial conurbations.

Arizona—*arida zona* in Spanish—is the driest, hottest, and by far the sunniest state in the United States. Bounded on the west by the Colorado River, which forms its border with southern California, on the north by Utah, on the east by New Mexico, and on the south by Mexico, Arizona is centrally located in the continent's arid Southwest. Central in the state and central in the drainage basins of the state is the location of modern Phoenix. Thus both political and commercial catchments are reinforced by a life-sustaining water basin. Today a 13,000 mi^2 watershed, as Figure 1 shows, provides for an irrigated area of 250,000 acres, which is the core of the conurbation.

Along the Salt River, after its confluence with the Verde River and before the two flow into the Gila

River system, lies a broad, dry, fertile, tilted plain. It is part of the Salt River Valley, sometimes known as the Valley of the Sun, and is now called metropolitan Phoenix. Today 17 distinct, autonomous municipalities occupy this 3000 mi^2 area—a heavily populated area of Maricopa County which is constantly expanding.

CENTRAL ARIZONA: THE PAST

Hunters, Food Gatherers, and the Hohokam. Phoenix is the largest and most central of these municipalities. "Phoenix" is, however, only the modern name of an ancient human settlement. Defined by its five small mountain clusters, the area was first occupied 15,000 years ago by hunters. With spears and darts they sought giant bison, camel, moose, or elephant in the tall grasses and hardwood groves. From mountain lookouts they located the wild herds, and they diligently patrolled "their" valley.

The climate had dramatically changed by the time the second group, the food gatherers, came. Although there was still hunting, the prey was now smaller animals and birds. The principal foods were berries, nuts, seeds, fruit, and the roots of mesquite, palo verde, and various cacti.

The first farmers arrived in the Salt River Valley several centuries before the beginning of the Christian era. Expanding from southeastern Arizona and

Figure 1. The state of Arizona with the 13,000 mi^2 watershed of the Salt River Project and the irrigated 250,000 acre core of Phoenix. Courtesy Salt River Project, History Center, Phoenix, Arizona.

southwestern New Mexico, a people known as the Hohokam brought stone hoes and a primitive knowledge of irrigation. The River Hohokam, who evolved as farmers along the river terraces of occasionally flooding streams, soon became distinguished from the semiagricultural Desert Hohokam, who were primarily food gatherers. With the former group a new farming technology evolved in settlements along the Gila River between 300 BC and AD 500. Between AD 500 and 700 the concept of canal irrigation emerged, opening the fertile valley of the Salt River for farming. The population shift from the Gila to the Salt River Valley was completed between AD 700 and 900. During these years the River Hohokam am-

bitiously initiated one of the first irrigation systems in North America. In a period of 500 years, they developed it into the largest irrigation system on the continent. Before the Hohokam, whose name means "the people who went away," actually went away, they had constructed an elaborate network of canals whose combined length, as Figure 2 reveals, measured more than 150 mi when examined 500 years later.

The Hohokam canal system brought water by gravity from the flowing Salt River into a broad, fan-shaped cultivation pattern on the desert floor. The canals were dug using neolithic implements: stone hoes, digging sticks, and baskets, and came in a great variety of sizes, the largest being both wider and deeper than those used today. The smallest ditches designed to deliver water to the crops had, of course, long since disappeared by the time the white man came. In many ways the Hohokam canal and dam construction techniques are similar to twentieth century techniques. Certainly the flow characteristics of water and the careful pitch of canals then and now require identical considerations. Figure 3 illustrates the use of brush, a primitive technique, to reinforce the foundation for an irrigation dam in 1906. The Hohokam canals were designed to prevent seepage, not just to save water. To avoid waterlogging in the land next to the canals, some of the canals were lined with clay, and in some cases attempts were made to fire the clay, thus making the project one of man's most ambitious ceramic undertakings. In these cases, after packing the sides with clay, the Hohokam would fill the canals with dry wood and brush which, when fired, gave them a burned adobe lining.

The first settlement patterns of the Hohokam bespeak their open society and lack of warfare with neighbors. Communities were scattered throughout the area: 22 large ones and many more small ones.

The early Hohokam villages were similar in their dispersion to the later Pima villages of Arizona. The houses themselves were constructed using post and beam, daub and wattle techniques. A framework of lightweight poles was woven with brush and thin branches and then plastered with mud inside and out. The floor was generally below the ground level so that the excavated dirt could often be used for the walls and roof. There were no windows, and possibly a blanket served for a door. Therefore most daytime activities were undoubtedly conducted out-of-doors under the free-standing porches or *ramadas,* constructed of poles with a brush roof which provided shade but took advantage of breezes. Here the routine domestic activities of weaving, pottery making, corn grinding, and meal preparing were carried out. In addition to cultivating beans, maize, squash, and cotton, these Hohokam collected wild foods and hunted for fish, birds, rabbits, peccaries, and especially desert bighorn sheep.

Later Hohokam communities were more compact and consolidated. The remains at Pueblo Grande typify a compound of the Classical Hohokam period from AD 1200 to 1400. Here massive walls using

Figure 3. Preparation, using brush, of the foundation of an irrigation dam at the Salton Sea on August 26, 1906. Courtesy Salt River Project, History Center, Phoenix, Arizona.

several construction techniques rose to a height of several stories. Housing was no longer dispersed but, rather, joined into a typical pueblo format, and defensive walls made their ominous appearance. Such "platform" structures used earthfill between retaining walls of caliche and river rock over 8 ft high. For the structures on top a variety of construction techniques, including wattle and daub, rubble and coursed masonry with and without mud mortar, as well as adobe, were used. The heaviest adobe walls were made using a puddled technique in which a double row of vertical posts served as a reinforcing core.[1] Each course of wet mud was moulded by temporary side forms until it became dried by the sun. Then the forms were raised to mould the next course of adobe, which was puddled into place.

Of special interest are the remains of the ball courts that have been excavated at both Snaketown and Pueblo Grande. The games undoubtedly served both ritualistic and intercommunity competitive roles. These ball courts, as well as the jewelry, pottery, weaving, and other artifacts of the Hohokam, tie them to cultures indigenous to their south, including the distant civilizations of Central America. The Hohokam constructions and land use patterns, as their later structures suggest, can also be linked to contemporary pueblo cultures to the east of the continental divide and along the Rio Grande. However, the urban structuring of the Hohokam never became as dramatically stylized as that evident in the ceremonial courts flanked by pueblo-wings at Casas Grandes in Chihuahua. Similarly, they developed neither the megastructural certainty nor the astronomical exactitude of Pueblo Bonito in Chaco Canyon, nor did they refine their crafts as deliberately as did contemporaries who lived at higher altitudes and thus experienced harsher winters and gentler summers.

The climate in the Salt River Valley during the Hohokam period was probably more temperate than it is today. There certainly was more rainfall, and, with the increasing intensity of the Hohokam irrigation, the water table rose. Then, between 1276 and 1299, there was a great drought. Finally, the Hohokam appear to have become the victims of their own neolithic megalamania and engineering prowess: their walls were eroded by salts, the land became waterlogged, and their crops rotted. Undoubtedly other factors, both climatic and human, also motivated their departure. Where they went no one knows. Their disappearance is as much a mystery to us as it was to their successors. By AD 1400 the

valley was deserted, and this third culture had abandoned the fertile desert.

The Refounding of Phoenix and Vicinity.   During the next four centuries, while the Europeans successively discovered and settled the rest of the continent, driving the native Americans out of their indigenous habitat, this site on the Salt River remained empty. Explorers and missionaries passed through, but no one stayed. One hundred miles to the southeast, Tucson had earlier been refounded with Indian, Spanish, and military encampments on a site almost as harshly arid, but until the second half of the nineteenth century there were virtually no American settlers, even there.

The Mexican–American War of 1846 and its concluding treaty of Guadalupe Hidalgo of 1848 established Arizona north of the Gila River as part of the territories belonging to the United States. The Gadsden Purchase of 1853–1854 gave the state's present boundaries to the territory called Arizona. However, it was a third midcentury event—the discovery of gold in California in 1848 and in Arizona in 1851—that gave rise to a flood of fortune seekers who streamed west by every route, thereby encouraging new settlements. This gold fever, as well as silver and copper fevers, increasingly contributed, toward the end of the nineteenth century, to the growth of local settlements throughout the state and to the need for a central city for supplies and services.

The precise founding or refounding of Phoenix was, at least, a double-barreled affair. In September 1865 a military post with mounted troops was established at Camp McDowell on the Verde River some 18 miles northeast of the Salt River Valley. This post was set up to control the movements of two of the more troublesome Apache tribes. But horses and men needed hay and food. Hence the enterprising post sutler, John Y. T. Smith, noticing the heavy growth of wild hay along the Salt River, obtained the hay contract in 1867 and proceeded to set up a "hay camp" roughly where 40th Street today meets the Salt River in Phoenix.

Earlier that year, the Salt River Valley had been surveyed by William H. Pierce, U.S. Government Surveyor. The inevitable gridiron is evident in all the early homestead maps. Later in 1867 and during that winter an entrepreneur from Prescott, wagon driver John W. Swilling, organized 16 of his friends at Wickenburg for the purpose of digging a canal and establishing a settlement. "Swilling's Ditch" was easily constructed, since it only involved cleaning out some prehistoric Hohokam canals. By March 1868 there was already a settlement of 50 persons "who have displayed great energy in the construction of their 'irrigation ditches' and the clearing of their land and will this year bring under cultivation a large extent of country. The settlement," according to the field notes of Wilfred F. Ingals, U.S. Deputy Surveyor, "though young, bears every evidence of thrift and prosperity."[2] The name "Phoenix" was suggested by Darrel Duppa, an educated Englishman pensioned by his family to stay away from home, who was a member of Swilling's party and observed the remains of a vanished people. He named the new settlement after the mythical bird reborn out of its own ashes. Phoenix was the first settlement. It was also central in the valley.

With a freshly plotted town site, an immediate regional supply business, and the refunctioning irrigation system, the new Phoenix was an instant, if modest, success. By 1872 the town had a bakery, a brewery, a butcher shop, a general store, county offices (complete with a sheriff and a jail), and many saloons. Modern Phoenix thus began, with little idealism, as an exploitative, speculative venture on a promising site.

Nearby, 9 mi to the east, the city of Tempe was founded when Charles Trumbull Hayden moved his freighting business from Tucson in 1870. In addition to operating a ferry across the Salt River, he built a flour mill. Already some small degree of specialization was giving an identity to each valley settlement. Tempe, first called Hayden's Ferry, received its classical name about 1877 from the same literate Darrell Duppa who christened Phoenix and who romantically imagined some resemblance between Hayden's site and the Vale of Tembi in Greece. Tempe developed first as a small agricultural community. With plentiful water and a railroad junction, it also became a livestock shipping point. With the establishment of the Territorial Normal School in 1885 (now Arizona State University) Tempe's career as an educational center began.

The early appearance of typical Salt River Valley settlements is seen in Figure 4, a photograph of Tempe taken 30 years after its founding. A characteristic desert haze veils the distant South Mountains.

Figure 4. Tempe looking southwest from the top of Tempe Butte on April 9, 1905. Courtesy Salt River Project, History Center, Phoenix, Arizona.

The general lushness of vegetation is perhaps typical of the irrigated desert. The spacious arrangement of buildings and streets, however, represents the uniquely American pattern of settling the West.

Five miles east of Tempe, Mormons founded Mesa with its wide streets and particular religious structures in 1878. In 1891 a Dunkard missionary, followed by 70 families, settled Glendale 10 mi northwest of Phoenix as a community for the temperate and industrious. Other communities in the valley had similar agricultural beginnings but without sharing the moral purposes of Mesa or Glendale.

Phoenix and all the surrounding communities such as Tempe were laid out on the gridiron of the surveyor's map. There was nothing unique about the plans. Even the striking broad streets were characteristic of all the western settlements founded at this time. Photographs of the early years do, however, reveal the importance of trees. By the late 1870s rows of closely spaced, ornamental shade trees already lined both the business and the residential streets of Phoenix, giving an almost sylvan appearance to the new desert community. Other Salt River Valley communities quickly developed an appearance similar to

that of the 1879 Jim Cotton's saloon at the corner of First and Washington streets, depicted in Figure 5.

Figure 5 also shows an open irrigation ditch. The early irrigation channels through the town of Phoenix were no more than open ditches with water flowing through them, which roughly divided the street from the sidewalk. Civic improvements, however, quickly bridged or enclosed these small water arteries. The original Swilling's Ditch became known as the "Town Ditch" and, running along Van Buren Street, was at least 8 ft wide—large enough for swimming, a Phoenician tradition increasingly discouraged by water managers because of the water's dangerous turbulence. Every summer, however, the tradition continues to be followed by growing boys. The volunteer vegetation along early canals provided a continuous strip of dense growth. By 1900 the Town Ditch, as Figure 6 shows, and many other canals became water avenues lined by large cottonwoods and thick undergrowth.

The land use patterns established by the end of the nineteenth century largely determined the structure which continues through the end of the twentieth. In effect, the Hohokam pattern of a series of dispersed

Figure 5. Jim Cotton's saloon at the corner of First and Washington streets in 1879, featuring trees as a major element of townscape. Phoenix Library Collection. From Herb McLaughlin and Dorothy McLaughlin, *Phoenix 1870–1970 in Photographs* (Phoenix: Herb and Dorothy McLaughlin, 1970), p. 32.

Figure 6. The Town Ditch *ca.* 1900, a water avenue lined by dense volunteer growth, which, more recently, has been deliberately eliminated as part of water management practices. Courtesy Salt River Project, History Center, Phoenix, Arizona.

settlements joined by open stretches of agricultural land was repeated by the white man. A number of small agricultural centers developed at convenient intervals throughout the richly productive, irrigated desert plain. During the territorial period, that is, until Arizona became the forty-eighth state, very little distinguished Phoenix from its neighboring towns except its central location, its superior size, and the number of its saloons. In 1910 Phoenix had only 11,000 people.

The early architecture of these Salt River Valley centers reveals an interesting progression away from building design related to the environment. The earliest white man's structures had adobe walls, and viga beams from the logs of local trees formed the roofs. Saplings or ocotillo were used as lattilas for roof decks which were covered by a clay roofing. These were the same types of structures that were built by the native Indians throughout the Southwest and adopted by early European settlers. However, in the Salt River Valley government buildings such as Fort McDowell were constructed of milled wood and shingles and often resembled eastern, temperate-

climate buildings. With such designs paving the way, brick quickly replaced the native adobe as the maintenance problems of wood in an alien desert were partially recognized.

Nevertheless, by the turn of the century, a building pattern emerged which was climatically responsive. As early as the 1880s, the business streets of Phoenix featured not only continuously raised sidewalks but also continuous overhead protection. These commercial walkways were often given further shade by pieces of canvas dropped along the sides of the walks, sometimes providing permanent panels just above eye level for signs and advertising.

This business veranda had its residential counterpart: whether modest or imposing, every valley home had some kind of porch. Although stylish houses of this period throughout the country sported verandas, the latter had a particularly tempering effect in the Phoenix climate. Often the simplest homes had porches all the way around. However, this architectural concept had its most exemplary application in hotel design. Here porches, as Figure 7 shows, were provided at every level and on every side and

Figure 7. The Adams Hotel, the pride of Phoenix, before it burned in the city's most spectacular fire in 1910. Courtesy Salt River Project, History Center, Phoenix, Arizona.

proved useful, not just for lounging during the daytime, but also for sleeping during summer nights. Hotels without porches outside each room provided beds on the roof, a sleeping arrangement that probably did very little to encourage female travelers. On the porches or the roof, by using wet sheets, it was possible to get some comfortable rest, even during the oppressive heat of summer. During the summer, the hotel room itself became a baggage repository and dressing room.

The Twentieth Century. One could trace the leadership of Phoenix among the growing surrounding communities up through the first half of the twentieth century, but in almost all respects it was typical and predictable.[3] Growth was gradual as the immediate agricultural economic base was increasingly augmented by the business attendant on the

city's role as state capital and regional distribution center. In 1908 the Carnegie Public Library became Phoenix's first library; in 1912 Arizona became a state; in 1913 there were almost 3000 winter visitors—the beginnings of an important present industry; and in 1914 Phoenix adopted a commission form of city government and swore in its first city manager.

The successive decades of the twentieth century reinforced the cultural, financial, and political leadership of Phoenix in the state. But architecturally, as well as in most other areas, the fashions of the day generated elsewhere dominated the area. Phoenix increasingly abandoned the particular environmentally related design characteristics that grew out of its desert setting and emulated every other aspiring city in the country.

Immediately after the success of Swilling's Ditch

Figure 8. Horseshoe Dam, completed in 1946 at a cost of $2.5 million, provides some of the domestic water supply of Phoenix, water for Phelps Dodge mining operations, and water for irrigation, but no hydroelectric power. Courtesy Salt River Project, History Center, Phoenix, Arizona.

Figure 9. The Salt River Project (in relief), showing the irrigated agricultural land now increasingly being turned to urban uses and the complex system of dammed lakes above the valley that stores and regulates water from a vast hinterland. Courtesy Salt River Project, History Center, Phoenix, Arizona.

in 1868, a number of other private water and irrigation projects were launched which, in effect, revived and revised virtually all of the remaining Hohokam canals. The highest and largest, the Arizona Canal, was dug and extended from 1884 to 1887 and was privately financed, like all the others, in a sometimes intense commercial rivalry. In 1903 the authority to distribute irrigation water of most of these private competing canal companies was transferred to the Salt River Valley Water Users' Association. In 1911 Teddy Roosevelt himself dedicated Roosevelt Dam, the first major investment in taming the Salt River and extending the Hohokam irrigation area. Thereafter, a series of other dams helped to form a necklace of lakes descending out of the mountains along the Salt River. Horseshoe Dam, shown in Figure 8, is only one of many remote construction projects that contribute to a complex regional water system. Not only a high degree of water management, but also the production of hydroelectricity resulted from this water system. The Salt River Project, still owned (in shares) by the holders of the land it irrigated, became the backbone of the

Phoenix Valley, providing life-giving water and a bounty of electricity, soon augmented by conventional power production methods. And, as land has been transferred from agricultural to residential uses, the water rights have been transferred to the new owners and users, allowing verdure to flourish throughout the different kinds of urban development.

The Salt River Project shown in Figure 9, represents the most highly developed planning agency in the Greater Phoenix region. Its quasi-governmental status, however, has only a subtle impact. Rather, its importance lies in the successful management of the most valuable resource of a desert community. Its policies early established regional development patterns. Its increasing role as a producer and vendor of electricity has reinforced its subtle regional influence; together with Arizona Public Service, the other electricity system, it has shaped the disposition of new development, especially commercial and industrial, to a much greater extent than has any of the local municipal planning boards.

The canal system has been equaled by another mechanical contrivance in its environmental impact on this arid place. The wet sheets of the old hotels and the towel-wrapped ice hidden under the hats of ladies and gentlemen were both forms of personal environmental control. A more general and practical contrivance is the evaporative cooler—a fan-driven ventilation system that cools air by passing it through porous, wet mats. Such a system typically has no return circuit, since the cool air produced is reasonably saturated. Exhaust is accomplished by leaving doors and windows ajar. Evaporative cooling was (and continues to be) a popular and successful technique that allowed openness and delivered comfort during most of the Phoenix summer. But, by late July or early August, when the heat of the valley becomes wetted by monsoon air, neither such evaporation nor nighttime reradiation is effective. The true deliverer of building comfort in the American arid zone was Willis Carrier, the inventor of air conditioning.[4] Although air conditioning was invented and developed earlier in the century, it took the World War II campaign in the South Pacific to develop mass production models. After the war not only Carrier but also a wide variety of other companies popularized and propagated air conditioning. Although in demand throughout the country, nowhere else did it make such an impact as in the arid Southwest. The dependence of air conditioning on electricity has reinforced the impact of the Salt River Project.

The postwar population explosion of Phoenix and its neighbors is virtually unprecedented in history. Air conditioning made life throughout the summer comfortable. Many of the pilots trained during the war on the Arizona desert and many of the steadily increasing number of winter visitors now wanted to come back and live permanently in the pleasant, clean, dry surroundings. The serene, strong landscape depicted in Figure 10 disappeared as the area grew by leaps and bounds as shown in Figure 11. As these comparative maps indicate, over the past two decades no city in history has sustained the

Figure 10. East of Mesa on the road to Apache Junction in the early years of the century, the landscape features a tree canopy (due to an irrigation ditch) shading the road as it passes through intensely farmed land. Courtesy Salt River Project, History Center, Phoenix, Arizona.

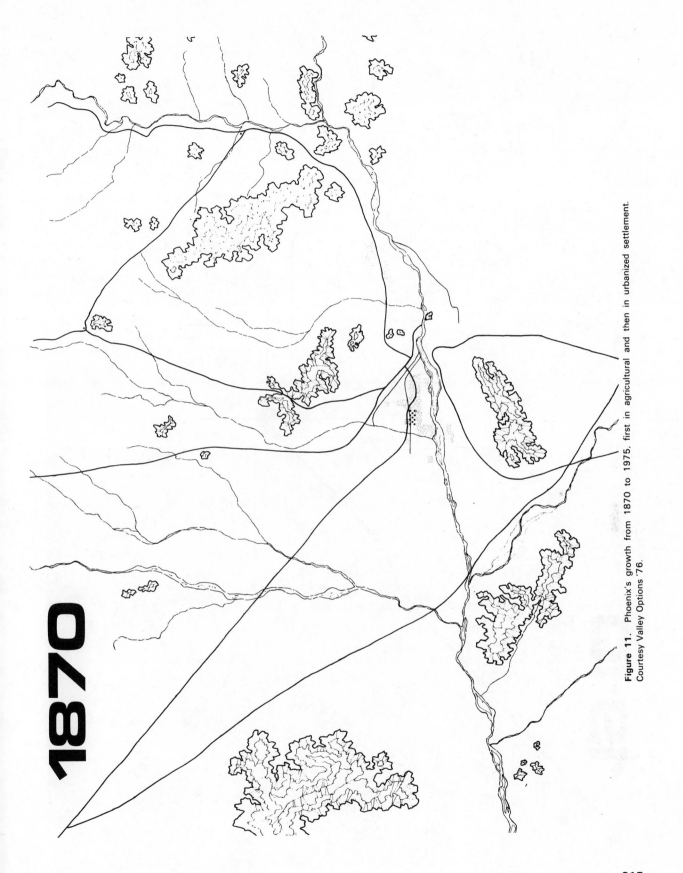

Figure 11. Phoenix's growth from 1870 to 1975, first in agricultural and then in urbanized settlement. Courtesy Valley Options '76.

1870

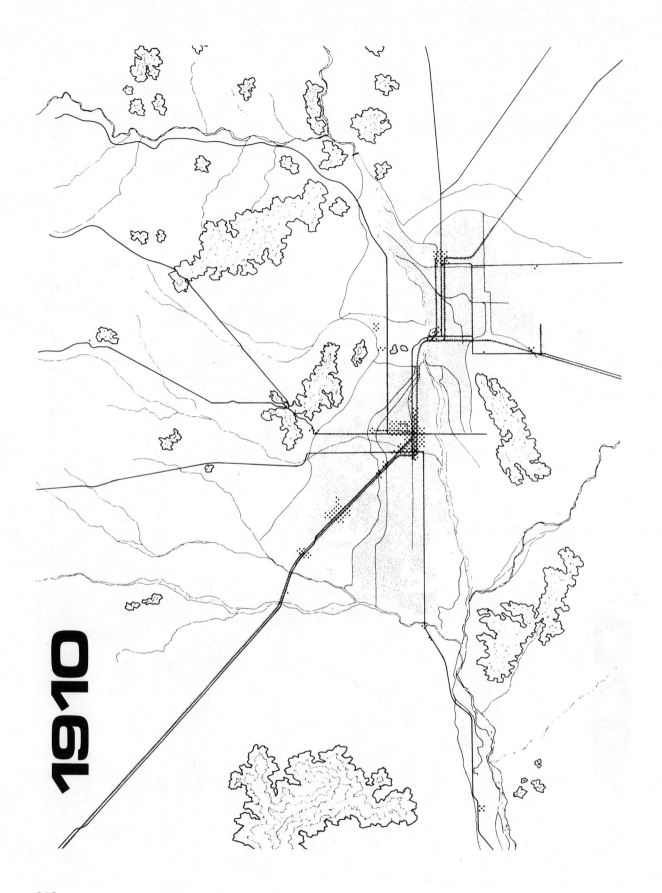

1910

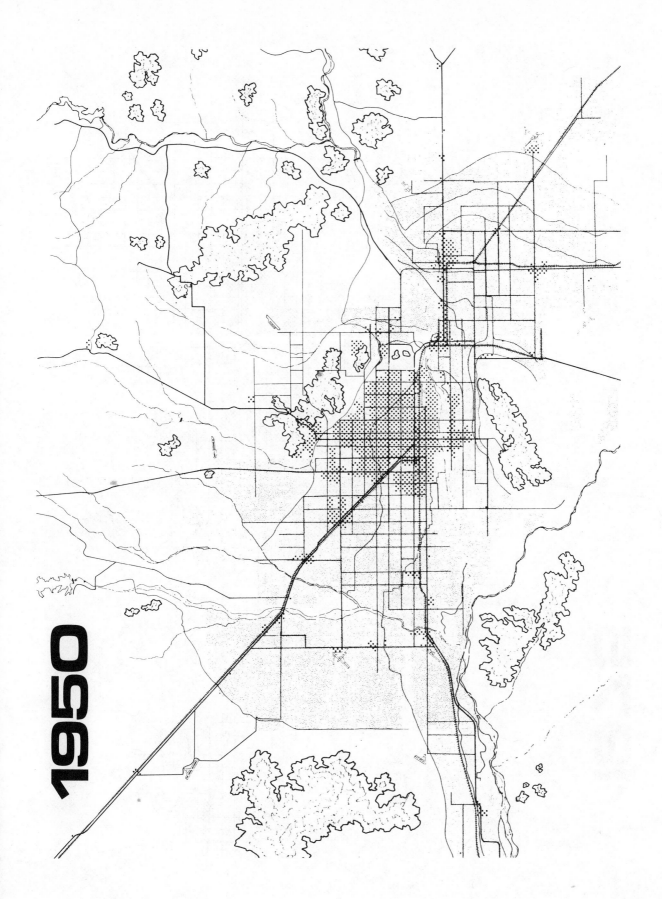

1950

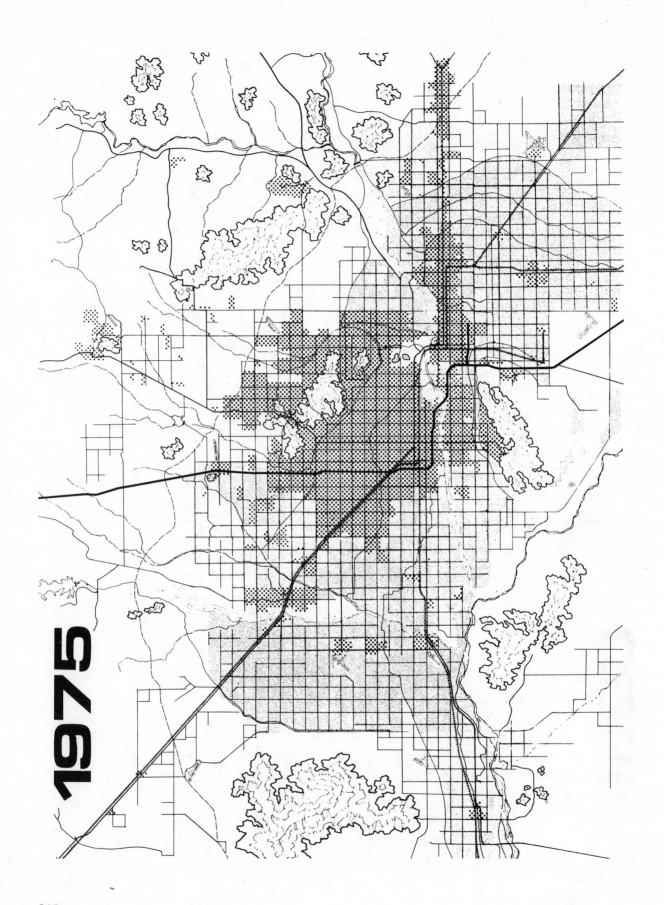

1975

continuous growth by emigration that has been experienced by Phoenix and Maricopa County, the city's metropolitan population jumping from 106,000 in 1950 to 1,355,000 in 1976.

Phoenix's growth is a wonder story told with great enthusiasm by all. The teller's only hesitation is due to his wanting to be the last immigrant, because every new resident—as well as every old one—knows that the continuous growth since World War II must ultimately destroy the qualities that make immigration so attractive in the first place.

It is an expansion story told with special exuberance by the land speculators and the real estate brokers. Indeed, Arizona is virtually their last frontier—the edge of the desert only lately surveyed and settled—in a vast country of richer and more obvious exploitative possibilities. By the 1950s the exploitation had begun, and today the Arizona land swindles are as infamous as the Florida swindles of the 1920s. Phoenix is the operating center of these national gyp operations, but the land near Phoenix has long since been promoted and speculated upon. Thus the swindles now involve land in some of the true wastelands of Arizona's lonely emptiness. Land speculation, however, does affect Phoenix: it is the source of the land development pattern so evident throughout the Salt River Valley, in which prime pieces of land, as well as those not so ideally located, are often ignored by developers who shrewdly never pay top dollar in acquiring building sites. Thus the Rosenzweig Center, a collection of commercial high rises, sits in the middle of a mile square block, not at an intersection in the grid pattern that characterizes and compartmentalizes the entire valley.

CENTRAL ARIZONA: THE PRESENT

Phoenix today is a very large and sometimes very attractive "new town." Almost everything built is very new. To those who crave antiques or old plumbing, Phoenix will seem a complete desert; such niceties must be imported from Iowa or Indiana. Phoenix is also a city without heavy industry. The old agriculture of citrus fruits and cotton remains, but the cattle lots, after a series of law suits, have been moved elsewhere, although some meat packing plants remain. The one distinct modern urban industry is electronics, particularly the production of semiconductors. This industry located in Phoenix largely because of the ease with which the product can be shipped from this city to anywhere. Retirement communities and corporate headquarters are today other important sectors of the economy. Both are postindustrial activities dependent on the climate and the attractiveness and independent of other natural resources. Service industries, including regional distribution and education, provide conventional economic support for the community's sustenance and growth.

Although each of the 17 autonomous municipal governments operates in its own peculiar way and at least some of these have made serious commitments to control land use, few obvious patterns separate Greater Phoenix from nonarid cities. The canal system is largely hidden from daily experience and is revealed only in plans such as Figure 12 or aerial views. If anything distinguishes the area, it is the admittedly infantile freeway system. This lack of development is in part a flattering commentary on the incredibly easy access afforded by the mile square, major street grid—a circulation matrix recently rediscovered in new-town planning abroad. It has been often suggested that the continuous street pattern of Los Angeles was one of the reasons for its phenomenal growth in the second quarter of this century. Compared to that of Phoenix, a road map of Los Angeles looks confused and complex.

Typically, the service industries and regional distribution centers are clustered along the freeway and next to the rail lines. The electronics plants are, however, dispersed, allowing the population scattered throughout the valley easy access to employment. This is perhaps more characteristic of the postindustrial period, than of an arid-region.

Typically, the residential slums of the area's three identifiable minorities (Indians, Mexicans, and blacks) are south of the tracks and south of the freeway, which runs near the river bottom. Unlike other major cities, however, Phoenix has few ethnic subcommunities: the minorities, in fact, have to work hard to keep together. In particular, there are few blacks, and there appear to be no major racial or ethnic discrimination problems. Nevertheless, in addition to the various self-imposed neighborhoods segregated on typical socioeconomic assumptions, Phoenicians also discriminate between lush irrigated landscapes and dry desert neighborhoods.

Life-Style. Because of abundant sunshine and generous irrigation, the cultivated landscape of Phoenix offers many opportunities, both aesthetic and physical. According to the National Climatic Center, "there is no evidence that irrigation has in any way

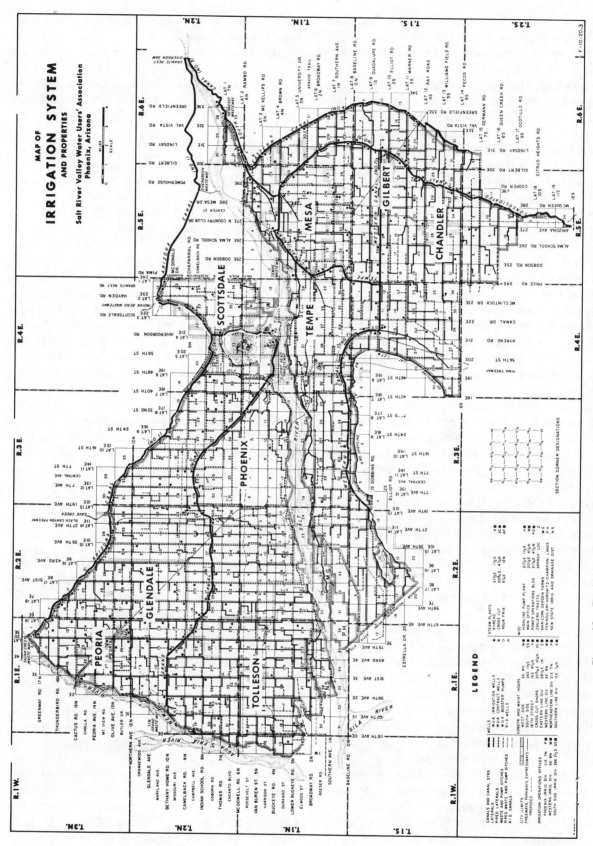

Figure 12. The hidden Phoenix canal system—the irrigation system of the Salt River Valley Water Users' Association—showing the form of the irrigation plan for a city laid out on a gridiron pattern, with the main distribution canals following Hohokam alignments along the most appropriate contours and the local ditches and laterals following the gridiron. Courtesy Salt River Project, History Center, Phoenix, Arizona.

affected the relative humidity in the Valley." Yet dramatic microclimatic variations have been recorded. Whereas the daytime temperatures in the Valley of the Sun can hit levels almost as high as those achieved on the open, dry desert, the nightly low temperatures in heavily irrigated regions can typically be 15 to 20°F lower than those for desert sites. Unfortunately, neither the present architectural design of buildings nor the habits and life-styles of the inhabitants recognize this natural advantage. At a regional scale, a simultaneous temperature profile can easily identify differences up to 20°F caused by the contrasting effects of man-made environments—thermal effects that have yet to be comprehensively understood but could ultimately be designed and planned for. In the meantime the agricultural patterns of irrigated land use, as in Figure 13, still make a pervasive imprint on urbanization.

The houses throughout Phoenix are typically built without cellars or basements. A slab laid on the grade is the most economical foundation. Even multistory dwellings seldom go below the grade. The potential for flooding and the saturation of flood irrigation probably reinforce the economy of this technique. Cellars, however, could give an important natural cooling feature to desert houses.

The shopping centers appear to be no different from those built elsewhere. Inevitably, the air-conditioned mall dominates. Other planning factors undoubtedly also contribute to the success of these malls. Although Phoenix is noted for the quantity and variety of its shopping centers, unfortunately a number of them not only are aesthetic disasters but also are financially unprofitable. Yet such units are often continued, their way being paid by the successful shopping centers operated by the same chain.

In housing and in shopping—indeed, throughout Phoenix—the pattern of life is virtually identical to that throughout the country. In the summer it is only persons in the building trades—carpenters, plumbers·

Figure 13. Flood irrigation farming south of Mesa in the 1920s, similar to both prehistoric Hohokam and present-day methods, using the straight run of the ditches, with the continuous earth berm that acts as a dike between them, a pattern that recurs in new land use designs for subdivisions or industrial parks. Courtesy Salt River Project, History Center, Phoenix, Arizona.

and masons—who begin work at 4:30 or 5:00 AM, as soon as it is light enough to see. By noon or 1:00 PM their workday is over before the temperature or the discomfort has climaxed. They ride home in air-conditioned pickup trucks, sleep through the heat of the afternoon, and enjoy a normal evening with friends or family. All other occupations, however, are almost scrupulously conventional, with offices and shops opening between 8:00 and 9:30 AM and closing at 4:00 to 5:30 PM throughout the year. Nor are many concessions practiced in regard to clothing or other habits. Bermuda shorts are much rarer in Phoenix than in New York. Businessmen and store clerks wear suits or sports jackets. Perhaps women's clothing tends more toward the informal and men's casual wear is more open than in some places, but these are national trends influenced by a less formal California life-style which Phoenix emulates. The influence of the arid climate appears secondary.

The virtual dependence of all Salt Valley residents on automobiles has had predictable results. Although cars, like people, can suffer from overheating, automobiles generally last longer in the desert climate than in temperate ones. The complete lack of rust and corrosion gives cars the longer life that retirees covet. The cars' exterior colors are virtually always light toned; there are none of the black or deep-colored exteriors seen elsewhere in the country. Car interiors are more of a problem. Again, off-whites and tans are preferred, but many models do not offer these colors. Air conditioning is virtually standard because of the summer heat, but this feature puts a premium on driving longer distances since it takes a minute or two for any cold air to be produced and several minutes to begin to cool out the intense solar buildup acquired by cars standing in the summer heat. Interior car temperatures in excess of 160°F during the summer can be destructive to plastic upholstery, people, and their belongings. Unfortunately car parks are seldom shaded.

The high mobility typical of a low-density city, a situation characterized by the large number of automobiles, is part of the Phoenix way of life. It has, in fact, only been since the 1974 oil-shortage scare that city bus service has been seriously considered. Taxis continue to be rare. The dispersed population necessarily reinforces the dispersed traffic grid.

High mobility is also reflected by certain social statistics. Phoenix now has more divorces than marriages. Since every divorce creates the need for two homes and also reduces the size of households, the result is lower population density and more diffusion.

In Phoenix, homes change hands with considerable frequency.[5] Both public institutions and private individuals operate with a relatively low debt base, since solvency seems a necessary part of mobility. Phoenix, with its clear skies, has the largest number of private airplanes *per capita* in the country, and Phoenix, without a major waterway, has the largest number of boats *per capita* in the nation. All of these statistics point to a life-style characterized by high mobility. Nevertheless socially Phoenix is not a loose or an open city. The fact that the majority of the adult population are first-generation Phoenicians may account for the conservative middle-class attitudes, which are much less tolerant than the attitudes in a more mature and stable arid city such as Albuquerque.

Downtown Phoenix. Since the end of World War II, the old downtown of Phoenix has been eclipsed as completely as has any American downtown during the same period. The lack of public transit or a place to park a car discouraged the use of the downtown business district, and the much more attractive new shopping centers offered a preferable alternative. The

Figure 14. Urban improvements on Washington St., Phoenix in the early 1880s: mature trees and new saplings, the ditch being formed in wood, and weatherproof sidewalk canopy with canvas drop wings. Courtesy Madison R. Loring Collection, Arizona Historical Foundation, Tempe, Arizona.

Figure 15. Downtown Phoenix in 1974 with the spine of Central Avenue on the right running due north. Courtesy Salt River Project, History Center, Phoenix, Arizona.

doom of the downtown area was sealed long before then, when the earlier urban desert amenities, as depicted in Figure 14, were eliminated. By 1900 the open irrigation ditches were already enclosed, the trees had disappeared, the colonnaded sidewalks had lost their porches, and asphalt and concrete had begun to make the downtown area a more oppressive desert than the actual one. Since 1970 the construction of a mediocre symphony hall and convention center and several new hotels and office buildings has infused some life into the old downtown. But little about their designs suggests their desert climate, and economically there are few winners. Physically, downtown Phoenix is all too similar to every "renewal" central business district, as can be seen in Figure 15. A series of new banks makes the financial community still the prime downtown activity aside from municipal, state, and federal offices.

Central Avenue Corridor. The successful commercial extension to downtown was the Central Avenue Corridor. Totally built by private developers, a series of skyscraper office buildings lining both sides of the north–south axis of Central Avenue was constructed during the 1950s and 1960s. These towers were kept apart by rigid zoning requirements for extensive car parking. Thus the resulting avenue appears

to be a more spacious version of Los Angeles' Wilshire Boulevard, linked to the regional gridiron by the 1 mi tartan of major roads. An architectural design proposal in Figure 16 suggests a complementary pedestrian green space linkage.

Proposals to allow high-rise development outside this corridor have so far been denied in Phoenix. Such proposals would permit the development of high-intensity nodes throughout the city—a planning concept very similar to that which transformed the skyline of Moscow during the 1950s. The only serious attempt besides the Central Avenue Corridor to engage in high-rise development has been in Scottsdale. The few towers built there, however, have not been convincing, either in architectural terms or in their planned relationship to the community. As a result, citizen opinion there is strongly set against further high-rise construction and totally committed to a low-profile if prolific future.

Sun City. The first of four residential prototypes found in the Valley of the Sun is the most startling example of residential segregation. Located 15 mi northwest of downtown Phoenix, Sun City is an exclusive enclave of voluntarily displaced old people who maintain high suicide and divorce rates, as well as an immaculate community that completely shuns

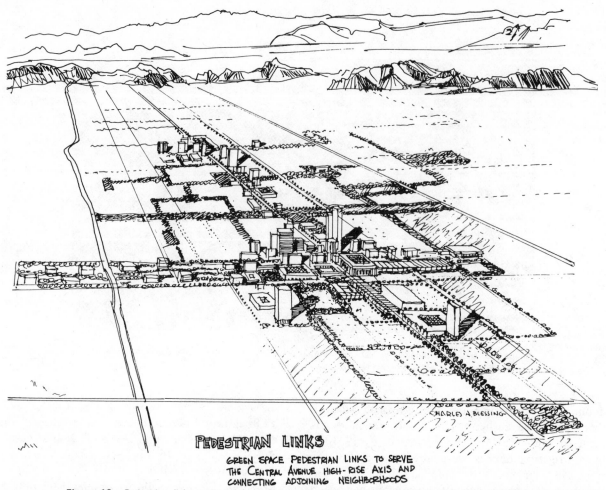

PEDESTRIAN LINKS

GREEN SPACE PEDESTRIAN LINKS TO SERVE
THE CENTRAL AVENUE HIGH-RISE AXIS AND
CONNECTING ADJOINING NEIGHBORHOODS

Figure 16. Pedestrian links proposed in a 3-day task force proposal by AIA Regional/Urban Design Assistance Team in 1974 to tie together the downtown area with the Central Avenue Corridor and a possible governmental crosstown mall to run east–west. Reproduced by permission of Central Arizona Chapter of the American Institute of Architects.

children. Construction was begun in 1959 (with the opening in 1960) by the Del E. Webb Corporation as developers and builders. Sun City is now advertised as the country's foremost retirement community—a claim based partly on its resort facilities. The financial success of Sun City has inspired emulation elsewhere. Undoubtedly the warm winter climate has been pivotal to the success of the Arizona site, but the sociological isolation of the elderly is a nationwide postindustrial phenomenon that is only reinforced here by the ideal climate of an arid region.

The La Ronde subdivision at Sun City, illustrated in Figure 17, has a circular form as arbitrary as the age qualification for home ownership. It provides building sites oriented to every degree of the compass without reference to the preferred angles in regard to the ever-present sun. Del Webb Boulevard provides

access to the central shopping center. An aerial view shows a complete lack of hedges or fences; neither security nor privacy is considered a problem for the duplexes on the right. The single-family homes on the left occasionally have individual rear yards (but even here only low hedges are permitted), and a green sward spotted with citrus provides a continuous verdant greenbelt backyard. The entire subdivision is defined by a golf course.[6]

Arcadia. Among the more conventional residential patterns, a most interesting arid prototype is the Arcadia district as seen partially in Figure 18.[7] This district is a surprisingly skillful conversion by speculative builders of several square miles of citrus orchard to single-family, one-story houses spaced two or three to the acre, largely built in the 1950s.

The houses themselves are without distinction. The retention of productive fruit trees, however, provides a lushness that would do credit to the most fertile oasis. The continuation of the flood irrigation system permits heavy green lawns, and the resulting vegetative ambience is particularly attractive to emigrants from the greener parts of the country. Furthermore, aside from the overabundance of fruit for one's own table, the Arcadia district presents the resident with a microclimatic advantage. The roll of the earth berm at the edge of each flood basin lends a particular character to the landscape, and the several inches of water that stand on the land once every 2 weeks in the summer and once every month in the winter give solace against the relentlessly sunny days. Although the houses were originally the modest homes of beginning families, increasing substance has not encouraged these people to move elsewhere, since no other neighborhood can offer a comparable lush, green setting. Thus land values have become high, and homes are continuously being upgraded and remodeled into more substantial properties.

"The Lakes" in Tempe.   A third arid residential prototype is "The Lakes" in Tempe, a 322 acre water-oriented development which has counterparts both in the development of the McCormick Ranch in Scottsdale and in the village plans for Litchfield Park, as well as elsewhere.[8] In these cases large, flat, agricultural sites have been shaped with earth-moving equipment by large developers to create modest hillocks as well as shallow lakes, whose edges are then intensively developed. (Figure 19 shows "The Lakes" under construction.) The microclimatic advantages are yet to be measured, but visually, as well as financially, these developments have been very successful. The cost of water evaporation of 110 in./year has proved so far not to be unreasonable. In fact, the water originates in the irrigation water rights attached to the land agriculturally. Now the water is circulated back into the canal system to assist in keeping "The Lakes" fresh.

A heavily landscaped, densely built edge of a 50 acre desert lake is a very attractive image in an arid context. A variety of residential types are provided,

Figure 17.   The La Ronde subdivision in Sun City, characterized by complete freedom in the planning of residential and commercial land uses due to the flat land and the subdivision's dependence on electricity, not the impact of the sun. Courtesy Del E. Webb Corporation.

Figure 18. The Arcadia district, a highly successful transposition from productive citrus orchards to lush residential neighborhoods with the regularity of tree plantings complimenting the gridiron land divisions. (At the lower right is an area developed using desert landscaping without the lushness provided by flood irrigation in Arcadia.)

from separate one-family houses to stacked town-houses and apartments. Some recreational facilities and restaurants also have lake frontage, and light sailboats add to the pleasant scene. Rigid covenants, restrictions, and bylaws are administered by "The Lakes" Community Association to ensure environmental continuity.

Paradise Valley. Paradise Valley, the fourth prototype, offers a rather different residential environment, one which is regarded as very exclusive both socially and financially.[9] It is located in a modest mountain valley, a naturally defined enclosure that lies approximately 8 mi to the northeast of the center of Phoenix. The most expansive and the most expensive houses are not located on the sides of mountains but are situated between them. The land is barren and rocky with considerable caliche, and it is higher than the highest canal and thus not irrigated.

This rather desolate wasteland is incorporated as the Town of Paradise Valley, where only residential and religious uses are permitted. (The residents must leave town to buy groceries, alcohol, and gasoline.) A minimum of 1 full acre is required for each dwelling—a seemingly wasteful ordinance that allows for an extensive sewage disposal field for each house, which is necessary because of the poor percolation qualities of the soil. The town provides no sewers, no water, no garbage collection, and no fire protection. Each of these, as well as security services to supplement the small police department, is available optionally from private agencies. The town, furthermore, collects no taxes and maintains itself quite adequately on its share of county revenue.

Such improvements as road widening and paving are universally resisted in the Town of Paradise Valley because they would increase through traffic, allow higher speeds, and perhaps force the imposition of

Figure 19. "The Lakes" under construction in Tempe in 1974: its extensive artificial waterfront, offering a unique environment in an arid region, increases land values. Courtesy the First National Bank of Phoenix.

227

taxes. The town is, however, now building an extensive bicycle network along its roadways. Of course, there are no sidewalks, since everyone drives everywhere because the distances are large, and typically there is at least one car per person. The capacity of the typical large car is used, for example, to ferry children to various activities, including play, since the density of children per acre is also very low.

The town's landscaping, which is based at least partly on native plant materials, is sustained by man-made, individual underground watering systems and is similar to the pattern in the lower right of Figure 18. Using arid-region plants not only is complementary to the terrain and aesthetically compatible with the wide spacing of buildings, but also is more economical when water is purchased at high cost from a private water company. Although arid-region vegetation can be densely cultivated and raked gravel lawns can minimize the upkeep and be extremely attractive, most homeowners try to have a small patch of grass or of some other lush landscaping materials that require heavy watering, typically in relation to a pool patio. Especially in Paradise Valley, every home has a swimming pool.

The Phoenix Grid. In general, the 1 mi square grid of major streets has kept the residential areas of the Phoenix metropolitan area free from traffic and has minimized the number of busy streets that school children must cross. Schools are dispersed, and the low density of housing throughout the town encourages the use of school buses. It is only within the last decade that townhouses and apartments have been built, and they are typically low (one to three stories) in profile. They are usually very heavily landscaped and feature swimming pools and other communal recreational facilities. The intensity of the landscaping gives them a green Casbah atmosphere and a potentially interesting future in arid-region development.

CENTRAL ARIZONA: THE FUTURE

Potentially, future planning for central Arizona will continue the present graceful acceptance of what is assumed to be inevitable—growth will not be challenged and may not even be directed. Regardless of the particulars, it is the existing overlapping patterns

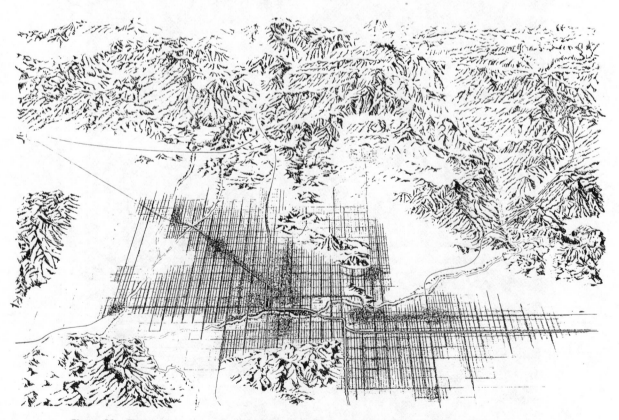

Figure 20. The trends concept. From Gruen Associates, *Growth Management* (Phoenix, [1975]), p. 95. Courtesy Maricopa Association of Governments and the Arizona Department of Transportation.

Figure 21. The corridors concept. From Gruen Associates, *Growth Management* (Phoenix, [1975]), p. 103. Courtesy Maricopa Association of Governments and the Arizona Department of Transportation.

of road grid and organic canal network that will structure any redevelopment of the existing metropolis, as well as its expansion. Indeed, extensive future growth is completely inevitable. Everyone connected with Phoenix expects it, and there are no active thoughts about resisting it.

An ever-expanding population is thus predictable as the first growth priority for the future. This will be complemented by improvements and more intensive development of land already absorbed in suburbanization and urbanization. Potentially the dialogues between new areas and existing development will provide, as everywhere else, the tension of constantly examined values—and a sharpening of wits absent from static planning situations. The potentials of these tensions were first sketched by Gruen Associates in a recent general regional report for the Maricopa Association of Governments entitled *Growth Management*. Gruen anticipated increasing present densities by 50 percent in three alternative futures:

1. Trends—a continuation of present land use and promotion without controls, as Figure 20 shows.

2. Corridors—an intensification of development along existing circulation corridors, as Figure 21 shows.

3. Centers—a nodal development emphasizing a series of identifiable urban cores, as Figure 22 shows.

Yet expansion over new land is hardly to be restrained by a growth ethic or by geography. To the north there is only 20 to 30 mi for building before major mountainous escarpments; to the south, South Mountain Park, once the world's largest municipal park, provides an unbuildable barrier, as Figure 23 shows. But along the east–west axis there are few natural physical edges. To the west the new "Brenda" section of interstate freeway, which substantially reduces both time and distance to Los Angeles, provides a freeway axis and access for development—already anticipated by Litchfield Park. However, perhaps more opportune is the southeast expansion of Phoenix toward Tucson, 110 mi distant. The existing interstate freeway provides the vector which has already encouraged new growth, especially on the facing edges of the two cities.

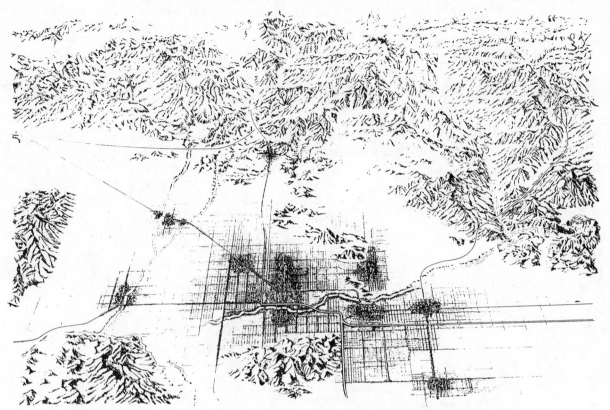

Figure 22. The centers concept. From Gruen Associates, *Growth Management* (Phoenix, [1975]), p. 101. Courtesy Maricopa Association of Governments and the Arizona Department of Transportation.

It is interesting to conjecture regarding the influence of climate on future development. Generally, the climate is already highly structured and extreme. It is to be hoped that in the future the man-made environment, whether for economic, political, or aesthetic reasons, will more completely interact with the climate.

Changes to the climate caused by increased human settlement appear not to be critical. At least they seem to be controllable. Phoenix now enjoys automobile emission pollution comparable to that of other major cities but has yet to seriously face the problem by enacting controls. More unpredictable would be the effects of major shifts in weather phenomena. Increased rainfall would reinforce growth; extended drought could be disastrous, although less than for other cities of comparable size because water management is already practiced.

Perhaps the human factors would be the most predictable. Frontier values, as expressed in the myth of rugged pioneering individualism, continue to be a major factor in planning and development attitudes. The adversary role of communal rights and responsibilities is best expressed by the texture of community

organization in the region. For instance, not only the many municipalities but also the school systems continue to resist consolidation. There are at present a total of 55 all but completely independent school districts, each with its own constituency, budget, and administration. In the balance between individual prowess and community responsibility, the "use it up and move on" attitude is pitted against "delayed gratification." In general, the most consistent attitudes about sustained yield are in evidence in the water management of the Salt River Project. They seldom govern individual action, however, immediate benefit is the goal. As a result, comprehensive planning proposals for the Phoenix region are relatively recent and are considered novel.

The Rio Salado Project. The Salt River no longer flows, except when unusual weather conditions bring more water to the mountains than the reservoirs will hold. A proposal to transform the wasted riverbed and its floodplain into a manageable continuous development is the theme of the Rio Salado Project. Initiated by the students and faculty of the College of Architecture at Arizona State University in 1966, the

Rio Salado is now an active plan for development, supported by the Valley Forward Association and a number of local, regional, and national agencies. Water is the central theme of the proposal, as shown in Figure 24. Its recreational uses are the most obvious, although most of the water would be recyclable sewage effluent. The program would provide almost all of a city's functions in an area larger than Manhattan. The Rio Salado would thus facilitate structured development on a 20,000 acre site within the city rather than at its perimeter, directing activity that would occur regardless.

Valley Options '76 Project. An equally ambitious proposal is the Valley Options '76 Project, also generated by the College of Architecture at Arizona State University. This study of the evolving future of metropolitan Phoenix develops some of the Gruen concepts by examining growth patterns along the perimeter and proposing an urban form for it by design rather than by default. By advancing regional goals as well as relationships between life-style and density, a "regional armature" is proposed. Figure 25 depicts two projected urban patterns. Valley 1 represents the continuation of the existing spontaneous growth; Valley 2, the proposed plan. In effect, Valley 2 continues the Rio Salado idea around the metropolitan area by following the natural water routes. There would be an attempt to attract higher than usual density development by providing particular services, amenities, and other incentives. This higher density would then support a regional transit net which could be extended to service the existing city. Figure 26 depicts the regional armature and attempts to show how this net could be expanded in response to additional urban growth.

Both of these projects—Rio Salado and Valley Options '76—would give form to future development and, in the process, provide definition to what already exists. Both are comprehensive, mixed-use planning programs to which transportation is a key.

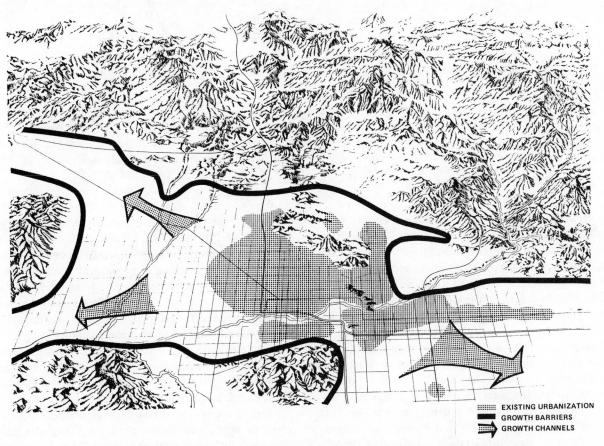

EXISTING URBANIZATION
GROWTH BARRIERS
GROWTH CHANNELS

Figure 23. Future paths of urbanization: the flood of continued growth over the remaining nonurbanized flatlands of the valley. From Gruen Associates, *Growth Management*, (Phoenix, [1975]), p. 93. Courtesy Maricopa Association of Governments and the Arizona Department of Transportation.

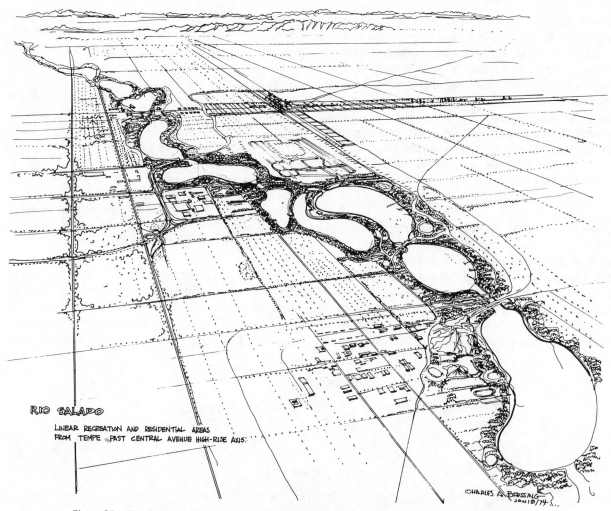

RIO SALADO

LINEAR RECREATION AND RESIDENTIAL AREAS
FROM TEMPE PAST CENTRAL AVENUE HIGH-RISE AXIS.

CHARLES A. BLESSING
JAN 10/74

Figure 24. The Rio Salado Project proposed for the comprehensive development of the now usually dry Salt River bed. Drawing from 1974 report of AIA Regional/Urban Development Assistance Team on Phoenix. Reproduced by permission of Central Arizona Chapter of the American Institute of Architects.

Both attempt to respond to the unique aspects of the arid location. In particular, both are strongly oriented to outdoor recreation and resort-type activities capitalizing on the pleasant daytime conditions that prevail for 8 months of the year. Both are corridor schemes in which increased mobility and lineal parkscapes are fundamental.

Freeways and Canals. Other proposals for the future development of the city of Phoenix have been surprisingly scarce. The most immediate project seems to be the next freeway—if and where. Although Phoenix is often honored as the next Los Angeles, freeway planning and building are already more than a generation late. Complicating the picture are the City of Scottsdale and the Town of Paradise Valley, which are adamantly opposed to

freeways crossing their incorporated areas. Similarly, the City of Phoenix bumbled for years planning a crosstown freeway in the Mooreland corridor—the right-of-way for which was painfully acquired—before the public voted against the freeway. Now the right-of-way stands idle. Furthermore, studies of public transit systems, the alternative, have quickly demonstrated their incompatibility with low-density development. Existing rights-of-way, however, include not only the wide streets but also railway lines and modern realignments of the ancient Hohokam fan of irrigation canals.

Phoenix today has turned its back on these canals. Their sweeping lines follow elevational contours providing a different geometry from the surveyor's gridiron and the orientation of all existing development toward streets. Again, proposals have been

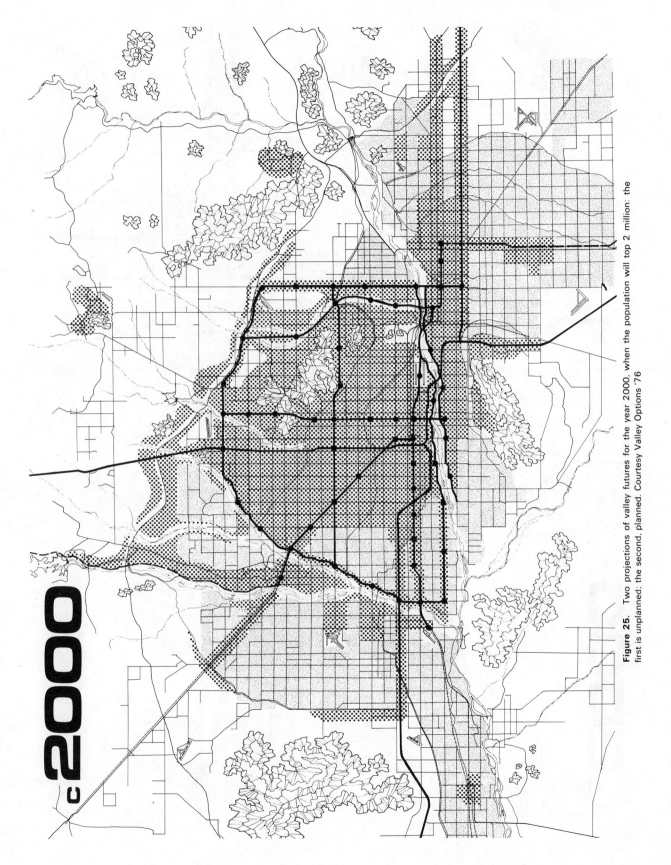

Figure 25. Two projections of valley futures for the year 2000, when the population will top 2 million: the first is unplanned; the second, planned. Courtesy Valley Options '76

233

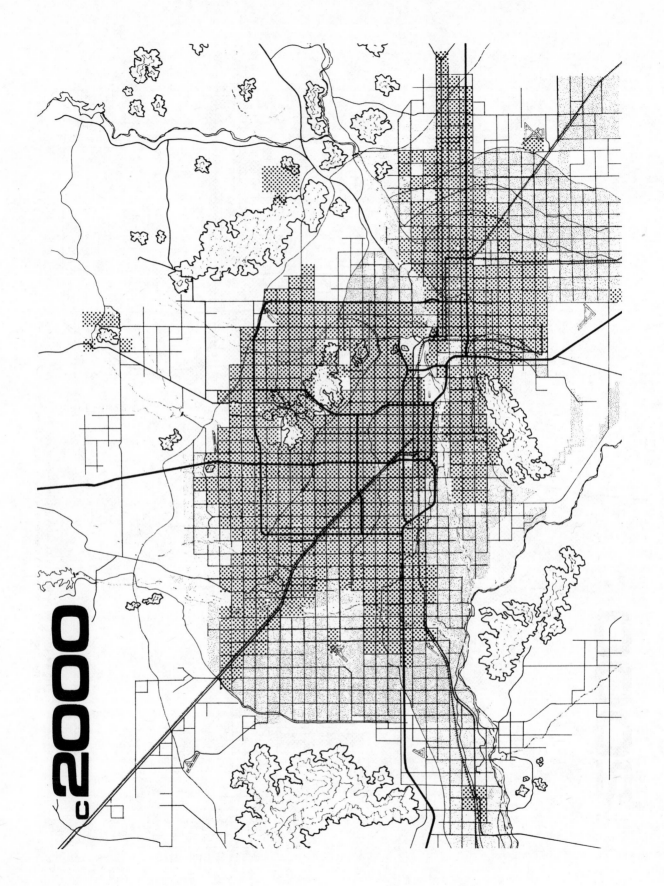

c2000

VALLEY LOOP

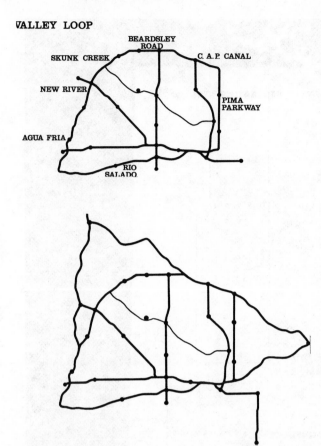

Figure 26. Valley Regional Armature Loop as a circulation corridor that provides both a frame for an infill network and a base for expansion into the undeveloped desert beyond. Courtesy Valley Options '76.

generated by the Arizona State University College of Architecture to revive the canals by providing lineal parks and trails and orienting both public and private uses toward the canals and away from the street pattern. Such a proposal could be furthered by a public transit program. However, the proposal does not recognize that canals are not always "pretty" things, for they constitute an open water-delivery system which is sometimes full of water and sometimes not because the pattern and the management of irrigation water differ from those of waterways used for recreation or commerce.

The Central Arizona Project and Water Needs. Water is also the theme of the Central Arizona Project (CAP), a federal program of the U.S. Bureau of Reclamation that already has a 50 year history,[10] As Figure 27 shows, CAP is designed to bring water from the Colorado River over the mountains to add to the water available in central Arizona half a state

away. The water would be lifted over 2000 ft vertically and travel in a giant, concrete canal 300 mi long. Aside from the audacity of the concept, the project's critics point out, first, that little water in the Colorado River would be available (in a year of average rainfall, none would be available); second, that the actual costs of building the project could be as much as 10 times what was planned; and, third, that the water really is not needed anyway. Yet contracts have already been let for part of the work, and ultimately Phoenix taxpayers will have to foot the bill.

It is often truly stated that subdivisions require less water than agriculture. Thus conversion of the agriculturally productive Salt River Valley to a megalopolis is certainly a possibility as far as water is concerned. Assuming a water use of 200 gal per person per day (currently, the rate in Tucson is 175 gal per person per day), sufficient water is available in Central Arizona, renewed by rainfall, to support a population of somewhere between 5.5 and 10 million people. Since the current population is well below 2 million, a tripled population is theoretically possible.

In Tucson it is another story, for that Arizona city's water is obtained from deep wells. The mining of prehistoric water, however, has a disastrously limited future, and Tucson, with neither a canal system, vast watershed territories, nor a reservoir system, may be in trouble. Phoenix, on the other hand, through the Salt River Project and the practice in the Southwest of separating water rights from land rights, has acquired water dominion over large, unpopulated areas. As a sprawling regional desert conurbation Phoenix thus draws her water resources from a vast watershed hinterland which may be extended even further by the Central Arizona Project.

Arcosanti. It is perhaps ironic that Paolo Soleri, the quasi-utopian architect and city planner, is a resident of Paradise Valley, for the compact, three-dimensional, megastructured cities called arcologies that he proposes are, as Figure 28 shows, in virtually every way·the antithesis of sprawling Paradise Valley and of Phoenix today. They represent an extreme alternative future for Phoenix. Soleri's sample arcology Arcosanti, which began for a modest 1500 and now is planned for 3000 residents, is already under construction 60 mi north of Phoenix.[11] The ethic of energy and resource conservation, however, ·is hardly any more in evidence at Arcosanti than in Phoenix itself.

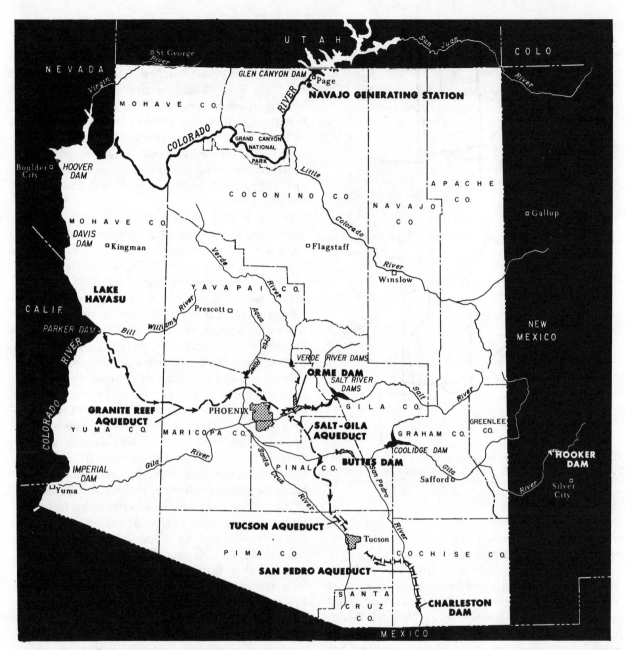

Figure 27. The Central Arizona Project. From *Central Arizona Project, Water for Cities, Farms and Factories* (Washington: U.S. Government Printing Office, n.d.).

Yet the concept of a symbiotic advantage that would accrue from building a dense three-dimensional, self-contained complex in which all services would be integrated is especially appropriate in a climate of extremes. Soleri's ethic of frugality has obvious applications to every successful desert culture. Yet the protective and generative benefits of an organically developed thickness to enclose a desert settlement represent a theory that has been examined to date only on the most modest scale.

Soleri's megalomanic scale begins to suggest some of the aesthetic potential of such a concept, but without any of the analytic quantitative inputs that would verify its particular viability.

CONCLUSION

Theoretically, the forces of energy and resource conservation that Soleri presumes to address remain the

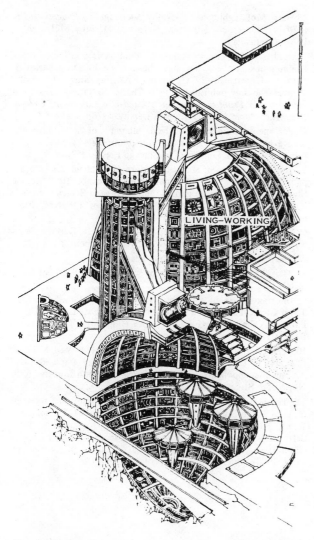

Figure 28. Section of Paolo Soleri's Arcosanti I, a desert megastructured community begun in 1970 and revised by Soleri in 1976 to better accommodate solar concerns. From Paolo Soleri, *Arcology: The City in the Image of Man* (Cambridge, Mass.: The Massachusetts Institute of Technology Press, 1970), p. 110. Reprinted from *Arcology: The City in the Image of Man* by Paolo Soleri, by permission of the MIT Press, Cambridge, Massachusetts.

most potent transformers in the future for Phoenix. Inevitably, population growth and boomtown policies will continue for at least another generation or more, simply because of existing momentum. Phoenix will certainly for a while continue to experience the major American urban trend of population dispersal. If the nation's suburbs prosper, Phoenix will, for it is mostly a continuous newly developed suburb. But ultimately the smaller households, the peculiarities of climate, and the need of people and plants for water may encourage a more particular life-style and a charm that can develop only through time.

The low density with many dispersed nodes that now exists should increasingly encourage more immediate contact with the climate and its bounty. The development of alternative transportation ties, including sidewalks, walkways, bicycle paths, and horse and hiking trails, is the most obvious immediate and economic means of developing more direct responses among people and greater interaction with their surroundings. The sunny, stimulating weather that prevails in all seasons except summer has been recognized only by local resorts—it should be the basis of daily activities for all residents, not just vacationers.

These potentials fit well the present diffuse matrix of many centers, whose focal capacities could benefit from more density. The reinforcements to Scottsdale's civic center in the past decade suggest the kind of program that can generate much more lively settlements. The design opportunities lie not just in architectural and landscape appropriateness but also in the social and economic planning of community activities in a complementary mix.

The development of such a multicentered arid megalopolis, with many more intense centers, would also coincide with recent realizations about energy and resources. With the potential decline in available fossil fuels, an increased premium will have to be exacted for energy consumed without producing real capital. Thus extensive private transportation based on nonrenewable energy or material sources would become prohibitive. A pedestrian-scaled settlement matrix would provide the most viable urban life-style—one of maximum potential in an arid climate. In addition, the solar energy potential of buildings means that the role of Phoenix as a major twenty-first century settlement is guaranteed by its abundant sunshine.

The planners of the many constituencies of Phoenix to date cannot be lauded for their vision or even their comprehension. The officials of the city of Scottsdale believe that low-cost housing begins at $35,000 per dwelling. And although especially Scottsdale (and now to some extent Tempe) is increasingly definitive about the quality of new development, the usual planning concern has to do with changes in the mix of residential and commercial uses that would affect the future tax base. Regional vision is thus noticeably absent even in applying the "growth ethic."

The great desert cities and cultures of man have evolved over long periods of time into particularly unique situations. Man has always lived in the deserts, but invariably in special adaptive ways.

Within the warp of history, the fourth human habitation at the place now called Phoenix has just begun. Its continued importance will be the direct result of continued adaptation.

The postindustrial period has provided some unique inputs to this phase of the evolution of this particular arid-region city. Desert cultures have always thrived on their diffusivity of resilient prototypes. Survival has always been selective and sparse. The dynamics of a desert area are, of course, more than meteorological. Such an area represents a definitive and predictable matrix for sometimes unpredictable human interaction. The 17 distinctive and autonomous municipalities known generically as Phoenix may evolve into the newest and most daring settlement that man has yet attempted in such a region.

NOTES

1. Universally, adobe is the indigenous construction material for buildings in arid regions. Local muds that contain a balance of sand and fine soil are mixed with water and then formed to dry in the sun. Adobe can be shaped into large bricks, which when cured are typically laid up in mud mortar; or adobe can be puddled directly on a wall one layer at a time, completely curing before the next is added. Thermally, adobe is an ideal desert building material because of its slow transmissivity of heat, which tempers the strong diurnal temperature fluctuations. Once cured, adobe is surprisingly stable, partially because of the lack of rainfall, but also because of the ease with which it can be repaired.

2. Herb McLaughlin and Dorothy McLaughlin, *Phoenix 1870–1970 in Photographs* (Phoenix: Herb and Dorothy McLaughlin, 1970), frontispiece.

3. Studies of the growth pattern of Phoenix in relation to other communities in the valley have been made by Dr. Charles S. Sargent, Department of Geography, Arizona State University, Tempe. The only published work is Charles S. Sargent, *The Conflict between Frontier Values and Land-Use Control in Greater Phoenix* (Tempe: Arizona State University, 1976).

4. For one partial account of the development of air conditioning, see Reyher Banham, *The Architecture of the Well-Tempered Environment* (Chicago: University of Chicago Press, 1969).

5. The best sources of statistical information about Phoenix are published by the Valley National Bank, Phoenix. Its "Arizona Statistical Review" is an annual, published each September; 1976 is its thirty-second year. Its monthly "Arizona Progress" highlights different sectors of the economy.

6. Sun City has yet to be studied comprehensively. Descriptive information is available from the Del E. Webb Corporation.

7. The Arcadia district has also not been studied.

8. "The Lakes" as a development was still, in 1976, not completely sold.

9. Information about Paradise Valley can be obtained from the Town Clerk, Town of Paradise Valley, 6400 East Lincoln Drive, Paradise Valley, or the Paradise Valley Homeowner's Association, Box 2071, Scottsdale, Arizona.

10. The Central Arizona Project Association, 111 West Monroe, Phoenix, is the proponent of this increasingly opposed plan. Among the opponents is the Maricopa Audubon Society, 6240 North 15th Street, Phoenix.

11. The best source of information about Arcosanti and the concepts of Paolo Soleri is the Cosanti Foundation, 6433 Doubletree Road, Paradise Valley. Among published sources, the most pertinent is Paolo Soleri, *Arcology: The City in the Image of Man* (Cambridge, Mass.: The Massachusetts Institute of Technology Press, 1970), which includes plans of Arcosanti I.

Index